Looking into the Past

Learner's Book
Grade 12

Yonah Seleti (series editor)
Peter Delius
Claire Dyer
Logan Naidoo
Jimmy Nisbet
Christopher Saunders

with Glynis Clacherty
as methodology consultant

MASKEW MILLER
LONGMAN

Maskew Miller Longman (Pty) Ltd
Howard Drive, Pinelands, Cape Town

Offices in Johannesburg, Durban, King William's Town, Pietersburg, Bloemfontein, representatives in Mafikeng and Nelspruit and companies throughout southern and central Africa.

First published in 1999

ISBN 0 636 03932 3

Cover design by Kathy Abbott
Cover photographs from Gallo Images (Pty) Ltd. (The Hulton Getty Collection) *left* and i-Afrika *right*
Typesetting and reproduction by Martingraphix
Printed by Creda Communications, Eliot Avenue, Epping II, Cape Town

Contents

THEME? : international relations & events

CHAPTER 4:   **The Cold War (1945–91)**   (1945 – 1976) 142

ESSAY)

CHAPTER 5:   **Decolonisation and independent Africa**   189

(SELF STUDY)

ESSAY)

CHAPTER 6:   **South Africa (1924–48)**   241

(FINAL EXAMS)

Foreword

This is the final book in the new *Looking into the Past* History Series for Grades 10, 11 and 12 (Further Education and Training). This unique series of books covers the interim curriculum introduced in 1995, but is firmly based on the ideas of the outcomes-based approach to learning. The books embrace the new curriculum by offering a competency-based interactive and learner-centred methodology. Learners are encouraged to become historians and use real sources drawn from paintings, old records, diary accounts as well as archaeological remains.

Content

The material content of the series takes a bold step beyond the syllabuses of the past; providing learners and teachers with a stimulating and original alternative for studying and teaching history.

There is a separate section on the history of Africa with emphasis on decolonisation and the problems of independence; a new perspective has been given to South African history and in Grade 12 the themes of segregation and resistance run through the period 1900 to the first democratic elections in 1994. New materials have been produced for the general history sections and the Cold War has been followed through up to 1991.

Looking into the Past and outcomes-based education

The study of history relates to the Human and Social Sciences learning area of the outcomes-based curriculum. At the beginning of each chapter the relevant specific outcomes are stated. These outcomes are divided into knowledge outcomes, concepts and skills outcomes, and value outcomes, which are promoted by the study of history. Exercises and tests are integrated into each unit, providing a vehicle for self-assessment. Various types of examination questions provide practice for the formal examinations. In addition, research assignments serve as an incentive for co-operative learning and continuous assessment.

Competencies and skills development

Historical competencies are developed systematically throughout the three books in the *Looking into the Past* series. The Grade 10 book introduces basic historical and analytical skills. These are developed further in Grade 11. The Grade 12 book develops more advanced skills of analysis and interpretation, while also emphasising the skills that learners will need for writing their final examinations. All three the books emphasise reference skills, information-finding skills and writing skills.

The grid on the next two pages outlines the competencies developed within the series of three books in the *Looking into the Past* series.

A note on the skills covered in this book

Historical competencies are dealt with developmentally throughout the *Looking into the Past* series. The following table summarises the skills that are taught in the series. In the Grade 10 book some basic competencies are introduced; these include the more technical skills of how to read a graph or a table. These skills are further developed in the Grade 11 book along with some skills concerning critical thinking. The Grade 12 book focuses on the development of more advanced critical thinking skills and finally also on skills related to the examinations that learners will write.

The skills outlined in this table correspond closely with the specific outcomes and range statements that form part of the Human and Social Sciences learning area.

Skills	Grade 10
Chronology	<ul><li>Timelines</li><li>Sequencing events</li><li>Dating sources</li></ul>
Evidence and sources	**Different types of sources**<ul><li>oral</li><li>primary</li><li>secondary</li></ul>**Written sources**<ul><li>travellers' accounts</li><li>documents</li></ul>**Visual sources**<ul><li>maps</li><li>graphs</li><li>photographs</li><li>statistics</li><li>cartoons</li></ul>
Critical Thinking	<ul><li>Questioning a source</li><li>Bias</li><li>Reliability analysis of a written text</li></ul>
Communication	<ul><li>Understanding change and continuity</li><li>Language: defining terms</li><li>Techniques for debating</li><li>Paragraphs: analysis and writing</li><li>Essay writing: basic techniques; analysis of questions; planning and writing</li></ul>

Grade 11	Grade 12
• As in Grade 10	• As in Grades 10 and 11 • Causes and consequences • Change/continuity: similarities/differences
Different types of sources • As in grade 10 • local history • newspapers **Written sources** • As in Grade 10 **Visual sources** • As in Grade 10	**Different types of sources** • As in Grades 10 and 11 • Primary and secondary sources • Archaeological sources **Written sources** • As in Grades 10 and 11 • Statistics **Visual sources** • As in Grades 10 and 11
• Chart and text analysis • Making value judgements • Research technique	**Development of advanced skills** • Questioning a source • Fact, opinion, propaganda • Bias, reliability • Generalisations and historical interpretations • Problem-solving
• Techniques for learning (synthesising information) • Developing empathy • Group work • Making an oral presentation • Essay writing	• As in Grades 10 and 11 • Looking at similarity and differences • Developing empathy • Essay writing • Examination technique

The rise of Soviet Russia (1917–39)

chapter 1

contents

Timeline

Romanov Imperial Dynasty	1914	First World War begins
	1917	February and October Revolutions
Soviet Russia under Lenin	1918	Civil war begins
	1921	Civil war ends; NEP introduced
The struggle for power	1924	Lenin dies; Power struggle begins
	1928	Stalin wins power struggle; First Five Year Plan begins
Soviet Russia under Stalin	1932	First Five Year Plan ends
	1933	Second Five Year Plan begins
	1934	Death of Kirov: purges begin
	1937	Third Five Year Plan begins
	1938	Purges halted
	1939	Second World War begins

chapter outcomes

Knowledge outcomes

As you work through this chapter you will be able to:
- explain how Russia became the first country in the world to have a successful communist revolution;
- discuss Lenin's political and economic policies;
- discuss the power struggle which emerged once Lenin had died;
- discuss Stalin's Five Year Plans;
- account for and describe Stalin's political terror.

concepts and skills outcomes

As you work through this chapter you will learn about and apply skills and concepts such as how to:
- explain the concepts of cause and consequence, and continuity and change;
- extract information from historical sources;
- compare various types of historical sources and reach conclusions based on this comparison;
- analyse events and issues of the past from the perspectives of those who lived in the past (that is, show empathy);
- interpret and evaluate evidence: be able to distinguish between fact and opinion and be able to detect bias and inconsistencies.

Value outcomes

As you work through this chapter you will get the chance to think about:
- the use and abuse of power, and whether absolute power corrupts absolutely;
- whether a goal should be attained no matter what the consequences are.

This chapter covers Specific Outcomes 2, 4, 5, 8 and 9 of the Human and Social Sciences learning area.

Unit 1 Conditions in Russia prior to 1917

Unit outcomes

- Discuss the political, social and economic conditions that prevailed in Russia before the outbreak of the 1917 revolution.
- Explain the cause and consequences of the 1905 Revolution.
- Discuss the consequences of Russia's participation in the First World War.
- Define the concepts capitalism, socialism and communism.
- Compare historical sources and reach conclusions based on this comparison.
- Interpret a historical cartoon.

▲ Diagram of the Hammer and Sickle

Introduction

1917 was a turbulent and decisive year in Russian politics. When it began Tsar Nicholas II was on the throne; when it ended the Bolsheviks, led by Lenin, were in power and beginning to establish the world's first communist state. How did this change come about? And how did Russia, a farming country and industrially backward in 1917, rise to become a superpower within a matter of three decades?

In this chapter we set out to answer these questions. But before we do, let us pause for a moment to think about the emblem of the new communist state that Lenin and the Bolsheviks set about establishing.

The Hammer served as a symbol of the industrial workers, who were also known as the proletariat. The Sickle represented the peasants who worked on the land. It was the belief of the communists that the workers and peasants would work together to shape a wealthy new society in which all would be equal.

If we are to grasp the changes that took place in Russia from 1917 – seen by many as a turning-point in the history of the twentieth century – we need to examine the political, social and economic conditions that existed in Russia before that date.

◀ **Source A**
Political map of the Russian Empire, 1900 (Adapted from: Mantin and Lankester. *From Romanov to Gorbachev: Russia in the 20th century.*)

Activities ·······················

1 How does the size of Russia compare with that of other countries in Source A?
2 Can you see from Source A how Russia was trying to solve the problem of its size?
3 How useful is Source A as a source of evidence to a historian studying the Russian Revolution?

··

The Tsar of Russia

At the beginning of the twentieth century Russia was ruled by Tsar Nicholas II. His family, the Romanovs, had been in power since 1613. Nicholas himself became king in October 1894, at the age of 26. Although he was well educated and widely travelled, Nicholas was not a strong ruler. He was full of goodwill and generosity, but he lacked the intelligence necessary for conducting affairs of state. He was, in addition, easily influenced by his wife and public servants which gave his regime a certain instability.

▲ The Tsar and Tsarina

Activities ·······················

Was Nicholas fit to govern an empire like Russia? Study the quotations provided in Source B and then decide for yourself.

·······················

▼ Source B

1 An extract from the Diary of Nicholas II on the day he became Tsar

What is going to happen to me, to all Russia? I am not prepared to be the Tsar. I never wanted to become one. I know nothing of the business of ruling. I have no idea of even how to talk to ministers.

2 From *Papa Tsar*, a biography of Tsar Nicholas II

Nicholas disliked making decisions and above all he disliked saying disagreeable things to people ... Nicholas made no attempt to see for himself what went on in his Empire. He never visited factories, schools or industrial areas in the towns.

3 Statement by Leon Trotsky, 1932

His ancestors did not bequeath him one quality which would have made him capable of governing an empire.

4 Comment by a Russian Cabinet Minister

Nicholas was not fit to run a village post office.

(All from: Mantin and Lankester. *From Romanov to Gorbachev*.)

···

Opposition to the Tsar

Like his predecessors Nicholas ruled as an autocrat, that is, he possessed absolute, total power. The decrees he passed were binding on the people and anyone who opposed his rule was shot or sent to Siberia to work on the salt mines. During his rule books and newspapers were censored and a secret police force, the Okhrana, spied on people. The church supported the Tsar's autocratic rule, and priests taught people that he was their 'Little Father' who had to be obeyed.

Before long there was a call for political reform. Demands were made for an elected parliament and greater civil liberties, but Nicholas consistently ignored these demands. Various groups then emerged to challenge Nicholas' autocratic rule.

- The Liberals wanted to replace Tsarist rule with a democratic parliamentary government.
- Another group, the Socialist Revolutionary Party, wanted to overthrow the Tsar and establish a socialist society.
- A third group was the Russian Social Democratic Workers Party (RSDWP) which wanted to replace Tsarist rule with a classless society in which all would be equal. The RSDWP believed in the ideas of Karl Marx, a German philosopher who challenged the exploitation and inequalities of capitalism. (You can find out more about Karl Marx and capitalism on pages 4 and 5.)

One of the leaders of the Social Democratic Workers Party, and a prominent interpreter of Marxism, was Vladimir Ulyanov, better known by his pen-name Lenin. At a congress of the party held in London in 1903, Lenin called for the formation of a small, well organised party of revolutionaries that would seek the support of peasants and workers for the Communist Revolution. Lenin's views at the congress caused the party to split into two groups, the Bolsheviks (meaning 'majority') and Mensheviks (meaning 'minority'). Lenin went on to lead the Bolsheviks, and his followers were known by this name only because he was able to get the majority of those present at the congress of 1903 to support his views. By 1905 the Bolsheviks and Mensheviks were holding separate congresses and by 1911 they had formally separated.

The groups in opposition to Nicholas put pressure on him to bring about change. But he refused to agree to their demands. Instead he denied them legal status and forced them to work in secret.

Profile: Lenin (1870–1924)

© RIA-Novosti Photos

Lenin was born in 1870 and eventually went to Kazan University to study law. He was a brilliant scholar who qualified as a lawyer in 1891. While at university he became involved in revolutionary activities and was frequently arrested because of this. He was in and out of prison, and it was at a prison camp in Siberia that he married Nadezhda Krupskaya. In 1900 he left Russia with his wife for exile in Europe.

Lenin was a follower of Karl Marx, and from exile in Europe he tried to spread Marxist teachings in Russia through newspapers such as *Iskra* (meaning 'The Spark') and *Pravda* (meaning 'Truth'). These were smuggled into Russia. After the revolution of 1905 Lenin returned to Russia, but the failure of the revolution made him more determined than ever to get rid of the Tsar.

The ideas of Karl Marx

The ideas of Marx, which were put forward in the *Communist Manifesto* (1848) and *Das Kapital* (1867), are summarised below.

1 Throughout history society has been characterised by a struggle between classes, between the 'Haves' (those who have wealth and power) and the 'Have Nots'.
2 The final struggle will be between the capitalists (land and factory owners) and the proletariat (working class).
3 The capitalists will not surrender their power without a fight. A violent revolution will be needed to overthrow them. (Marx anticipated these revolutions occurring in the industrialised countries of Western Europe because of the huge numbers of proletariat. The first successful revolution, however, took place in Russia which, ironically, comprised a majority of peasants).
4 After the revolution, a socialist government would take over the country. Land, factories and the banks would be nationalised.
5 In time competition among people for wealth and power would give way to cooperation. Society would reach a final stage of communism – a perfect society (utopia) in which there would be no shortage of foods and goods; no class struggle since everyone would be equal; and no government to regulate the conduct of people.

Understanding capitalism, socialism and communism

Capitalism

Capitalism is an economic system that encourages individuals to compete for wealth and power against each other.

In theory, each individual in a capitalist society can make as much wealth as he or she wishes. In practice it is only a few who really become wealthy. In a capitalist society, therefore, the distribution of wealth is uneven. Because of this, classes emerge and the distinction between classes is quite sharp. Some people are very rich and some very poor.

In a capitalist society the relationship between capital and labour is problematic. Labour may complain about poor pay and bad working conditions. For this reason workers form trade unions to bargain with employers.

Profile: Karl Marx (1818–83)

© RIA-Novosti Photos

Karl Marx was born in Germany in 1818. He was a brilliant intellectual who held radical political views. He was constantly in trouble with the authorities and eventually fled Germany with his family. He went to London where he spent most of his time writing articles for journals and newspapers. In 1848 he published the *Communist Manifesto* which he co-wrote with Friedrich Engels. He went on to write *Das Kapital* which was published in three volumes.

Marx was an ardent socialist who was extremely critical of capitalism. Marx said that all history is about struggles between different classes. In feudal times, where people lived off the land, the struggle was between land owners and peasants. When society became industrialised the struggle was between the capitalists (those who owned the means of production, distribution and exchange) and the proletariat (workers).

Marx believed that workers would not tolerate being exploited forever and would overthrow the capitalists in a violent revolution. They would then seize power and, after establishing a socialist government, would prepare society for a final stage of communism in which class conflict would cease to exist. Despite the strength of his ideas Marx lived in poverty for much of his life.

Socialism

Socialism is a political and economic system that advocates state ownership and control of the means of production (farms and factories), distribution (railways, shops), and exchange (banks).

Socialism claims to prevent social inequality. Socialism was a product of the industrial revolution which first began in England. The revolution created a capitalist society in which only a handful of people became wealthy. The majority of people were workers and they were exploited by the capitalists. They worked long hours for extremely low wages and were forbidden to form trade unions. Because people earned so little, they were unable to afford decent houses and usually lived in poor housing.

People calling themselves socialists condemned this ill-treatment of workers. They believed that if society was organised differently it would eliminate inequalities among people. Socialists believed:

- that people should cooperate rather than compete with each other. Individuals are to use their talents and skills not for their own self-interest, but for the good of the community or country.
- that there should be no private ownership of property: that all property, land, banks and industry should be controlled and owned by the community.

Communism

In a narrow sense, communism is a social and economic system in which people live and work in communes on an equal footing and share in the profits of their collective labour. In a broader political sense, communism refers to the creation of a perfect society (utopia) achieved when the workers – in a revolution – overthrow the capitalists and take control of the farms, factories, railways, shops and banks.

When society reaches the stage of communism there would be no shortage of food and goods. No one person or group would have more than another. Hence class struggle would disappear and a classless society would emerge. In this classless society people would cooperate with each other according to the following principle: '*From each according to his ability, to each according to his needs*'. In other words, people would give freely to society what they were best able to do, and take, in return, what they needed to survive and no more. In this perfect society people would live in complete harmony with each other. Consequently there would be no need for government or the security forces to regulate social relationships. The institution of government, according to Karl Marx, would eventually 'wither away'.

Activities

1 Make a list of the different features of each system. Choose one issue, for example, ownership of land, and compare the positions of the three systems on this issue.
2 Which economic system do you prefer? Give reasons for your choice.

Social and economic conditions

At the beginning of the twentieth century the population of Russia was approximately 140 million. In Source C you will find a breakdown of the composition of Russian society at that time. Study the table and make a careful note of the composition of the different groups.

▼ *Source C* Russian society in 1900

Nobles	1,5%
Priests	0,5%
Middle class	10,0%
Peasants	78,0%
Working classes	10,0%

(From: H Mills. *Twentieth century world history in focus.*)

Activities ....

1 What percentage of the population were nobles?
2 What percentage of the population were peasants?

....

It is quite clear, on looking at the table, that the majority of Russians were peasants. These peasants lived in villages such as the one in Source D.

Activities ....

Look closely at Source D.
1 What kinds of houses do these people live in?
2 What do you notice about their clothes?
3 How big is the family?
4 Does the farm look prosperous?

....

Peasants and workers

Of all the groups in Russia peasants were, by far, the poorest and least educated. Though freed from serfdom (slavery) in 1861 they were always in debt, and life was a constant struggle. Although they made up the majority of the population, the peasants only shared in about 10 per cent of the nation's wealth. The greater share of the country's wealth – over 50 per cent – was controlled by the nobles. The distribution of wealth was clearly uneven.

The lack of money caused the peasants much hardship, and diseases such as typhoid and cholera saw two out of every five peasant children die in infancy. On occasions, reforms were introduced to ease the burden of the peasants, such as those introduced by Peter Stolypin, Prime Minister to Tsar Nicholas II. Although Stolypin allowed peasants to break away from the communal system (the MIR) and own their own lands, the peasants were no better off. Large numbers of peasants then left the countryside for the towns where they hoped to find employment and a better life.

The situation in the towns was hardly any better. By the time Nicholas II came to the throne industrialisation had already started. Huge iron foundries and textile factories were set up. For the majority of workers conditions in the mines and factories were very bad. Wages were very low – under twenty roubles a month – the hours very long, and there was a lack of decent housing. In addition, workers were not allowed to strike or form trade unions.

▼ *Source D* Photograph of peasants in the late nineteenth century
(From: C Culpin. *Making History. World History from 1914 to the Present.*)

Tsar Nicholas II did little to improve the conditions of his people. It was therefore not surprising to see groups such as the Bolsheviks exploit the bad socio-economic conditions. To the oppressed workers and peasants, the Bolshevik vision of a classless society seemed extremely attractive.

The revolution of 1905

In the first few years of the twentieth century there were few signs that the simmering discontent in Russia would result in a revolution against the Tsar. However, the outbreak of war between Russia and Japan in 1904 brought the discontent to the surface.

When war broke out, patriotic fever gripped the Russians. It looked as if the war might strengthen the Tsar's authority, but it was not to be. The Russians, who were expecting to win easily, suffered a humiliating defeat at Port Arthur on the Chinese coast. This defeat triggered off a number of strikes and public demonstrations. For example, on Sunday, 9 January 1905, a group of 250 000 people marched towards the Tsar's palace in St Petersburg. They wanted to hand him a petition in which they demanded shorter working hours, better pay for women and free medical aid.

Bloody Sunday

The march, led by Father Gapon, was a peaceful one. However, when the marchers reached the palace they were given two orders to disperse. The marchers defied the orders. The soldiers then opened fire while Cossack troops charged the crowd with heavy swords. Over a hundred marchers were killed and several hundred more were wounded. Father Gapon, who escaped, wrote this of the massacre known as 'Bloody Sunday': 'This is the work of our Little Father, the Tsar. There is no longer any Tsar for us.'

The two sources below provide two different descriptions of 'Bloody Sunday'.

▼ *Source E*

Extract from the diary of Tsar Nicholas II, 9 January 1905

9 January, Sunday. A painful day! There have been serious disorders in St Petersburg because workmen wanted to come up to the Winter Palace. Troops had to open fire in several places in the city. There were many killed and wounded. God, how painful and sad! Mama arrived from town, straight to Mass. I lunched with all the others. Went for a walk with Misha. Mama stayed overnight.

(From: Mantin and Lankester. *From Romanov to Gorbachev.*)

▼ *Source F*

Description of 'Bloody Sunday' by the revolutionary, Leon Trotsky

'Let us through to the Tsar!' The old ones fell on their knees. The women begged and the children begged. 'Let us through to the Tsar!' – and then it happened! The guns went off with thunder ... The snow reddened with workers' blood ... Tell all and sundry in what way the Tsar has dealt with the toilers of St Petersburg.

(From: Mantin and Lankester. *From Romanov to Gorbachev.*)

Activities ....

1 What differences do you notice between the descriptions of 'Bloody Sunday' in Source E and Source F?
2 Why do you think the two descriptions are different?

....

A Duma is formed

The massacre angered the nation and sparked off widespread riots and rebellion. Sailors on the battleship Potemkin – and on other ships – mutinied. The first Soviet (Council of Workers and Soldiers) was set up in Petrograd and it organised a series of strikes. Revolutionaries like Trotsky returned to Russia to help overthrow the Tsar. It appeared as if the Tsar would lose his throne, but Nicholas acted quickly. Using troops and the secret police, he arrested the leaders of the Soviets and stopped the riots in the streets. In an effort to please the masses he published the October Manifesto. He promised to improve the situation of factory workers and peasants. He also agreed to constitute a Duma (parliament) in which all classes would be represented. The rebellion died down as the hopes of a troubled nation came to centre on the proposed Duma.

The Duma, when it was finally constituted, was dominated by nobles and the middle class. Nevertheless, it demanded a greater say in the running of the country. Nicholas made it clear that he was not willing to share power with the Duma. He declared: 'To the Emperor of all Russia belongs supreme autocratic power.' The first Duma was soon closed down, as was the second one in May 1907. The next two Dumas, dominated by landlords, caused the Tsar few problems and therefore completed their five year terms. By his actions Nicholas demonstrated that he was unwilling to introduce a political system in keeping with the needs of his people.

The First World War (1914–18)

Elsewhere in Europe events began to take a turn for the worse. Rivalry among the major powers made war inevitable. The war finally broke out in July 1914, a month after the assassination of the Austrian Archduke, Franz Ferdinand. Austria blamed the assassination on Serbia and, after failing to resolve the murder through diplomatic means, declared war on Serbia on 28 July. Russia, for reasons of her own, chose to help Serbia and on 30 July Tsar Nicholas ordered a general mobilisation. Germany, Austria's ally, viewed this as a hostile act and declared war on Russia on 1 August.

Among the Russians there was tremendous enthusiasm for the war. But within a year, after military defeats at Tannenburg and Galicia, initial Russian enthusiasm turned to despair. Russia was also not well prepared for the war, and in the first ten months of the war alone 3,8 million men were lost. From the beginning, too, there were complaints about a shortage of equipment, ammunition and boots. Most of these complaints were genuine, and the government's delay in attending to them caused soldiers to desert in their thousands.

In August 1915 Nicholas II took over as commander-in-chief of the army, contrary to the advice of his ministers. With Nicholas at the war front the Tsarina Alexandra assumed responsibility for governing Russia. Against her better judgement she allowed Gregory Rasputin, a Siberian holy man, to interfere in the affairs of state. Rasputin had become the Tsarina's close confidant and spiritual advisor after he had seemingly cured the Tsarina's only son and heir, Alexis, of haemophilia (a disease which prevents blood from clotting). Rasputin's importance caused deep resentment, especially among the nobility at the Imperial Court. In two years Rasputin hired and fired 21 ministers, turning government into a joke and undermining the credibility of the throne itself. After several unsuccessful attempts on his life, Rasputin was finally murdered by Prince Yusupov.

Meanwhile, the war had taken a heavy toll on the Russian economy. Food and fuel were in short supply. Prices rose, and strikes occurred more frequently. To make matters worse, troops who deserted from the front joined the striking workers, prompting Rodzianko, President of the Duma, to warn Nicholas that 'chaos reigns every-

▼ Source G

A cartoon of 1915 showing Rasputin holding Nicholas and Alexandra as puppets

© David King Collection

where'. There was little Nicholas could do: he was still at the war front. He didn't realise that the social and economic structure of Russia was on the verge of collapse; or that the food riots in Petrograd would lead to a spontaneous revolution which would remove him from power.

Activities

1 What is the cartoonist trying to say about Rasputin's power in Source G?
2 What effect would Rasputin's power have on people's feelings about Nicholas?
3 Nicholas and Alexandra were not really puppets on the knees of a giant Rasputin. What does Source G actually tell us about what was going on in Russia?
4 Why is it unlikely that Source G would be seen in Russia?

Unit 2

The revolutions of February and October 1917

Unit outcomes

- Describe the course and explain the consequences of the February Revolution.
- Explain the 'Dual Authority' that assumed control of Russia.
- Give reasons why Germany helped Lenin return to Russia.
- Discuss Lenin's April Theses.
- Discuss the cause and consequences of the July uprising.
- Explain the reasons for the Kornilov Insurrection (rebellion).
- Compare historical sources.
- Trace the steps the Bolsheviks took to seize power in October 1917.
- Discuss the consequences of the October Revolution.

The February Revolution

The First World War (1914–18) provided the catalyst for political change. As news of the military failures filtered through, there were demands for a more democratic and competent government. Nicholas II would not yield to these demands and cries of 'Down with the Tsar' soon filled the air.

When the revolution came, it was spontaneous. It started on 22 February 1917 in the Russian capital, Petrograd. News of a shortage of bread sparked off rioting and demonstrations on the streets. Almost simultaneously, workers from the Putilov engineering works went on strike. As the streets filled with demonstrators, shops and bakeries were looted in full view of soldiers sent to the city to restore order. This time, unlike the revolution of 1905, the soldiers sympathised with the demonstrators, and refused to fire on them when ordered to do so.

On 27 February a regiment mutinied and killed its officers in the process. Anarchy continued, and before the end of the week the entire city of Petrograd was in the hands of the mob.

▼ Source A

A tired old man, carrying a dinner basin tied up in a red handkerchief, tried to push his way through the crowd. A soldier stopped him ... The old man explained that

if he could reach the other side of the river, his daughter might let him have a little food ... The soldier refused and turned away. The old man trailed wearily after him ... This annoyed the officer: he ordered the soldier to take the old man away. The soldier did not move ... The officer rode up to the old man and slashed him furiously across the face with his whip. The old man dropped his basin and began to cry. Without a word, the soldier drew his sabre and killed the officer.

Pandemonium broke loose. Soldiers killed all their officers. The crowd went mad and tried to rush the bridge.

(From: N Poliakoff. *Coco the Clown.* In C Culpin. *Making History.*)

Activities

Source A describes just one incident of the February Revolution.

1 What happened to the officer?
2 Why did the soldier kill the officer?
3 Analyse how useful Source A is in helping us to understand the February Revolution.

The President of the Duma, Rodzianko, then cabled the Tsar who was still on the war front. Rodzianko's message called for the formation of a government that would enjoy the confidence of the people. But Nicholas ignored Rodzianko's call for a new government for Russia. He decided instead to dissolve the existing Duma. However, the deputies serving in the Duma refused to disperse.

As his authority grew weaker, Nicholas tried to hurry back to Petrograd. But his train was detoured to army headquarters at Pskov. There, on the advice of his generals, he decided to abdicate (give up his throne). He abdicated eventually in favour of his brother, the Grand Duke Michael. But Michael refused to reign without popular consent, and subsequently declined the throne. Consequently, after 300 years, the Romanov Imperial Dynasty came to an end. Tsar Nicholas requested that he and his family be allowed to go to Britain, but they were arrested and sent to exile in Siberia. A provisional (temporary) government was then formed by members of the Duma.

The Dual Authority

The provisional government which assumed power planned to rule Russia until the election of a Constituent Assembly (a body that would draw up the Constitution). Prince Lvov, leader of the Zemstvos' Union, became prime minister of the new government. Paul Milyukov became foreign minister, and Alexander Kerensky, leader of the Socialist Revolutionary Party, became minister of justice. The provisional government, however, was not the only institution of authority in Russia. The power vacuum created by the collapse of the monarchy was also filled by the Petrograd Soviet of Workers' and Soldiers' Deputies. Whereas the provisional government represented the interests of the middle class, the Petrograd Soviet represented the ordinary workers, soldiers and peasants.

▲ Alexander Kerensky

The provisional government and Petrograd Soviet together made up the 'Dual Authority' that was to rule Russia over the next few months. However, the Petrograd Soviet sometimes acted as if it were the national government. It issued its own proclamations and orders, for instance Order No. 1 which ordered all soldiers to obey only the Soviet. The provisional government found itself unable to reverse this Order, and its acceptance of the Soviet Order showed that it lacked legitimacy.

The provisional government nevertheless won the support of the Petrograd Soviet for the reforms it introduced. It granted amnesty to political and religious prisoners, abolished capital punishment, as well as all discriminatory laws based on class, creed and national origin. It granted freedom of speech and the press, instituted an eight-hour working day, and granted labour the right to strike. It restored the independence of Finland, granted the Poles semi-independence, and made preparations for the election of a Constituent Assembly.

These were sweeping reforms that might have marked the beginning of constitutional democracy in Russia. However, any effort at the development of democracy in Russia was undermined by the government's decision to continue with the war, and to postpone a final decision on the ownership of land until after the Constituent Assembly had met.

This was the situation Russia found herself in when the more radical revolutionaries began to return from domestic and foreign exile.

Return of the exiles

The return of the exiled revolutionaries was to alter the course of Russian history. Like most people they were taken by surprise by the events of February 1917. Nevertheless, they were eager to return to the land of their birth. The most prominent of the revolutionaries were Leon Trotsky, who returned from the United States, and Lenin, who returned from Switzerland. Lenin returned to Russia in a 'sealed train' (from which no one was allowed to get on or off until it reached its destination) provided by the German government. The Germans hoped that Lenin would seize power from the provisional government and take Russia out of the war. If this happened, it would ease the pressure on the Germans of fighting a war on two fronts.

▼ Source B

Painting of Lenin returning to Russia in April 1917

Lenin did not drive the train that took him back to Russia in April 1917 as shown in Source B.

1 In what ways has the artist made him look a hero?

2 Why did Germany help Lenin to return to Russia?

....

Lenin arrived in Petrograd on 3 April 1917 to an enthusiastic welcome from the crowd that had gathered at the railway station. In his address to the crowd, he said: 'We don't need any parliamentary republic. We don't need any bourgeois democracy. We don't need any government except the Soviet of Workers' and Soldiers' Deputies.'

The April Theses

Lenin wasted no time in preparing his followers, the Bolsheviks, for the seizure of political power. At a congress called by the Bolsheviks at the Tauride Palace the day after his arrival, he unveiled his blueprint (master plan) known as the April Theses. He demanded an end to the war. He called for the nationalisation of land and industry, and for the merger of all banks into one national bank under Soviet control. He also urged his followers to withdraw their support of the provisional government. Finally, he advocated the transfer of all power to the Soviets which would take control of production and distribution.

The April Theses were instantly criticised, particularly by those Bolsheviks who seemed not to grasp the key to it all. For Lenin the bourgeois-democratic phase of the revolution was over (in this case, the February Revolution). What had to be done now was to prepare for the transition to the socialist phase. The only thing that remained uncertain, of course, was the timing of the socialist revolution. Despite these criticisms a special All-Russian Party Conference approved, by 37 votes to 3, the essential points of Lenin's April Theses.

The demands of Lenin and the Bolsheviks soon found expression in the slogans 'Down with the Provisional Government', 'All Power to the Soviets', and 'Peace, Land, Bread'. In the circumstances of the time the slogans had a powerful effect. Lenin offered what the people wanted. By July, when an uprising shook the country, the membership of the Bolshevik party had risen to 100 000, from just 20 000 in February.

New words

disgruntled having grievances

The July Uprising

In June the minister of war, Alexander Kerensky, ordered a new military offensive. This was intended to boost the army's morale and to distract attention from the country's domestic problems. Led by General Brusilov, the offensive against the Austro-Hungarian forces in Galicia got off to a successful start. The Russians captured several thousand prisoners and a few towns. But when the Germans sent in reinforcements to help the Austrians, the Russian forces panicked and fled.

The failure of the military offensive sparked off the 'July Uprising'. **Disgruntled** soldiers from the Petrograd garrison and sailors from the Kronstadt naval base issued a call for an uprising. Almost instantly, a large, leaderless mob answered the call. Thousands of demonstrators – many of whom were Bolsheviks – took to the streets demanding that the provisional government resign and power be handed to the Soviets. The Petrograd Soviet, however, would not support the call. Lenin himself watched these develop-

◀*Source C*

Rioting on the streets of Petrograd in July 1917

© David King Collection

ments with interest but took no steps to either control or direct the excited mob. With no one to give the mob leadership and direction, the uprising, which caused several deaths, quickly fizzled out.

Activities

1 Describe what you see happening in Source C.
2 Why are these people rioting?
3 .Where are people running to or what are they running from?

The provisional government re-establishes its authority

The provisional government chose to use the uprising to re-establish its authority. Because of the involvement of some Bolsheviks in the uprising, the government decided to suppress the Bolsheviks. Bolshevik offices were raided by government forces and the Bolshevik newspaper, *Pravda*, was banned. Lenin was called a German spy and the government ordered his arrest on a charge of encouraging armed insurrection. Lenin protested his innocence but had to flee to Finland to escape arrest. He remained there until mid-October 1917. Many prominent Bolsheviks, including Trotsky and Kamenev, were arrested.

Shortly after the uprising Prince Lvov resigned as prime minister and a new coalition government was formed. Alexander Kerensky took over as prime minister and led a cabinet of sixteen ministers, none of whom were Bolsheviks. The actions taken by the government against the Bolsheviks severely weakened them, but it proved to be only a temporary setback.

The Kornilov Insurrection

Whatever support and status the Bolsheviks lost through the July Uprising, they soon regained through the Kornilov Insurrection of September 1917. General Lavr Kornilov had succeeded General Brusilov as commander-in-chief of the Russian armies. He was convinced that the Soviets, especially the one in Petrograd, were the biggest threat to Russia and the source of all her troubles. In a speech given in 1917 he said: 'It is time to hang the German supporters and spies, with Lenin at their head, and to disperse the Soviets of Workers' and Soldiers' Deputies so that they can never reassemble.'

Kornilov hoped not only to **oust** the Petrograd Soviet but to overthrow Kerensky and establish a military dictatorship. When Kerensky learnt of Kornilov's plans he dismissed him from his post.

But the General refused to surrender his post and instead ordered his troops to march on Petrograd. In desperation, Kerensky appealed to the Bolsheviks for help. Once they agreed, he released the Bolsheviks, including Trotsky, from prison and sent arms and ammunition to the Petrograd Soviet.

All socialist organisations in Petrograd – Mensheviks, Bolsheviks and Socialist Revolutionaries – decided to jointly oppose the threat posed by Kornilov. They mobilised the Petrograd garrison, alerted the Kronstadt sailors, armed the Petrograd workers, dug trenches across the city and disrupted the rail and telegraph systems. With little effort both government and revolutionary forces stopped Kornilov's troops from entering the city of Petrograd. When Kornilov's most loyal troops refused to fight, the whole expedition fell apart. Kornilov himself was subsequently arrested but released later that year.

New words

oust to eject; drive out; seize the place of

© Gallo Images (Pty) Ltd. (The Hulton Getty Collection)

▲ General Kornilov

Kerensky's reliance on the Bolsheviks weakened his own position as prime minister. Once again, the Bolsheviks benefited from the turn of events. It appeared to many that the Bolsheviks had saved the revolution from military dictatorship. Within a week of the coup the Bolsheviks won control of the Moscow and Petrograd Soviets. By October Trotsky had become chairman of the Petrograd Soviet, and membership of the Bolshevik Party surged to 200 000.

Understanding historical skills and concepts

Comparing historical sources

In trying to explain past events historians make use of sources. A number of sources are available to the historian, such as written sources (documents, diaries and newspaper reports) and visual sources (photographs and paintings).

Activities ....
Find examples in this chapter so far of a written and a visual source.

....

By questioning the sources a historian gathers evidence with which to explain past events. Only when he or she has done this will a historian offer an opinion about an event. Not all historians will give the same opinion or reach the same conclusions, even though they may consult the same sources. This illustrates the point that history is a matter of interpretation. Of course, some interpretations are more plausible (believable) than others.

Throughout this chapter you will be asked to compare various types of historical sources and to reach conclusions based on this comparison. The idea is to develop your ability to make judgements about events that are supported by evidence. It is wise not to accept the sources at their face value. Remember, it is a poor historian who bases his or her judgement on just one source of information. Wherever possible consult other sources to confirm your point of view.

The sources below on the Kornilov Insurrection illustrate the difficulty facing historians when they try to gather evidence about past events. Study the sources, and then answer the questions which follow.

▼ *Source D*
Many people had the mistaken idea that Kerensky was defending democracy against reaction. In reality, the struggle between Kerensky and Kornilov arose not so much out of political differences as out of political similarities. While the Right looked upon the Supreme Commander as a dictator who would save the country from anarchy, Kerensky simply thought that he himself was the better qualified candidate for that office. His shift to the Right had been accompanied by the adoption of an increasingly conservative programme (discipline, sacrifice, labour) and also by a growing taste for personal power ... It is possible that he had all along intended to turn the Kornilov plot to his own

advantage – in any case he admitted that he had known about it since the end of the Moscow Conference [15 August] ... But while Kerensky was more than willing to make use of Kornilov's services and to include him in the cabinet, he was not at all disposed to take second place to him. That was why on August 26, when Kornilov's true aims could no longer be mistaken, he ordered him to 'surrender your post' ... Kornilov was stunned ... he refused point blank to resign his post, and in doing so transformed his fight with the Soviet and the working class into open rebellion against the Provisional Government ...

(From: M Liebman. *The Russian Revolution.*)

▼ *Source E*
Kornilov's rapid rise made him suspect to the Soviet ... [He] became an early focus for all counter-revolutionary forces. His programme was simplicity itself. 'The time has come to hang the German agents and spies, headed by Lenin' he told his aide-de-camp, 'to disperse the Soviet of Workers' and Soldiers' Deputies so that it can never reassemble' ...

(From: L Kochan. *Russia in Revolution.*)

▼ *Source F*
Kerensky's telegram to the country, 27 August 1917

I hereby announce:

On August 26 General Kornilov sent ... a demand for the surrender by the Provisional Government of all civil and military power, so that he may form, according to his wishes, a new government to administer the country ... [which] was confirmed subsequently by General Kornilov in his conversation with me by direct wire ...

I hereby order:

1 General Kornilov to surrender his post ...

2 The city ... of Petrograd to be placed under martial law ...

(From: *Vestnik Vremmenago Pravitelstva*, 29 August 1917.)

▼ *Source G*
Kornilov's response to the telegram, 27 August 1917

People of Russia! Our great motherland is dying. The hour of death is near. Obliged to speak openly, I, General Kornilov, declare that under the pressure of the Bolshevik majority in the soviets, the Provisional Government is acting in complete accord with the plans of the German General Staff, and simultaneously with the imminent landing of the enemy forces at Riga, it is destroying the army and is undermining the very foundations of the country.

(From: El Martynov. *Kornilov.*)

▼ *Source H*

Memories of U Kraintsev, a member in 1917 of the Extraordinary Commission of Inquiry into the Kornilov putsch

Kornilov catalogued all the measures which the high command, responsible for waging the war, had proposed to the government in order to rebuild the army and which that command had adopted itself independently to that end.

Finally, Kornilov came to the most important part, a part so unexpected that it literally staggered us. He informed us that in the interests of maintaining order in the capital he had reached an agreement with Kerensky to move a large military force to Petrograd so that disturbances, if they occurred, could be suppressed immediately. It was quite clear from Kornilov's account that the Soviets (the Soviets of Workers' and Soldiers' Deputies) were regarded as the main source of the possible disturbances and that by suppression of disturbances was understood the suppression of none other than the Soviets and, moreover, that this was so understood not only in Stavka, but also by Kerensky himself.

(From: *Novoye Russkoye Slovo.*)

Activities ....

1 Which of the two secondary sources (D or E) would you regard as the more reliable and why?
2 What sources would you need in order to check on the important revelation given in the second paragraph of Source H?

3 Consider the following three interpretations of the Kornilov rebellion.
  a Kornilov acted alone throughout.
  b Kornilov and Kerensky acted together against the Bolsheviks, but did not trust each other.
  c Kerensky turned to the Bolsheviks because he had failed to control Kornilov in a bid for dictatorship.
Use the evidence presented in the sources and your own understanding of the nature of the Kornilov Insurrection to demonstrate which of the three interpretations is most likely.

....

The October Revolution

After the Kornilov Insurrection conditions in Russia deteriorated. On the war front the mainly peasant army began to desert in large numbers. In the countryside, peasants seized the land of the nobility, and simply murdered them if they resisted. Promises by the provisional government to refer the land issue to a Constituent Assembly had not been fulfilled, and the peasants had run out of patience. The situation in the factories was no better. A shortage of raw material forced many factories to close down. As unemployment increased many workers resorted to violence. The more daring ones seized control of industrial plants.

It was the Bolsheviks, more than anyone else, who sought to exploit the discontent and the prevailing anarchy. Lenin, still in exile, decided that it was time for the Bolsheviks to seize power. He said, 'History will not forgive us if we do not seize power now.'

Elections for the long-awaited Constituent Assembly were scheduled for November. Lenin realised that if he wanted the socialist revolution to succeed, it would have to take place before November.

◀*Source I*
A Red Guards detachment

In October Lenin returned from exile in Finland. At a secret meeting held on 10 October, he called for an immediate violent revolution by the proletariat – led and organised by the Bolsheviks – to coincide with the Second All-Russian Congress of Soviets. He saw the revolution as introducing the Marxist stage of a dictatorship of the proletariat in which the proletariat seizes power, overthrows capitalism, and uses terror and violence to eliminate its enemies, the bourgeoisie. For Lenin, the revolution was to be a transfer of power to the working class – a revolution for and by the proletariat supported by the poor peasants. Apart from a few dissenting voices, the meeting agreed in principle to an uprising. On 16 October a military revolutionary committee (MRC) was established by the Petrograd Soviet under the chairmanship of Leon Trotsky. Working from the Smolny Institute, a former convent school

for young women, Trotsky organised the uprising to its last detail. Soldiers from the Petrograd garrison as well as the sailors from the Kronstadt naval base pledged support for the uprising .

Activities ....

1 How many soldiers can you count in Source I?
2 Where do you think those who were not soldiers obtained their weapons?

....

The Bolsheviks seize power

Final arrangements for the uprising were being put into place when, on 18 October, Zinoviev and Kamenev, two Bolsheviks who were opposed to the uprising from the beginning, leaked details of the uprising to a newspaper.

◀ *Source J*

'The Proletarian Hammer hits on …': a contemporary cartoonist's view of October 1917

Lenin was furious. He branded the two men 'traitors' and demanded their expulsion from the Bolshevik Party. Trotsky categorically denied the existence of any impending uprising, but the provisional government was not convinced. It proclaimed a state of emergency, declared the MRC to be illegal, and ordered the arrest of Trotsky and other Bolshevik leaders.

At this point troops loyal to the Bolsheviks swung into action. On the night of 24 October, and the morning of 25 October, the troops occupied strategic points in the capital: the telephone exchange, railway stations, power stations, bridges and public buildings. They met with little resistance. At 10 a.m. on 25 October, Trotsky formally announced the overthrow of the provisional government, by which time Kerensky had fled in a car provided by the United States Embassy. It was only later that evening that the Bolsheviks were able to seize control of the Winter Palace, a former palace of the Tsar used by the provisional government as its headquarters. It had been an almost bloodless coup.
(NOTE: Up to February 1918, Russia used the Julian calendar which at that time differed from the Gregorian calendar used in the West, by thirteen days. The Revolution took place on 25 October 1917 according to the Russian calendar – hence October Revolution – or 7 November, according to the Western calendar.)

Activities

1 What is happening in Source J?
2 Who does the man with the hammer represent?
3 Who are the people flying into the air?
4 Do you think the cartoonist is sympathetic to the proletarians or not?

▼ Source L
The capture of the Winter Palace

By 7 November 1917 the provisional government had dwindled to a meeting of ministers in the Winter Palace ... the provisional government was not overthrown by a mass attack on the Winter Palace. A few Red Guards climbed in through the servants' entrance, found the provisional government in session and arrested the ministers in the name of the people. Six people, five of them Red Guards, were casualties of bad shooting by their own comrades.

(From: AJP Taylor. *Revolutions and Revolutionaries.*)

▶ Source K

Map of Petrograd at the time of the October Revolution
(From: E. Campling. *The Russian Revolution.*)

★ Night of 6 November: first objectives, including main bridges and telegraph station, seized
■ Day of 7 November: second objectives, including railway stations, seized
▲ Evening of 7 November: third objectives, including Winter Palace (HQ of Provisional Government) seized

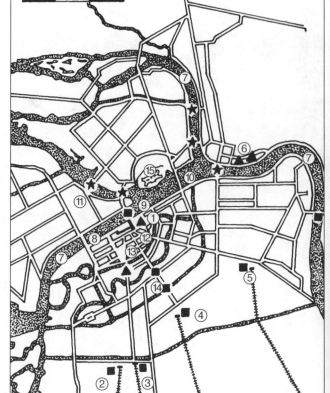

1 Winter Palace	8 Nicholas Bridge
2 Baltic Station	9 Dvortsovyi Bridge
3 Warsaw Station	11 Trotsky Bridge
4 Tarskoye Selo Station	12 Telegraph Station
5 Nicholas Station	13 Post Office
6 Finland Station	14 State Bank
7 River Neva	15 Peter & Paul Fortress

Activities

Study Source K, and then answer questions 1 and 2.

1 Identify, by letter, the building where the Bolsheviks set up their headquarters.
2 Suggest reasons why Trotsky decided to seize
  a those parts of the city labelled ★ first;
  b those parts of the city labelled ■ next;
  c the headquarters of the provisional government (marked ▲) last.
3 Study Source L, describing the capture of the Winter Palace. What evidence, contained in the extract, suggests that the capture of the provisional government did not amount to a 'storming'?

Activities

Study Source M, a photograph taken in Petrograd in June 1917, and then answer these questions.

1 What was the system of government in Russia at the time that this photograph was taken?
2 a What does this photograph show of the political life of Russia at the time that it was taken?
  b How was this different from the situation which had existed at the beginning of 1917?
3 The second banner reads: 'Down with the Capitalist Ministers. All Power to the Soviets'.
  a With which political group in Russia at this time were the slogans, which were written on the second banner in the procession, most closely associated?
  b Who led this group at the time of the photograph?
4 a What do you understand by the word Soviets on the second banner?
  b Explain the importance, during the year 1917, of the slogan on the banner of which this word forms a part.
5 When did capitalist ministers stop holding office in Russia?

◀ **Source M**
Petrograd, June 1917

Unit 3

Lenin's political and economic policies (1917–24)

Unit outcomes

- Trace the steps taken by the Bolsheviks to consolidate their power.
- Explain the terms of the Treaty of Brest-Litovsk.
- Discuss the first Soviet constitution.
- Discuss the cause, course and consequences of the Russian civil war.
- Discuss the cause and consequences of War Communism.
- Discuss the New Economic Policy.

The Council of People's Commissars

The ease with which the Bolsheviks seized power surprised Lenin. Nevertheless he moved quickly to consolidate his power. When the Second All-Russian Congress of Soviets met, he organised the election of the first Soviet government known as the Council of People's Commissars. Lenin was elected chairman of the new government. The government also included Rykov, as commissar (minister) for the interior; Trotsky as commissar for foreign affairs, and Joseph Stalin, as commissar for nationalities.

Winning power in Petrograd was not enough. In the whole of Russia the Bolsheviks were still a minority party. Consequently, the revolution had to be extended countrywide. Hundreds of Bolshevik commissars were sent to towns throughout Russia. But the process of seizing power in the provinces was not as quick as it had been in Petrograd. In certain areas there was strong resistance to the Bolsheviks. In Moscow, for instance, the Bolsheviks only won control after several days of fighting. It did not seem possible that Lenin would hold onto power, but he did. This was largely due to his exceptional skill and judgement.

Elections for a Constituent Assembly

It was during this period of the Bolshevik consolidation of power that Lenin proceeded with the long-awaited elections for the Constituent Assembly. The holding of the elections suggested that Russia might still become a liberal democracy after years of Tsarist autocracy. It was not to be: autocracy was to continue – but under

new masters. The elections, which were held on 12 November, yielded the following results:

▼ *Source A*
The election results

Votes cast	
Social revolutionaries	58%
Bolsheviks	25%
Mensheviks	4%
Others	13%
Number of deputies	
Social revolutionaries	370
Bolsheviks	175
Mensheviks	16
Others	146

(From: Mantin and Lankester. *From Romanov to Gorbachev.*)

Activities ....
1 Which party won the most seats in source A?
2 Why do you think the Bolsheviks won so few seats?
....

Although less than half the electorate had voted, the results showed that the Bolsheviks were still a minority. When it finally met for its first session on 5 January 1918, the Constituent Assembly lasted just one day. On Lenin's instructions, Bolshevik Red Guards dissolved the Assembly. In response to why the Constituent Assembly had to be dissolved, Trotsky remarked: 'We have trampled underfoot the principles of democracy for the sake of the loftier principles of a socialist revolution.' For the Bolsheviks, socialism and parliamentary democracy had become opposing concepts. In dissolving the Constituent Assembly the Bolsheviks turned Russia into a dictatorship of the proletariat. In so doing they made more enemies than friends.

Treaty of Brest-Litovsk

The day after the October Revolution, the Bolsheviks approved the decree on peace, which proposed an end to the First World War without annexations or indemnities. For the Bolsheviks, peace was crucial. Without peace, they could not proceed with building a socialist society in Russia. The new Soviet government, however, lacked international recognition, and no one took their peace efforts seriously. To demonstrate their seriousness, and to force the major powers to negotiate, the Bolsheviks published several secret agreements between the former Tsar's government and its allies. They followed this up on 7 November 1917 with a proposal to the Central Powers of unilateral and immediate cease-fire. The Germans agreed to negotiate with the Bolsheviks, and on 26 November concluded a 30-day armistice (cease-fire) with Russia.

The peace conference between Russia and Germany eventually took place on 9 December at Brest-Litovsk, over 100 km east of Warsaw. Negotiations took a while to conclude. Part of the delay was caused by Trotsky who was sent to negotiate with the Germans. Trotsky's stalling tactics upset the Germans who then renewed military operations all along the eastern front. Lenin decided not to delay matters any further and urged Trotsky to conclude peace regardless of the cost.

Peace was eventually achieved – but on German terms. On 3 March 1918 Russia and Germany concluded the Treaty of Brest-Litovsk. It was a draconian (harsh) peace treaty which the Russians condemned as a blow to the working class. The treaty provided for diplomatic recognition between Russia and the Central Powers; allowed for an exchange of prisoners of war; and provided for a reparations payment by Russia of six billion German mark. Russia was also to recognise the independence of the Ukraine, Georgia and Finland; hand control of Estonia, Latvia, Lithuania and Poland to Germany and Austria-Hungary; and allow Turkey to take control of Kars, Ardahan and Batum. In effect, Russia lost 62 million people, 26 per cent of her railroads, 32 per cent of her arable land, 33 per cent of her factories, and 75 per cent of her coal and iron. Although their losses were catastrophic, it must be remembered that the authority of the Bolsheviks did not extend to the areas it handed over to the Germans. Geographically speaking, Russia was pushed back from the Black Sea and virtually cut off from the Baltic.

The acceptance of the terms caused bitter conflict within the Soviet government and Bolshevik Party. But Lenin was convinced that Russia needed breathing space with which to consolidate communism at home, before embarking on the spread of communism worldwide.

▼ Source B

Map showing boundary changes caused by the Treaty of Brest-Litovsk (Adapted from: Mantin and Lankester. *From Romanov to Gorbachev.*)

▼ Source C   Betrayed

BETRAYED.

THE PANDER. "COME ON; COME AND BE KISSED BY HIM."

1 Look at Source B and suggest reasons why Lenin moved the Russian capital from Petrograd to Moscow.
2 What reason does Source C suggest for the Bolshevik peace offer to Germany?
3 Do you agree with the cartoonist's point of view?

The first Soviet constitution

With Russia out of the war, Lenin began to concentrate on the task of building a socialist society in Russia. As one of his first tasks, Lenin nationalised (made into state or national property) agriculture and abolished private ownership of all land. Peasants were free to work the land, but all property rights in land were held by the state. His

Nevertheless, anyone could believe in any or no religion. The new constitution also offered workers and peasants universal and free education.

Although the new constitution proclaimed the equality of all citizens before the law, it openly favoured workers. In the election of Soviets at every level (from the basic village and city Soviet right to the All-Russian Congress of Soviets) the constitution assigned urban areas a five-to-one advantage over all districts. Finally, supreme political authority was placed in the All-Russian Congress of Soviets, which elected an Executive Committee, which in turn chose the Council of People's Commissars (Sovnarkom).

By their very actions, the Bolsheviks destroyed the roots of Tsarist autocracy that had existed in Russia for centuries. But they also had not laid the

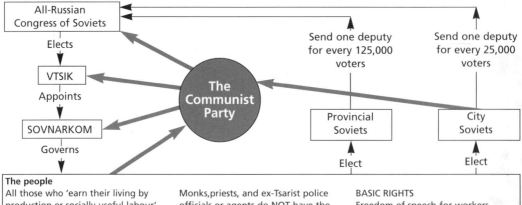

Source D Diagram of Lenin's constitution (From: *Russia in Revolution.*)

next task was to nationalise industry. Some industries – like the metallurgic and paper industries – were completely nationalised. Others, such as the textile industry, had individual factories, rather than the entire industry, nationalised by the state. Private trade and banks were also nationalised. Through his programme of nationalisation Lenin ensured that the means of production, distribution and exchange passed into the hands of the state.

All of these changes were incorporated in the first Soviet constitution of 10 July 1918. The constitution provided for a Federation of Soviet National Republics in which all class divisions were abolished. Women were declared the social equals of men, and as symbols of this new equality, people were to call each other 'comrade' or 'citizen'. The constitution no longer recognised the Church as a juridical (legal) person. It could own no property and was separated from the state. The teaching of religious doctrines in school was prohibited.

foundations for a liberal democracy. Instead, in line with Marxist principles, they laid the foundations for a classless society which would be reached after society first passed through the transitional stage of the dictatorship of the proletariat.

Activities .....
1 Do you approve of or disagree with Lenin's constitution as shown in Source D?
2 What are the potential problems that you could predict?
3 What are the advantages of this constitution?

'Just when it seemed there would be a rest from the turmoil of the preceding months, counter-revolutionary forces, with the assistance of foreign powers, plunged the nation into a bloody civil war.

The civil war

In 1918, as Lenin proceeded with the socialist reconstruction of Russia, a civil war broke out that threatened to engulf the Bolsheviks and destroy all that they had accomplished. The civil war, which continued until 1921, went through a number of phases, each phase being accompanied by bloodshed and loss of life.

Initial phase of the civil war

The initial phase of the civil war was accompanied by Allied intervention in Russian affairs. The Allies were disappointed with the signing of the Treaty of Brest-Litovsk. They feared that the collapse of the Eastern Front would enable Germany to concentrate on the Western Front. For this reason the Allies were determined to intervene in Russia and help any group which would end Bolshevik rule and take Russia back into the war. Apart from this, the Allies also intervened to capture a huge arms cache sent to the Russians when the Tsar was still in power. There was a danger of these arms falling into German hands.

However, this was not the only reason for Allied or Western intervention. The Western powers hated the communists, which is what the Bolsheviks began calling themselves from 1918. The Western powers intervened, hoping to stamp out communism in Russia and prevent it from spreading into central and western Europe.

The first of the Allied forces, the British, landed in Murmansk in March 1918, to be joined later by French, American, Czechoslovak and Serb forces. In April, the first Japanese and British troops arrived in Vladivostok, where they were later joined by French, Italian and American troops. English forces also landed at Estonia, and at Baku in the south. Soviet Russia was thus hemmed in from north, south, east and west, cut off from the seas, and isolated from contact with other countries.

Activities

Study Source E closely.
Which side do you think had the best chance of winning the war at the start? Explain your answer by referring to the map.

The Red Terror

The arrival of the Allied troops gave fresh hope to those groups in Russia who were fed up with Lenin's policies and who sought to overthrow the Bolshevik regime. Known as 'Whites' (in contrast

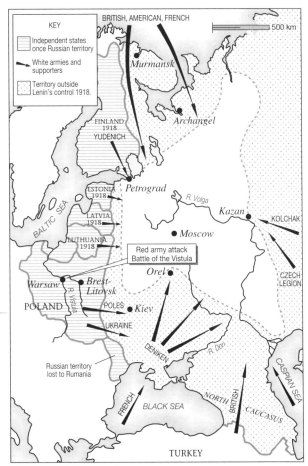

▲ *Source E*

Map showing the two sides in the civil war, 1918
(Adapted from: Mantin and Lankester. *From Romanov to Gorbachev.*)

to the Bolsheviks who were known as the 'Reds'), they included richer peasants, workers, Mensheviks, Monarchists, Liberals and Socialist Revolutionaries. The Whites, however, were a divided lot – each group had its own agenda – and were united only by their common hatred for the Bolsheviks. One of their first actions was to assassinate high-ranking Bolsheviks in Moscow and Petrograd. Their prime target was Lenin, who was shot and wounded on 30 August 1918, by a Jewish girl, Dora Fanny Kaplan.

The Bolsheviks replied to these actions by launching a terror campaign of their own. In July 1918, with the assistance of the Cheka (secret police), they arrested and executed a number of Socialist Revolutionaries, nobles, clergymen and wealthy peasants. The most prominent victim of this Red Terror was Nicholas II. On 16 July 1918, Nicholas and his entire family were executed near Ekaterinburg.

New phase in the civil war

From November 1918, following Germany's defeat in the First World War and Russia's repudiation of the Treaty of Brest-Litovsk, the civil war turned into a series of uncoordinated battles. The first to mobilise against the Red Army was Admiral Kolchak. Supported and supplied by the British, he reached Kazan, and came to within 40 kilometres of the Volga River. His attack then stalled, and by summer the Red Army – organised and led by the able Trotsky who rushed from front to front in a special train – had him on the run. He surrendered his command in January 1920 in favour of General Denikin, and was later court-martialled and executed.

After disposing of Kolchak, the Bolsheviks turned their attention to Generals Denikin and Yudenich. The former came to within 300 kilometres of Moscow, while the latter, attacking from Estonia in the north-west, reached the outskirts of Petrograd. The situation was so critical that Lenin considered abandoning Petrograd and withdrawing to Moscow, but Trotsky stepped in, rallied the Red Army, and forced Yudenich to retreat. Yudenich's retreat weakened Denikin's position.

▼ Source F

A civil war poster entitled 'Have you volunteered?'
(From: *Europe and the Modern World.*)

He subsequently fled across the Ukraine and, with British help, eventually reached the Crimea. On 4 April 1920 he turned over his command to General Wrangel and promptly left the country.

Activities ·······························

What do you think the Soviet government hoped to achieve through propaganda posters such as Source F?

··

Wrangel's task was a difficult one. Any chance he might have had of victory was compromised by the withdrawal of British and French forces from the Black Sea and Transcaspian area. Nevertheless, with an army of 70 000 he scored several victories over the Bolsheviks in the north. But he was fighting a lost cause. By mid-November 1920, the Red Army had him on the run. His troops fled for destinations unknown, and the Russian civil war was virtually over.

Poland enters the civil war

Before Wrangel's collapse, a surprise attack was launched by Poland in April 1920. The frontier between Poland and Russia had not been resolved at the Paris Peace Conference (1919) and the Poles decided to take advantage of the chaos in Russia by moving their frontier as far east as possible. On 7 May the Poles took Kiev. But the Red Army hit back, recaptured Kiev and had the Poles on the retreat. On the Vistula, however, the Poles, with French help, fought back. The Red Army was forced to retreat from Warsaw, and in October the Poles and Russia concluded an armistice. The Treaty of Riga on 18 March 1921 ended hostilities, but forced Russia to recognise an extended eastern boundary for Poland.

The Reds had won the civil war. There were several reasons for this: Trotsky's brilliance in leading the Red Army; the disunity among the Whites; and the appeal of the Bolsheviks to the patriotism of the Russian people. The average Russian was very patriotic and young men joined the Red Army to fight for Russia against the foreigners.

War Communism

The Bolsheviks realised that if they were to win the civil war, they would need to keep the Red Army equipped and fed. To ensure that this situation was never compromised, the Bolsheviks decided to tighten the state's control over the economy. A policy known as War Communism was then implemented, which according to Lenin, was 'dictated not by economic, but by military needs and considerations'.

Under War Communism, all large-scale enter-prises were nationalised. Private trade was banned, and all public and private wealth was conscripted. Labour was sent to wherever it was most needed – in factories or the armed forces. Wages were paid in kind, since money had become worthless. Finally, the government re-quisitioned foodstuffs and grain from the peas-antry to keep the Red Army well supplied. The secret police simply shot those peasants who hoarded their food or refused to cooperate.

War Communism had disastrous conse-quences. Industrial production fell by 50 per cent or more, and in the oil and metal industries it was no more than 10 per cent of its pre-war level. Since private trade was banned, **black markets** flourished everywhere. There was a drastic shortage of fuel, leading to an almost complete breakdown in transport. In agriculture, peasants saw no need to produce more than they could consume. The area under cultivation thus decreased, leading to widespread **famine** that eventually claimed the lives of four million peo-ple. Along with the economic collapse went the depopulation of the larger towns as millions fled to the countryside to escape the deteriorating conditions in the towns and cities.

▼ *Source H*
Output of selected goods

Products	1913	1921
Oil (million tons)	9,2	3,8
Coal (million tons)	29,1	9,5
Steel (million tons)	4,2	0,2
Machine tools (1 000 units)	1,8	0,8
Leather shoes (million pairs)	60,0	28,0
Grain (million tons)	86,0	36,2
Cows (million)	28,8	24,8

(From: Oxenfeldt and Holubnychy. *Economic Systems in Action.*)

Activities
In small groups, study Source G above, showing the Whites being swept off Russia at the end of the civil war, and then complete the activities below.
1 Explain what you understand by the term 'Whites'.
2 What term is used to describe the large figure on the left of the cartoon?
3 How appropriate was the cartoonist's choice of terrain as background for the episode to which the cartoon refers?
4 a Which country does the tall figure in the bottom right hand corner of the cartoon represent?
  b Explain the reasons for this country's intervention in the Russian civil war.
  c How different were the political beliefs of this coun-try from Russia at the time of the civil war?
5 How accurately has the cartoonist portrayed the out-come of the civil war?

New words

black markets unlawful trade in goods or curren-cies; place where such trade takes place
famine scarcity of food accompanied by widespread starvation

Activities
1 a Study Source H and then compare the output of goods in 1921 with that of 1913.
  b Why is there this difference in output?
2 Source I is a picture that was posed for. What does this mean in terms of its value to the historian?

Discontent slowly built up, and flared into the open in March 1921, when sailors from the Kronstadt naval base mutinied. It was, according to Lenin, 'the flash which lit up reality better than anything else'. The sailors had been among the Bolsheviks' most loyal supporters, and though Trotsky put down the mutiny using brute force, Lenin realised that a change of policy was needed. He consequently introduced the New Economic Policy or NEP.

▼ *Source I* Victims of the famine, 1921

© Gallo Images (Pty) Ltd. (The Hulton Getty Collection)

The New Economic Policy

In the face of discontent from the masses, Lenin abandoned War Communism in March 1921, and replaced it with the New Economic Policy (NEP). Through the NEP Lenin relaxed strict Marxist ideology and introduced elements of capitalism in the economy. In doing so he had to endure vigorous opposition from radicals within the Communist Party (the Bolsheviks were now calling themselves communists). But he was realistic enough to recognise the need for concessions and compromise. The NEP, in his own words, meant 'one step backwards in order to make two forwards'.

The NEP replaced grain requisitioning with a grain tax. Once he paid this tax, the peasant could sell his surplus grain on the open market. The profits were his to keep. The poorest peasants were exempted from taxation, and the confiscation of livestock as a penalty for non-payment of taxes was prohibited. The NEP restored land tenure, and peasants were free to lease their land, extend it, or use hired labour to cultivate it. Although the government did not intend these measures to be permanent, Lenin was determined to forge an alliance with the peasantry. As it turned out, these measures contributed to an astonishing agricultural recovery. In 1925 agricultural production in the northern Caucasus reached 77,5 per cent of its 1916 yield. For Kazakhstan, Siberia and the Ukraine, the figures were 71,9 per cent, 92,2 per cent and 96,1 per cent respectively. By then, too, a new class of wealthy peasants called kulaks had emerged, busy enlarging their farms, and hiring poorer peasants to work for them.

In industry, enterprises employing anything from ten to twenty workers were returned to private ownership. Private trade became legal again, and money was restored as the medium of exchange. Forced labour was abolished, and Russia returned to a free labour market with a wage economy. Trade between town and country was re-established, but virtually all this trade was conducted through brokers known as Nepmen. Despite these concessions, the state remained in control of what Lenin called the 'commanding heights' of the economy, that is, all large-scale industry, foreign trade, banking, transportation and credit facilities. The changes that Lenin brought about created the necessary confidence in workers, and stimulated industrial production, which in 1925–26 reached the pre-war level.

▼ *Source J*
Output of selected goods

Products	1913	1921	1928
Oil (million tons)	9,2	3,8	11,6
Coal (million tons)	29,1	9,5	35,5
Steel (million tons)	4,2	0,2	4,2
Machine tools (1 000 units)	1,8	0,8	2,0
Leather shoes (million pairs)	60,0	28,0	58,0
Grain (million tons)	86,0	36,2	73,3
Cows (million)	28,8	24,8	29,2

(From: Oxenfeldt and Holubnychy. *Economic Systems in Action.*)

Activities

1 Study Source J above, and then compare the output of goods in 1928 with that of 1913 and 1921.
2 Had the NEP been a success?

The overall effect of the NEP was the creation of a mixed economy, in which the state virtually dominated industrial life but left agriculture in the hands of the peasants. The impression created was that the peasant – who merely had the obligation of a taxpayer to the state – was being favoured over the proletariat who had to endure rationing and unemployment. It was for this reason that not all Bolsheviks welcomed the NEP. Its critics – the most vocal being Trotsky – argued that the emergence of wealthy peasants and small entrepreneurs was a betrayal of true Marxist principles and threatened the rise of a classless society. Although Lenin tried to reassure his colleagues that the NEP was merely a temporary retreat to capitalism forced by the circumstances of the moment, the NEP left a deeply divided Communist Party. These divisions were still there when Lenin died in 1924, after failing to recover from a series of crippling strokes. At the time of his death a new constitution had already been introduced, making Russia a federal state, the Union of Soviet Socialist Republics (the USSR or Soviet Union).

Lenin was only 53 when he died. His death was a setback for the Bolsheviks whom he had led since 1903. There is no doubt that he had changed the course of world history. He had carried out a communist revolution in a country that had not yet reached the stage of industrial development that Karl Marx believed was a necessary precondition for a successful communist revolution. In this respect he provided hope for other nations – that they did not have to wait to be industrialised to become communist. He went on to lead the Bolshevik state, against all the odds, through its first seven years (1917–24). He was not inflexible as a communist leader. When he abandoned War Communism in favour of the NEP, he showed that he was prepared to compromise his communist principles for the sake of the country.

Lenin was, nevertheless, a ruthless man. His use of the secret police and widespread terror not only recreated many of the worst features of the Tsarist era, but also set a pattern for the mass terror that followed later under Joseph Stalin.

▼ Source K

On 10 October Lenin showed that the moment was ripe for the seizure of power. Kamenev and Zinoviev alone acted as cowards and opposed the resolution.

The uprising was carried out with military precision and in full accord with Lenin's instructions. Lenin's genius as a leader of the masses, a wise and fearless strategist, was strikingly revealed.

(From a biography of Lenin published in the USSR in 1976. In C Culpin. *Making History.*)

▼ Source L

Lenin was one of the most sinister figures that ever darkened the human stage. This evil man was the founder and mainstay of Bolshevism. He was a revolutionary whose thirst for blood could never be quenched.

(From Lenin's obituary in the *Morning Post*, a British Newspaper, January 1924. In C Culpin. *Making History.*)

Extension activity

'A genius' (Source K) or 'an evil man' (Source L). Which of these opinions of Lenin do you most agree with and why?

Activities

With a partner study Source M on the next page – an extract from an editorial in *Izvestia* on the day of the Bolshevik coup in Russia, and then answer these questions.

1 Who led the Bolsheviks at the time of this editorial?
2 Of which institution was *Izvestia* the official newspaper?
3 State two reasons, put forward in this extract, why the writer of the editorial disapproved of the Bolshevik plot.
4 a Explain the term 'Constituent Assembly'.
  b How did the preparation for the election of the Constituent Assembly come about?
5 a With which nation did the Bolsheviks promise peace, and which war would thus have been brought to an end for Russia?
  b Explain the connection between the discontent of soldiers and workers and the Bolshevik promise of land.
6 How far did the Bolsheviks succeed in their attempt?
7 How right, during the five years which followed the writing of this editorial, were the prophecies that the Bolsheviks would be unable to keep their promises, and that dictatorship and terror would result?

▼ Source M

It is only three weeks to the Constituent Assembly, only a few days to the Congress of Soviets, and yet the Bolsheviks have decided to stage a new coup d'etat. They are making use of the wide discontent and great ignorance that exist among the masses of soldiers and workers. They have taken upon themselves the boldness to promise the people bread, peace and land. We have no doubt whatsoever that they are unable to keep a single one of their promises, even if they succeed in their attempt ...

The Bolshevik uprising can lead only to civil strife. Is it possible that people do not understand that dictatorship and terror are not the way to organise a country? Is it not clear that an attempted uprising, at the time of the preparation for the election of the Constituent Assembly, can be regarded as a non-criminal act only because it is a mad act?

(From: Watson, Rayner and Stapley. *Evidence in Question: European History 1815–1949.*)

Stalin's rise to power (1924–29)

Unit outcomes

- Explain the ideological difference between Trotsky and Stalin.
- Discuss why it was Stalin, and not Trotsky, who won the struggle for power.

Introduction

Lenin died on 21 January 1924 at approximately 6 p.m. His death brought to the forefront the deep divisions that existed within the Communist Party. For a while after his death, Party leaders tried to heal the divisions and maintain unity. But the competing personalities of the leaders ensured that peace within the Party would not last long.

The main contenders

The main contenders to follow Lenin were Trotsky and Stalin. However, several other prominent figures, like Kamenev and Zinoviev, were also involved. Of all the leaders, Trotsky seemed the man most likely to succeed Lenin. He had been Lenin's right-hand man during the revolution and civil war. He was also, in his own right, a gifted orator, writer and organiser, as well as a brilliant intellectual. But for all his talents, he was not very popular with other top leaders.

Compared to Trotsky, Stalin had not been an outstanding Bolshevik leader. Although an editor of *Pravda* and commissar of nationalities in Lenin's government, he was, in Trotsky's cutting phrase, 'the Party's most eminent mediocrity'. His talent lay in administration, and in 1922 he was appointed general secretary of the Communist Party's Central Committee. Although not immediately apparent to all leaders, Stalin had achieved a position of real power. As general secretary with a staff of over 600, he appointed his own followers to key posts in the Party. He also began to coordinate the Party's top-level activities, and, in so doing, shifted the power base away from the Politburo (the Party's central decision-making body) to the Secretariat.

Ideological differences

There were deep ideological differences between Trotsky and Stalin. Trotsky believed in 'Permanent Revolution', that Russia had a duty to spread communism throughout Europe without delay. He thought that this was the only way capitalism could be ended. Stalin saw Trotsky's scheme as impractical. He advanced, instead, his own theory of 'Socialism in one country'. He called for the consolidation of socialism in Russia first. He felt that only when Russia was strong enough, should she pursue her goal of promoting revolutions abroad.

Stages in the power struggle

After a bitter struggle, Stalin eventually triumphed over Trotsky. This was achieved in different stages. In the first stage of the power struggle, which began in 1923 and ended in January 1925, Stalin allied himself with Zinoviev and Kamenev against Trotsky. During this period Trotsky was forced to resign his post as commissar for war and assigned to lesser duties in the Council of National Economy. In the second stage – from the middle of 1925 until December 1927 – Zinoviev and Kamenev broke with Stalin and allied themselves with Trotsky. As a result, Trotsky, Zinoviev and Kamenev were removed from the Politburo. By December 1927 all three **dissident** leaders were expelled from the Communist Party. In a third stage – from 1927 until 1929 – Trotsky and his family were exiled to Alma Ata in Central Asia, and then expelled from the country altogether. Trotsky finally ended up in Mexico where he was murdered in 1940. By December 1929, Stalin was the unquestioned leader of Russia. What finally emerged after the power struggle had ended was a united Communist Party committed to Stalin's doctrine of 'Socialism in one country'.

> ### New words
> **dissident** not in agreement with; conflicting

Profile: Leon Trotsky (1879–1940)

© Hulton Getty

Leon Trotsky's real name was Lev Bronstein. (Trotsky was the name of one of his gaolers.) He was born in 1879, the son of a wealthy Jewish farmer. He was expelled from school in Odessa but went on to finish his education at a local secondary school. At the age of nineteen he was arrested for participating in revolutionary activities and was banished to Siberia. He managed to escape and with a forged passport he made his way to England. It was here that he first met Lenin in 1902.

In 1905 Trotsky returned to Russia where he helped set up the St Petersburg Soviet. He was the outstanding leader of the revolution of that year, but after its failure he was imprisoned and then banished to Siberia for a second time. He escaped again and eventually reached Vienna, where he lived and worked. For the next ten years he lived mainly in Europe, during which time he supported the Mensheviks.

When the February Revolution broke out, Trotsky was in New York. He quickly returned to Russia where he offered his services to Lenin. He joined the Bolsheviks in July 1917 and was elected president of the Petrograd Soviet. He then went on to play a key role in the revolution that broke out in October. After the October Revolution, he was made commissar of foreign affairs, later becoming war minister. He negotiated the Treaty of Brest-Litovsk with Germany, after which he successfully led the Red Army against the Whites in the civil war.

After Lenin died in 1924, Trotsky lost the leadership race to Stalin who, prior to banishing Trotsky in 1929, had him stripped of all positions of power. Trotsky lived in exile until his brutal murder in Mexico in 1940.

Profile: Joseph Stalin (1879–1953)

© Hulton Getty

Joseph Stalin's real name was Joseph Djugashvili. ('Stalin' means 'Man of Steel'.) He was born in the same year as Trotsky to poor Georgian serfs. When he was fifteen, his mother sent him to a theological college to become a priest. But in view of his Marxist leanings, he was expelled from the seminary.

He first saw Lenin in 1905, and in the revolution of that year, he organised a number of terrorist attacks on police in his home town of Georgia. He also carried out a number of armed robberies to help bring in money for the Bolshevik Party.

He was in exile in Siberia when news of the February Revolution reached him. He was the first of the Bolshevik leaders to arrive in Petrograd. He played only a minor part in the October Revolution, helping to pick Red Guards to take up key positions. After the October Revolution, he was made commissar for nationalities. In 1922 he became general secretary of the Communist Party's Central Committee, and used this position to amass great power. After Lenin's death he became involved in a struggle for power with Trotsky over whom he finally triumphed.

▼ Source A

From Lenin's 'Political Testament' written in late 1922

Comrade Stalin, having become General Secretary has concentrated enormous power in his hands; and I am not sure that he has always known how to use that power with sufficient caution. On the other hand comrade Trotsky is, to be sure, the most able man in the present central committee – but is also too self-confident.

(From: Mantin and Lankester. *From Romanov to Gorbachev.*)

▼ *Source B*

Stalin is too rude, and this shortcoming, though bearable in internal relations amongst us Communists, becomes quite unbearable in a General Secretary. I therefore suggest to you, Comrades, that you remove Stalin from his post and replace him with someone else who is superior to Stalin in this respect; namely, is more tolerant, more loyal, more polite, and more attentive to the needs of the comrades, is less capricious, etc. This may seem a trifling detail. But as regards the avoidance of schism and as regards the relations between Stalin and Trotsky, which I have discussed earlier, this is not a mere detail, but a detail which might one day acquire decisive importance.

(From: J Quinn. *The Russian Revolution.*)

Activities . . . .

1 What complaints does Lenin make against Stalin in Source A?
2 Which of the two leaders, Stalin or Trotsky, do you think Lenin prefers?
3 Is this source biased in any way? Explain your answer.
4 Study Source B – an extract from a letter written in December 1922 and translated from the Russian, and then answer these questions.

a Which Russian leader wrote this letter?
b What political position did the author hold?
c Why is the year 1924 important in connection with this extract?
d Of what organisation was Stalin general secretary at the time this letter was written?
e Trace Stalin's emergence within this organisation in the years before this letter was written, identifying one main political office he had held before becoming general secretary.
f Why was the advice contained in this letter never acted on?
g What ideological differences helped to cause the schism between the two men, Stalin and Trotsky?
h How did the development of this schism affect the political career of Trotsky?
i Show how the later career of Stalin revealed that he was neither tolerant nor loyal as is suggested in the letter.

. . . .

Extension activity . . . .

Do some research to help you complete the following activity.

A study in the course of revolution shows that after the initial revolutionary outburst there is a retreat into dictatorship. The Russian experience is no exception. Discuss this point of view.

. . . .

Economic development and planning (1929–39): The Five Year Plans

Unit 5

Unit outcomes

- Explain the reasons for collectivisation and analyse its consequences.
- Discuss the methods Stalin used to achieve his targets for industry and agriculture.
- Discuss the achievements and shortcomings of the Five Year Plans.
- Extract information from historical sources.
- Interpret a historical cartoon.
- Extract information from statistics.
- Analyse past events from the point of view of those who lived in the past.

Introduction

In 1928 Russia was on the eve of a new revolution, one that would radically transform the Russian economy and lay the foundations for her emergence as a superpower. Joseph Stalin, his power struggle with Trotsky virtually over, stood at the head of this new revolution. His policy of 'Socialism in one country', adopted as official policy by the Communist Party's Fourteenth Congress, was the foundation on which the economic revolution was to be built. To ensure the success of the economic revolution, the NEP, with its mixture of capitalism and socialism, was to be abandoned altogether.

Changes in agriculture

Stalin recognised that if Russia was to be a country with a strong industrial base, it would mean making sweeping changes to agriculture. He believed that peasants would have to provide not only food, but also workers for the new industries. He also believed that there would have to be an increase in agricultural exports if Russia was to acquire the capital necessary for large-scale industrialisation.

The manner in which the Bolsheviks had divided the land in 1917 and 1918 made an increase in agricultural production impossible. The break-up of the large estates had created some 25 million individual peasant farms. Most of these farms were small – roughly 30 acres – and were worked by peasants using primitive farming equipment. In such circumstances, peasants produced barely enough for their own needs.

Collectivisation

To solve the problems in agriculture, and eliminate the private farming encouraged by the NEP, Stalin introduced a system of farming called collectivisation. Under the new system, the tiny individual farms and small-holdings were joined to form collective farms in which the land was jointly owned and worked by the peasants who lived on it. To increase production on the collective farms, peasants could rent machinery from so-called 'Machine Tractor Stations' (MTS). A collective farm (known also as a kolkhoz) consisted on average of 75 families, each of which could personally own a house, vegetable garden, poultry, tools and a few animals. Each kolkhoz was managed by a committee elected by the local Communist Party. The committee drew up the budget, paid taxes and expenses, and divided the common income according to the amount and quality of work performed. Each farmer had to fulfil a certain quota. Discipline was strict, and enforced by so-called 'labour brigades'.

The policy of collectivisation initially met with some success. Between 1 June 1928 and 1 June 1929, the number of collective farms rose from 33 000 to 57 000, incorporating over a million peasant homesteads. But this success was restricted to the poorest of peasants, the Bedniaks, who owned no land, livestock, or agricultural implements, and who had everything to gain by entering the new system.

Kulaks oppose collectivisation

Those peasants who were most hostile to collectivisation were those who stood to lose the most, namely, the kulaks (the most prosperous peasants). The kulaks numbered almost 800 000, and showed their dislike for collectivisation by sowing less. This decision by the kulaks to sow less came at a time when Stalin announced plans for

КРОКОДИЛ

© Petrushka, Moscow

rapid industrialisation. Stalin would not allow the kulaks to hold hostage his plans for the industrialisation of Russia. He stated: 'We must break down the resistance of this class [the kulaks] in open battle and deprive it of the productive sources of its existence ... This is the turn towards the policy of eliminating the kulaks as a class.'

Activities
The kulak with his fertile plot is in the background in Source A.
1 How does Source A portray the kulaks?
2 What effect do you think Source A was meant to have on the attitude of ordinary peasants towards the kulaks?

To eliminate the kulaks as a class, Stalin ordered thousands of police and soldiers into the countryside. Kulaks who refused to join the collective farms were rounded up by police, exiled to distant parts of Siberia, or shot and killed if they physically resisted. The kulaks retaliated by burning their crops, killing their cattle and destroying their homesteads. They chose to do this rather than let their property fall into the hands of the state. There was chaos in the countryside, and the situation resembled an all-out civil war. The chaos frightened Stalin, and in March 1930 he called a halt to proceedings.

Famine

In 'Dizziness with Success', published on 2 March 1930, Stalin blamed local party officials for the tragedy that had occurred. In future, he said, collectivisation would be carried out on a voluntary basis. As a concession, he allowed collective farms to sell surplus wheat, meat and vegetables on the open market, once they had delivered their fixed quotas to the state. In addition, peasants who wished to withdraw from the collective farms were allowed to do so. Between March and April 1930, some nine million households took advantage of this offer. Nevertheless, by the end of 1932, the number of collectivised peasant households rose to almost fourteen million, with three-quarters of the arable land under cultivation by collective farms. All of this came too late to save the country from a terrible man-made famine that claimed the lives of five to fifteen million people.

Industry

By the time the famine broke out, the industrialisation of Russia was already well under way. Under Stalin's direction, Gosplan (the State Planning Commission) produced a series of Five Year Plans for the overall development of Russian industry. The First Five Year Plan had swung into operation on 1 October 1928, with industries having to meet, at all costs, the targets set for it. Class A industries – coal, iron, steel, oil and machine-building – were ordered to triple their output, while class B industries, producing consumer goods, were to double theirs. In addition, six times as much electricity was to be produced.

▼ *Source B*

Some industrial targets in the First Five Year Plan

Industry	1927–28	Target for 1933	'Optimal variant'
Electricity (milliard kWh)	5,05	17,0	22,0
Coal (million tons)	35,4	68,0	75,0
Oil (million tons)	11,7	19,0	22,0
Pig iron (million tons)	3,3	8,0	10,0
Steel (million tons)	4,0	8,3	10,4

(From: A Nove. *An Economic History of the USSR.*)

Activities

1 Use Source B to calculate how much each industry was required to increase its output.
2 Do you consider the targets for 1933 to be realistic or unrealistic? Explain your answer.

The First Five Year Plan was declared completed on 31 December 1932, a year ahead of schedule. During the four years of the plan's execution, the industrialisation of Russia made rapid progress. A huge iron and steel works was built at Magnitogorsk, while a hydro-electric plant on the Dnieper river was built with the assistance of an American engineer, Hugh Cooper. The Turksib railway, connecting Turkestan and Siberia, was opened on 1 May 1930; the Dnieprostroy dam in 1932. There was success in other undertakings as well. Tractors were built at Kharkov while cars were manufactured at Nizhni Novgorod on the basis of a contract with the American Henry Ford, who supplied parts and technical advice. More oil wells were opened in the Caucasus, while coal mining in the Donetz Basin was speeded up by mechanisation. All told, 1 500 new plants were built, while over 100 new towns had appeared.

To ensure the success of the Plan, a huge education programme was started. Primary schooling was made compulsory. Schools were set up in factories and workers were taught while they worked.

By the time the Plan ended, the output of machinery had quadrupled, oil production had doubled, and electric power was two and a half times greater.

▼ *Source C*

Some industrial production figures in 1932, at the end of the First Five Year Plan

Industry	
Electricity (milliard kWh)	13,4
Coal (million tons)	64,3
Oil (million tons)	21,4
Pig-iron (million tons)	6,2
Steel (million tons)	5,9

(From: A Nove. *An Economic History of the USSR.*)

Activities

1 Compare the figures in Source C with the figures in Source B. Calculate the differences in production.
2 Were the targets set in 1928 met by 1932?

The First Five Year Plan fell short of expectations in certain areas. Instead of the projected 8,3 million tons in steel production, only about 6 million was attained. The output of coal was also below target, and so, too, the output of consumer goods. Critics also pointed to the low productivity of workers, and to the poor quality of goods. Doubt was also expressed about the official figures given to substantiate the advances made. New towns may have emerged, but the living conditions were deplorable, with amenities virtually non-existent.

Throughout the Plan the impression created was one of haste, of keeping the tempo going and not slackening. In a speech in February 1931, Stalin explained the need to avoid slowing down: 'We are fifty to a hundred years behind the advanced countries,' he said, 'We must make good this lag in ten years. Either we do it or they crush us.'

Extension activity ....

Study the cartoon in Source D, and then answer the questions which follow. The cartoon is a Russian 'before and after' cartoon. In the top half of the cartoon the foreign capitalist calls the First Five Year Plan a ridiculous dream.

1 What has happened in the bottom half of the cartoon?
2 Do you agree with the 'after' part of the cartoon? Give reasons for your answer.

▼ Source D

Before and after the Five Year Plan

The Second Five Year Plan

A Second Five Year Plan was launched in 1933. Like the First Plan, the emphasis remained on heavy industry. In addition, there was to be an improvement of railroads, canals and highways, and a greater concentration on quality. This last aspect was considered important, as some 40 per cent of production in the First Plan had to be scrapped because of poor workmanship.

As in the First Plan, industries were set targets, and the performance of the Second Five Year Plan was in many ways like that of the first. Some industries – steel and automobiles – reached their targets, while others – oil, coal and textiles – lagged behind. Although not all targets had been reached, the country had, in less than ten years, made incredible progress.

▼ Source E

Some industrial production figures in 1937, at the end of the Second Five Year Plan

Industry	
Electricity (milliard kWh)	36,2
Coal (million tons)	128,0
Oil (million tons)	28,5
Pig-iron (million tons)	14,5
Steel (million tons)	17,7

(From: A Nove. *An Economic History of the USSR.*)

Activities ....

Compare Source E with Sources B and C.
1 Which industry increased its output the most over the years, and which the least?
2 What does Source E tell you about the success of Stalin's industrialisation programme?

Understanding historical skills and concepts

Extracting information from historical sources: the use of statistics

Statistical material is an important source of historical information and is one that appears in a variety of forms: tables, graphs, and, more recently, computer printouts. Tables of statistics, arranged in columns or rows, make it possible to compare facts quickly. However, such tables have to be checked and analysed carefully. The title or heading tells you what the table is designed to show, e.g. Source F shows the amount of harvest and the numbers of livestock which existed in two separate years – 1928 and 1933. Why have these two years been chosen?

Note the units: tons of grain and millions of head of livestock. It is important that any comparison is made between the same units.

As you read across the table, note the direction and amount of any change.

▼ Source F

	1928	1933
Grain harvest	73 mil	68 mil
Livestock (head)		
Cattle	70,5 mil	38 mil
Pigs	26 mil	12 mil
Sheep and goats	147 mil	50 mil

(From: A Nove. *An Economic History of the USSR.*)

Activities ....

In 1937 the grain harvest output for the USSR was 97 million tons. How far would this change your opinion of Stalin's agricultural policies as shown in Source F?

Workers who reached and surpassed the targets were rewarded with medals, better pay, housing and holidays. In 1935 Stalin found a role model for workers in Alexei Stakhanov, a coal miner. Stakhanov decided that he would do all the cutting, leaving the rest of his team to do the other work. In a six-hour shift that normally produced about 7 tons of coal, Stakhanov cut 102 tons. Stalin at once made a national hero out of him. Stakhanovite workers were rewarded with extra pay, extra food and free holidays. Stakhanovism, however, was against the principles of communism. Marx had written that people should be paid according to their needs. But to Stalin anything which increased production was allowed. Stakhanovism soon spread to other sectors of the economy, and the government set production quotas on the results achieved by Stakhanovites. But this hurt the average worker who felt he was being exploited. Workers then retaliated by murdering Stakhanovites.

New words

publicity stunt an act designed to gain the public's attention, generally for show or with the intention of misleading, deceiving or cheating

Extension activity

1 If you had been a Russian worker and found out that Stakhanov's effort had been nothing but a huge **publicity stunt**, how would you have reacted?
2 Write a letter to a newspaper from either the point of view of a Russian peasant or a Russian factory worker in 1937, expressing your views on twenty years of communist rule.

Labour camps

Many workers were crushed under the enormous burden of work. People resented being forced to work so hard and showed their anger by destroying machines. Sometimes they just did not show up for work. The government got tough with such people. People who were regularly absent lost their food cards or were sent to gaol. When targets were not reached, a worker or manager was branded a 'wrecker' and sent to labour camps (Gulags) run by the NKVD (secret police). It is believed that the NKVD managed a convict labour force of some eight million people.

◀ Source G
A labour camp

© RIA-Novosti Photos

Conditions in the labour camps were harsh. No wages were paid and there was not enough food. Stalin's methods were similar to those used by Lenin during the period of War Communism – a mixture of brute force and propaganda. Only the economic policies pursued by the two men were different. Nevertheless, the industrial achievements – along with the success of collectivisation in 1938 – convinced many Russians, especially the young people, that their country was 'going places' at last.

▼ *Source H*

At the end of the day, there were corpses left on the worksite. The snow powdered their faces. One was hunched over beneath an overturned wheelbarrow; he had hidden his hands in his sleeves and frozen in that position. Two were frozen back to back, leaning against each other. At night, the sledges went out and collected them. And in the summer, bones remained from corpses which had not been removed in time and together with the shingle, they got into the concrete mixer.
And in that way, they got into the concrete of the last lock at the city of Belomorsk and will be preserved there for ever.

(From: Alexander Solzhenitsyn. *The Gulag Archipelago*. In C Culpin. *Making History*.)

Activities ....
1 Look carefully at Source G. What are the working conditions like?
2 What does Source H tell you about work and life at the labour camps?
3 How useful is Source H for finding out about conditions in the labour camps?

The Third Five Year Plan

A Third Five Year Plan was launched in 1938, with the government seeking to correct some of its earlier shortcomings, like addressing the housing shortage (the urban population had risen to over 50 million) and increasing the supply of consumer goods. But the plan had to be cut short when the Second World War broke out in September 1939. Industries had to switch to producing arms for the war.

By the end of the 1930s Russia had emerged as a strong industrial nation, with a greater ability than ever before to produce iron, steel, coal and electric power. But the great industrial advance was only achieved at a tremendous cost to the Russian people. Through the Five Year Plans, Russia now ranked among the world's foremost industrial powers. The Plans helped Russia survive the German onslaught in 1941, and helped her achieve the status of a superpower after the Second World War ended in 1945.

Activities ....
Study Source I – an extract from a Soviet History, and the officially published statistics it contains, both of which concern Russia in 1928, and then answer the questions below.
1 Explain the following terms: 'kulaks' and 'white-guardists'.
2 What attitude is shown in this extract towards priests, and how do you explain this?
3 Why did the authorities consider someone who had 'hid[den] grain' to have committed a serious offence in Russia at this time?
4 Explain the importance of the Party line in the USSR.
5 For what did the initials NEP stand?
6 For what reasons, and in what circumstances, was the NEP abolished?
7 What do the statistics show of the organisation of Russian agriculture in 1928, and how did this differ from that before 1917?
8 In what ways, and for what reasons, would the statistics have changed by the end of the 1930s?

▼ *Source I*

The kulaks undertook large-scale agitation, asserting that Soviet power impoverished the peasant, did not allow him to improve his income, that NEP was being abolished. Kulaks, priests, former white-guardists endeavoured to utilise in their counter-revolutionary agitation certain cases of distortion of the Party line in credit and tax policy ... In the village of Troitskoye in the Don area there was unmasked a priest who hid grain and organised in the cemetery a kulak meeting.

Statistics	
Percentage of sown area	
Individual peasants	97,3
Collective farms	1,2
State farms	1,5

(From: Watson, Rayner and Stapley. *Evidence in Question*.)

Extension activity ....
Some people have argued with regard to the Five Year Plans that the end justified the means. Debate this assertion with other learners in your class.

Stalin's political terror (1934–39)

Unit outcomes

- Explain the reasons for the terror (purges).
- Discuss the steps taken by Stalin to rid himself of his opponents.
- Compare various types of historical sources and reach conclusions based on this comparison.
- Explain the concept of continuity and change.

Introduction

As Russia underwent far-reaching changes to her industry and agriculture, there occurred, almost simultaneously, a purge (cleansing) of the Communist Party and security forces. Started by Stalin, the purge was more a reign of terror in which thousands – if not millions – of people from all walks of life, were forced to confess to crimes of which they were usually innocent, and either banished to labour camps in Siberia, or simply executed.

Reasons for the terror

Various explanations have been offered for this brutal purge. One view is that Stalin resorted to violence in order to cover up his economic failures. Another view is that Stalin embarked on a terror campaign to eliminate all opposition to his rule. A third school of thought is that Stalin's own madness was to blame for the bloodshed. Whatever his motives, Stalin was convinced it was the right thing to do.

The purges begin

The event which triggered off the purges, was the assassination of Sergei Kirov, chairman of the Leningrad Soviet, and a rising star in the Communist Party. At 4.30 p.m. on 1 December 1934 Kirov arrived at the Smolny Institute in Leningrad. As he walked down a corridor, a man came from around a corner and shot him dead. The assassin was a young communist named Leonid Nikolaev. On 30 December Nikolaev was promptly executed, along with thirteen alleged accomplices.

A wave of arrests followed the death of Sergei Kirov. One of those arrested was Victor Serge, a poet. Shortly before his questioning by the secret police, he gave the following account of his arrest:

> I went out in the cold morning in Kazan to do some shopping. I am aware of being followed, which is quite natural. Except that by this time 'they' are trailing so close behind me that I begin to be worried. As I come out of the chemist's shop they stop me. This is on the pavement of the October 25th Prospect, with everybody bustling past all around me. 'Criminal Investigation. Kindly follow us, citizen, for purposes of identification.'

(From: V Serge. *Memoirs of a Revolutionary 1901–1941.*)

Show trials

The purge continued throughout 1935 and into 1936. In August 1936, sixteen leading members of the Party, including Kamenev and Zinoviev, were accused of trying to kill Sergei Kirov, and of plotting with Germany and the exiled Trotsky to murder Stalin. As incredible as these charges seemed, the accused were arraigned (indicted) for a public trial at which they confessed to their crimes. All sixteen were found guilty, sentenced to death, and executed. This was the start of the famous 'show trials' which were intended to serve as an example and a warning to the Soviet people.

At the beginning of 1937 a further seventeen prominent communists were brought to trial and accused of scheming with Nazi Germany to sabotage Stalin's industrialisation programme. All seventeen pleaded guilty. Thirteen were executed, and four received long-term sentences. The trial of the seventeen implicated others – this time in the armed forces. In June 1937 several military leaders, including Marshal Tukhachevsky, Chief of the Red Army, and Admiral Orlov, Chief of the Red Navy, were arrested. They were accused of espionage (spying) on behalf of Germany and Japan, found guilty and executed.

About two-thirds of all Red Army officers above the rank of colonel were subsequently executed or sent to labour camps.

A Russian joke on the purges

According to the story, Stalin lost his pipe. He thereupon telephoned the NKVD [secret police] and demanded it be found immediately. Two hours later, he found the pipe himself – it had merely fallen into one of his boots behind the sofa in his apartment. He telephoned the NKVD again and asked what progress had been made.

'We have arrested ten men already,' the Minister reported, 'and the investigation is continuing.'

'As it happens,' said Stalin, 'I have found my pipe. So free them instantly.'

'But, Comrade Stalin, seven of them have already confessed!'

(From: H Montgomery Hyde. *Stalin*.)

Activities

1 What point about the purges is Source A making?
2 Do you think that this portrayal of Stalin is valid or not?
3 If you had been a high-ranking official during the purges, what action would you have taken?

The end of the purges

A third show trial was held in 1938 in which Politburo members Bukharin and Rykov were purged, along with Yagoda, former head of the NKVD (secret police). All three faced charges of espionage, and of conspiring to kill Lenin and Stalin in the early 1920s. All three confessed to their crimes and were executed. It was only after this incident that the wave of arrests and executions began to die down.

The show trials were given wide publicity in Russia and abroad. Those in the West who read of the trials, were puzzled by the fact that nearly all the main figures confessed their guilt. What these people did not realise, is that long before the accused appeared in court, they were subjected to repeated interrogation, denial of sleep, and physical torture. If the accused, after all this, still refused to admit his or her guilt, death threats were made to the victim's family and friends.

The exact number of those who perished in the purges will probably never be known but it is estimated that hundreds of thousands – if not millions – were killed. Through the purges the Party – and therefore the government – lost its most able and experienced workers. In the Red Army, the replacement of senior officers by men with no war experience was to have disastrous consequences during the German invasion of Russia in 1941. At another level, the purges terrified people, and caused all protests to Stalin's rule to be silenced.

The tyranny of Stalin was similar to that of Tsar Nicholas II and, to a lesser extent, that of Lenin. It was Lenin who created the Cheka and who ordered the shooting of the sailors of Kronstadt in 1921. Stalin merely carried to extremes what others had begun. Even when the Second World War (1939–45) ended, Stalin continued with the purges. He was never at ease, always suspicious of those around him. He finally died in March 1953, by which time Russia (known officially as the Union of Soviet Socialist Republics) had established herself as a superpower, second only to the United States of America. But the country was still caught up in the dictatorship of the proletariat, chasing that elusive, utopian dream of a perfect society.

Activities

In small groups study the following sources, and then answer the questions below.
1 What reasons for the purges are given in the sources?
2 Read Sources D and F. Compare the way in which they describe Stalin.
3 'Isaac Deutscher (Source E) would have taken a different view of the purges had his biography on Stalin been published after Stalin's death in 1953.' Do you agree with this statement? Explain your answer.
4 Look at Source C. In what ways can this cartoon be useful to a historian studying Stalin's purges?
5 'Trotsky's view of Stalin (Source F) is less reliable than Isaac Deutscher's opinion (Source E) because Trotsky was biased.' Do you agree with this statement? Explain your answer.
6 Do the sources portray Stalin as a monster? Explain your answer.

▼ *Source B*

Critics can also seize upon the economic weakness of Stalinism. His agricultural policies were cruel and counter-productive, and collectivisation is something for any country to avoid. If the pace and strategy of economic development by his methods required the horrors of terror and Purge, then the pace and strategy were wrong.

(From: Alec Nove. *Stalinism and After*. In Mantin and Lankester. *From Romanov to Gorbachev*.)

▲ **Source C**

The caption for this cartoon reads: 'Visit the USSR's Pyramids! ...' The shape is formed by the skulls of those who died in the purges

▼ **Source D**

But do we need any sensational revelations to understand Stalin? No, the explanation of his life is as banal as many of Stalin's own speeches: he was corrupted by absolute power. Absolute power turned a ruthless politician into a monstrous tyrant. The terror was necessary, not only to keep men obedient, but even more to make them believe. Without terror, who would have failed to notice the patent absurdity of Stalin's rule.

(From: Adam B Ulman. *Stalin the Man and his Era*. In Mantin and Lankester. *From Romanov to Gorbachev.*)

▼ **Source E**

But why did Stalin need the abominable Purge? It has been suggested that he sent the men of the old guard to their death as scapegoats for his economic failures. There is a grain of truth in this, but no more. For one thing, there was a very marked improvement in the economic condition of the country in the years of the Purge.

Stalin's real and much wider motive was to destroy the men who represented the potentiality of alternative government, perhaps not of one but several governments.

(From: Isaac Deutscher. *Stalin: a political biography*. Published in 1949 when Stalin was still alive. In Mantin and Lankester. *From Romanov to Gorbachev.*)

▼ **Source F**

Undoubtedly characteristic of Stalin is personal physical cruelty, which is usually called sadism. After he had become a Soviet dignitary he would amuse himself in his country home by cutting the throats of sheep or pouring kerosene on antheaps and setting fire to them.

(From: Leon Trotsky. *Stalin*. In Mantin and Lankester. *From Romanov to Gorbachev.*)

Extension activity ....

A great leader or an evil tyrant? Hold a class debate to try to decide how Stalin should be remembered.

....

Understanding historical skills and concepts

Change and continuity

The early years of radio – people gathered together to listen to news of important events
(Photo: Gallo Images (Pty) Ltd (The Hulton Getty Collection).)

People listening to a radio in front of a mine hostel
(Photo: Eric Miller/i-Afrika.)

The photographs above are good examples of the concept of change and continuity. In both photographs there is evidence of technological change. The first photograph shows a large and heavy radio while the second shows a modern, portable radio. It is clear that in the years between the two photographs radio manufacturing underwent great change. However, it is worth noting that the function of the radio did not change: it still brought people together, whether it was to gather information or simply for entertainment. This is an example of continuity.

The history of Russia is a story of continuity and change. As an example one could compare the Russia of Tsar Nicholas with that of Stalin. Both men ruled Russia with the same autocratic style, making use of the secret police to deal with opponents. In this respect there is continuity between the regimes of the two men since some aspects of Tsarist Russia were still present under Stalin. However, there had also been considerable change in Russia. Under Tsar Nicholas Russia was a backward agricultural country with very few industries. When Stalin was in power Russia became a country with a strong industrial base, one that was strong enough to withstand the German invasion during the Second World War.

Activities

Complete the exercise below. How much change was there in Russia between 1923 and 1939? What things stayed the same?

Russia under Lenin	Russia under Stalin
1 Russia was called the Soviet Union.	1
2 Wealthy peasants called kulaks thrived.	2
3	3 A secret police force crushed all opposition.

Unit 7
A cult of personality

Unit outcomes

- Compare historical sources.
- Recognise bias and propaganda.

Introduction

About the same time as thousands of people were suffering in the purges, Stalin proceeded with burnishing (improving) his own image. Through careful use of propaganda, he encouraged the growth of a personality cult. Towns were named after him – like Stalino and Stalingrad. Huge portraits of him were displayed in all public buildings, while his statues were erected in prominent public places. Special paintings commissioned by the Soviet government gave prominence to him. Finally, heroes of yesteryear were turned into traitors through the careful 'doctoring' of pictures.

Study the sources below, and then answer the questions which follow. You need to consider the sources carefully, and to determine their reliability for the historian.

Activities

1 What 'image' of himself was Stalin trying to put across through the sources below? Give evidence from the sources to support your answer.
2 a Refer to Source C. Who does Source C suggest were the key leaders in the October Revolution?
  b Source C was completed around 1935. How reliable is the painting as a source of historical evidence about the Russian Revolution, and what particular significance can be attached to the year in which the painting was done?
3 Refer to Source D. Stalin's picture was added to the photograph years after it was taken. Suggest reasons why Stalin chose this particular photograph of Lenin to which to add his picture.
4 Source D has been altered. Does that mean it is of no use to a historian as a source of evidence? Explain your answer.
5 Look at all the sources, and then answer the following question. Do the sources show Stalin to have been popular among his people, and honest about his past? Explain your answer fully.

▼ Source A

Stalin, the schoolboy, is the one leading the group holding his cap

▼ *Source B*

Return of Lenin with Stalin in the painting
(From: Petrushka, Moscow.)

© SMOLNY Museum, St Petersburg

▼ *Source C*

Lenin and Stalin with Red Guards, November 1917
(From: Mansell/Time Inc.)

© SMOLNY Museum, St Petersburg

▼ *Source D* Lenin and Stalin

(From: Mansell/Time Inc..)

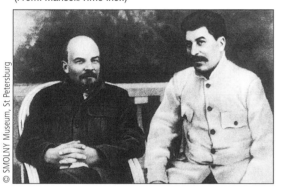

© SMOLNY Museum, St Petersburg

Extension activity

In Russian history there are a number of similarities and differences. What similarities and differences are there:
1 between War Communism and the NEP?
2 between the First and Second Five Year Plans?
3 between Lenin's leadership style and Stalin's?

Understanding historical skills and concepts

Essay writing

Good essay writing skills are not things that you are born with, but are acquired through practice and effort. The most important thing to remember is that history essays are not about repeating the pages of facts that you somehow managed to cram into your head. History essay questions are carefully designed around a problem or question which requires you to work out an answer and to use, select and adapt the relevant historical information.

The following skills are tested in essay writing in history:

- accurate and adequate historical information (factual information which is usually presented in chronological order)
- the skill of comprehension and analysis (the ability to distinguish the various aspects of the historical problem posed by the question)
- the skill of selection (the ability to use what is relevant and important for the answer to a particular question)
- the skill of synthesis (evidence of logical thought and effective argument in putting together a structured answer)
- the skill of communication (adequate style and presentation with good language usage).

Guide to writing a history essay

1 Before you can decide on what content to include in your essay you must analyse the question.
- Underline the key instruction words.
- Underline those words that indicate the subject matter (that is, names, places and dates).

Underlining these key words will enable you to identify the problem or topic around which you are being asked to develop an argument, then identify what relevant information you need and how to organise that information.

The most important words to identify in the essay topic are the instruction words. These will direct you towards:
- what you are required to do (for example, discuss, analyse, evaluate, etc.)
- how much information to include (for example, discuss briefly, give a detailed account of, etc.).

Many essay questions will use more than one instruction word. It is important to identify and analyse each instruction word on its own, then in relation to each other and to the topic as a whole. These are a few of the most commonly used instruction words and what they mean:

- **account for** – give reasons for
- **give an account of** – describe
- **analyse** – break down into the component parts and show how they are related and why they are important
- **comment on** – discuss, giving valid views on something. This instruction word is often used with a quotation or statement and you are expected to give an opinion about it which is backed up with historical evidence.
- **compare** – show the similarities and the differences between two or more things
- **contrast** – show the ways in which two or more things are different from each other
- **criticise** – give your opinion of something, showing its good and bad points, strengths and weaknesses, and supporting your opinion with facts and careful argument
- **describe** – write a detailed account in a well structured logical sequence in which the event(s) can be seen clearly
- **discuss** – examine in as much detail as possible within the allowed time limits
- **evaluate/assess** – give your opinion on some expert's opinion of the truth, importance or value of a concept or theory including the advantages or disadvantages
- **explain** – give reasons, or provide an analysis of the facts
- **relate** – show connections between terms, ideas and/or events showing how one is like the other
- **summarise** – give a brief, condensed account of the main ideas and events leaving out details and examples.

2 Plan your answer. Even when time is tight you should take a few minutes to note down a few key words and ideas which you can organise into a logical, well-constructed argument.

3 Structure your essay according to these guidelines.

A The introduction
You cannot write an introduction for an essay unless you already have an answer in your mind. Your introduction should be no longer than ten to fifteen lines and it should address the topic, showing the reader how you are going to argue.

B The body (paragraphs)
Each paragraph in your essay must have:
- a topic sentence or controlling idea
- evidence (information and opinions) to support the point made in the topic sentence
- a concluding sentence which focuses on the topic and links the point of the paragraph to the overall argument.

C The conclusion
No essay is complete without a conclusion. Do not try to introduce any new ideas in the conclusion. It should sum up your overall argument in the essay.

The style of your essay
- Use formal and correct language – no slang or clichés.
- Keep your sentences short and uncomplicated.
- Pay attention to paragraphing.
- Make sure that you understand the meaning of the words that you are using.
- Avoid using words that do not add to the meaning of a sentence, for example, obviously, clearly, definitely, actually, etc.
- Use facts and logic, not vague impressions or your personal feelings, to construct the argument in an essay.

How to improve your essays
- When you receive back your marked essays with your teacher's comments, make sure that you read through these carefully.
- Check with your teacher whether your essay shows problems with:
  a content (extent of detail) or structure
  b lack of focus
  c style
  d expression
  e a combination of these things, so that you can work on these areas.
- When you prepare your next essay refer back to your teacher's comments about previous essays to avoid making the same mistakes.

If you follow the above guidelines to essay writing you will find that many of the problems or weaknesses that you have previously encountered in your essays will disappear. The most important thing is to focus on what the essay topic is asking of you and to organise your answer carefully around this.

CHAPTER ASSESSMENT

These essay questions will help you to assess your understanding and progress in Chapter 1. In groups discuss the different essay topics and then work out essay plans for each topic. Then choose one of the essay topics and write about it.

1 'Land, Peace and Bread' were the three aims put forward by the Bolsheviks in the early months of 1917.

Explain the relevance of these aims, and assess to what extent Lenin had achieved them by 1924.

2 'October 1917 was a turning-point in the history of Russia. It enabled Lenin to come to power and set Russia on a new course.'

Discuss the immediate events which made Lenin's assumption of power in October 1917 possible, and the changes he introduced up to 1924 which 'set Russia on a new course'.

3 'There is no doubt that during the period 1928 to 1938 Stalin performed an economic miracle as he transformed a backward, mainly agricultural Russia into a major industrial power.'

With reference to Stalin's Five Year Plans, discuss this assertion and show to what extent he achieved this 'economic miracle'.

4 'History records Stalin to be an ambitious figure, an emancipator and a tyrant, a man determined to a ‧cause, yet extremely brutal and indifferent to human suffering'.

Examine Stalin's role in Russia in the period 1928 to 1939 with particular reference to his Five Year Plans and terror campaigns, and then assess whether the above description of him as 'an ambitious figure ... and a tyrant' can be justified.

Further reading

C Culpin. *Making History: World History from 1914 to the Present.* London: Collins Educational, 1996.

B Dmytryshyn. *A History of Russia.* New Jersey: Prentice-Hall Inc., 1977.

T Howarth. *Twentieth Century History: The World Since 1900.* Essex, England: Longman, 1983.

W Kirchner. *Russian History.* Harper Collins, 1991.

L Kochan. *The Making of Modern Russia.* Middlesex, England: Penguin Books, 1975.

P Mantin and C Lankester. *From Romanov to Gorbachev: Russia in the 20th century.* London: Hutchinson, 1989.

G Parker, ed. *The Times Illustrated World History.* London: Times Books, 1992.

G Stern, ed. *Communism: An Illustrated History From 1948 To The Present Day.* London: Amazon Publishing, 1991.

H Ward. *World Powers In The Twentieth Century.* London: Heinemann, 1985.

The rise of the USA (1917–41)

chapter 2

contents

Timeline

		US Presidents
First World War	1910	
	1913	Wilson
	1914	First World War begins
	1917	April, USA enters war
	1918	First World War ends
	1919	Treaty of Versailles
The Roaring Twenties / Foreign Policy of Normalcy	1920	
	1921	Harding
	1923	Coolidge
	1929	Wall Street Crash; Great Depression begins Hoover
Great Depression / Neutrality Acts	1930	
	1933	New Deal begins Roosevelt
The New Deal	1939	Second World War begins
	1940	
	1941	December, Attack on Pearl Harbour; USA enters war
Cold War	1945	Second World War ends April, Roosevelt dies Truman
	1950	

chapter outcomes

knowledge outcomes

As you work through this chapter you will be able to:

- explain the development of the United States of America (USA) to super-power status;
- describe how the USA abandoned its policy of isolationism and became involved in world affairs;
- discuss how the US economy prospered, then suffered and recovered from the Great Depression;
- discuss the principles and effectiveness of the New Deal;
- describe economic concepts such as laissez-faire, tariffs, mass-production, specula-tion, and depression;
- evaluate how the life and attitudes of the American people changed.

concepts and skills outcomes

As you work through this chapter you will learn about and apply skills and concepts such as how to:

- analyse, organise and critical-ly evaluate historical sources;
- work effectively in a group;
- show empathy for people;
- use effective research meth-ods and solve problems;
- assess bias and reliability;
- understand causes and con-sequences;
- organise and communicate the results of historical study.

value outcomes

As you work through this chapter you will get the chance to think about:

- the extent to which a gov-ernment should control the economy and provide social welfare;
- the effects of new technology and the role and effect of the media.

This chapter covers Specific Outcomes 2, 4, 5, 7 and 9 of the Human and Social Sciences learning area.

FOREIGN POLICY

Isolationism: Early United States foreign policy

Unit outcomes

- Describe isolationism and the open door policy as principles of US foreign policy.
- Explain the geographical imperialism of the USA in Asia and Central America during the nineteenth century.
- Interpret a historical cartoon.

Introduction

The foreign policy of most governments starts with three basic aims.

1 To remain independent and defend the country from attack.
2 To protect its citizens abroad.
3 To promote its own trading interests overseas.

This was certainly the case with the USA.

The USA and isolationism

From the time of the War of Independence (1775–83), the USA followed a foreign policy of isolationism, or what today would be called neutralism or non-alignment. In the early years after 1783, the need for economic development seemed to justify avoiding foreign entanglements, and the priority of internal political and economic tasks, all of which were reinforced by the opening of the West and the subsequent drive to the Pacific. Foreign policy was of secondary importance.

During the nineteenth century, too, there developed an intense belief in democracy – a strong feeling that it was the American destiny to spread, by example, freedom to all people and to lead the world out of the wicked ways of the Old World. Europe stood for war, poverty and exploitation; America for peace, opportuni-

THE UNITED STATES OF AMERICA

ty and democracy. America was to be an example of a morally superior democratic pattern of international behaviour; undemocratic states were inherently warlike and evil; democratic nations, in which people controlled and regularly changed their leaders, were peaceful and moral. Therefore, America had to guard her democratic purity and not get involved in the affairs of Europe.

Americans turned their attention toward the outside world only with the greatest reluctance and only when provoked – that is, when the foreign threat had become so clear that it could no longer be ignored. Once Americans were provoked, however, and the United States had to resort to force, the employment of this force could be justified only in terms of the **universal moral principles** which the United States, as a democratic country, identified in itself. Resorting to war could only be justified by presuming noble purposes and completely destroying the immoral enemy who threatened the integrity, if not the existence, of these principles. As a result, American wars were total wars – that is, wars aimed at the total destruction of the enemy. Wars became ideological crusades to make the world safe for democracy. Once that aim had been achieved, the United States could again withdraw into itself, secure in the knowledge that American works had again proved to be 'good works'.

▼ *Source A*

In this cartoon the Russian bear and the British lion fight over the Chinese dragon. As other imperialist nations join in the contest, the American eagle, at left, watches them. (From: Patrick and Berkin. *History of the American Nation from 1877, Volume 2.*)

Courtesy of Library of Congress, USA

Activities

1 What does Source A tell you about the characteristics of US foreign policy?
2 Why do you think that trade with China was so desirable?

New words

universal moral principles laws about truth and goodness which are accepted worldwide
sphere of influence area where power of one country is dominant

The Monroe Doctrine (1823)

The idea of isolationism was stated clearly by President James Monroe in his message to Congress on 2 December 1823. He made it clear that any foreign power must 'keep off' territory which the USA regarded as her **sphere of influence.**

1 Any attempt by any European country to establish colonies in the New World or gain political control of any American country would be viewed as an unfriendly act towards the USA.
2 The USA would not interfere in the affairs of European nations or in the affairs of their colonies already established in the Americas.

This implied that the USA would not become involved in any alliances in Europe which might involve the country in a European war. However, this policy did not rule out establishing valuable commercial and trading links with foreign countries. To promote these trade links, during the late nineteenth century, the USA acquired several overseas territories, for example, Alaska (1867), Midway Island (1867), American Samoa (1878–99), Hawaii (1898), Puerto Rico (1898), the Philippines (1898), Guam (1898) and Wake Island (1900).

The Open Door Policy (1899)

The US secretary of state proposed that all nations should have equal commercial rights in China. This favoured the USA and was accepted with reluctance by the European nations and Japan, who were already trading in China.

Corollary to the Monroe Doctrine (1904)

President Theodore Roosevelt confirmed the Monroe Doctrine and stated that the American government assumed the right to intervene in the affairs of neighbouring states if their internal affairs did not correspond to the criteria of a civilised society; as a result, the USA became involved in the revolutions in Panama and Mexico.

So, by 1900 the USA had moved away from strict isolationism and would now play a role as an international police power – particularly when it suited her interests to do so.

Activities

1 Define the word 'isolationism'.
2 Study Source B and note the position of the various territories taken over by the USA. What do they show you?
3 In your own words, explain the meaning of the Open Door Policy and the Corollary to the Monroe Doctrine.

▼ *Source B*

US possessions in 1900

(Adapted from: Patrick and Berkin. *History of the American Nation from 1877, Volume 2*.)

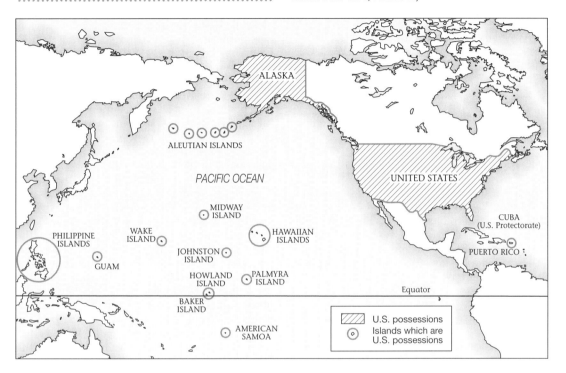

Unit 2 The First World War

Unit outcomes

- Analyse the reasons why the USA avoided involvement and then entered the First World War.
- Assess the US contribution to Allied victory.
- Recognise bias and propaganda.
- Judge the importance of causes and consequences.
- Analyse historical sources both written and visual.
- Create an empathetic picture.

The USA stays out of the First World War

When war broke out in Europe in August 1914, President Woodrow Wilson urged Americans to remain 'neutral in fact as well as in name', that is, not to take sides. He did not wish to involve the United States in the problems of Europe. The USA should stay at peace as an example to the warring nations.

Activities ....

1 Identify the two figures and the building shown in Source A.
2 Explain the various comments and the attitude of the two figures.
3 Do you think that Source A is biased in any way? Give reasons for your answer. (See page 50.)

Many Americans found it difficult to remain neutral. About 32 million Americans were for-eign-born or were the children of immigrants. Eight million of these people were German-Americans. Over 4 million were Irish-Americans who hated the British control of Ireland; there were millions of Jews and Poles who had fled from the persecution of the Tsar of Russia, whose autocratic rule was disliked by most Americans. There was hostility between Japan and the USA in the Pacific – and Japan was one of the Allied powers.

Most Americans seemed to favour the Allies. Cultural ties and a common language had helped to bind the Americans and British together. Americans admired the French and they remembered France's help during the American Revolution. Allied propaganda also played a part in making Americans sympathise with the Allied cause. Britain controlled the **transatlantic cables** which carried most of the news published in America about the war, so Americans read war news which favoured the Allies – there was emphasis on the devastation caused by the Germans in Belgium and the inhumanity of Germany's submarine warfare.

There were also financial and trade consider-ations. Many US banks raised huge loans for the Allies who then spent the money in the USA – on munitions and other supplies. By April 1917, American investors had bought Allied war bonds worth over two billion dollars. An Allied defeat would mean the loss of this money. American prosperity had become closely tied to the success of the Allies.

New words

transatlantic cables wires which carried telegraphic messages across the Atlantic Ocean

◀ *Source A* The only way we can save her

Source B▶

A cartoon showing Henry
Ford, the car manufacturer,
with the pacifists he sent to
Europe to try to keep the
USA out of the war. In the
background a German
U-boat calls 'Welcome'.
(From: Peter Lane. *The USA
in the Twentieth Century*.)

Activities

1 Describe what you see in Source B.
2 Who was Henry Ford and why did he want peace?
3 Can you suggest the significance of the two birds –
   the parrot and the dove?
4 The cartoon comes from *Punch*, a British magazine.
   Does this mean that the cartoon is biased? If so, how?

Legally, both the Allies and the Central Powers could purchase supplies from the USA. But Britain held the advantage because of her strong naval power. Ships of the Royal Navy controlled the sea lanes leading to Germany, where German and neutral (including American) ships were stopped, searched and any military supplies seized.

'Military supplies' were defined widely and even included food. This British blockade annoyed American merchants and in the early years of the war, the American government repeatedly protested against this interference with trade. But no stronger action was taken, in spite of the lack of response from the British – and the blockade continued.

Submarine warfare

The German reply to the British blockade was the use of undersea boats or 'U-boats'. These U-boats were slow-moving and lightly armoured; if they were caught on the surface of the water, they were easily destroyed. The submarine's effectiveness depended on surprise attack and quick retreat. For a submarine it was difficult to halt an enemy or neutral ship, search its cargo, and remove its cargo before sinking it.

In February 1915 when Germany announced that merchant ships found in a war zone around Britain and Ireland would be sunk without warning, the American government protested vigorously. The full significance of submarine warfare was brought home to Americans by the sinking of the 'Lusitania'. On 7 May 1915 this British passenger ship was torpedoed and sunk by a U-boat off the coast of Ireland. Of the almost 1 200 men, women and children who died, 128 were Americans. Some Americans urged an immediate declaration of war, but President Wilson remained calm. He warned the Germans that surprise U-boat attacks must be stopped or America would end its neutrality. In spite of German assurances, submarine attacks continued: in March 1916, a French passenger ship, the 'Sussex', was attacked without warning and many people were injured, including some Americans. Another strong warning from Wilson brought the 'Sussex pledge' from the Germans that merchant vessels would not be sunk without warning.

Meanwhile, German secret agents in the USA carried out sabotage (the destruction of property) to stop the flow of arms and supplies to the Allies. Bombs were placed on ships bound for Britain; strikes were stirred up among workers in munitions factories; and explosions and fires destroyed factories producing war materials.

President Wilson knew that the USA was in a dangerous situation and the country must be prepared for war. In June 1916 a National Defence Act was passed by Congress and about $500 million was voted to improve the navy, but Wilson was still determined to keep the country at peace. He won the presidential election in 1916 with the campaign slogan 'he kept us out of the war'.

Activities ·····································

1 Read the section on bias. What kind of bias is shown in Source A and Source B?
2 Write a short paragraph in which you give the views about the European War from the point of view of:
   • an Irish-American
   • a Jewish immigrant from Russia
   • an American businessman with interests in the Pacific.

·····································

Understanding historical skills and concepts

Facts, opinions, bias and propaganda

Facts and opinions
Most historical sources are a mixture of fact and opinion.

• A historical fact is information that is commonly accepted to be true.
• A historical opinion is a personal judgement about some aspect of a historical event.

Some opinions may be very personal and emotional statements which can be challenged by other people. Others may be personal observations based on a balanced judgement or interpretations based on an assessment of available information.

Bias
Bias is a 'leaning of the mind, an inclination or prejudice' (Oxford Dictionary).

Everyone has a tendency to see and judge events from his or her own point of view. Sometimes this is clearly noticeable, but often people are unaware of this. In their writings, all historians are influenced by their nationality, religion, race, culture, social class, experience and values.

So the learner must accept that bias is always present, and that a historian will have a prejudice (that is, an advance judgement) in favour of a particular viewpoint.

Propaganda
Propaganda is the deliberate spreading of certain ideas to achieve a specific purpose. In real life you are the target of propaganda every day. Television and newspaper advertising that urges you to buy a particular motor car or a toothpaste, or to wear certain kinds of clothes, is propaganda.

Posters telling you why something is good or harmful for you are another kind of propaganda. Propaganda is made to influence you either for or against an idea, an action or a product. It often emphasises one point over others. We can say that it is always biased, and sometimes untruthful.

Wartime propaganda
Propaganda has always been important in times of war. Leaders sometimes have to ask their people to do something unpleasant – to make some special sacrifice – and so they try to get public opinion on their side.

Both sides used propaganda during the First World War; for example, the Germans bought several American newspapers and used them to print stories that made Britain or France appear cruel and evil. On the other hand, Allied soldiers were subjected to posters and information describing the atrocities committed by the Germans. The USA also used propaganda. You will find two examples on the next page.

Bias diagram
Throughout this book you will find examples of biased sources. Use the diagram below to help you decide in what ways a source is biased.

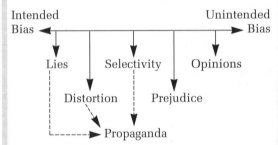

How do you oppose or counter propaganda?
Below are some questions you should ask.
• Who produced the piece of writing?
• Is the author likely to be trustworthy?
• What is the author's purpose or intention:
   – to arouse people's feelings?
   – to persuade people to act or think in a particular way?
   – to present only one point of view?
   – to present events in their most favourable light?

© Peter Newmark's Military Pictures

© Peter Newmark's Military Pictures

The two posters are appealing to young Americans to join the armed services. Notice the feelings of patriotism – your country needs you! Even girls would like to join the US Navy.

The other poster (on this page) encourages German submarine attacks on US ships. It was made just before the US entered the First World War. How would this influence American public opinion?

The USA enters the First World War

Early in 1917 Wilson increased his efforts to end the war. He insisted all the warring nations state their terms for stopping the fighting, but the various replies differed greatly and Wilson had to outline his own ideas. He suggested 'a peace without victory', but this was unacceptable to both the Allies and the Central Powers.

The outlook for continued American neutrality faded when, on 31 January 1917, Germany announced its decision to resume unrestricted submarine warfare. This was a gamble by the German leaders. They realised that this action would bring the USA into the war, but they calculated that the new submarine sinkings would starve Britain into surrender, and they thought that the German armies would crush the war-weary Allies on the Western Front before any sizeable American reinforcements arrived in Europe.

▼ German poster encouraging the use of U-boats against Allied ships

(From: Patrick and Berkin. *History of the American Nation from 1877, Volume 2.*)

© Peter Newmark's Military Pictures

On 3 February 1917 President Wilson ended all American diplomatic relations with Germany, but he still hesitated to declare war. Late in February, the British government notified Wilson that they had intercepted a secret message sent from the German Foreign Secretary Zimmermann to the German minister in Mexico. This note proposed that if war broke out between Germany and the USA, Mexico should enter into an alliance with Germany. In return, Germany would help the Mexicans recover their 'lost territory in New Mexico, Texas and Arizona'. On 1 March this note was released to the newspapers. Americans were angered and calls for war grew louder.

▼ Source C

Extract from the Zimmermann message of 19 January 1917

... we propose an alliance ... with Mexico: that we shall make war together ... and ... Mexico is to reconquer the lost territory in New Mexico, Texas and Arizona ... The employment of ruthless submarine warfare now promises to compel England to make peace in a few months.

Still Wilson hesitated: 'if there is any alternative', he said, 'let us take it'. In March 1917 a revolution toppled the Tsar of Russia from power, and a provisional (or temporary) government was set up. Submarine warfare continued and, during March, five American ships were sunk. Wilson could find no alternative and on 2 April 1917, he asked Congress to declare war on Germany. The resolution declaring war was signed on 6 April 1917. Wilson declared to Congress: 'The world must be made safe for democracy. Its peace must be planted upon the tested foundations of political liberty. We have no selfish ends to serve, we desire no conquest, no dominion.'

Activities

1 Who was Zimmermann and to whom was he sending Source C?
2 To whom and when had Mexico 'lost the territory'?
3 Write about ten lines on 'the submarine warfare' and what happened to England.
4 Explain how the revolution in Russia in March 1917 influenced the Americans.
5 Read the section on causation that follows. Below is a list of the reasons why the USA entered the First World War.
   a Indicate whether each reason is a long-term, short-term or trigger, economic, social, political or intellectual cause. There may be an overlap.
      • the loans and supplies given to the Allies
      • the Zimmermann note
      • submarine warfare
      • the March Revolution in Russia
      • the views of President Woodrow Wilson
      • the need to defend democracy.
   b Explain which cause you consider to have been the most important.

Understanding historical skills and concepts

Causes and consequences

Causes

Events happen because of interactions and relationships between various conditions, factors and people. However, events which follow each other do not necessarily have a causal link.

Historians usually divide the causes of events into long-term (or background) and short-term (immediate or 'trigger'). Some causes are about the way the government uses its power (political causes); some are about the lifestyle and standards of living of the people (social causes); some are about the way the wealth of the country is produced and shared out (economic causes). There are also intellectual causes when new ideas create an atmosphere for events to happen. People can make things happen in history – as, for example, President Woodrow Wilson did – but the individual's role is usually limited.

Usually there are several causes and some may be more important than others. This means that you have to make your own judgement based on your own personal viewpoint or values.

Different causes may interact with one another and this can cause other events to happen.

Consequences

Sometimes you will be asked to judge the importance of an event. On what basis will you decide? You should distinguish the immediate consequences, longer-term and wider effects. Factors to consider include the following.
• Did the event influence a large number of people?
• Did the effects last a long time?
• Did people at the time think that the event was important?
• Is the event relevant to people today?
• Does the event have importance against some general standard, for example, of freedom, of equity, of justice?

As you work through the pages of this book, you will be asked to decide about the causes and consequences of events.

Involvement in the First World War

The USA's decision to fight was the turning-point in the First World War. Americans were convinced that they were on the side of good, destined to destroy evil and somehow create a better world.

But the country was not prepared and there was little enthusiasm for the fighting. The horrors of trench warfare were well-known and patriotic propaganda such as that on page 51 did not raise enough troops. In spite of opposition, in May 1917 Congress passed the Selective Service Act that made all men between the ages of 21 and 30 years liable for military service. In June, ten million young men registered for the draft.

Training this vast number of men – the building of training camps, the provision of equipment, munitions and food required a great re-organisation of American life – industry, labour unions, railroads, farmers and housewives. Soon the entire economic life of the country was under the control of various federal agencies. To ensure the support of the people, a Committee on Public Information was set up. It mobilised advertising men, artists, authors, songwriters, actors, orators and motion picture companies 'to sell the war'.

Millions of pamphlets explained the causes of the war and American war aims. Inevitably, American troops were slow to arrive at the war front in Europe. General John Pershing, commander-in-chief, reached Paris with his staff in June 1917 and the first regular army units arrived soon afterwards. After training in trench warfare, the first Americans saw action in October 1917. In 1918, the increasing number of American troops helped stop the German advance towards Paris and, later, they formed a large part of the Allied attack which led to the armistice in November.

At sea, the US navy concentrated on attacking the U-boats. Using the new **hydrophones** and **depth charges** as well as the **convoy system**, the navy successfully transported over two million American soldiers across the Atlantic (see Source D). An anti-submarine minefield was laid across three hundred miles of the North Sea. As the thousands of US troops arrived in France, the effect on morale was enormous – it lowered German morale and boosted the Allies.

▼ *Source D*

The Americans in France (1918)

(Adapted from: Nichol and Lang. *GCSE Modern World History*.)

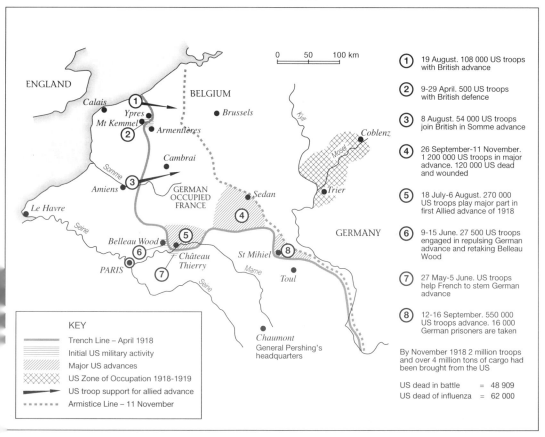

KEY
- Trench Line – April 1918
- Initial US military activity
- Major US advances
- US Zone of Occupation 1918-1919
- US troop support for allied advance
- Armistice Line – 11 November

1. 19 August. 108 000 US troops with British advance
2. 9-29 April. 500 US troops with British defence
3. 8 August. 54 000 US troops join British in Somme advance
4. 26 September-11 November. 1 200 000 US troops in major advance. 120 000 US dead and wounded
5. 18 July-6 August. 270 000 US troops play major part in first Allied advance of 1918
6. 9-15 June. 27 500 US troops engaged in repulsing German advance and retaking Belleau Wood
7. 27 May-5 June. US troops help French to stem German advance
8. 12-16 September. 550 000 US troops advance. 16 000 German prisoners are taken

By November 1918 2 million troops and over 4 million tons of cargo had been brought from the US

| US dead in battle | = 48 909 |
| US dead of influenza | = 62 000 |

New words

hydrophone instrument for detecting sound waves in water
depth charge bomb which exploded under water – for use against a submerged submarine
convoy system a system by which a number of merchant vessels sailed together under navy escort

▼ Source E

A Boost for British Morale: In *Testament of Youth*, Vera Brittain, who served as a nurse behind the British lines, described her first sight of American troops as follows:

I was leaving quarters to go back to my ward, when I had to wait to let a large contingent of troops march past ... though the sight of soldiers marching was now too familiar to arouse curiosity, an unusual quality of bold vigour in their swift stride caused me to stare at them with puzzled interest.

They looked larger than ordinary men; their tall, straight figures were in vivid contrast to the undersized armies of pale recruits to which we had become accustomed ... Had yet another regiment been conjured out of our depleted Dominions?

Then I heard an excited exclamation from a group of Sisters behind me.

'Look! Look! Here are the Americans!' ...

The coming of relief made me realize how long and how intolerable had been the tension, and with the knowledge that we were not, after all, defeated I found myself beginning to cry.

Activities

Study Sources D and E and then answer the questions below.

1 Draw up a timeline showing the involvement of the American troops on the Western Front during 1918.
2 How many American troops were in France by November 1918, and how many of them were killed in battle?
3 On the basis of the information in Source D, which do you think was the most important contribution made by the Americans?
4 Who was General Pershing and where were his headquarters?
5 Put yourself in the position of a German soldier in the trenches, and write about ten lines describing your first battle with the American soldiers.

Extension activity

Hold a group or class discussion to explore the question: "To what extent and how do you think that 'the Americans won the war'?"

▶ During the war, many women took on factory jobs
(From: Patrick and Berkin. *History of the American Nation from 1877, Volume 2.*)

Women in the workplace

Before the First World War, about eight million American women earned wages. They were employed in 'female' areas such as domestic service (maids), dress-making, secretarial work, nursing and teaching. Many more worked in unpaid jobs – in their homes and on farms.

The war did not greatly increase the number of women workers, but it changed the type of work that they did. To replace the men who were sent overseas to fight, women moved into highly-paid jobs in war factories and shipyards, where they helped to build tanks, guns and aeroplanes. Black women took over the jobs white women had left.

Some American men did not want women workers in the factories because they said that women slowed down production. However, women constantly proved their ability to work hard and quickly. Other men did not like the independence that women factory workers came to enjoy.

Women factory workers hoped to continue their new jobs after the war, but most were quickly replaced by returned soldiers at the end of the fighting in 1918. In the end, the war brought few changes in the work patterns of American women.

One area where the war did have an influence was in the struggle of women to gain the vote. How could President Wilson aim to 'make the world safe for democracy' when American women did not have the vote? Women were finally given the vote throughout the USA in 1920.

New opportunities for blacks

The war opened up new opportunities for black male workers in railroad yards, meat packing houses, steel mills and coal mines. To get these jobs, however, black families had to leave the south and move to northern cities. Between 1910 and 1920, the black population of Detroit grew by 600 per cent as over half a million black southerners chose to move. Unfortunately, they were not always well-received in the north, and after the war, there were race riots in some American cities.

Activities ....

Put yourself in the position of an American working woman or a black male worker. Describe how your life changed during and after the war.

....

The Paris Peace Conference and President Woodrow Wilson

Unit outcomes

- Assess President Woodrow Wilson's successes and failures at the Paris Peace Conference.
- Compare the ideal of the Fourteen Points with the reality of the peace settlement.
- Interpret historical cartoons.
- Debate differing viewpoints.
- Describe the constitution of the USA.

Profile: *Woodrow Wilson*

© INPRA

Woodrow Wilson was the son of a Presbyterian minister. He became professor of history and later president of Princeton University. He entered politics in 1910 and was elected president of the United States in 1912 as a Democrat.

Wilson was an idealist. He believed that the war was being fought to 'make the world safe for democracy' and to safeguard the rights of mankind. He wanted 'peace without victory' by which he meant that the winners must not humiliate the losers. He outlined his ideas in his 'Fourteen Points' in January 1918 and it was on this basis that the Germans signed the armistice which halted the fighting on 11 November 1918.

▼ *Source A*
The Fourteen Points

1 There should be no more secret treaties.

2 Absolute freedom of the seas at all times.

3 Free trade between nations.

4 All armaments to be reduced.

5 The rights and opinions of people living in colonies to be considered when settling colonial claims.

6 The Germans must withdraw from Russian territory.

7 Belgium must be free and independent.

8 France will regain the territory of Alsace-Lorraine.

9 The border between Austria and Italy to be readjusted.

10 The peoples of Eastern Europe must have self-determination in their own independent nations.

11 Romania, Serbia and Montenegro must be liberated and their territory guaranteed by international agreement.

12 The people in the Turkish Empire must decide upon their own future.

13 Poland should be an independent nation with access to the Baltic sea.

14 An association of nations – the League of Nations – to be set up to settle all disputes between countries.

The Paris Peace Conference

Wilson arrived in France in December 1918 and he received an enthusiastic welcome from crowds of ordinary people. He told them that he had come to Europe to make an eternal peace that was both just and right.

However, other Allied leaders had their own objectives. Clemenceau, Prime Minister of France, was determined that the power of Germany must be reduced and France made secure against another German attack. Lloyd George had promised the people of Britain that

Germany would pay for the great destruction caused by the war. Sometimes he exercised a moderating influence between the views of Wilson and Clemenceau. Orlando of Italy wanted territory along his northern borders.

Wilson was forced to make concessions (see Source B) and his Fourteen Points were continually modified. But he was successful in making the League of Nations an inseparable part of the final Treaty of Versailles. In this way he hoped that any faults in the treaty would be resolved by negotiation and that peace would be maintained by nations joining together under the principle of collective security. To guarantee a lasting settlement, it was vital that the USA should be a member of the League.

▼ *Source B*
How the Fourteen Points were changed

1 *Even the Council of Four met in secret – in spite of Wilson's promise of 'open diplomacy'.*

2 *Lloyd George, thinking of Britain's naval and trading interests, refused to accept 'absolute freedom ... in peace and war ...'*

3 *Tariff barriers were not removed.*

4 *There was no guarantee given by anyone on disarmament.*

5 *The interests of the colonial peoples were rarely considered.*

6 *The Allies (including the USA) sent forces against the new Bolshevik government.*

9 *Italy received some territory but there remained a dispute over the town of Fiume.*

13 *The new Poland contained over two million Germans, an issue which was to play a part in the onset of the Second World War in 1939.*

14 *A League of Nations was formed – but was weaker than Wilson had hoped.*

Domestic politics upset Wilson's plans. The American Constitution requires that all treaties signed by the president must be approved by two-thirds of the Senate. In November 1918, elections had resulted in Republican majorities in the Senate and in the House of Representatives. The isolationist outlook was still strong in many Republican areas of the mid-West; many recent immigrants criticised Wilson for not doing enough to satisfy the demands of their previous homelands; and

other critics complained that Wilson had not broken up the British and French Empires in the peace settlement.

The debate in the Senate was bitter and in September 1919, Wilson set off on an exhausting countrywide tour to try to sell the idea of the League to the American people. Wilson's health broke down under the strain and he suffered a stroke. He was absent from politics for months and he remained an invalid for the rest of his life, until his death in February 1924.

In March 1920, the Senate finally voted against the Treaty of Versailles and the League of Nations. The issue was raised again in the presidential election of November 1920: the Democratic candidate, James Cox, supported the League, while the Republican candidate, Warren Harding, offered a policy of 'isolation' and a return to 'normalcy'. Harding won decisively.

In 1921, the USA and Germany signed a separate Treaty of Berlin. It contained most of the Versailles clauses except for references to the League and certain territorial changes. The USA had effectively excluded herself from the rebuilding of Europe in the 1920s.

An isolationist view of the League

Senator Henry Cabot Lodge of Massachusetts, chairman of the very influential Senate Foreign Relations Committee, was one of the most skilful and determined opponents of the League and Wilson personally. In this speech to the Senate in August 1919, he stated some of his objections:

I object in the strongest possible way to having the United States agree, directly or indirectly, to be controlled by a League which may at any time ... be drawn in to deal with internal conflicts in other countries, no matter what those conflicts may be ... It must be made perfectly clear that no American soldiers ... can ever be engaged in war or ordered anywhere except by the constitutional authorities of the United States.

▼ *Source C*
Speech by President Wilson in Colorado on 25 September 1919

– mothers who lost their sons in France have come to me ... they rightly believe that their sons saved the liberty of the world. They believe that, wrapped up with the liberty of the world, is the continuous protection of that liberty by the concerted powers of all civilised people. They believe that this sacrifice was made in order that others' sons should not be called upon for a similar gift – the gift of life.

Courtesy of John Frost Historical Papers

The Tiger: "Curious! I seem to hear a child weeping!"

Activities

Study the text and the sources with a partner and then complete the activities below.

1 Consider each of Wilson's Fourteen Points in Source A and explain why each was changed or retained by the Peace Conference.

2 The Germans called the Treaty of Versailles 'a dictated peace'. Do you consider this to be a justified comment? Explain your answer.

3 Describe the cartoon and explain the cartoonist's viewpoint in Source D.

Extension activity

Hold a group discussion and debate. One group find arguments in favour of Wilson's viewpoint, and the second group find arguments in favour of the view of Senator Cabot Lodge. Consult the text and Sources C and D.

How the USA is governed

The constitution was drawn up in 1787 by the founders of the USA. The USA is a republic and the two most important features are federalism and the separation of powers.

'Republic' means that there is no hereditary monarch like a king or queen. Instead, there is a president who is elected every four years.

'Federalism' means that there are two distinct layers of government. The Federal Government is based in Washington DC and is responsible for issues affecting the whole country, for example, economic policy, defence, and foreign policy. Each state has its own constitution, capital city and congress. States raise their own taxes and run their own affairs, such as education and police. Many states do not like federal interference, although they do accept financial help from the federal government.

The constitution divides the powers of the government among three separate branches – legislative (makes the laws), executive (runs the country) and judiciary (decides if laws are constitutional). Each branch is able to balance or obstruct the activities of the others, so that no one branch can completely dominate the country.

The president is the most important figure in the government. He is elected for four years and has great powers, for example, he is commander-in-chief of the armed forces, he appoints his own cabinet and ambassadors; he also appoints judges to the Supreme Court when there is a death or retirement. However, he has very little direct control over what laws are passed by Congress, and he frequently has to enter into a process of bargaining with Congress to get what he wants. This is sometimes difficult, as in Woodrow Wilson's case, because one or both houses of Congress may well not be dominated by his own political party.

There are two major political parties – the Republicans and the Democrats. Their policies are similar on many issues, and the role of individual personalities is an important one. The Republicans are more conservative, tend to gain support from the wealthy, big business and those who distrust government interference in their lives. The Democrats usually gain support from liberals, racial minorities, the poor, weak and jobless and those who believe the government should be active in solving problems.

The Electoral College is a body of electors chosen by state voters to elect the president and vice-president.

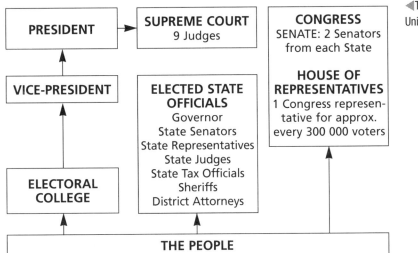

◀The structure of the United States government

PRESIDENT → SUPREME COURT 9 Judges

VICE-PRESIDENT

ELECTED STATE OFFICIALS
Governor
State Senators
State Representatives
State Judges
State Tax Officials
Sheriffs
District Attorneys

CONGRESS
SENATE: 2 Senators from each State

HOUSE OF REPRESENTATIVES
1 Congress representative for approx. every 300 000 voters

ELECTORAL COLLEGE

THE PEOPLE

Activities

Consider Source E below and answer the following questions.

1 Who is 'the boss' that Woodrow Wilson is going to talk to?
2 Why does he have to go to 'the boss'?
3 What happened to Wilson's plans?

Extension activity

How does the US system of government compare to South Africa's system of government? Find out more about how our system operates.

▼ Source E

Woodrow Wilson going to talk to the boss
(From: Bragdon and McCutchen. *History of a Free People*.)

'Normalcy': Republican foreign policy (1920–32)

Unit outcomes

- Describe the Republican foreign policy of 'normalcy' (1920–32).
- Interpret a historical cartoon.
- Participate in a group discussion.

The nation was spiritually tired. Wearied by the excitements of the war ... They hoped for quiet and healing. Sick of Wilson and his talk of America's duty to humanity, they hoped for a chance to pursue their private affairs without governmental interference and to forget about public affairs. There might be no such word in the dictionary as normalcy, but normalcy was what they wanted.

(From: Frederick Allen. *Only Yesterday*.)

In the years between the wars, Americans believed that they had returned to 'normalcy', that is, avoided involvement in the affairs of other countries. In his first speech as president, Warren Harding had stated, 'we seek no part in directing the destinies of the Old World'.

However, no country of the size and with the wealth of America could realistically cut herself off from all **entanglements**. In spite of rejecting the League of Nations, America became involved in the promotion of world peace and in international finance.

> ### New words
>
> **entanglements** relationships in which the USA might become trapped
> **renounce** abandon; refuse to recognise
> **tonnage ratio** quantity used to compare the numbers of naval vessels

Cooperation with the League of Nations

It soon became apparent that committees of the League were discussing issues of vital interest to the USA. Unofficial American observers were sent to the League headquarters at Geneva and by 1930, five permanent officials were present to look after American interests.

A World Court had been set up in 1920 to consider all future international disputes. An American lawyer helped to outline the organisation and functions of the Court and there was a long Senate debate about American membership. In the end, the Senate did not approve American membership.

Promoting peace

America had declared war on Germany on 6 April 1917. Exactly ten years later, the French Foreign Minister, Briand, suggested that the two countries solemnly **renounce** war as a means of settling any future disputes. The American Secretary of State, Kellogg, met Briand in Paris in 1928, and along with fifteen other nations, signed the Kellogg-Briand Pact which renounced war as an instrument of policy. Subsequently, 62 countries signed the Pact, but no method of enforcing the Pact by peaceful means was ever found.

Disarmament

After the First World War, Britain and Japan made plans to increase their naval forces in the Pacific, and the USA developed a similar programme. It seemed as if there was going to be a new arms race. President Harding convened a conference in Washington (1921–22). Three treaties were signed, the most important of which laid down that the battleships of the USA, Britain and Japan should be scrapped until the **tonnage ratio** of 5: 5: 3 respectively was reached. There were further disarmament conferences in Geneva and London in 1924, 1927, 1930, 1932 and 1935. In 1936, Japan withdrew from the naval disarmament conference. Britain and France began new naval construction programmes.

+ open door policy (china not property of Japan)

Russia

Communist Russia, under Lenin's government, had withdrawn from the war with Germany by the Treaty of Brest-Litovsk (March 1918). The Allies sent troops and supplies to help the 'White' Russians fighting against Lenin's forces.

American forces were withdrawn by 1920. In 1921, the US government, assisted by private donations, sent medical assistance and food supplies to help overcome the famine caused by the fighting in the Russian civil war. However, it was not until 1933, that the USA formally recognised the communist regime in Russia.

War debts and reparations

During the First World War, many Allied countries borrowed money from the USA to purchase military supplies – from April 1917 to the end of the war, the Allies borrowed nearly seven billion dollars. Britain and France, who owed the largest sums of money, expected to pay their debts out of the war reparations to be collected from Germany. The Germans soon fell behind in their payments: the French invaded the Ruhr in 1923 to extract payment in kind, and the German economy was about to collapse. The Dawes Plan of 1924 scaled down the amount of German reparations and granted a loan to Germany – very largely financed by American banks. In 1929, German reparations were reduced still further (the Young Plan) and the period of payment extended. However, the Great Depression upset these plans, and in 1931, all payments were suspended for a year. Eventually, the USA had to cancel most of her investment in reparations and war debts.

Many Americans were bitter about this – they agreed with President Coolidge's statement – 'they hired the money, didn't they?' Altogether, Germany paid about four and a half billion dollars in reparations to Britain and France. In turn, the Allies paid about two and a half billion dollars in war debts to the USA.

Latin (South) America

Relations between the USA and Latin America were not always good during the 1920s. In fact, war almost broke out with Mexico. In 1925, the Mexican government enacted a law which stated that all petroleum and mining deposits were owned by the Mexican nation; most of these were actually owned by US companies. Some Americans called for military intervention, but the US Senate preferred a peaceful settlement. President Coolidge sent a special ambassador, DW Morrow, to Mexico. He was able to persuade the Mexican government to revise its policy towards American oil rights. Relations with Mexico improved, and in 1928 the American government renounced the Theodore Roosevelt corollary to the Monroe Doctrine. It said that the Monroe Doctrine was 'not an instrument of violence and oppression, but a guarantee of freedom from international intervention in the area'.

▼ *Source A*
The Japanese invasion of Manchuria (1931)

In Nicaragua, however, American troops were used. In 1927 marines were sent to restore order when civil war broke out. Peace was eventually restored, but the marines were not withdrawn until 1933.

In his first inaugural address in 1933, the new President, Franklin Roosevelt, promised that the USA would be a 'good neighbor' in the family of nations. This concept was confirmed by the US secretary of state who said that 'no state has the right to intervene in the internal and external affairs of another'. Thus the Roosevelt government abandoned the right of intervention introduced by Theodore Roosevelt as a corollary of the Monroe Doctrine.

Words were soon translated into deeds: the USA withdrew the marines from Haiti and wrote a new treaty with Cuba; the right to send police to Panama was abandoned as was control of the finances of the Dominican Republic. In 1938, a collective security pact was signed between all the American nations. Cultural exchanges were promoted between the USA and South America and President Roosevelt himself attended a conference in Buenos Aires. A new friendliness was developed in the Americas.

Activities

1 Give a definition of 'normalcy'.
2 Study Source A on page 61 which describes the Japanese invasion of Manchuria. Explain how this invasion destroyed the various agreements made by the USA during the 1920s.

Extension activity

The basic aims of any government's foreign policy (as stated before) are:
a to remain independent and defend the country from attack
b to protect its citizens abroad
c to promote its own trading interests overseas.
Hold a group or class discussion in which you list the various areas where the USA abandoned the policy of isolation in the 1920s and early 1930s, and decide which of the above aims persuaded her to do so.

Unit 5

The foreign policy of President Franklin Roosevelt

Unit outcomes

- Describe the foreign policy of President Franklin Delano Roosevelt.
- Analyse and synthesise events of the 1930s.
- Interpret historical sources and assess differing viewpoints.

The road to war in Europe

In the early 1930s, recovery from the Great Depression was the main concern of most Americans. They were worried by the rise of Fascism in Italy, Nazism in Germany and a military government in Japan; but they were unable or unwilling to do anything about these developments. A senator from Minnesota summed up how most people felt when he said: 'to hell with Europe and the rest of those nations'.

Roosevelt's attention was focused on the Depression at home, and he allowed the isolationist group in Congress to pass several Neutrality Acts which were designed to keep the country out of any possible war. In the later 1930s, American attitudes began to change as developments in Europe (and the East), became more alarming and began to threaten US interests.

Activities

1 You are an American news commentator during the 1930s. Your views are isolationist, but you want to present a fair picture to your readers. Study Source A and prepare some brief comments on the world events and the American response. You will be asked to present these comments to the class.

2 a What is the meaning of Source B?
  b Comment on each of the figures who are securing the ropes.
  c Suggest a date for this cartoon.

▼ *Source A*   World events and American responses

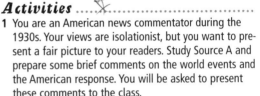

World event	Date	American response
Italy invaded Abyssinia (Oct)	1935	1st Neutrality Act (Aug) – arms not to be sold to warring nations; US citizens not to travel on ships belonging to nations at war
Spanish civil war began – *germany + italy inv.*	1936	2nd Neutrality Act – no war loans or credits
	1937	3rd Neutrality Act – 'cash & carry' act Belligerents to pay cash and carry goods in own ships. Roosevelt calls war a disease which must be 'quarantined', that is, isolated to prevent its spread
Hitler occupied Austria and the Sudetenland	1938	Roosevelt telegraphed Hitler and Mussolini urging a peaceful settlement
Germany took over Czechoslovakia (March) Germany attacked Poland (Sept) Britain and France declared war on Germany	1939	4th Neutrality Act: 'cash & carry' to continue. Atlantic Ocean to remain open *could buy weapons + ammunition*
Germany conquered most of Europe Battle of Britain (Aug–Sept) German submarine attacks began	1940	Rearmament started (April) Peacetime Draft approved 50 Destroyers for Bases deal
Germany attacked Russia (June) Germany declared war on USA (Dec – after Pearl Harbour attack)	1941	Active aid to Britain Lend-Lease Act (March) – war supplies leased to Britain Atlantic Charter (Aug) – statement of War Aims by Churchill and Roosevelt

◀ *Source B*
Sleeping Uncle Sam
(From: Nigel Smith. *The USA 1917–1980.*)

Labels in image: 5TH COLUMNISTS, NAZI SYMPATHIZERS, DEFEATISTS, HATE ENGLAND CROWD, ISOLATIONISTS, APPEASERS, BUSINESS AS USUAL

The road to Pearl Harbour

In January 1933 Roosevelt made it clear that he intended to stand by the 'Open Door' policy of trade with China. However, the weakness of America's Pacific Fleet and the small number of American troops in China meant that he could not use force to defend China against Japan. On 7 March 1933 Roosevelt warned his Cabinet that his policy was to avoid war with Japan.

During the 1930s, aggressive steps by Japan drew a weak response from the USA.

< (138)

1933 Japan completed occupation of Manchuria (invaded in 1931)

1934 the Amau Declaration: Japan claimed responsibility for peace in the area, contrary to the Open Door Policy; Japan withdrew from the Washington Naval Treaty and began unrestricted naval expansion

1936 Japan joined the Anti-Comintern Pact (with Germany and Italy), directed against Russia

1937 Japan attacked China after Marco Polo Bridge incident; US warship 'Panay' sunk by Japanese aircraft (Japanese government later apologised)

1939 President Roosevelt cancelled a trade agreement with Japan

1940 Japan joined the Berlin-Rome Axis

1941 Japan occupied French Indo-China; USA cut export of war materials (including oil) to Japan. Further credit was refused; Japanese assets in USA were frozen

1941 Japanese attacked Pearl Harbour (7 December); Japanese invasion of Philippines, Hong Kong, Malaya began; Germany and Italy declared war on the USA (11 December).

Finding out from sources

Study the sources about Pearl Harbour and then complete the activities which follow.

Pearl Harbour

On Sunday 7 December 1941, two American radar operators were surprised to see a mass of 'blips' on their screens. Their officer, however, told them not to worry, but those 'blips' were, in fact, 214 Japanese planes which, in the space of a few hours, destroyed most of the American

Roosevelt elected - 1932
- 1936
- 1940
- 1944
die - 1945

Pacific fleet and military installations at Pearl Harbour in Hawaii.

In the attack, 2 400 Americans were killed and 1 178 wounded; 7 battleships, 5 other ships and 180 aircraft were lost.

To the Americans, this was an act of murderous treachery.

Activities

Look carefully at Source C.
1 Describe what it shows.
2 What do you think is the perspective of the cartoonist drawing Source C?

▼ Source D

An American view of Pearl Harbour by a sailor who was in the harbour at the time

At Hickam Field, the airfield so near Pearl Harbor that it is virtually the same target, a long row of hangars and bombers invited the Japanese. A bomb hit on a hangar announced the news to the thousands on the post. Men came pouring out of the barracks – men in slacks, men in shorts, some in their underwear only, some without anything on at all. What was going on? Another

mock war? No, bombs! Everyone ran for clothes and then for his battle station.

I cannot tell you how many ships were lying in Pearl Harbor on that peaceful Sunday morning. That is a naval secret, but you know that Pearl Harbor is the United States' largest naval base – battleships were there, destroyers lay near them, mine-layers, cruisers and all types of ships.

From somewhere a wave of torpedo planes eased down towards the ships and released their torpedoes, glittering like fish in the sun, plunging with a loud splash into the sea. Each plane had its object carefully selected in advance for the approaching planes separated and each went to a definite attack.

A massive battleship rocked as if hit by a mighty fist. Almost simultaneously jets of oil spouted all over the ship. In two minutes the deck of the ship was covered with flames. Flames leapt as high as the crows nest on which a lone sailor stood. Groping, he leaped into the oil-covered, flaming water below, just missing the deck. When he clambered up on the beach, all the hair had been singed from his head.

▼ *Source E*

A Japanese view of Pearl Harbour
(From: John O'Keeffe. *America 1870–1975.*)

▼ *Source F*

President Roosevelt speaks to Congress (8 December 1941)

Yesterday, December 7, 1941 – a date that will live in infamy [evil crime] – the United States was deliberately attacked by the naval and air forces of the Empire of Japan. This unprovoked attack left no doubt that our people, our territory and our interests are in grave danger ...

We didn't want to get into this war – but we are in it and we're going to fight it with everything we've got!

Activities

1 What evidence can you find in the sources that this was a well-planned attack?
2 What does Source E tell you about the Japanese pilot?
3 What important type of ship (shown in Source E) was not in Pearl Harbour at the time of the attack?
4 Imagine that you are either a Japanese attacker or an American defender. Write a short description of your part in the action.

5 How do you think these people would have reacted to the news of the Japanese attack on Pearl Harbour?
  • Winston Churchill, Prime Minister of Britain
  • President Roosevelt (in private – and in public)
  • young Americans.
6 Group discussion. Consider the viewpoint that the Japanese attack was justified.

Extension activity

1 What would have happened if the USA had remained neutral in the First World War? Find evidence to support your viewpoint.
2 Draw up two lists of the events which brought the USA into the Second World War – one for Europe and one for Asia. In a class discussion pick out similarities and differences.

THE US ECONOMY

Unit 6 The boom of the 1920s

Unit outcomes

- Describe the political and economic conditions of the 1920s.
- Describe the 'good life' and the conservative reaction to it.
- Analyse the reasons for the industrial boom.
- Explain the effect of new technology on American life.

Introduction

The 1920s were a period of prosperity and glamour in the USA. They were sometimes called the 'Roaring Twenties' since the country was busy and booming in many ways. Americans bought millions of new cars and filled the highways, the cities and even the country lanes with the sound of roaring engines. In the factories machines whirred and clanked day and night. Sports crowds roared with excitement as professional boxers battled each other or when baseball players hit home runs. Other forms of entertainment were often loud; the popular music of the time, 'hot jazz', seemed to pound through the night-clubs where couples danced the Charleston or the foxtrot.

After the restrictions of the war years, Americans felt that this was a time to enjoy life. They seemed to be saying: we are young and growing richer and more powerful every day.

Politics

The presidents who were elected to office during this period reflected the mood and morality of the times. In the 1920 election, the Republican candidates won an overwhelming victory – Warren Harding became president and Calvin Coolidge vice-president.

These men believed that governments should not interfere in the running of the country's economy. Businessmen should be left to make their own decisions which would result in the production of more profit and wealth. This system is sometimes known as *laissez-faire* or private enterprise and, it was argued, was the most efficient way to run an economy.

President Warren Harding (1921–23) wanted a 'return to normalcy'. One aspect of 'normalcy' was that the special powers given to the government during the war should be removed; one of his first acts was to cancel all the war taxes on the rich. Harding was considered to be a 'nice' man – friendly, handsome and with a kind heart. Harding's cabinet was very largely made up of businessmen who intended to look after the interests of business as well as themselves. Several of them were involved in dishonest deals and various scandals were discovered which forced some cabinet members to resign.

Harding died in August 1923 and Vice-President Calvin Coolidge became president. He was a conservative man who was sometimes called 'Silent Cal' because of his quiet, unimaginative nature. An unkind political opponent, Walter Lippmann, said of him: 'Mr Coolidge's genius for inactivity is developed to a very high point. It is far from being apathetic inactivity. It is a grim, determined, alert inactivity which keeps Mr Coolidge busy all the time.'

During the 'Roaring Twenties', the economy seemed to be going well and people were interested in changing nothing. In 1928, the Republican candidates for president and vice-president were elected: Herbert Hoover and Charles Curtis.

Activities

1 Suggest three ways in which the USA 'roared' during the 1920s.
2 The USA is rich in resources. Use source A to give a percentage figure (for the 1920s) of the US production of the world's supply of corn and petrol, and the use of petrol, cars and rubber.
3 Give a definition of the following terms:
   - normalcy
   - a *laissez-faire* economy.

▼ *Source A* The wealth of the USA
(Adapted from: BBC. *Twentieth Century History*.)

KEY
🛢 Cars
 Coal
 Corn
 Cotton
 Electricity
 Films
 Fish
 Fruit
 Iron
 Petrol
 Rubber
 Silk
 Sugar
 Telephones
 Timber
 Tobacco
 Wheat

In the 1920s the United States contained only 6 per cent of the world's population but

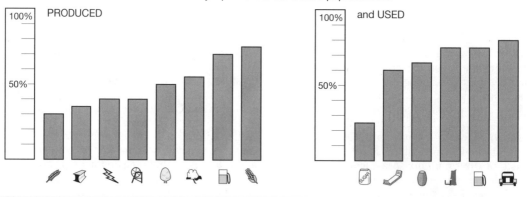

PRODUCED

and USED

---

4 Write a short paragraph about each of President Harding and President Coolidge and their policies.

5 Do you consider the statement about President Coolidge (made by Walter Lippmann) to be reliable (trustworthy)? Explain your answer.

· ·

The economy

At the end of the First World War, the American economy slowed down briefly as industry changed from the production of wartime to peacetime goods. By 1921, the change had been made and for the next eight years, most Americans lived better than ever before. Wages rose and, in many industries, the working day was shortened. The output of industry rose by over one-third: by 1929 America produced about 46 per cent of the world's industrial goods. A policy of strict tariff barriers (import taxes) restricted the entry of foreign imports so that they could not compete with American-produced goods. New methods of payment – by instalment or hire-purchase – made it possible for many more people to buy consumer goods that they had previously not been able to afford. Advertising techniques became more advanced to persuade consumers to spend even more of their money.

Economic indicators: 1922 and 1929
(From: Harry Mills. *Twentieth Century World History in Focus.*)

Indicator	1922	1929
National income (billions of 1926 dollars)	61,2	75,9
Income per head (1926 dollars)	563,0	625,0
Employment (millions)	40,0	47,9
Average hourly earnings in manufacturing (dollars)	0,52	0,57
Bank deposits (billions of dollars)	41,1	57,9
Business profits (billions of dollars)	3,9	7,2

The boom in business was led by three new industries: motor cars and related industries, electrical goods and chemicals. The increase in car production was particularly dramatic. Between 1909 and 1928, fifteen million Ford Model Ts were built. For the first time cars came within the reach of ordinary people. This was all possible because Henry Ford revolutionised car production.

Henry Ford was the son of an Irish father and a Dutch mother. From an early age he was fascinated by steam engines. In 1896, he built his first motor car and he founded the Ford Motor Company in 1903. The first Model T was produced in 1909.

▶ *Source C*

Part of the assembly line for the Model T
(From: Neil Demarco. *The USA: A Divided Union.*)

The secret of Ford's remarkable success was the assembly line. On the assembly line, workers stood beside a carefully timed conveyor belt or moving platform. Each worker had one task, for example, to put one piece in place or to tighten one set of bolts. When a worker finished with one car, it moved down the belt to the next worker and another car came along. When the car rolled off the assembly line, it was ready to be sold.

This process cut the time needed to make a car – from 14 hours to only 93 minutes – and during the 1920s this production time continued to decrease. In 1927 the Model T was replaced with the improved Model A. By 1929, one out of every five Americans owned a car.

Activities

1 What do the economic indicators in Source B tell you about the economy in 1922 and 1929? Explain each figure in the table.
2 a Describe the process of mass-production shown in Source C.
   b Why is it a cheap way of production?
3 Explain why the car industry was so important both economically and socially.
4 How are motor cars produced today? Do some research to find out the answer to this question.

The motor industry created a huge demand for steel, rubber, glass and oil and, as a result, all these industries boomed. Roads had to be built for the cars to travel on, and this created more jobs.

Another area where mass-production was applied was in the manufacture of domestic appliances such as refrigerators, vacuum cleaners and washing-machines. This led to a fall in

prices which encouraged people to spend more money. Radio broadcasting began in 1921 and this created a demand for radio sets – a boost for the electrical industry. Sales of radios rose from about $2 million a year in 1920 to $6 million in 1929.

Foreign competition

In 1922, during Harding's period of office, the Fordney-McCumber Act was passed to protect USA industry against foreign competition. High tariffs (or taxes) were put on foreign goods entering the country. In this way, foreign goods were made more expensive. American industry profited in the short term, but foreign countries fought back by imposing their own tariffs on American imports, and in this trade war, fewer goods were sold.

Hard times

For some Americans, however, the 'Roaring Twenties' were years of hard times. Many farmers, who made up 25 per cent of the population, did not share in the good life. With the end of the war, Europeans began to grow food again so there was less demand for American produce. The prices of farm products in America fell. At the same time, the cost of running a farm was increasing as farming machinery and fertilisers became more expensive. Like other American families, farmers wanted to own motor cars and have attractive houses, but most farmers did not earn enough to buy these things. About 600 000 farmers lost their farms in 1924. By 1929, about 12 million families had an average annual income of only $1 500.

There was also poverty and hardship among the unskilled workers in the cities and among black people in the north and south. Workers in the coal-mining and textile industries were often retrenched, and even in booming industries, wages of the workers went up more slowly than the price of goods they had to buy.

It was the wealthy people who gained most from the booming American economy.

Activities

1 Why did more people buy domestic appliances during this period?
2 a Describe what you see in Source D.
  b Part of this photograph is an advertisement. Do you consider this to be valid (trustworthy)?
  c Identify and explain the line of people standing at the front of the photograph.
3 Why was the US economy not dependent on other countries during this period?

▼ *Source D*
World's Highest Standard of Living
(From: Neil Demarco. *The USA: A Divided Union.*)

'The Good Life'

During the 1920s the everyday life of the American people changed in many ways. Americans wanted to forget about the war, and they set out to enjoy themselves as never before. The use of the new domestic appliances gave Americans more free time. There were many new forms of entertainment which became popular: the radio, talking movie films, sports events and holidays away from home. Attitudes to life changed.

▼ *Source E*

Detail from *Contemporary America* by Thomas Hart Benton, 1930 (From: Neil Demarco. *The USA: A Divided Union.*)

Motion pictures (movies) had been popular since they began in about 1900, but until 1927 they were silent. Sometimes a few printed words were shown on the screen, and a piano player in the theatre often played music to fit the action. In 1927, *The Jazz Singer*, starring Al Jolson, was the first motion picture with sound.

Jazz emerged on to the national scene from its African American roots in New Orleans. Young people everywhere enthusiastically adopted the new music with its sexy songs and dances such as the Charleston. Young women, known as 'flappers', upset older Americans – they cut their hair short and wore much shorter and looser clothing; they wore make-up and openly flirted with men.

Late in 1920, a Pittsburgh radio station made the first commercial broadcast: this was so successful that millions of Americans decided to buy radio equipment, and by 1929 over $842 million worth of radio sets had been sold. The radio changed evening activities in most American homes. It brought the world closer to farm families, and families throughout the country sat around their radios listening to their favourite programmes.

Activities ....

1 Discuss the possible effects of the new technology on the life of an American family during the 1920s.
2 Describe and explain what you see in Source E.
3 Describe the attitude and activities of the 'flapper' girls in Source F.
4 Choose one of the American heroes mentioned in the text. Do some research and find out about his or her life and success.

....

The boom of the 1920s

© Gallo Images (Pty) Ltd. (The Hulton Getty Collection)

It was a time of happiness and optimism – in the words of a popular song: 'You've got to *accentuate the positive*. Eliminate the negative!' People identified with heroes – men and women who had faced the trials of competition, hardship and danger, and won – aviator Charles Lindbergh; sports stars such as Babe Ruth (baseball); Jack Dempsey (boxing); Helen Wills (tennis); and Bobby Jones (golf).

Conservative reaction

Many small-town and farm people in the 1920s were alarmed at the changes taking place and the way in which American morality was on a downswing. This conservative reaction was shown in various ways.

The Red scare
Americans had been alarmed by the Russian Revolution of 1917; and when, after the end of the war, the American Communist Party began to recruit new members, there was a real fear of a communist take-over. Trade unions were seen

as breeding grounds for communism and there was considerable opposition to union demands for higher wages. Mitchell Palmer, Attorney-General of the USA, began a campaign in 1919 to rid the country of communists. In a dramatic raid on 2 January 1920, Palmer and government agents arrested 2 700 people suspected of 'anti-state' activities. Many of them were later released because of lack of evidence, but about 300 were deported. After this, trade union membership fell and the effectiveness of the unions declined.

Immigration restrictions
In 1921 President Harding approved a limitation on the number of immigrants and in 1924 a 'quota' system was introduced. This restrictive system was based on national origins and favoured newcomers from Northern Europe, especially those who were White Anglo-Saxon Protestants ('WASPS'). The restriction was caused by racism, religious intolerance and the fear of socialist political ideas streaming in from Europe.

The Ku Klux Klan

The Klan had been founded immediately after the civil war, to prevent the newly freed slaves from gaining equal rights with other Americans. In the 1920s the Klan re-emerged and by 1925 it had built up a membership of about five million. Members wore white hoods and cloaks and used violence against blacks, Catholics, Jews and foreign immigrants – all who might claim equal rights. Only a WASP was eligible for membership; and many people in the small towns of the west, mid-west and south joined the Klan and took part in its secret rituals.

The Klan's favourite methods included whipping, branding and lynching (hanging). Support for the Klan declined rapidly after 1925 when one of its leaders was convicted of kidnapping and murder.

Activities

1 a Describe what is happening in the photograph of the Ku Klux Klan (Source G).

   b What can we learn about the Ku Klux Klan from this photograph?

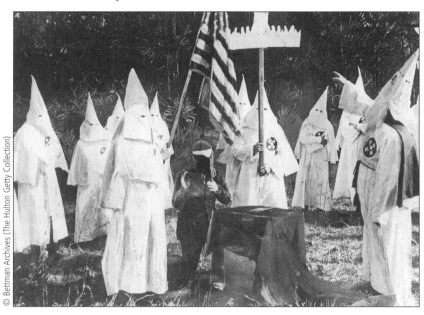

◄*Source G*

A Ku Klux Klan ceremony

© Bettman Archives (The Hulton Getty Collection)

In 1923 Hiriam Evans became the Klan's leader or 'Imperial Wizard'. He wrote:

> The Klan has now come to speak for most Americans of the old pioneering stock. These are a blend of various peoples of the so-called Nordic race [Northern Europeans] ... There are three great racial instincts which must be used to build a great America: loyalty to the white race, to the traditions of America and to the spirit of Protestantism ... The pioneer stock must be kept pure. The white race must be supreme not only in America but in the whole world ... The world has been so made that each race must fight for its life, must conquer or accept slavery or die.

> The Klan believes the Negroes are a special problem. The Klan wants every state to bring in laws making sex between a white and black person a crime. Protestants must be supreme ...

Prohibition

In 1917, during the war, Congress passed a law against alcohol which to many Americans seemed an appropriate sacrifice for the war effort. In January 1920, the Eighteenth Amendment to the Constitution came into force, prohibiting Americans from selling or making alcohol.

Prohibition became law because of pressure from religious organisations like the Anti-Saloon League. It claimed that alcohol was evil and against Christian teaching, and led to drunkenness and violent behaviour. Alcohol undermined traditional American values such as hard work, saving money, respect for the family and for God. People in small towns and the countryside were in favour of the law, but in the cities, people were not enthusiastic.

As soon as the law went into effect, Americans began to find illegal sources of alcohol. Speakeasies – secret clubs where liquor could be bought – sprang up by the thousands.

Bootleggers – those who supplied illegal drink – smuggled huge quantities across the border from Canada, while other people operated illegal breweries and stills. Federal agents had the impossible task of destroying gallons of illegal liquor.

Meanwhile, crime syndicates saw the immense profit to be made from selling illegal liquor. There were wars between rival syndicates, especially in Chicago, where Al Capone built up an empire of illegal activities which, by 1927, produced an income of $27 million. But Capone's profits depended on violence against all who stood in his way – he is thought to have been behind about 130 murders in Chicago in 1926–27. Capone was never convicted of any violent crime; in the end he was arrested for not paying income tax and sent to prison for eleven years.

In December 1933 President Roosevelt formally ended prohibition.

Activities

1 a How would you define conservatism?
  b Give one example from American life at this time.
2 a What was a 'speakeasy' in the days of Prohibition?
  b Describe some of the effects of Prohibition.

Conclusion

In the 1920s America was a land of contrasts. Permissiveness and prohibition existed side by side: in contrast with the confident city 'flapper', there was the elderly farm wife who was fearful of the change she saw around her. Some people became very rich, others continued to live in poverty.

But the boom roared on. In the words of President Hoover in March 1929: 'I have no fears for the future of our country ... it is bright with hope.'

The Great Depression

Unit outcomes

- Describe the Wall Street Crash.
- Analyse the reasons for and consequences of the Great **Depression**.
- Create an empathetic picture.
- Interpret written and visual sources.

Introduction

During the 1920s the main feeling in the USA was one of success. In his 1928 presidential election campaign, Republican candidate Herbert Hoover could claim: '... during eight years' rule ... we have done more to increase production, expand export markets and reduce industrial and human misery, than in any previous quarter of a century. Prosperity is written in full wage packets, high business profits and record share values.'

The Wall Street Crash

Wall Street in New York City is the financial centre of the USA where shares in companies are bought and sold. Most companies are owned by shareholders who buy and sell their shares (or stock) on a stock market. If a company makes a good profit, it pays shareholders a dividend and the value of its shares on the stock market goes up. During the 1920s the prosperity in the USA brought a general rise in share values. Many investors turned to speculation, that is, they bought shares in the hope that they could sell them again after the price rose and make a quick profit. This seemed an easy way to make money; and this 'get-rich-quick' craze swept the country.

▼ *Source A*

Wall Street fever sweeps America

It would be a mistake to exaggerate the number of people who 'played the market' in 1929, but there was certainly a 'Wall Street mentality' which was widespread, and accepted that speculation was desirable and foolproof:

The rich man's chauffeur drove with his ears laid back to catch the news of an

impending move in Bethlehem Steel; ... The window-cleaner at the broker's office paused to watch the ticker, for he was thinking of converting his laboriously accumulated savings into a few shares of Simmons. Edwin Lefevre (an articulate reporter on the market at this time who could claim considerable personal experience) told of a broker's valet who made nearly a quarter of a million in the market, of a trained nurse who cleaned up thirty thousand following the tips given her by grateful patients; of a Wyoming cattleman, thirty miles from the nearest railroad, who bought or sold a thousand shares a day.

(From: FL Allen. *Only Yesterday*. In John Vick. *Modern America*.)

New words

depression a serious decline in economic activity
dividend a share of the profit made by a company

People were assisted by two factors: first, they could usually borrow money from their bank manager and buy shares with this credit; secondly, stockbrokers usually demanded only a fraction (perhaps about 10 per cent) of the total values of the shares, that is, people were buying 'on margin'. This was fine if the share prices rose – the remaining part of the share value as well as the bank manager could be paid and there would be a useful profit for the investor. However, if share prices fell, there could be a disaster!

During September 1929, some Stock Exchange traders decided that they would cash in their shares at the current high prices and they unloaded large blocks of shares onto the market. Suddenly, everyone wanted to sell but nobody wanted to buy; share prices fell dramatically and panic broke out on the Stock Exchange. On 24 October 1929, thirteen million shares were sold. Between September and December 1929, share values fell by $40 000 million. The Crash had a disastrous effect on individuals – large numbers of people were financially ruined.

PRICES OF STOCKS CRASH IN HEAVY LIQUIDATION, TOTAL DROP OF BILLIONS

PAPER LOSS $4,000,000,000

2,600,000 Shares Sold in the Final Hour in Record Decline.

MANY ACCOUNTS WIPED OUT

But No Brokerage House Is in Difficulties, as Margins Have Been Kept High.

ORGANIZED BACKING ABSENT

Bankers Confer on Steps to Support Market—Highest Break Is 96 Points.

Frightened by the decline in stock prices during the last month and a half, thousands of stockholders dumped their shares on the market yesterday afternoon in such an avalanche of selling as to bring about one of the widest declines in history. Even the best of seasoned, dividend-paying, shares were sold regardless of the prices they would bring, and the result was a tremendous smash in which stocks lost from a few points to as much as ninety-six.

Loss in Market Values.

The absolute average decline of active and so-called inactive issues yesterday was 2.995, or roughly three points. Using this figure as a base and taking the percentage of shares listed on the Exchange in relation to the percentage of issues traded in, the loss in value of listed securities amounted to $2,210,675,184. This, however, does not measure up to the full value of the loss, for the reason that many lesser-known issues of small capitalization did not figure in the sharp declines. It might be conservatively estimated that the actual loss in market value on the New York Stock Exchange ran to about $4,000,000,000.

▼ Source B

Share prices in cents from the Wall Street Journal, 1928–29
(From: Peter Lane. *The USA in the Twentieth Century.*)

COMPANY	3 March 1928	3 Sep 1928	3 Nov 1929
MONTGOMERY WARD	132	450	49
UNION CARBIDE AND CARBON	145	413	59
ELECTRIC BOND AND SHARE	90	204	50
RADIO CORPORATION OF AMERICA	94	505	28
WOOLWORTH	181	251	52

▼ Source C

In March 1929 shares in a cigarette company were selling for $115 each. The market collapsed. The $115 share dropped to $2 and the company president jumped out of the window of his Wall Street office.

(From: *Hard Times – memories of the Depression.*)

TOTAL VALUE OF STOCKS ON THE NEW YORK STOCK EXCHANGE, 1922–1932

◀ Source D

Total value of stocks (shares) on the New York Stock Exchange, 1922–32 (From: Patrick and Berkin. *History of the American Nation from 1877, Volume 2.*)

YEAR

BILLIONS OF DOLLARS

The Crash also affected the economic system. Banks were not able to recover the loans that they had made to Stock Exchange speculators, and people who had deposited their savings in the banks tried, without success, to withdraw their money. Banks were unable to pay – 650 banks went bankrupt in 1929. Banks were also unable or unwilling to lend money to factories in industry so industrial production fell and workers became unemployed. The downward spiral of economic activity continued.

The Depression

The Wall Street Crash did not cause the Great Depression, but it did make it worse. A depression can be defined as a serious decline in economic activity. The basic cause of this Great Depression, which began in 1929, was **over-supply** of goods related to **under-demand** – a situation which had been building up during the 1920s. Study the diagram which shows how this situation had arisen and how the Crash contributed to it.

◄ *Source E*

Photograph of a crowd in Wall Street, outside the New York Stock Exchange, 1929

© Gallo Images (Pty) Ltd. (The Hulton Getty Collection)

Activities
Study the sources carefully.
1 As one of the individuals mentioned in Source A, explain how you made money on the Stock Exchange.
2 In Source B, calculate which share showed the greatest percentage loss between 3 September 1928 and 13 November 1929.
3 Look at Source D.
  a How much more was stock worth in 1929 than in 1922?
  b How much value did stocks lose between 1929 and 1930?
4 Explain the role of the banks in the Wall Street Crash.
5 Put yourself in the position of either one of the people outside the bank or of the bank manager inside the bank (Source E). Explain your major problem on this day in October 1929 and what you are trying to do about it.
6 Explain the link between the Wall Street Crash and the Great Depression (see flow chart on page 78).

New words
over-supply too great a supply of goods relative to the demands of the market
under-demand too little demand for goods relative to the supply on the market

Causes of the Great Depression

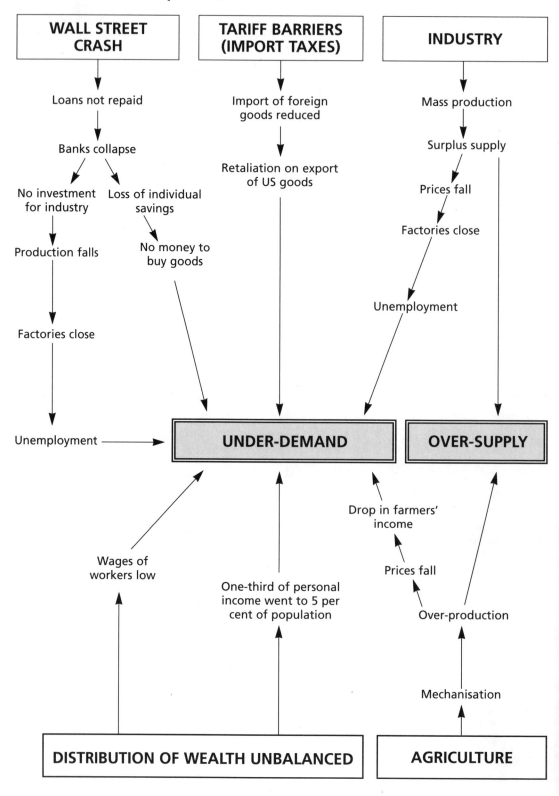

The effects on people

The major effect of the Depression for the individual American was unemployment. Millions of men lost their jobs. By the spring of 1930, four million men were unemployed, and by the winter of 1932–33, the figure had reached over thirteen million.

Consider the case of Mr Stephen Harper.

In 1929 Mr Harper, a salesman for a clothing manufacturing firm, lived in his own home (which he had bought with the help of a mortgage from the bank), had a car (which he was buying on an 'easy payment' plan), and had saved some money for a rainy day in a savings bank. On the advice of a broker friend, he also was 'taking a flyer' on the stock market, buying on margin. His immediate plans included the purchase of an expensive cabinet radio, and his long-term ambitions included sending his two teenage children to college. But when the stock market crashed in the autumn of 1929, Mr Harper lost every cent he had put into the stock market, since his margins were wiped out.

So Mr Harper and thousands of others stopped buying such luxuries as new radios. Radio companies therefore closed down plants or ran them only part-time, laying off thousands of workers and cancelling orders for copper, wood and glass tubes. Thus copper miners, lumberjacks and glassworkers lost their jobs.

So many men decided to mend their old suits instead of buying new ones, that Mr Harper's company eventually closed down and he was laid off. He was lucky enough to find work elsewhere, but at such low pay that in order to continue mortgage payments on his house, he stopped paying instalments on his car, which therefore became the property of a finance company. His savings bank failed and so he lost the money with which he had intended to send his children to college. Multiply Mr Harper by millions and one can see how there developed a chain reaction that closed down more factories, drove more firms into bankruptcy, and put more men out of work. (Story adapted from: HW Bragdon and SP McCutchen. *History of a Free People, 6th edition.*)

Mr Harper found another job. Millions of other Americans were not so lucky. In order to live, they first used up their savings, then they had to get food and clothing in whatever ways they could. Men left home to look for work, they built shacks on the edge of cities; they scrambled for food outside restaurants or waited in lines for the issue of soup and bread.

Farmers

American farm families faced hardships like those in the cities. Farm prices dropped more sharply than ever. The situation was made worse by dry weather and a severe drought. The rich farmland of the Great Plains lost its covering of grass and became known as the 'Dust Bowl'. To make matters worse, fierce winds blew the dust across the plains. Hundreds of small farmers were ruined. They and their families packed up and went to California to find work as farm labourers. Poor black farmers from the south moved north to hunt for what little work there was in the cities.

Migration

A great migration took place during the early 1930s as people looked for jobs in other parts of the country. In 1932, it was estimated that about two million hobos (wandering workers) were travelling along the roads and on goods trains. Farmers from Oklahoma (known as Okies) and Arkansas (Arkies) moved to California in search of work.

In despair, some Americans emigrated to Europe, and in the early 1930s, the Russian trading agency in New York received 350 applications a day from Americans who wished to settle in the Soviet Union.

Government action

When the Great Depression began in 1929, President Herbert Hoover was reluctant to take action. He believed that hard work and minimum government interference – which had worked well in the past – would soon restore prosperity, that is, the theory of *laissez-faire.* He declared that things would soon get better and he urged businesses and wealthy individuals to give generously to charities which were feeding the unemployed.

When it became clear that voluntary action would not be enough, Hoover began to take action. He set up the Reconstruction Finance Corporation with four million dollars of government money to help banks and businesses. More funds were provided for building roads and dams, for example, the Hoover Dam in Colorado.

These actions did not go far enough and came too late. As the Depression grew worse, more and more Americans blamed Hoover and his government for their troubles. It was no surprise when he lost the presidential election in 1932.

▼ Source F

Graphs of unemployment; business failures and; bank failures
(1920-41) (From: Harry Mills. *Twentieth Century World History in Focus.*)

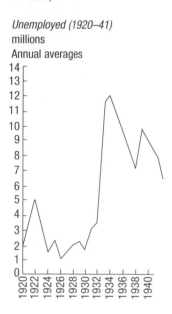

Unemployed (1920–41)
millions
Annual averages

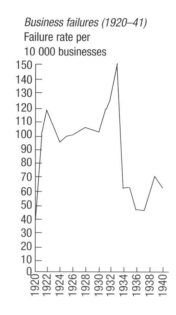

Business failures (1920–41)
Failure rate per
10 000 businesses

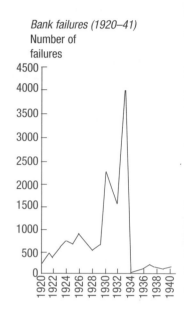

Bank failures (1920–41)
Number of
failures

▼ Source G

Two young residents at a 'Hooverville' shantytown in Washington DC

First, the bread lines in the poorer districts. Second, those bleak settlements ironically known as 'Hoovervilles' in the outskirts of the city and on vacant lots – groups of makeshift shacks constructed out of packing boxes, scrap iron, anything that could be picked up free in a diligent combing of the city dumps. Third, the homeless people sleeping in the doorways or on park benches, and going the rounds of the restaurants for leftover half-eaten biscuits, pie crusts, anything ... Fourth, the vastly increased numbers of thumbers on the highway, and particularly of freight-car transients on the railroads; a huge array of drifters ever on the move, searching half-aimlessly for a place where there might be a job.

(From: FL Allen. *Since Yesterday.*)

Extension activity

1 Look at page 41 in Chapter 1 again and prepare yourself for writing a test essay. Test essay topic: Discuss the causes of the Great Depression.

By mid-morning a gale was blowing, cold and black. By noon it was blacker than night ... a wall of dirt one's eyes could not penetrate [see through] ... When the wind died and the sun shone forth again, it was a different world. There were no fields, only sand drifting into mounds ... In the farmyard, fences, machinery and trees were gone, buried. The roofs of sheds stuck out through drifts deeper than a man is tall.

I do not exaggerate when I say that in this country there is now no life for miles upon miles; no human beings, no birds, no animals. Only a dull brown land with cracks showing. Hills furrowed with eroded gullies – like a picture of ruins of lost civilisations.

(From: Roger Smalley. *Depression and the New Deal.*)

Activities

1 Give a figure for the number of unemployed in the years 1929, 1930, 1931, 1932 (Source F and text).
2 Read the story about Mr Harper.
   a Describe his life before the Crash.
   b List the misfortunes which happened to him as a result of the Crash.
   c How did his situation contribute to the Depression?
3 Explain the name 'Hooverville' as used in Source G, and give a description of one.
4 a Describe the situation in Source H.
   b How did people cope with these problems?

Extension activity

Hold a group discussion to evaluate the actions of the Hoover government and what they achieved. What further action should have been taken?

Unit 8

The New Deal

Unit outcomes

- Describe the background, principles and effects of the New Deal.
- Interpret written and visual sources.
- Create an empathetic picture.
- Describe the role and effect of the media.
- Analyse opposition to the New Deal.
- Organise research work.
- Take part in a discussion.
- Assess the reliability of a source.

The 1932 presidential election

President Hoover believed that American business had produced the boom of the 1920s because it had been left alone by the government. He now believed that business would also produce the answer to the Depression. But as the election drew near, things became worse. The Democratic Party nominated Franklin Delano Roosevelt to stand against Hoover in the election.

▲ Herbert Hoover

▲ Franklin D. Roosevelt

Roosevelt was born in New York in 1883, the son of wealthy parents. He trained as a lawyer and served in the administration of President Woodrow Wilson during the First World War. In 1905 he married Eleanor, a niece of former President Theodore Roosevelt. In 1921 he was struck down with poliomyelitis: both his legs were paralysed and for the rest of his life he was unable to stand or walk without help. This is why photographs of Roosevelt usually show only his head and shoulders.

This experience seemed to give Roosevelt genuine sympathy for the unfortunate. After his painful battle towards recovery, no opposition and no obstacle could dismay him.

In spite of his handicap, Roosevelt showed great confidence and a cheerful optimism. During his election campaign he 'pledged a New Deal for the American people'.

The phrase, 'a New Deal' caught the imagination of the American people and FD Roosevelt (FDR) was elected with a convincing majority.

▼ Source A

Roosevelt during the 1932 election campaign

I pledge you, I pledge myself to a New Deal for the American people. This is more than a political campaign; it is a call to arms. Give me your help, not to win votes alone, but to win in this crusade to restore America.

▼ Source B

Roosevelt, during his speech at his inauguration

... the only thing we have to fear is fear itself. Nameless, unreasoning, unjustified terror which paralyses needed efforts to convert retreat into advance ... our greatest primary task is to put people to work.

Activities

Study Sources A, B, C and D carefully.

1 If you had been an American voter in the 1932 presidential election, for whom would you have voted? Explain why.
2 Comment on the photograph (Source C), particularly on the actions and situation of Franklin Roosevelt.
3 Look at the cartoon (Source D) and answer these questions.
   a Who are HH and FDR?
   b Explain the importance of the date of publication.
   c Describe what each figure is doing.
   d Explain the meaning of the various items in the dustbin.
   e Do you think that the cartoonist (Jerry Doyle) is a supporter of HH or FDR? Explain why you think so.

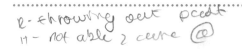

◀ **Source C**
Photograph of Roosevelt campaigning
(From: Harry Mills.
Twentieth Century World History in Focus.)

▼ **Source D**
Getting rid of the rubbish (1933)
(From: Neil Demarco. *The USA: A Divided Union*.)

The New Deal

Roosevelt came into office with no carefully worked out programme of how he was going to deal with the economic crisis. He gathered round him a 'brains trust' of advisers – university professors, lawyers, businessmen, experts from industry and social workers. Their leader was Harry Hopkins and other members were Raymond Moley, Rexford Tugwell, Harold Ickes and Frances Perkins (the first woman to be a member of the cabinet). These people were confident and able and they generated many new ideas – sometimes the ideas worked, sometimes they did not! Throughout the discussions, Roosevelt supported several major principles:

- the lack of **purchasing power** of so many Americans must be remedied;
- relief should be found for the poor and the unemployed;
- the government must exercise more control over the economy, although he continued to favour a 'balanced budget';
- the repeal of the Prohibition Law which had led to so much crime.

New words

purchasing power the ability (that is, the money) to buy goods and services

During the next few years, many measures were introduced by President Roosevelt. Some were laws, others were government policies, and others were organisations or agencies – known as the 'alphabet agencies' after their initials. Sometimes Roosevelt's programme is summed up in the three words – Relief, Recovery, Reform; but it will be easier to understand the measures if we consider the problems which they aimed to solve:

1 the collapse of the banking and financial system;
2 widespread poverty and unemployment;
3 the depression in industry;
4 the state of farming;
5 the collapse of foreign trade.

Activities
1 Describe what is happening in Source E.
2 Is the cartoonist in favour of or against FDR?

1 The collapse of the banking and financial system

Roosevelt's first concern was the banking crisis. Since 1930, five thousand banks had run out of money and had been forced to close. One reason for this was that businesses to whom the banks had loaned money had gone bankrupt, another was that savers who were worried about the safety of their money, withdrew their deposits.

Immediately after his inauguration in March 1933, Roosevelt declared a four day 'bank holiday'. All banks were closed and only those approved by the government were allowed to re-open.

At the same time, Roosevelt used the first of his radio 'fireside chats' to explain that it was 'safer to keep your money in a re-opened bank than under the mattress'. As they listened to Roosevelt's compelling voice over the radio, Americans felt the warmth and understanding of his personality. In simple, friendly language, Roosevelt explained his policies and carried the people with him. Confidence returned and more money was put into the banks than was taken out.

Several further financial measures were important.

- In 1934, Roosevelt set up the Securities Exchange Commission to control the Stock Exchange.

- The Banking Act of 1935 set up the banking system which exists today; one measure ensured that if people were not able to repay their loans and mortgages, banks would not be able to seize their goods and houses.
- The Reconstruction Finance Corporation channelled government funds into the projects of the New Deal.

2 Widespread poverty and unemployment

The poor needed food, clothing and housing. The Federal Emergency Relief Administration (FERA), set up in 1933 and directed by Harry Hopkins, distributed $500 million to the individual states to provide better relief.

The Civil Works Administration (CWA), in operation from 1933–34, gave employment to about four million people building roads, schools, hospitals and sewers. This lasted only a year and, in 1935, was replaced by the Works Progress Administration (WPA). This ran many projects and employed three million people, with a budget of $5 000 million.

The Civilian Conservation Corps (CCC), set up in 1933, was one of Roosevelt's favourite schemes. This provided three million young employed with food, lodgings and a dollar a day, building dams and canals, planting trees and working on other improvements to the National Parks. The Social Security Act (1935) provided national insurance against sickness and unemployment for 28 million workers; it also provided old age pensions for all people over 65 years old.

3 The depression in industry

One of Roosevelt's first acts in 1933 was the National Industrial Recovery Act (NIRA). This set up the National Recovery Administration (NRA) which operated in two areas. The first regulated relations between industrialists and workers: hours of work, wages and conditions were agreed for many industries, and eight-hour days and agreed minimum wages became general. Collective bargaining by workers was agreed. This Act was declared unconstitutional in 1935, so a new act, the Labour Relations Act or Wagner Act was passed, strengthening the rights of the trade unions.

The second function of the NRA was carried out by the Public Works Administration (1935) which spent millions of dollars on large-scale projects such as slum clearance, building dams, roads and bridges.

▼ *Source F*

An NRA poster
(From: Nigel Smith. *The USA 1917–1980*.)

Activities

Explain how Source F sums up the purpose of the NRA.

4 Agriculture

In the previous ten years, the prices of farm products had fallen much faster than factory goods, so many farmers faced ruin. The Agricultural Adjustment Administration (AAA), set up in 1933, granted subsidies to farmers for reducing production and in this way, prices rose. Farmers could then afford better machinery to improve their farms.

This Act was a great success. Although the original Act was declared illegal by the Supreme Court in 1936, new laws enabled the AAA to continue.

The Farm Credit Administration (FCA) provided new loans for farmers at low interest rates.

One of the most important successes of the New Deal was the Tennessee Valley Authority (TVA) of 1933. This area had been over-farmed and much of the soil was useless. The TVA built a string of dams to control river water, and provide electricity and irrigation. Farmers were trained in soil conservation and thousands of jobs were provided.

Activities

Study Source G and describe two aspects of the New Deal's work with the environment.

5 The collapse of foreign trade

In 1933, the new Roosevelt government was faced with a world where countries were setting up trade barriers with high tariffs. With inevitable retaliation, their own industries and farmers were cut off from potential markets. A London Economic Conference was called to discuss this issue in 1933, but Roosevelt refused to

▼ *Source G*

New Deal Agencies and the environment (Adapted from: Brian Catchpole. *A Map History of the United States*.)

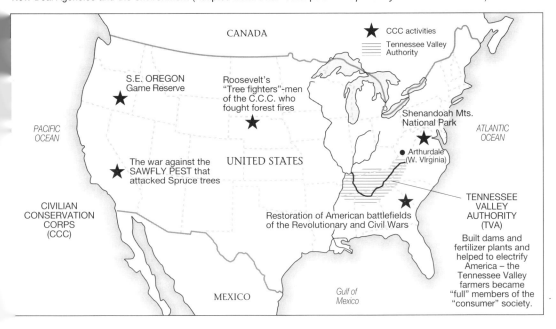

allow the American delegates to take the lead and tariffs remained at a high level. A Trade Agreements Act passed by Congress in 1934 allowed Roosevelt to fix tariffs freely. But a great opportunity for economic stimulation was missed.

In 1934, Roosevelt devalued (reduced the gold content of) the US dollar. In this way, he hoped to increase American exports by making them cheaper.

Activities ....

1 Link the appropriate New Deal agency with the function in the second column.

   a **TVA**   regulated the Stock Exchange

   b **SEC**   provided conservation jobs for young men

   c **FERA**   encouraged farmers to reduce production

   d **NRA**   promoted the growth of trade unions

   e **AAA**   developed huge areas of farmland in the Tennessee Valley

   f **CCC**   provided relief for the poor

2 The New Deal has been summed up in the three words: Relief, Recovery, Reform. Study the function of each of the agencies mentioned in the text and place it in one of the above three categories. There may be an overlap.

3 Research. Choose one of the five areas of Roosevelt's reforms and describe in detail the success and failure of the various measures.

4 Study the description of Roosevelt's 'fireside chat' in Source H below.

   a What were two of Roosevelt's aims in making radio broadcasts to the American people?

   b Suggest at least two reasons why the source may not be reliable (trustworthy).

....

▼ *Source H*

'A fireside chat': Frances Perkins describes Roosevelt in action in front of the radio microphone

His voice and his facial expression as he spoke were those of an intimate friend. His mind was focused on the people listening at the other end. As he talked, his head would nod and his hands would move in simple, natural gestures. His face would smile and light up as though he were actually sitting on the front porch or in the par-

lour with them. People felt this and it bound them to him in affection. (1946)

Opposition to the New Deal

Most Americans supported Roosevelt and he won the 1936 election easily. However, he faced opposition from various organisations and groups. These opponents can be divided into three groups.

1 Businessmen, the rich upper classes, and Republicans. They complained that:

   • the cost of the New Deal was too high and taxes had to be increased; the rich paid more than the poor; some policies seemed wasteful, for example, the destruction of crops under the AAA; and there seemed to be no overall plan; the government was interfering in business affairs and trade unions were being encouraged;

   • the federal government was assuming too much power and overruling the rights of individuals and the states – contrary to the American constitution.

▼ *Source I*

The Banyan Tree: Increased federal powers during the New Deal (From: Harry Mills. *Twentieth Century World History in Focus.*)

2 Small political groups led by individuals who challenged Roosevelt's approach and methods. In general they thought that he was not doing enough to help the poor.

   • Governor Huey Long of Louisiana proposed a 'Share our Wealth' scheme which proposed taking money from the rich and giving it to the poor. Long intended to challenge Roosevelt in the 1936 presidential election, but he was assassinated in 1935.

- Dr Francis Townsend proposed that everyone over the age of 60 should be given a pension of $200 a month. Father Charles Coughlin was a Catholic priest who accused Roosevelt of failing to keep his promises and of being a communist. Townsend and Coughlin formed the Union Party to challenge Roosevelt in the 1936 election, but their candidate received few votes.

3 The Supreme Court

- Between 1935 and 1937, the Court judged that seven of the New Deal laws were unconstitutional on the grounds that the federal government was going beyond the powers given to it by the constitution.
- Roosevelt tried to overcome this by asking Congress to increase the number of judges on the Court from nine to fifteen. The new judges would, obviously, be nominated by the president. However, Congress rejected the plan by a large majority and there were accusations that Roosevelt was trying to become a dictator like Hitler in Germany.
- The strength of the opposition to his plan surprised Roosevelt. However, some of the judges retired voluntarily and the Court became less hostile to New Deal measures.

The 1937 recession

In 1937, Roosevelt decided to cut back on several New Deal programmes in an attempt to 'balance the government's budget', that is, where income would equal expenditure. However, industrial production started to fall and unemployment began to rise again. In 1938, Congress voted $4 million to retrieve the situation.

After 1938, Roosevelt failed to pass a single New Deal law. In 1939 with the outbreak of the Second World War, his attention became focused on foreign affairs.

Women and the New Deal

Two women played an important part in shaping the New Deal. Frances Perkins became the secretary of labour in Roosevelt's cabinet and she helped prepare the 1935 Social Security Act. She frequently favoured the trade unions during negotiations with the president. Eleanor Roosevelt, the president's wife, held strong opinions and constantly urged her husband towards more liberal policies. She

© INPRA

▲ Frances Perkins and members of Roosevelt's war cabinet

© INPRA

▲ Eleanor Roosevelt

received hundreds of letters from ordinary Americans and travelled widely through the country, listening to the views of the people. She provided women administrators with invaluable access to the president.

But, for the ordinary American woman, conditions improved little under the New Deal. Working women were thought to be depriving unemployed men of jobs. In most industries, women were paid much less than men, even in the same jobs, and the Social Security Act gave no protection in domestic work. Only 8 000 women were employed in the Civilian Conservation Corps, out of the 3 million involved in the scheme.

► *Source J*

New Deal II

(From: John Vick. *Modern America*.)

Blacks and the New Deal

Black people gained little from the New Deal. Most of them were in unskilled jobs, and black women worked for even lower wages than white women. About 30 per cent of the black population were on relief during the Depression.

Roosevelt claimed that he wanted to do more to help blacks, but he could not do so, because of fear of upsetting white congressmen from the southern states. In the mid-1930s prejudice, racism and lynch mobs continued. Blacks and whites could not serve together in the same unit of the armed forces.

© Punch Library

Activities ....

1 Choose one of the cartoons (Sources I or J).
   a Describe in detail what is happening, including the attitudes of the various figures.
   b Explain the cartoonist's viewpoint.
   c Is this viewpoint biased towards or against Roosevelt, and is it a valid comment?
2 Do some research and write a short life history of either Frances Perkins or Eleanor Roosevelt, explaining her contribution to the New Deal.
3 Discuss to what extent (if at all) black Americans benefited from the New Deal.

How successful a president was Franklin Roosevelt?

He always had the firm support of the majority of the population. In his four presidential elections, he had huge victories.

He had the 'common touch' and he made people feel that he was interested in their problems. His fireside chats over the radio were immensely popular and he was able to stimulate new hope in the American people. He developed a close relationship with newspaper reporters and always had their support.

Roosevelt received 5 000 to 8 000 letters a day. A typical one read:

Dear Mr President,

This is just to tell you that everything is alright now. The mortgage can go on for a while longer. I never heard of a President like you, Mr Roosevelt. My wife and I are old folks and don't amount to much, but we are joined with those millions of others in praying for you every night. God bless you, Mr Roosevelt.

▼ Source K

David Kennedy, writing in 1970 (Kennedy had been a government official in Roosevelt's first administration)

There was a very, very serious down-turn in 1937. We really had not made a substantial recovery from the deep Depression in the early 1930s. Unemployment was still very high. The New Deal programmes were not stimulating in the way people thought. There was a sort of defeatist attitude – that the government just had to do all this for the people. It was not until the war, with its economic thrust, that we pulled out of it. The war got us out of it, not the New Deal policies.

At the time, I felt we were relying too much on the government to save us. I felt people were losing their initiative.

▼ Source L

American historian, writing in 1954

The New Deal operated on no consistent economic theory, it was damned by laissez-faire economists and by socialists. Yet, looking back, we can see that something in between traditional capitalism and socialism had emerged, combining features of both.

The essential structure of private ownership was disturbed only in the area of production and distribution of electricity. Elsewhere the ownership of the means of production and distribution of goods and services continued in private hands. Profit remained the dominant motive.

(From: Bragdon and McCutchen. *History of a Free People*.)

▼ Source M

CD Hill, an English historian writing in 1967

The New Deal was an episode of international importance. It was a democratic and peaceful revolution, the achievement of a free people whose voters put Franklin Roosevelt into power and freely confirmed him in office at a time when Europe was being forced and deceived into submission by the dictators Hitler, Mussolini and Stalin.

(From: Roger Smalley. *Depression and the New Deal*.)

▼ Source N

Graph of American industrial growth 1929–41

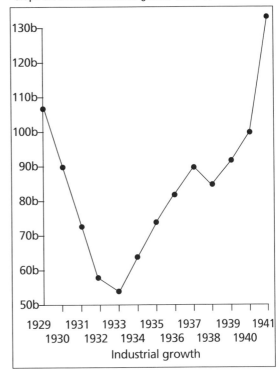

Industrial growth

▼ Source O

Figures of: (i) unemployed, (ii) employees of the federal government

(From: Roger Smalley. *Depression and the New Deal*.)

Year	Unemployed (in millions)	Unemployed (% of workforce)	Millions employed by federal government (1933–42)
1929	1,5	3,2	
1930	4,3	8,7	
1931	8,0	15,9	
1932*	12,1	23,6	
1933	12,8	24,9	4,3
1934	11,3	21,7	1,1
1935	10,6	20,1	4,0
1936*	9,0	16,9	3,8
1937	7,7	14,3	2,7
1938	10,4	19,0	4,3
1939	9,5	17,2	3,3
1940*	8,1	14,6	2,9
1941	5,6	9,9	1,8
1942	2,6	4,7	0,4
1943	1,8	2,3	
1944*	1,0	1,2	

*Presidential election years.

Activities

1 Study the sources and the text on the preceding pages and complete the table below. Give details of how these people gained or lost from the New Deal.

	Gained	Lost
The unemployed		
Businessmen		
Farmers		
Bankers		
House-owners		
Women		
Black people		
Foreign traders		

2 Use the information from the table above to write an essay discussing the successes and failures of the New Deal.

3 It has been said that the New Deal was 'another name for socialism'. Explain to what extent you would agree with this comment.

4 Write a critical appreciation of the achievements of Franklin Roosevelt in the years 1933–41 using Sources K to O to help you.

CHAPTER ASSESSMENT

In small groups write essay plans for the following topics, and then choose one of the topics to complete. Each learner in your group should write on a different topic.

1 Discuss the development of the US economy between 1920 and 1929, and explain why the USA became a major industrial power.

2 'During the period 1921 to 1932 the Republican presidents of the USA applied a strict policy of isolation.'
Critically comment on the above statement.

3 'Thursday 24 October 1929 was a black day for the USA due to the fact that millions of shares were for sale on the New York Stock Exchange.'
Explain the reasons for this crisis and the course of events.

4 'President Roosevelt was the darling of the poor, who saw him as their saviour whilst the industrialists and the affluent regarded him as an enemy.'
What opinions do you have about the above statement? Support your opinions with evidence drawn from your knowledge of Roosevelt's New Deal.

Further reading

B Catchpole. *A Map History of the United States.* London: Heinemann Educational, 1972.

N Demarco. *The USA: A Divided Nation.* Harlow, Essex: Longman, 1994.

CU Macdonald. *Modern America.* Hemel Hampstead: Simon and Schuster Education, 1987.

J O'Keeffe. *America 1870–1975. Modern Times. Sourcebooks.* Harlow, Essex: Longman, 1984.

N Smith. *The USA 1917–1980.* Oxford: Oxford University Press, 1996.

J Vick. *Modern America.* Slough: University Tutorial Press, 1985.

Totalitarianism and the road to the Second World War (1919–39)

contents

Timeline

First World War	1914	First World War begins
	1918	First World War ends
	1919	Treaty of Versailles signed
The rise of totalitarianism	1922	Mussolini takes power in Italy
	1928	Stalin takes power in the USSR; the Wall Street Crash in the USA
	1929	The Great Depression begins
	1933	Hitler takes power in Germany
	1935	Italy invades Abyssinia
	1936	German troops enter the Rhineland
	1937	Japan invades China
	1938	Germany and Austria merge; the Munich Agreement; Germany invades Czechoslovakia
Second World War	1939	Germany invades Poland; Second World War begins
	1941	Japan attacks Pearl Harbour
	1941	Germany invades the USSR
	1944	Allies invade France
	1945	United Nations set up
	1945	Atomic bombs dropped on Japan; Second World War ends

chapter outcomes

knowledge outcomes

As you work through this chapter you will be able to:

- explain the main factors in a society that lead to political instability;
- show the relationships between political, economic and social factors in a society;
- discuss the main characteristics of a totalitarian state;
- explain the relationship between domestic politics and foreign policy;
- describe the factors that influence international relations.

concepts and skills outcomes

As you work through this chapter you will learn about and apply skills and concepts such as how to:

- analyse a variety of sources and different forms of evidence;
- deduce and bring together information from sources and evidence;
- detect bias in sources and evidence;
- compare different points of view;
- use sources and evidence to construct an argument.

value outcomes

As you work through this chapter you will get the chance to think about these issues:

- should we blame the dictators for what happened, or the people of their countries for allowing them to come to power?
- should the democracies accept some responsibility for the war?
- how should the individual respond to state persecution and the violation of the human rights of others?
- the responsibilities of democratic citizens – making choices, facing the consequences, taking responsibility;
- the problems of establishing a democratic tradition, climate, and confidence in democracy.

This chapter covers Specific Outcomes 3, 8 and 9 of the Human and Social Sciences learning area.

Unit 1

The factors leading to the collapse of democracy in Europe and Japan after the First World War

Unit outcomes

- Explain the effects of the peace settlement at the end of the First World War.
- Describe the political and economic instability between the two world wars.
- Report on the main characteristics of a democracy and a dictatorship.
- Explain the emergence of the left and right political movements in Europe.
- Interpret historical maps and cartoons.

Introduction

The First World War (1914–19) was the most terrible war the world had known. Millions had died and there was destruction of property on a scale never seen before. The survivors of the war, particularly on the side of the victors, were determined to build a 'brave, new world' – a world that would be democratic. The Allies established the League of Nations in the belief that nations would work together to ensure lasting peace and to set up measures to stop future aggressors. The Allies attempted to meet the hopes of various nationalities in Europe by establishing independent, national states, believing that this would ensure the growth of democratic societies in Europe and help bring about political stability.

Instead, two decades later, in most of Europe, democracy had not survived. In the face of poverty, unemployment and violence, many people chose instead to support individuals and their parties that advocated dictatorships and absolute control over all aspects of society. These individuals and parties claimed that they would restore national pride and bring glory to their countries. The consequence was another world war which broke out in 1939.

Activities

1 Compare Sources A, B and C. Which sources are primary and which are secondary?

2 In your own words briefly summarise the perspectives (points of view) in Sources A and B.

3 Refer to all three sources. Draw two columns and draw

up two lists indicating which factors would contribute to future peace and which would not.

▼ Source A

More than 1,700,000 men are dead; over 1,200,000 are mutilated ... That's the balance sheet of what was meant to be the 'war to end war'.

We say to every kind of citizen, but especially to fiancés and to mothers. War against War! We say to the millions of soldiers who returned home after their torments, Stand up against War! We openly declare that we, the 'victims of war', are opposed to all wars because ... [we] have been condemned by war to disability and death.

All of us, the mutilated and the crippled, cry out with one heart 'War on War!'

(From: An ex-soldiers' newspaper, *Le Poilu cévenol* (*The Cévennes Soldier*), 25 March 1921. In J Brooman. *The Era of the Second World War.*)

The failure of democracy

The concept of democracy is not fixed in meaning. There are many forms of democracy and the stages towards democratic government can be analysed within any society. It is important to note that no country in Europe had achieved what we understand as democracy by the First World War, even though this war was won by the Allies in the name of democracy.

Even in the most democratic states, such as Britain, people were still excluded from the franchise (voting) on the basis of class or race or gender. While the idea of democracy found favour with some groups, such as the middle class and many of the working class, it was not fully supported by either the old ruling classes of Europe or by extreme socialists who looked towards a radical transformation of society. The old ruling elite looked back to the old order and wished to retain or take back power from the broader population, while others believed that democratic forms of government were just the first stage of the revolution of the masses.

British Empire Union.
"ONCE A GERMAN-ALWAYS A GERMAN!"

REMEMBER!
This Man, who has shelled Churches, Hospitals, and Open Boats at Sea; This Robber, Ravisher and Murderer. AND This Man, who after the War, will want to sell you his German Goods,
ARE ONE AND THE SAME PERSON!
Men and Women of Britain! Have Nothing to do with Germans Until the Crimes Committed by Them against Humanity have been expiated! Help to Boycott Germans and German Goods by joining the
British Empire Union, 346, Strand, London, W.C. 2.
COPIES OF THIS POSTER 6d. EACH, SMALL SIZE 3d. EACH.

◀ *Source B*
Issued in 1918 by the British Union, this cartoon warns people not to buy from German business-men after the First World War
(From: J Brooman. *The Era of the Second World War.*)

How have historians explained the failure of democracy between the two world wars?

Many historians and many school textbooks have focused on the collapse of democratic governments in those countries which they saw as responsible for the Second World War – in other words – Germany, Italy and Japan. They have presented the right-wing Fascist governments of those countries as an aberration – as something out of the ordinary. They have explained the factors in those societies that contributed to the decline of democratic governments and the rise of forms of dictatorships in those countries.

However, it is important to realise that the situation in Europe in the 1920s and 1930s was much more complex than that. Democracy was much more fragile – many countries throughout the world during the 1920s and 30s were not democratic, and many peoples in those regions which formed part of the empires of democratic nations did not enjoy any democratic rights. Countries like France and Britain also saw a growth of right-wing and left-wing parties that wanted to destroy democratic parliamentary government. By 1939 when the Second World War broke out, almost the whole of Europe was ruled by dictatorships of various forms – both from the right and the left.

An important issue to consider is why people

	Soldiers killed	Other Damage
Allies		
France	1 400 000	North-east France ruined by fighting
Britain	750 000	Spent nine billion pounds on the war (some of which was borrowed money)
Belgium	50 000	Suffered great damage from fighting and German occupation
Italy	600 000	North-east Italy devastated by fighting
USA	116 000	Entered the war late in 1917 and suffered least
Russia	1 700 000	The war led to revolution, a communist take-over and the loss of much land
Central powers		
Germany	2 000 000	Little damage but revolution and hunger at the end of the war
Austria-Hungary	1 200 000	
Turkey	375 000	
Bulgaria	100 000	
TOTAL	Approximately 20 000 000 soldiers and civilians died due to the war	

◀ *Source C*

The aftermath of the First World War (From: K Shepherd. *International Relations 1919–1939*)

of different classes and under different conditions in different parts of the world chose to support political parties that denounced or condemned democracy as a workable form of government. They instead supported dictatorships of various forms that denied them any democratic rights.

The main characteristics of a democracy

Remember that there are different forms of democracies but all share these main characteristics.

- The basis of the political system is a constitution, in which the powers of the state are set out.
- The constitution sets out the powers of the different branches of the state and the limits on those powers.
- The different parts of the state are separate from each other and there are a series of balances and checks on each.
- The constitution sets out the rights of the individual in the society, including freedom of thought and expression, the right of protest, the right to belong to a political party, trade union or any other association and the freedom of religion, freedom of the press and information among other rights.
- All citizens have the franchise – the right to vote – and participate in elections to choose the government from a number of political parties.
- Voters have the choice between several (at least two) political parties.
- A government is in power for a limited period of time, before a new election must be called.
- The government is responsible – answerable – to the people.

The main characteristics of a dictatorship

In a country governed by a dictator, people do not have a say in how the country is run.

- There are no regular elections. Only one party is allowed – the one led by the dictator.
- People are represented only by organisations which the dictator allows to exist.

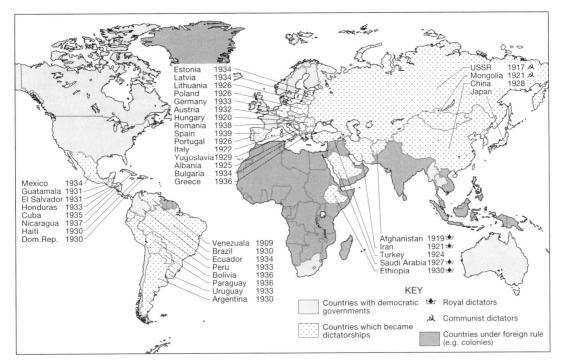

Estonia 1934
Latvia 1934
Lithuania 1926
Poland 1926
Germany 1933
Austria 1932
Hungary 1920
Romania 1938
Spain 1939
Portugal 1926
Italy 1922
Yugoslavia 1929
Albania 1925
Bulgaria 1934
Greece 1936

USSR 1917
Mongolia 1921
China 1928
Japan

Mexico 1934
Guatamala 1931
El Salvador 1931
Honduras 1933
Cuba 1935
Nicaragua 1937
Haiti 1930
Dom.Rep. 1930

Venezuela 1909
Brazil 1930
Ecuador 1934
Peru 1933
Bolivia 1936
Paraguay 1936
Uruguay 1933
Argentina 1930

Afghanistan 1919
Iran 1921
Turkey 1924
Saudi Arabia 1927
Ethiopia 1930

KEY

Countries with democratic governments

Countries which became dictatorships

Countries under foreign rule (e.g. colonies)

Royal dictators

Communist dictators

▲ Source D

The spread of dictatorships in the 1920s and 1930s
(Adapted from: J Brooman. *The Era of the Second World War.*)

- In a dictatorship people have very few rights.
- There is no freedom of speech. If people criticise the dictator or the dictator's party they are likely to be arrested.
- There is no freedom of information. The dictator controls the newspapers, books, films, etc.
- Not all religions are allowed.
- There is no legal freedom. The police can arrest whom they wish and keep them in prison without trial.
- People can only join associations allowed by the dictator.

Activities

Look closely at Source D and complete these activities with a partner.
1 Which countries were not democratic by the end of the 1920s?
2 Which countries were not democratic in the 1930s?
3 What conclusion can you reach about the state of democracy as a form of government in the 1920s and 1930s?
4 Draw up a table comparing the main characteristics of democracy and dictatorship.
5 In pairs or groups, discuss the possible circumstances under which people would choose one form of government or the other.

Reasons for the collapse of democracy

Historians have focused on a number of factors in order to explain the collapse of democracy. We will look at the extent to which each of these factors contributed to the collapse of democracy.

The First World War

When discussing the collapse of democracy some historians point to the unique nature of the First World War itself. For the first time in the history of the world, entire nations were involved in the war effort. Societies were organised around the war and economies were changed to meet the needs of war. Governments in the democracies used emergency powers in order to mobilise the population and the economy. Some historians argue that this provided a model for future dictators.

The political effects of the First World War were to force change on societies. The immediate trend was to democracy, but it took many forms. In many countries, including Britain and France, it meant the extension of the franchise, first to the remaining voteless men, and later to women.

The arrangements for future peace

The formal end to the First World War between the main Allied powers, Britain, France, the United States, Italy, Japan and other minor allies and Germany came with the signing of the Treaty of Versailles in 1919. Later, the United States Congress refused to ratify the treaty and a separate treaty was signed between the United States and Germany. Separate treaties were signed with Germany's allies – Austria (1919), Bulgaria (1919), Turkey (1919 and 1923) and Hungary (1920).

The overall aim of the treaties, particularly with Germany, was to ensure future world peace. However, a great deal of criticism has been directed at the peacemakers – both at the time by those countries which were directly affected, and by historians later – who saw in the treaties the foundations of future instability and conflict. Even contemporary observers and participants were divided on whether the treaties were too harsh or too lenient (moderate).

humiliation. Many members of the armed forces and the administration criticised the new government and looked for ways to restore German national pride. Hitler and Mussolini used the bitterness of ex-soldiers and the general feeling of national humiliation to win support for their parties. They both adopted militaristic symbols for their parties and supporters and ran their parties along militaristic lines.

Activities ....

Look closely at Source E and complete the following activities.

1 Draw up a table listing the various conditions of the Treaty of Versailles affecting Germany and the possible effects on the German economy and society.
2 Explain how these arrangements would contribute to a sense of German nationalism.

....

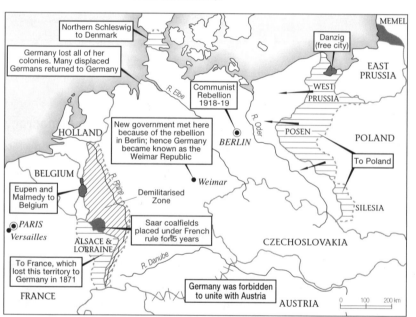

◀*Source E*

The price of defeat: Germany's territorial losses by the 1919 Treaty of Versailles

(Adapted from: *A Map History of the Modern World*.)

Germany and the Treaty of Versailles

Of those countries directly affected by defeat, Germans were the harshest critics. They referred to the Treaty of Versailles as the 'Diktat' or 'Dictated peace'. The members of the new German government, who had signed the treaty, were criticised as traitors. The terms of the treaty were certainly harsh on Germany – the loss of German territory inside Europe and the dismantling of the German Empire, the exclusion from the League of Nations, the heavy restrictions on the German army and navy, and the War Guild Clause and reparations – all added to German

Italy and the Treaty of Versailles

The Italians, who had been on the side of the victors, were also very angry at the terms of the treaty. In their view, Italy had been promised in a secret agreement with the Allies a large portion of the Dalmatian coastline and hoped for territory in Africa. They had received the Tyrol from Austria, and Trieste. The treaty became known as 'the mutilated peace' and gave cause for complaint to those Italians who had fought in the war. The Italian government that signed the treaty was also seen to be too weak to represent Italy's demands strongly enough at Versailles.

Japan and the Treaty of Versailles

Many Japanese were also angered by the Treaty of Versailles. Japan, also an ally, had received under **mandate** from the League of Nations, all the former German islands in the Pacific north of the equator. Japan was recognised as a Great Power and granted a permanent seat on the Council of the League, but many Japanese nationalists were insulted by the refusal of the Western powers to include a clause guaranteeing racial equality in the Covenant of the League. They took this to be a direct racial slur on Japan. This was to help fuel anti-Western feelings in the 1920s and 1930s and to justify independent, aggressive policies in the region.

> ### New words
>
> **mandate** right to govern overseas territories, previously held as colonies, but without necessarily the permission of the people living there
> **surplus capital** wealth created from profits which could be used for other capitalist ventures

Other countries and the Treaty of Versailles

In other countries the Treaty of Versailles was also regarded as inadequate. In the United States, conservative Republicans who represented big business interests saw the treaty as too binding on the United States' foreign interests. They were looking for investment markets to invest **surplus capital** and did not want the United States unable to act because of any deals that bound them with one side against another.

The voters in Britain and France had been influenced by wartime propaganda that it was all the fault of the Germans and thus their demands at Versailles were harsh: reparations were regarded as non-negotiable. Both Britain and France acquired more colonial possessions from the old German Empire – including parts of Africa – and the old Turkish Empire (most of the Middle East).

Some historians argue that the break-up of the old multinational empires, particularly the Austro-Hungarian Empire – left a political vacuum and a loss of identity. While the peacemakers at Versailles were committed to the principle of **self-determination**, the new nations turned to the Catholic Church for inspiration and a sense of continuity once old **authoritarian** governments had disappeared. The common thread was a rejection of liberal democracy and Marxist socialism. Conservative church-based parties were common in Europe in the 1920s and 1930s, for example, in Poland, Hungary, Austria, Spain and Portugal.

> ### New words
>
> **self-determination** right of a nation to rule itself and to choose its own form of government independently
> **authoritarian** those governments that retained most powers in the hands of a few
> **liberal** (liberalism) political philosophy in which the basic rights of the individual are protected and the powers of the state are limited
> **constitution** body of fundamental/basic principles by which a state is governed, setting out clearly the rights of the individual and the laws governing the responsibilities and powers of the state
> **coalition governments** governments that are made up of a number of political parties, none of which has a clear majority in order to govern on its own

New governments cause political confusion

It is important to note that the emergence of mass-based parties on the left and the right in Europe at the end of the war threatened the establishment of democracies. The communist parties were committed to the principle of socialist revolution in order to establish 'a dictatorship of the proletariat'. Communists regarded democratic governments as instruments of middle class capitalist interests which had to be overthrown.

On the other hand, the far right parties were also committed to the end of parliamentary multi-party democracies, perceiving them to be weak and useless. Their goal was to establish single-party dictatorships or military governments and they rejected the idea of restricting state power. They were prepared to use any means to attain power – either legitimately through the constitutional process, or by violent overthrow of the democratic system.

One of the main obstacles to political stability and democracy in Europe was the weakness of the new governments in Germany and Italy and in many other European countries after the war.

The Weimar government

In Germany, the new Weimar government as it became known, struggled with problems from the start. A provisional or temporary government had been established in 1918 to fill the political vacuum after the abdication of the Kaiser, and it faced enormous problems. Before the war, Germany was not a strong democracy. There was an elected parliament or Reichstag but the real power lay in the hands of the upper house and the Kaiser. A strongly **liberal** democratic **constitution** was drawn up and the Weimar Republic came into being in 1919. The Weimar government was faced with internal political conflict.

Parties on the left – the communists – and parties on the right never supported parliamentary rule and there was a very real threat of attempted *coups d'état* from extremists on both the left and the right wing.

The politicians had little experience of a strong parliamentary tradition, and in the face of continued crises, **coalition governments** seemed unstable and weak. It was clear from their actions that members of the judiciary, the army and the civil service either did not care about or were even disloyal to the new democracy. Judges gave mild sentences for violence and rebellion and political murder to members of right-wing groups (as in the Kapp Putsch of 1920, and the Bavarian (Beerhall) Putsch organised by Hitler in 1923).

The Italian government

In Italy, a strong parliamentary tradition was also lacking. Until 1919, the Vatican had forbidden Catholics from voting in elections. In the elections of 1919, mass-based political parties on the left and right emerged. Weak, short-lived coalition governments were unable to solve the great postwar economic and social problems facing the population. The newly formed Communist Party, as in Germany, would not work with the socialists, and alone the socialists were unable to work out strategies to keep out the extreme right wing.

In both Germany and Italy, democratic governments and parliamentary rule were unable to solve serious social and economic problems and stronger alternatives were looked for. The emergence of extremist parties was not restricted to these countries. Not only did the far left and right emerge in the new democracies of Eastern Europe, but also in Spain, in Britain, France and, to an extent, in the United States.

▼ *Source F* The 'political spectrum'
(From: K Shepherd. *International Relations 1919–1939.*)

▼ *Source G*
An explanation of the political terms 'left' and 'right'

> The terms are familiar and even overworked in historical and political discussion. They entered European politics at the time of the French Revolution. In the National Assembly of 1789 a division of views soon made itself apparent over the question of the royal veto. One section of the members took the radical view that the will of the elected representatives of the people should prevail on questions of reform. Another, composed of the nobility and higher clergy, upheld royal power. The first of these groups sat or stood to the left of the speaker's chair, the second to the right. In the centre, before the speaker, gathered moderate and uncommitted men. The extremists agreed in condemning their moderation as a weakness springing from lack of principle or corrupt self-seeking.
>
> This historical spectrum has become the classical stereotype of European political opinions. The left is radical, democratic and reforming. The right is resistant to change in these directions, even reactionary. The centre, in fortunate times, holds the balance. In times of crisis power falls to one or other of the extremes, usually not without a conflict.

(From: D Smith. *The left and right in twentieth century Europe.*)

Activities ....

1 Summarise the definitions of the 'left', 'right' and 'centre' as outlined in Source G.

2 How do these definitions match up with the diagram in Source F?

....

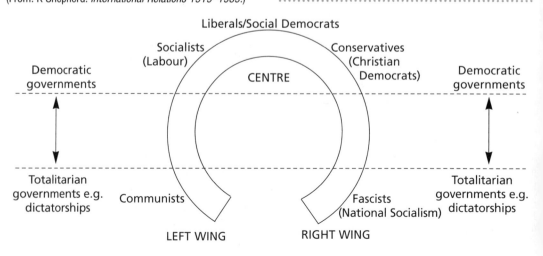

Liberals/Social Democrats

Socialists (Labour)

Conservatives (Christian Democrats)

Democratic governments

CENTRE

Democratic governments

Totalitarian governments e.g. dictatorships

Communists

Fascists (National Socialism)

Totalitarian governments e.g. dictatorships

LEFT WING

RIGHT WING

Economic instability

Remember that economic instability has a direct effect on voters' lives. When economic problems persist and the government is perceived to be unable or unwilling to solve them, voters will turn to alternative parties that promise quick solutions.

At the end of the First World War, there was a general worldwide economic depression. Countries faced the costs of the war and faced rising costs of living and the problem of reabsorbing returning soldiers into the economy. There was a worldwide influenza (flu) epidemic resulting in the deaths of millions of people.

Countries in Europe, particularly those like France and Belgium, had the added problem of rebuilding their infrastructures that had been shattered by the war. This made France, in particular, determined that Germany should pay reparations for the war. Britain and France also faced the huge task of repaying large amounts to the United States for loans granted during the war.

In Britain, much blame had been laid at the Kaiser's door and Germans in general during the war. Wartime propaganda had done its work during the war, but afterwards the government faced many economic and social problems. The government in Britain faced rising worker unrest after the war. Not only were millions of men given the vote but fears of working class action prevented the government from offering asylum (safety) to the Tsar of Russia and his family – close relations to the British royal family.

France and Britain had insisted on Germany accepting responsibility for starting the First World War and demanded reparations from Germany for losses as a result of the war. The reparations amount was not set at Versailles, but turned out to be so high that it was impossible for Germany to pay. The new Weimar government immediately faced an economic crisis with soaring **inflation** and the collapse of the German currency. It also faced the added humiliation of the French occupation of the Ruhr, Germany's major industrial area, in 1923, which attempted forced payment in industries instead of money. As a result of this crisis, many Germans, particularly those in the middle class who could have been strong supporters of democracy, lost faith in the ability of this government to handle such problems, and in turn questioned the nature of parliamentary democracy. Support for extremist parties, including the Nazis, grew.

However, after 1925, there was a brief period of economic recovery in Germany, under the leadership of Gustav Stresemann. Following German promises of French security, the bad feelings towards Germany began to decline. Germany was admitted to the League of Nations in 1926. The United States negotiated several deals with Germany by which American loans were used to bring about economic recovery and the reparations repayments were reduced. There was relative political stability during this time, but the German economy was dangerously dependent on the wellbeing of the economy of the United States.

New words

inflation general increase in prices; increase in the supply of money leading to declining value

◀ **Source H**
German Mark notes for sale as waste paper in Germany in 1923

Look at Source H and answer the following questions.

1 Is this a primary or secondary source? Give reasons for your answer. (See *Looking into the Past Grade 10* on primary and secondary sources.)
2 Can this source be considered useful by historians? Explain your answer.

....

Extension activity ....

How would this inflation affect the following groups?
a workers
b the middle class with savings
c German voters.

....

The decline of democracies in Europe before 1929

The post-war economic and resulting political problems that we have looked at did not only affect Germany and Italy. There was widespread worker unrest throughout Europe, caused by the high levels of inflation and unemployment. In 1926, Britain experienced large-scale general workers' strikes. In Britain and France conservative governments came to power. Working class actions led to increasing fears of communist revolution and, in turn, many middle class and ex-soldiers looked to right-wing parties for action. By 1929, before the Wall Street Crash and the ensuing Great Depression, right-wing governments or dictatorships had been established in most new democracies in Eastern Europe.

The historian David Thomson's argument can be found in Source I below.

▼ *Source I*

*So widespread, indeed, was this drift toward military or royal or **clericalist** dictatorships between 1926 and 1929 – in the years of relative economic prosperity – that the eclipse of democracy in Europe clearly cannot be attributed to the world economic depression that only began at the end of*

*1929. A tendency that appeared simultaneously in Spain and Portugal, in Poland and Lithuania, in Austria and Yugoslavia, was not merely regional in character. It was, like the earlier **reversions** to dictatorships in Italy and Hungary, mainly due to the unsettled economic and social conditions after the war, to the shallow roots of the new democratic constitutions and the **ineptitudes** of parliamentary politicians ... The tide of authoritarianism in Europe before 1929 had a nineteenth century flavour, royalist and militarist and clericalist. The effect of the Great Depression was to intensify this trend and to carry it very much further in the extremist direction of Fascism and totalitarian government.*

(From: D Thomson. *Europe Since Napoleon.*)

New words

clericalist influenced by the church
reversions returns
ineptitude lack of skills

Activities ....

Discuss the following questions in small groups.

1 What is the main point of Source I?
2 What three things does Thomson give in Source I as contributing to the rise of dictatorships in the 1920s in Europe?
3 Refer to Source D on page 95.
   a How many countries had established dictatorships by 1929?
   b Does this support Thomson's point or not?

....

Extension activity ....

A number of causes have been highlighted as explanations for the failure of democracy in Europe between the two world wars.
Write an essay on the following topic: 'To what extent did the First World War contribute to the political instability in Europe and the rise of dictatorships until 1929?'

....

The rise of the Fascists in Italy, the Nazis in Germany, and the militarists in Japan

Unit 2

Unit outcomes

- Understand the nature of Fascism, Nazism and militarism.
- Explain why these movements rose to power.
- Analyse a variety of sources.

The rise of Fascism in Italy

Mussolini used the post-war economic problems and the seeming inability of the government to handle the social and economic problems to his own advantage. There was a major increase in political violence as groups of left-wing and right-wing sympathisers clashed. Returning soldiers and the middle class were disillusioned with the corrupt and inefficient elected governments, while the working class and agricultural labourers were strongly attracted to the Communist Party which increased its support dramatically. The Catholic Church did not support the democratic governments as a result of a long-standing conflict over land. It forbade members to vote in elections and about 40 per cent of the adult population did not vote.

Mussolini presented his party – the Fascist Party – as the solution to Italy's problems. The party, formed in 1919, deliberately created a militaristic image with its black uniforms and demonstrations. Its members targeted communists, disrupting political meetings and beating up communist supporters. As the government was faced with increasing unemployment, rising prices and increasing political instability, the Fascists increased their support in parliamentary elections and control of local governments. They seemed to be the only group who was prepared to oppose the left-wing socialist strike in 1922. At this stage, the Fascists only had 35 seats (out of 535) in parliament.

Mussolini seizes political power

Despite their minimal parliamentary representation, Mussolini decided to take control of the government in October 1922. He planned a march on Rome by columns of Fascist supporters, without antagonising the army which was loyal to King Victor Emmanuel III. He demanded that six Fascists be included in the coalition cabinet. The prime minister requested that the king declare martial law to deal with the situation, but, fearing a civil war, the king refused. Mussolini saw his opportunity and increased his demands. He insisted that the Fascists took complete control of the government. On 29 October 1922 the king invited Mussolini to form a new government.

This decision was still within the democratic constitution. However, Mussolini used this opportunity to consolidate his position, destroying the democratic process, and creating a dictatorship within a short period of time.

Creation of a dictatorship

Soon after taking up his position, Mussolini was granted full powers to reform the government by the parliament. He established a new national militia out of existing Fascist groups. He introduced a new electoral law whereby two-thirds of the seats in the lower house of parliament were given to the party with the most number of votes. This was to strengthen his political position. He persuaded the parliament to vote overwhelmingly in favour of these measures. In the 1924 elections Mussolini's Fascists gained nearly 4,5 million votes against the 3 million of the other parties.

Violence against his opponents continued. In 1924 an outspoken socialist opponent, Matteoti, was assassinated. This brought criticism from other governments and newspapers in Italy. Mussolini imposed censorship of the press and successfully rode out the political storm. This was made easier by the deep divisions between the other parties. By 1925 he was in a position to eliminate the opposition. All opposition parties were broken up and opponents were imprisoned. The constitution was amended to enable Mussolini to rule as a dictator. He was responsible to the king alone. He issued laws by **proclamation**, nominated all ministers and leading officials and commanded all branches of the armed forces.

In 1928, further amendments to the constitution were introduced. The king remained the head of the state and parliament, in theory the legislative body. However, in practice real power rested with the Fascist Grand Council, a body made up of 22 leading Fascists with Mussolini as head. He now assumed the title of 'il Duce' – the leader. All decisions were taken within this council and were simply ratified or approved by parliament.

The electoral system was also changed. Only the names of those who belonged to Fascist organisations were put forward to the Grand Council as possible candidates. A list of 400 was drawn up and presented to voters as a whole. The voters were only able to accept or reject the list as a whole. The effect was the creation of an all-Fascist parliament which simply approved the decisions of the Grand Council. The former elected Chamber of Deputies was disbanded and replaced by a Chamber of Fascists and Corporations made up of nominated members. Parliamentary democracy was effectively destroyed and opposition essentially eliminated.

Mussolini further enhanced his position with an agreement with the Catholic Church. This was a major success as the Church had never recognised the state of Italy and the loss of its own territories. By the Lateran Treaty of 1929, the Pope and Mussolini reached agreement on the official position of the Church as Italy's State Church. The **sovereign independence** of the Vatican City was recognised and the Church was compensated for lost territories. Importantly, the Church recognised the existence of the Kingdom of Italy. This agreement won Mussolini enormous popularity in the Catholic-dominated country. Between 1924 and 1929, Mussolini was able to establish a dictatorship in Italy and to lay the foundations of a totalitarian state.

▼ Source B
Mussolini's call to Italian Fascists before the march on Rome

Fascist Italians! The hour of the decisive battle has come. The army of Blackshirts does not march against the police or army but against the class of stupid and weak-minded politicians, who for four years have not known how to give a government to the nation. Fascism wishes to impose discipline only on the nation as a whole and to give aid to all those forces which will encourage the nation's economic growth and well-being.

(From: K Shepherd. *International Relations 1919–1939.*)

▼ Source C
Mussolini commenting on the Catholic Church

The Pope? He is one of my helpers. He looks after the dead. I look after the living. To him the kingdom of souls. To me the kingdom of the living.

(From: K Shepherd. *International Relations 1919–1939.*)

New words

proclamation decree; law issued without reference to parliamentary procedure
sovereign independence right to govern itself as an independent state

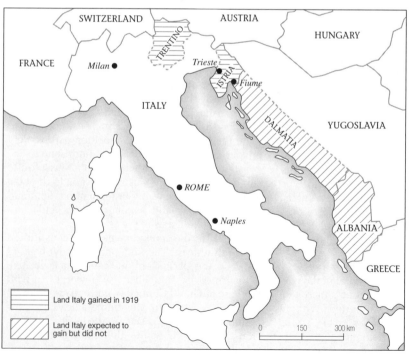

◀ Source A
Italy and the peace treaties
(Adapted from: K Shepherd. *International Relations 1919–1939.*)

© INPRA

Activities

1 Look at Source A. Why would Italian nationalists have seen the peace treaties of 1919 as a 'betrayal'?
2 What sentiments does Mussolini appeal to in Source B?
3 Look at Source C.
   a What was Mussolini's attitude to the Catholic Church?
   b Draw up a list of reasons why the Lateran Treaty of 1929 could have been advantageous to both Mussolini and the Church.
4 Study Source D very carefully and then answer these questions.
   a What seems to be the relationship between Mussolini and the Church representatives? Give reasons for your answer based on evidence from the source.
   b Read through the sections headed 'The rise of Fascism in Italy' and then give possible reasons for the relationship between Mussolini and the Church.

relied upon extravagant foreign loans in order to rebuild and modernize German industry ... [But] the whole German economy rested not on financial solvency but on the opposite – lavish and mostly short-term borrowing; and for this reason it now stood on a precarious footing, which the first shock to international confidence would rock and probably shatter.

(From: D Thomson. *Europe Since Napoleon.*)

New words

bankruptcy the economic state of individuals or businesses whose debts are greater than their assets
insolvency the economic state of a debtor who can no longer pay any debts or costs
abeyance temporarily set aside

The rise of the Nazi Party in Germany after 1929

The Great Depression was to have its harshest political impact on Germany. The German economic recovery in the 1920s had been an artificial one.

Having ruined almost the entire middle class by the currency collapse of 1923, at the same time liquidating all public and many private debts, German policy now

The Wall Street Crash of October 1929, and the worldwide economic depression, had immediate and disastrous consequences for Germany. America stopped short-term loans and stopped lending money to Germany completely. There was an immediate rise in **bankruptcies**. By 1931, the German government faced **insolvency**. An attempt was made to cut public expenditure and impose new taxes, but by 1932 industrial production had halved since 1929, and unemployment trebled from two to six million. There was a crisis of confidence in the government's ability to handle the crisis and many people feared a new currency collapse, such as they had experienced in 1923.

After 1929, there was a succession of weak governments, forced to rule with the help of emergency powers. In the Weimar Constitution, Article 48 set out emergency powers to the president in an emergency.

Should public order and safety be seriously disturbed or threatened, the President may take measures necessary to restore public order and safety; in case of need he may use armed force ... he may, for the time being, declare the fundamental rights of the citizen wholly or partially in **abeyance**.

This power was intended as an extreme measure only to be taken if the republic itself was under threat. Its use during the depression and political crisis that followed set a precedent which seriously undermined the tradition of parliamentary democracy. While emergency powers were denied to the socialist government in 1929, they were granted to the more conservative Catholic Centre party which governed as a minority government between 1930 and 1932.

Both the Nazi Party and the communist parties made great headway after 1929 (see Sources E to H). The communists won increasing support from the rising numbers of unemployed and employed workers while the Nazis appealed to a wide spectrum of the German population, from industrialists, to the middle class, to the unemployed and the youth. Hitler's potential support base was much broader than that of the communists. Through effective propaganda and promises to all to solve all grievances, membership of the party grew and in the elections between 1930 and 1932, the Nazis won an increasing number of seats. In the presidential elections of April 1932, Hitler won nearly 13,5 million votes against the president in power, the senile 84-year-old President von Hindenburg, who won 19,25 million.

Despite a massive increase in support, the Nazis remained outside the government, although they supported a right-wing coalition under Franz von Papen who represented landowners, industrialists and army officers. Von Papen was beaten in the November 1932 elections and the Nazis, unlike the communists, lost votes. Von Schleicher replaced Von Papen who immediately began plotting to get back into power. None of the political parties took Hitler particularly seriously and the other right-wing parties, while enjoying Hitler's backing to put them in power, looked down on Hitler and his 'rabble supporters'.

In a desperate attempt to return to power, Von Papen persuaded the president to call new elections in January 1933. Again the Nazis increased their support. They now had 37 per cent of the seats in the Reichstag. Von Papen proposed a right-wing coalition government of nationalists and Nazis. Hitler should be given the position of Chancellor, with three cabinet positions for the Nazis, while Von Papen would be vice-chancellor, and the nationalists would hold the remaining nine cabinet seats. The chief supporters of the right-wing nationalists believed that Von Papen would be able to control Hitler, who, they felt, was inexperienced and likely to fail in high office.

On 30 January 1933, Hitler became the new German Chancellor. After twelve years of political struggle he was now in a position to carry out his aims. It would, however, take him two more years before he was able to destroy the remaining democracy in Germany and to establish a totalitarian state.

Motives for joining the Nazi Party

▼ *Source E*
I observed many things in Berlin which could not be noticed – or only to a lesser degree – in small towns. I saw the Communist danger, the Communist terror, their gangs breaking up 'bourgeois' meetings; the 'bourgeois' parties being utterly helpless, the Nazis being the only party that broke terror by anti-terror. I saw the complete failure of the 'bourgeois' parties to deal with the economic crisis ... Only national socialism offered any hope. Anti-Semitism had another aspect in Berlin: Nazis mostly did not hate Jews individually, many had Jewish friends, but they were concerned about the Jewish problem ... Nobody knew of any way to deal with it, but they hoped the Nazis would know. If they had guessed how the Nazis did deal with it, not one in a hundred would have joined the party.

(From: A letter by the Headmaster of Northeim's Girls' High School, 1967. In W Allen. *The Nazi Seizure of Power*.)

▼ *Source F*
It was the depression and business was bad. The Nazis used to ask my father for contributions and he refused. As a consequence of this he lost business. So he joined the Nazi Party. But this lost him other customers, so he was discouraged by

the whole situation. He probably wouldn't have joined of his own choice.

(From: The owner of a printing shop in Northeim. In W Allen. *The Nazi Seizure of Power*.)

▼ *Source G*

For three months I had managed to avoid saluting the swastika flag ... I tried it once too often, however ... I caught sight of an approaching procession of Nazi nurses, carrying banners. Without stopping to think, I turned my back on it and walked in the opposite direction, only to face four Brownshirts crossing towards me from the other side of the street.

'Trying to get out of it?' said one. 'Arm up! And now – ?'

'Heil Hitler,' I said.

I could have spat at myself as I strode past the procession with arm uplifted.

In Berlin alone thousands of Socialist and Communist officials were dragged from their beds at night ... and led away to Brownshirt barracks. There they were worked over with boot and whip, beaten with steel rods and rubber truncheons until they collapsed unconscious ... Many were forced to drink castor oil or had urine directed into their mouths. Others had their bones broken.

(From: *Listen! Read! Pass it on! Hitler's Crimes*, an underground pamphlet circulated by communists in 1933)

Activities ·

1 Study Sources E to H and analyse the reasons given for the support or hatred of the Nazi Party.
2 Draw a timeline showing the rise of the Nazi Party between 1929 and 1933.

· ·

The rise of the military in Japan

The term 'militarism' describes a system of government in which the military dominates. It also refers to the country's goals which are aggressive and expansionist, relying on the military to be attained.

The Great Depression had important consequences for Japan. In the 1920s it had seemed that democratic parliamentary government would take root. Universal male suffrage was granted in 1925. Political parties took control of the government. Despite opposition from anti-Western ultra-nationalists, Japan seemed to enjoy a good relationship with the major powers,

▼ *Source H*

Unemployment in Germany, 1928–33, and seats won by the Nazis in the Reichstag, 1928–32
(From: *Discovering the Past Y9: Peace and War*.)

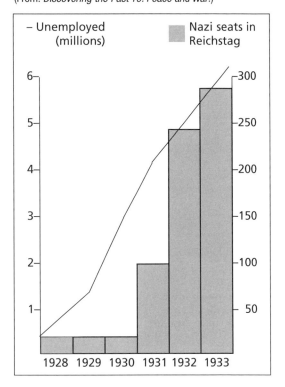

(See chapter 1, page 33 on the use of statistics)

although some agreements troubled the nationalists. For example, the Washington agreements (1921–22) limited the size of the Japanese navy to a proportion of the American and British navies and resulted in the Japanese agreement to withdraw from Shantung in China.

Several extremist organisations were established in the 1920s ranging from socialist to ultra-nationalist, aiming to protect traditional Japanese values, a sense of unity among the Japanese and an aggressive foreign policy. They attracted support from young officers in the army. The Cherry Society planned a *coup d'état* in 1931 but was betrayed. These groups won increasing support during the Great Depression as a result of widespread unemployment and the collapse of the silk and rice industries in the rural areas. Widespread unrest followed. The Japanese politicians were seen as corrupt and ineffective.

The Japanese army began to act independently of the government when it occupied the city of Mukden, in the Chinese province of Manchuria in September 1931. The cabinet gave

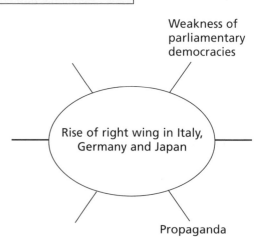

◀ **Source I**
Japan, Manchuria and China

its approval to the step, but the prime minister was later assassinated by a group of young army and naval officers. The army now simply refused to cooperate with the government unless it approved of the people in the government. Constitutionally, the army could prevent the formation of governments as it had the right to appoint the minister of war. After the assassination in May 1932, the heads of the governments were all non-party men, usually from the armed forces. Civilian politicians became increasingly reluctant to oppose the demands of the military, particularly after an attempted *coup d'état* by sections of the army in 1936. After this, the armed forces dictated a foreign policy which became increasingly anti-Western and aggressive. Japanese expansionism began to grow stronger.

Weakness of parliamentary democracies

Rise of right wing in Italy, Germany and Japan

Propaganda

Activities
Discuss these questions as a class.
1 Why did the Japanese army target Manchuria in 1931?
2 Why do you think that the army's action in Manchuria was popular with Japanese people?
3 Complete the spider diagram highlighting those factors which contributed to the rise of Fascism, Nazism and militarism in the 1920s and 1930s.

Extension activity
Use the spider diagram to draw up a detailed essay plan of the following essay topic:
'Economic factors played a major part in the rise of right-wing groups in the 1920s and 1930s. However, these were not the only factors.' Discuss.
Remember: Your essay plan should have an introduction, body and a conclusion. Indicate the content of each paragraph in point form, but write out each topic sentence in full.

The nature of totalitarianism and the main features of Nazism

Unit outcomes

- Describe the nature of totalitarianism.
- Discuss the nature of Nazism and Italian Fascism.
- Use a variety of sources to reach a conclusion.

The nature of totalitarianism

A totalitarian state is one in which the state assumes all power over every aspect of life in the society. The state deliberately destroys parliamentary democracy and replaces it with a one-party system, usually led by a dictator. It takes control of the courts which have to carry out its laws, however unjust. It prohibits all opposition and imposes restrictions on the freedom of the press and all forms of communication. The totalitarian state takes control of the economy and dictates production and price controls if necessary. It usually abolishes the right to collective bargaining and may replace trade unions with a state-controlled labour organisation. It takes control of cultural aspects of society, including education and religion, to further its own aims. The state will make use of propaganda and/or force to retain and expand its power. It will use a secret police force in order to protect its interests and will take direct control of the armed forces.

The nature of Nazism and Italian Fascism

It is extremely difficult to define the exact nature of Nazism and Italian Fascism which both fall under the banner of 'Fascism' – a term which historians have used to describe a number of political movements in Europe between the two world wars. However, Nazism and Italian Fascism did share certain characteristics.

They shared a hatred for communism and for parliamentary democracy, which they characterised as weak and ineffectual. Emphasis was placed on leadership and a cult of the leader was deliberately constructed in both parties. Both parties were strongly authoritarian,

promoting obedience and submission of the individual will to that of the party. Both parties presented a fervent nationalism and patriotism and a strongly militarist image. They shared a strongly held view of racial superiority and a sense of destiny. In the case of Hitler, anti-Semitism was to play a major part in the growth of Nazism. Each movement projected itself as dynamic, decisive and based on action rather than words and thoughts. From a feminist perspective, both movements projected themselves as masculine, emphasising strength and aggression. Compassion and conciliation were seen as weak, and therefore feminine. Nazism in particular reinforced the notion of the role of women as wives, homemakers and mothers, who did not take part in decision-making and the economy. Other Fascist parties in Europe shared many of these characteristics.

▼ Source A
Mussolini spoke these words

> *Fascism is not only a party, it is a regime; it is not only a regime but a faith; it is not only a faith but a religion.*

(From: K Shepherd. *International Relations 1919–1939.*)

▼ Source B
The role of the leader (Führer) – Ernst Huber, Nazi political theorist

> *The Führer is the bearer of the people's will; he is independent of all groups, associations, and interests, but he is bound by laws which are **inherent** in the nature of his people ... He shapes the collective will of the people within himself and he embodies the political unity and entirety of the people in opposition to individual interests ...*

(From: DM Phillips. *Hitler and the Rise of the Nazis.*)

New words

inherent existing in; a part of

▼ Source C

Attitude to women

We do not consider it correct for the woman to interfere in the world of the man, in his main sphere. We consider it natural if these two worlds remain distinct ...

The sacrifices which the man makes in the struggle of his nation, the woman makes in the preservation of that nation in individual cases. What the man gives in courage on the battlefield, the woman gives in eternal self-sacrifice, in eternal pain and suffering. Every child that a woman brings into the world is a battle, a battle waged for the existence of her people.

(From Hitler's 'Address to Women' at the Nuremberg Party Rally, 8 September 1934. In *History at Source – Nazi Germany.*)

Activities ....

1 What did Mussolini imply when he equated Fascism with religion in Source A?

2 In your own words sum up the role of 'the leader' as expressed in Source B.

3 a What are the implications for the rights of the individual as seen in Source B?

   b What is your attitude to this? Explain your answer.

4 Summarise the main points of Source C explaining the attitude of Nazis towards the role of women in society.

5 Look closely at Source D.

   a What image did Mussolini and Hitler present in public?

   b Why do you think the photograph was taken from this angle?

6 What are the main characteristics of Nazism and Fascism?

7 Why would these parties attempt to establish totalitarian states?

....

◄ Source D

Hitler and Mussolini, the Fascist partners

© INPRA

The political consolidation of power and the creation of dictatorships

Unit 4

Unit outcomes

- Explain how Hitler was able to consolidate political power in Germany.
- Identify the factors that enabled Hitler to create a dictatorship in Germany.
- Analyse a variety of sources.

Introduction

It is important to note that until Hitler and Mussolini were able to consolidate political power, they were not in a position to transform society according to Fascism. Germany and Italy did not automatically become totalitarian states when Hitler and Mussolini came to power. In fact, both came to power by constitutional means and they then proceeded **systematically** to destroy the democratic state.

> ### New words
>
> **systematically** according to an overall plan; deliberately and methodically

The overthrow of the democratic state 1933–34

Hitler clearly stated his strategy when he said: 'Unlike most revolutions which aim to transform society by capturing power from below, this was a revolution from above, in which the power of the state would be used, not to resist change, but to promote it.'

Hitler was not in a strong enough political position to implement his goals immediately. He had not seized power on his appointment as chancellor in January 1933, but had managed to get the position through political intrigue. The triumphal march of the Nazis through Berlin after his appointment did not reflect his somewhat weak position. The Nazis had only captured 37 per cent of the German vote and there were only three Nazis besides him in the cabinet. It was quite clear that the army would not allow the constitution to be overthrown at this stage.

In order to strengthen his position in the Reichstag, Hitler called for new elections to be held in March 1933. He immediately drafted 50 000 SA (Sturmabteilung – Brownshirts) and

SS (Schutzstaffel – Black Guards) into the police and used all the state power at his disposal, particularly the radio, to support the Nazi campaign. His main target was the Communist Party.

On the night of 27 February, the Reichstag building in Berlin spectacularly burnt down. Historians have never been able to establish the involvement of the Nazis, but given the advantage that this afforded Hitler at this time, it seems likely that Nazis were involved. The incident gave Hitler the excuse to act against the Communist Party, as a young Dutchman, who was allegedly a communist, was arrested and later executed for the crime. On Hitler's advice, President von Hindenburg issued a decree which suspended all rights of the individual, including freedom of speech and the press. It gave the government the right to search private houses and to confiscate private property. Hitler attempted to use the 'Communist Threat' during the election campaign, but he was disappointed by the election results: the Nazis were only able to increase their proportion of the vote to 44 per cent. With the support of the nationalists, he was able to establish a small majority in parliament.

With this advantage, he was able to prevent the communists from taking up their seats. He was in a strong position to persuade the parliament to enact the Enabling Law, on 23 March 1933, by which the cabinet, and therefore in effect, Hitler, was granted the power to govern and enact legislation without the consent of parliament. With the removal of the communists from the Reichstag, Hitler was able to get the necessary two-thirds majority. Only the Social Democrats voted against the Bill. Parliamentary government had effectively been destroyed.

At the same time, Hitler proceeded to create a centralised system of government. Under the Weimar Constitution, the German states were granted state legislative power. This meant that the Nazis could face opposition from State Diets (state parliaments) in the future implementation of their policies. For them, a strong centralised system of government with the only legislative power was the only option. Throughout 1933, the State Diets were dismissed and Nazi governors appointed with full powers. In January 1934, a Law for the Reconstruction of the Reich destroyed the State Diets.

Removal of opposition

Hitler proceeded to eliminate all opposition. In May 1933, the trade unions were banned and replaced by a Nazi Labour Front, controlled by party officials. Strikes were made illegal. The trade union movement was one of the biggest obstacles to total Nazi control. Many union leaders were arrested and imprisoned, and union funds and property were confiscated. Workers were bombarded with Nazi propaganda and encouraged to make every sacrifice for 'the fatherland'.

With the powers of the Enabling Act, Hitler was able to act against his political opponents. Many politicians were arrested in the months after the Enabling Act. Concentration camps were established. The Social Democratic Party was dissolved by decree in June 1933 and the other parties announced their own dissolution in the weeks that followed, including the nationalists who formed part of Hitler's coalition. The Nazi Party was now the only party. This was formalised by a law on 14 July 1933, which prohibited the formation of any other party. A one-party state had been achieved. Hitler wrote:

> The German Government has enacted the following law, which is herewith promulgated:
>
> Article I: The National Socialist German Workers' Party constitutes the only political Party in Germany.
>
> Article II: Whoever undertakes to maintain the organisational structure of another political Party or to form a new political Party will be punished with penal servitude up to three years or with imprisonment up to three years, if the action is not subject to a greater penalty according to other regulation.

(From: DM Phillips. *Hitler and the Rise of the Nazis.*)

Activities

1 Consider the consequences for democracy and individual rights as a result of each of Hitler's actions between 1933 and 1934. (Refer to the main characteristics of a democracy on page 94.)
2 Do you think that opposition parties are an important part of a democracy? Explain your answer.

Extension activity

Do some research to find out if/how our South African constitution prevents the actions of someone like Hitler.

Elimination of potential opposition within the party

During 1934, it became clear to Hitler that the SA under Ernst Röhm was no longer necessary to his plans and had become a political embarrassment. The SA had been set up to achieve political goals – to terrorise opponents and to break up political meetings. Given the image that the party was now projecting, many members were regarded as unacceptable. Moreover, Röhm continued to preach a form of socialism and the 'second revolution' which could alienate the industrialists and business community on whom Hitler relied for funds and support for his economic programme. An even greater danger was the possible alienation of the Wehrmacht (the army). Hitler needed the neutrality of the army and even their support for his ongoing constitutional changes. It was also obvious that President von Hindenburg would die soon, and Hitler needed the support of the army in order to take over the presidency and create a dictatorship.

Ernst Röhm openly demanded that the army should be taken over by the SA. In June 1934 Hitler plotted to eliminate Röhm and any other potential rivals. The SA members were given a month's leave so that they were dispersed and could not regroup and the SS was called on to carry out the purge. On the night of 30 June 1934, Röhm and many others were brutally executed. Hitler openly admitted in the Reichstag that 77 had died, including Röhm and Von Schleicher, the previous chancellor. He simply stated that all the victims were engaged in a plot against the Reich and that this was what would happen to those who plotted against him. It is likely that between 400 and 1 000 people were executed on The Night of the Long Knives. It was now clear that Hitler would not permit any opposition and placed himself and the party above the law. The rule of law had come to an end. Hitler also achieved his aim of satisfying the army, and this was to work in his favour in August.

The creation of a dictatorship

President von Hindenburg died on 2 August 1934. Three hours later, it was announced that according to a law enacted by the cabinet the 'previous' day, the offices of the chancellor and the president had been combined and that Hitler had taken over as head of state and commander-in-chief of the armed forces. The title of president was abolished and Hitler would be known as the Führer and Reich Chancellor. To tie the army closer to his regime, he ordered that all officers and men of the armed forces swear

▲ *Source A*   Nuremberg Rally
(From: Judith Stech. *The Rise and Fall of Adolf Hitler.*)

an oath of allegiance – not to Germany or the constitution – but to Hitler himself:

> *I swear by God this sacred oath, that I will render unconditional obedience to Adolf Hitler, the Führer of the German Reich, and people, Supreme Commander of the Armed Forces, and will be ready as a brave soldier to risk my life at any time for this oath.*

According to the constitution, Hitler should have called for an election for the office of the presidency. The armed forces tied themselves to the person of Hitler, and had lost their neutrality. Hitler called for a plebiscite/referendum – to endorse his actions. On 19 August, 90 per cent of the electorate – 38 million people – voted in favour of this unconstitutional action. Only 4,25 million voters voted against.

At a massive rally in Nuremberg on 4 September, Hitler's proclamation was read out: 'The German form of life is definitely determined for the next thousand years. The Age of Nerves of the nineteenth century has found its close with us. There will be no other revolution in Germany for the next one thousand years.'

▼ *Source B*

From Hitler's speech in the Reichstag, July 1933, in which he explained his actions against the SA (Night of the Long Knives)

> *If anyone reproaches me and asks why I did not resort to the regular courts of justice for conviction of the offender, then all that I can say to him is this: in this hour I was responsible for the fate of the German people, and thereby I became the supreme Justiciar of the German people!*
>
> *Everyone must know for all future time that if he raises his hand to strike the State, then certain death is his lot.*

(From: DM Phillips. *Hitler and The Rise of the Nazis.*)

Activities

1 What justifications does Hitler make in Source B to excuse his attitude to the law?
2 Do you think that the state (as in Source B) is justified in putting itself above the law? Explain your answer.
3 What were the links between 'The Night of the Long Knives' and Hitler's new position in August 1934?
4 What was Hitler trying to achieve by getting the army to take an oath of allegiance to him personally?
5 What can you deduce about Nazism from the rally shown in Source A?

Unit 5 The totalitarian state in Germany in the 1930s

Unit outcomes

- Explain the main characteristics of the totalitarian state in Germany in the 1930s.
- Assess the extent to which the Nazi state was completely totalitarian.
- Analyse the process of the destruction of individual rights.
- Examine the nature of prejudice and persecution of minorities.
- Detect bias and prejudice in a variety of sources.
- Empathise with a variety of different perspectives.

Introduction

In order to understand the nature of the Nazi totalitarian state in Germany, it is essential to understand the concept of *Gleichschaltung* – the coordination of the state. The Nazis were able to transform Germany into a totalitarian state rapidly and with very little opposition. Hitler used the Weimar Constitution, which he despised, to carry out the transformation of all aspects of life in the state. He used the emergency presidential decree of February 1933 which had suspended all civil rights to rule Germany through thousands of decreed laws.

Hitler's views on race

Hitler's views on race were expressed in his famous book *Mein Kampf* and signalled the means by which he planned to achieve racial purity.

▼ Source A

The whole organization of education and training which the People's State is to build up must take as its crowning task the work of instilling into the hearts and brains of the youth entrusted to it the racial instincts and understanding of the racial idea. No boy or girl must leave school without having attained a clear insight into the meaning of racial purity and the importance of maintaining the racial blood unadulterated. Thus the first indispensable condition for the preservation of our race will have been

established and thus the future cultural progress of our people will be assured.

(From: DM Phillips. *Hitler and the Rise of the Nazis.*)

▼ Source B

The Ideal German Girl: A 1938 poster encouraging the building of the Youth Hostels and Homes

© Peter Newark's Historical Pictures

Activities

1 Summarise Hitler's views on race as expressed in Source A.
2 What are the main features of the 'Ideal German Girl' as shown in Source B?

Extension activity

Do some research to help you write an essay on the following topic: 'The term "totalitarianism" refers to a totalitarian system of government, that is, a dictatorial one-party system based on the totality of the state.'
Explain in detail how Mussolini was instrumental in the establishment of a totalitarian state in Italy.

Features of Nazi Germany 1933–45

Anti-Semitism

A policy was adopted deliberately and systematically against the German Jewish population from the moment the Nazis came to power. This racist policy had its roots in *Mein Kampf*, in which Hitler explicitly stated his hatred of the Jews. He used anti-Semitism as a political tool to win support among the German population, and as an organisational weapon of the party to win followers. A crucial part of the Nazi philosophy which served their political ends, was the emphasis on uniting all Germans across class, religious and ideological grounds. The emphasis was on a new and unified 'national community' based on ties of blood and race, with a common world view. Thus Germans were expected to conform to an Aryan (German) norm, with an emphasis on biological purity. The ideal German was to be healthy, active, socially responsible and politically and ideologically reliable.

Jews were portrayed as the common enemy of the German people. Hitler blamed the German Jews for all Germany's ills, including the signing of the Treaty of Versailles, the rise of communism in Europe, and the so-called decline of moral standards. Jews were blamed for the economic problems faced by other Germans. Vicious anti-Semitic propaganda formed the backbone of Nazi statements. 'Racial Science' was developed as the academic legitimisation of anti-Semitism and was introduced in schools and universities. The German 'Master Race', the Aryan people, were destined to save mankind from the 'Jewish-Bolshevik' yoke and racial purity was emphasised as part of achieving this goal.

The German Jewish population

The Jews formed less than 1 per cent of the total German population. It could not be argued that the Jews dominated the cultural or economic life of Germany as the Nazis claimed.

According to the historian William Carr:

Certainly Jews were prominent in the cultural and economic life of Berlin. And in certain professions there was a higher proportion of Jews than Aryans. For example, 17 per cent of all bankers were Jews – a much lower percentage than in the closing years of the nineteenth century; 16 per cent of all lawyers – but rarely was a judge Jewish; and 10 per cent of all doctors and dentists – but few held university or hospital posts. In the clothing and retail trades Jewish influence was pronounced ... Nor were the Jews particularly wealthy, many of them were as poor as their Aryan neighbours, despite a well-earned reputation for hard work.

(From: 'Nazi Policy Against the Jews'. In R Bessel, ed. *Life In The Third Reich*.)

Nazi Policy against the Jews

While vicious physical attacks on Jewish people and businesses were a trade mark of the Nazi supporters, particularly the SA, in the first few years, Hitler was forced to compromise on his policy of isolating Jews from German society because of political and economic factors. Between 1933 and 1935 deliberate SA attacks on Jews were slowed down. In 1933 a coordinated boycott of Jewish shops was limited to one day – partly because of public lack of interest, a fear of foreign reaction, and the danger of damaging the economy even further. In July, the cabinet agreed to continue to offer public contracts to Jewish firms. In spite of the restrictive legislation, Jews continued to live relatively freely in Germany. However, by 1935 the situation had changed drastically. Hitler was now in an untouchable political position. President Hindenburg, who had tried to limit the initial discriminatory legislation, was dead. After 1935, anti-Semitic legislation touched every aspect of Jewish life in Germany. As Hitler expanded German borders into Austria and Eastern Europe, anti-Semitism formed an integral part of Nazi reorganisation of society.

The Nuremberg Laws (1935)

These laws were designed to alienate Jews completely from German society. They included:

- *The Law for the Protection of German Blood and Honour.* This forbade marriages between Jews and other Germans and cancelled all 'mixed marriages' even if they had happened outside Germany. Jews were forbidden to employ German women as domestic servants and were forbidden to display the national flag or national colours.
- *The regulation under Reich Citizenship Law.* This denied German Jews the right of citizenship, removed the right to vote, and forbade Jews from holding any public office.

In 1936, the anti-Jewish campaign slowed down during the Olympic Games held in Berlin that year. All anti-Jewish signs were removed.

By 1938, the government stopped all public contracts with Jewish firms. No Jewish businesspersons were allowed to sell their business. No Jewish doctor, dentist or lawyer could offer services to an Aryan. Jews had to add Israel or Sarah to their names. Jews were forced to carry identity cards and all Jewish passports were stamped with the letter 'J'. The situation was made far worse after the assassination of a German embassy staff member in Paris by a young Jewish man whose parents had been deported from Germany to eastern Poland, where they suffered enormously.

This assassination led to a brutal reaction in Germany. On the so-called *Reichskristallnacht* (Night of Broken Glass), savage attacks were launched on the Jews. At least 91 Jews were murdered, 20 000 thrown into concentration camps, synagogues were burnt down all over Germany, and thousands of shops vandalised. Jews were fined for the destruction of their property by others. Legislation was extended. A 'Jew-free' economy was created: Jews were forbidden to practice trades or to own shops or manage businesses. Jewish businesses had to be sold to Aryan competitors. Furthermore, Jews were excluded from schools, universities, all places of entertainment and sporting facilities. In many cities, Jews were forbidden to enter Aryan areas and particular streets.

In 1938 and 1939, forced mass emigration of the Jews was attempted. In 1934, a branch of the SS had been put in charge of Jewish matters, under Heinrich Himmler. The SS forcibly expelled 45 000 Jews from Austria after the annexation, 78 000 from Germany and 30 000 from Bohemia and Moravia (the old Czechoslovakia) and confiscated their property. A major obstacle for Jews who wanted to leave were the restrictions imposed on Jewish immigration by many governments, including the United Party in South Africa. With the outbreak of war in 1939, persecution of the Jews reached terrible new heights. In countries under German occupation, ghettos (separate urban areas) were designated, Jews were forced to wear yellow stars on their clothing and mass forced removals were carried out. By 1941, mass exterminations had begun. Over 2,5 million Jews were shot. The exact timing of the decision to embark on what became known as the 'Final Solution' is not known. But further emigration was forbidden and an extermination programme was set up under the SS. Transports of Jews to forced labour camps and death camps were begun. By 1945, between 5 and 6,5 million European Jews had perished in a systematic, brutal way.

Policies against other Germans

While the Nazis targeted the German and other European Jews as 'aliens' on the basis of race and religion, other Germans who did not fit the Nazi ideal were also brutally exterminated. These were regarded as aliens in biological terms or because they did not conform to Nazi political and ideological ideals, or because they were regarded as social misfits.

The emphasis on race and racial strength was not simply a Nazi sentiment. Racial theories, the idea of improving the 'race' through the encouragement of selective breeding, was influential in many countries in the 1920s and 1930s. This was known as eugenics. In many cases, policies continued long after the Second World War. The policy involved sterilisation of anyone considered to have mental disabilities and later social defects, such as **habitual criminality**, alcoholism, prostitution and extreme poverty. The first concentration camp was established in March 1933. In Germany from 1934 to 1945, between 320 000 and 350 000 men and women were sterilised under Nazi law. Then this policy was taken further: a 'euthanasia' programme was adopted in 1939, which resulted in the systematic murder of 72 000 mentally sick and handicapped men, women and children in 1941. This policy was then abandoned due to increasing public opposition.

Other groups considered outcasts were also targeted, particularly the gypsies. Over half a million European gypsies were murdered by the Nazis. People who were designated social misfits, such as beggars and tramps, were put into concentration camps, particularly during the Olympic Games of 1936 and then during 1938. Few survived the camps. People who were regarded as sexual deviants were also brutally murdered.

New words

habitual criminal a criminal who continues to commit crimes in spite of repeated punishment

Extension activity

In small groups discuss why particular religious, foreign or ethnic groups in a society are so often targeted as enemies and persecuted. What about groups of particular sexual persuasion?

Anti-Semitism in Nazi Germany

© Bundesarchiv Koblenz

◀ *Source C*

A storm trooper outside a Jewish-owned shop. The placard tells Germans not to shop there (From: N Kelly. *The Second World War.*)

▼ *Source D*

A mathematics problem from a German text-book published in Nazi Germany

> *A bomber on take-off carries 144 bombs, each weighing ten kilos. The aircraft makes for Warsaw, the centre of international Jewry. It bombs the town. On take-off with all bombs on board and a fuel tank containing 1,500 kilos of fuel the aircraft weighed about 8,000 tons. When it returns from the crusade there are still 230 kilos of fuel left. What is the weight of the aircraft when empty?*

(From: N Kelly. *The Second World War.*)

▼ *Source E*

Picture of a Jew from a German school textbook published during the Nazi period (From: N Kelly. *The Second World War.*)

◀ *Source F*

A German classroom. Jewish boys stand embarrassed at the front of the class (From: N Kelly. *The Second World War.*)

▼ Source G
Goebbels blames the Jews

The Jews wanted their war. Now they have it. But what is also coming true for them is the Führer's prophecy which he voiced in his Reichstag speech of 30 January 1939 ...

In this historic conflict every Jew is our enemy, no matter whether he is vegetating in a Polish ghetto, or still supporting his parasitical existence in Berlin or Hamburg, or blowing the war trumpet in New York or Washington. By reason of their birth and race, all Jews are members of an international conspiracy against National Socialist Germany ... There is a difference between humans and humans, just as there is a difference between animals and animals. We know good and bad humans, just as we know good and bad animals. The fact that the Jew still lives among us is no proof that he is one of us, no more than the flea's domestic resilience makes him a domestic animal ...

So superfluous though it might be, let me say once more:

The Jews are our destruction. They provoked and brought about this war ... Every German soldier's death in this war is the Jews' responsibility ... The Jews enjoy the protection of the enemy nations. No further proof is needed of their destructive role among our people.

(From: J Goebbels' article 'The Jews Are to Blame' in *Das Reich, 16 November 1941*. In *Anne Frank in the World*.)

▼ Source H
Nazi cartoon of a Jewish department store
(From: *Anne Frank in the World*.)

▼ Source I
A German explains his father's suicide, from 'After Hitler' by Jürgen Neven-du-Mont, 1968

My father took his life in 1938, on Crystal Night. When my parents met the inflation was at its worst. They got gifts like eggs and a blanket. My father had lost his business and earlier he had lost his leg when he had been run over when he fell from a train. The loss of his leg was one big handicap, the other was that he was a Jew. In 1938 he took his life to save his Aryan wife and his half Jewish children. In his farewell letter he wrote 'This is to save you'... My father died because he was a Jew.

(From: *Anne Frank in the World*.)

Activities ·····························

These activities are based on Sources C to I.
1 From the sources identify and explain various examples of anti-Semitism.
2 Look at the cartoons in Sources E and H. How does the cartoonist show his or her bias and prejudice?
3 Put yourself in the position of the Jewish people in Source F.
   a Describe how you would have felt.
   b What in your view was the purpose of this form of Nazi discrimination?
4 Carefully analyse Gobbels' justification of anti-Semitism in Source G. Discuss the propaganda techniques in use.
5 Carefully read Source I.
   a Do you think that the father's actions were justified?
   b What might you have done in similar circumstances?
···

Nazi treatment of the Christian churches
The main goal of the Nazi state was uniformity and obedience to the party and Hitler. The Christian churches represented a challenge as Christianity bases its belief on a higher spiritual authority. Catholics, in particular, would potentially have had divided loyalties, particularly if the Pope directly opposed Hitler's policies. Initially Hitler, like Mussolini, entered into an agreement with the Pope known as the Concordat. Signed in July 1933, this guaranteed religious freedom for Catholics in Germany and the right of the Church to govern its own activities. Within a few days, Hitler had broken the accord. The Sterilisation Law was enacted and the first steps were taken to dissolve the Catholic Youth League. In the next few years, thousands of Catholic priests and nuns were arrested, Catholic publications were banned and the Gestapo ignored the sanctity of the confessional, spying on those who were making

their confessions. In March 1937, Pope Pius XI issued a papal encyclical (a papal declaration), in which he condemned the Nazi state.

Germany was largely a Protestant country and there were many different branches of Protestant churches. While many Protestants initially supported Hitler, some turned against the regime when it became clear that the Nazis aimed at complete transformation of the Church along party lines.

One group, the German Christians, continued to support Nazism and the establishment of a Reich Church which would unite all Protestants. This group had considerable support from 1933. The constitution of the Reich Church was drawn up in July 1933, and it was ratified by the Reichstag that month. The Nazi Party directly involved itself in the administration of the Church, including the election of the Reich Bishop. Included in its programme were the following points:

- *that Mein Kampf should be placed on the altar, alongside a sword, as 'It ... not only contains the greatest but it embodies the purest and truest ethics for the present and future life of our nation.'*
- *'On the day of its foundation, the Christian Cross must be removed from all churches, cathedrals and chapels ... and it must be superseded by the only unconquerable symbol, the swastika.'*

(From: W Shirer. *The Rise and Fall of the Third Reich.*)

One group, the Confessional Church, led ultimately by Pastor Niemöller, opposed the Nazification of the Protestant churches, the Nazi racial policies and the anti-Christian doctrines of leading Nazis. The Nazis were determined to get rid of any opposition and hundreds of pastors who were members of the Confessional Church were arrested in 1935 and 1937, when Dr Niemöller himself was imprisoned, freed, and then interred in a concentration camp until the end of the war. By 1938, most public opposition from pastors in the Confessional Church had died out.

With many imprisoned, the majority finally bent to Nazi terror. They were ordered by the respected Bishop of Hanover to swear a personal oath of allegiance to Hitler in 1938. Opposition from within the Protestant churches was essentially silenced.

Activities

1 Summarise the Nazis' attitude towards religion.
2 Do you think that the state should be involved in religion?

The role of the courts in Nazi Germany

Under the Weimar Republic, the judiciary, the legal system of courts, magistrates and judges, were independent from the state. They were subject only to the law itself and were safeguarded from arbitrary removal. However, when the Nazis came to power in 1933, it immediately became clear that Germany was no longer a society based on law.

Most judges had been opposed to the Weimar Republic and democracy but now faced the stripping away of their independence. 'Hitler is the law', and 'the law and the will of the Führer are one' were common statements from the party. Two Civil Service laws, in 1933 and 1937, removed not only Jews from holding office but also any court officials thought to be politically suspect. Jurists had to join the League of National Socialist Jurists. The hesitancy of Supreme Court judges to find communists guilty of the Reichstag fire in March 1933 spurred Hitler to set up a new court in which crimes of treason (covering an increasingly broad range) were tried. This People's Court was made up of two professional judges and five others from party officials, the SS and the armed forces. There was no appeal and usually cases were held in camera (behind closed doors). Another court, the Special Court, was established to try ordinary political crimes. The three judges and even the defence lawyers were party members.

Significantly, Hitler had the right to stop criminal proceedings against anyone he did not want prosecuted. This opened the way for the corruption of party officials who could arrange to have charges dropped. The Gestapo were also above the law. The courts were unable to interfere in their actions. It was the right of the Gestapo to arrest and detain anyone without trial in 'protective custody'.

Nazi Germany as a police state

Hitler had given increasing support and power to the SS (the *Schutzstaffel*) under the leadership of Heinrich Himmler. Its main task before 1933 was to break up political meetings and act as Hitler's personal police force. Concentration camps were established in 1933 and political opponents and other dissidents were interned. Hitler appointed Goering as minister of the interior in Prussia, the largest German state. Immediately Goering created an auxiliary police force of 50 000 men mostly drawn from the SA and SS. After the annihilation of the SA in the Night of the Long Knives, the SS became even more powerful.

Goering created the Secret State Police, the Gestapo, as an instrument of terror in Prussia to arrest and murder opponents of the regime. He appointed Heinrich Himmler as deputy chief of the Prussian secret police and the Gestapo began to expand. It had about 3 000 full-time members but relied on hundreds of thousands of ordinary citizens who acted as part-time members, informing the Gestapo of any suspicious activities. It was placed above the law. In June 1936, a unified police was established in Germany, including the former state police. In effect the SS now controlled the police, and that institution also became an instrument of the party. Germany had become a police state.

▼ Source J
Pastor Niemöller (1892–1984)

First they came for the Jews.

I was silent. I was not a Jew.

Then they came for the Communists.

I was silent. I was not a Communist.

Then they came for the Trade Unionists.

I was silent. I was not a Trade Unionist.

Then they came for me.

There was no one left to speak for me.

(From: *Anne Frank in the World*.)

▼ Source K
Albert Einstein (1897–1955)

The world is too dangerous to live in – not because of the people who do evil, but because of the people who sit and let it happen.

(From: *Anne Frank in the World*.)

Activities ....
Discuss the views of both Pastor Niemöller (Source J) and Albert Einstein (Source K) towards individual responsibilities in society.

1 What do these views have in common?
2 Do you agree with their views? Give reasons for your answer.

....

Education in the Third Reich
Education was used by the Nazis as an important form of **indoctrination**. Hitler appointed a senior Nazi and close friend, Bernard Rust, as the minister of science, education and popular culture in 1934. All education institutions were quickly Nazified. Textbooks were rewritten and curricula changed. History was completely rewritten and the 'racial sciences' became an integral part of the curriculum. Teachers were sent for re-education in Nazi doctrine and *Mein Kampf* became the guide for all teaching. All teachers were required by law to join the Nazi-controlled National Socialist Teachers' League, and later all male teachers were required to serve in the SA, the Labour Service or the Hitler Youth. They were required to take an oath of loyalty to Hitler. All education appointments, including universities, were placed under the Nazi minister of education. Jews were forbidden to teach.

Many academics accepted the new order but some rejected the loss of academic freedom or were dismissed. A significant group left Germany, including Albert Einstein and other scientists who played a central role in the development of the atomic bomb in the United States.

New words
indoctrination a process by which individuals or groups are taught to accept particular beliefs without questioning; brainwashing

The youth in Nazi Germany
The Nazis considered the youth a priority, particularly in terms of building a nation committed to Nazism and all for which it stood. Traditionally there had been many youth organisations in Germany, both church-centred and secular. Hitler was determined to replace these with a single youth movement controlled by the Nazis. In 1936, the Catholic Youth League, along with all others, was outlawed. The intention was clear:

> ... *All of the German Youth in the Reich is organised within the Hitler Youth. The German Youth, besides being reared within the family and schools, shall be educated physically, intellectually and morally in the spirit of National Socialism ... through the Hitler Youth.*

(From: W Shirer. *The Rise and Fall of the Third Reich*.)

There were various levels within the youth organisation. The emphasis was on building loyalty to the state, physical training and service on the land or in the military. The aim was to indoctrinate the youth completely through building a new identity across class differences. All wore uniforms which clearly identified them.

Boys between six and ten went through a preparatory stage, at the end of which they took an oath of loyalty to Hitler: 'In the presence of this blood banner, which represents our Führer,

I swear to devote all my energies and my strength to the saviour of our country, Adolf Hitler. I am willing and ready to give up my life for him, so help me God' (Shirer).

At fourteen, boys entered the Hitler Youth in which they were exposed to intensive ideological training and physical exercise. After that, they moved into the army or the Labour Service.

Girls were also exposed to physical training. However, part of their political training was the indoctrination of the role of women in the new society. The Nazi view of the role of women was extremely conservative: they were to be good wives and future mothers of strong, healthy children. At fourteen, they became members of the League of German Maidens. At eighteen, they were required to do a year's service on the farms as agricultural and domestic helpers or to spend a year in domestic service in the towns.

Intense pressure was put on parents to enrol their children. They were threatened with heavy prison sentences or with having their children taken from them and put into orphanages. By late 1938, the Hitler Youth had 7 728 259 members, although some four million children managed to remain outside of the organisation.

▼ Source M

'The German Student Fights for Leader and People.' A propaganda poster for the Hitler Youth, encouraging students to join the Socialist Students' Society

© Peter Newark's Military Pictures

▼ Source L Timetable in a girls' school

Time	Monday	Tuesday	Wednesday	Thursday	Friday	Saturday
8.00–8.45	German	German	German	German	German	German
8.50–9.35	Geography	History	Singing	Geography	History	Singing
9.40–10.25	Race Study	Race Study	Race Study	Ideology	Ideology	Ideology
10.25–11.00	Break, with Sports and Special Announcements					
11.00–12.05	Domestic Science with Mathematics, daily					
12.10–12.55	Eugenics, alternating with Health Biology					

Activities

Look closely at Sources L and M.

1 Why do you think that the Nazis specifically targeted German children and youth for their own purposes?

2 What message is being portrayed in the propaganda poster, Source M?

3 Assess the school curriculum in Source L.
   a What do you think the underlying purpose was in terms of choice of subjects?
   b Is this a form of indoctrination? Explain your answer.

The German economy in the Third Reich

Hitler's increasing popularity in the 1930s had a lot to do with the transformation of the German economy. This also contributed at home and outside the country to the positive image of the Nazis – that they, like Mussolini's Fascists, could get things done. When Hitler came to power in 1932, there were six million unemployed. By 1936, there were less than one million people unemployed. How was this achieved?

Remember that the Nazis were not restricted by any organised opposition or by parliament, in which economic policies could have been debated or challenged. Unlike in the United States, where aspects of Roosevelt's New Deal were challenged by big business in the courts, the Nazi state was able to take control of the economy and direct it as it wanted to. Although the ideological reasons were different, the economic transformation processes in Germany and Russia in the 1930s share some similarities – control of capital, production and labour by the state.

Hitler appointed Dr Schacht, a financial genius, to direct the economic recovery and then Goering, in 1936, to create a German war economy. It was Dr Schacht who provided the financial means to develop a war economy, through printing banknotes and setting up profitable barter deals with many countries.

The first years were spent trying to solve the unemployment crisis by creating massive public works programmes and the stimulation of private enterprise through tax relief incentives. All business and trade associations were brought under the control of the state in February 1934, under the Reich Economic Chamber. All businesses were forced to become members. In 1937, all small businesses and corporations with small capital were forced to dissolve and new ones were forbidden. One-fifth of small businesses disappeared, despite the fact that it was this group which had initially been one of Hitler's strongest supporters.

The ministry of economics devised a Four Year Plan in 1936 and issued thousands of decrees and laws to control businesses. Germany went over to a war economy – the purpose of which was to make Germany self-sufficient in four years: imports were drastically reduced, price and wage controls introduced, and companies established to produce synthetic rubber, textiles, fuel and other products to ensure Germany's economic self-sufficiency. Steel production, essential for the war machine, grew quickly. The war programme, called *Wehrwirtschaft* (defence economy) was carefully planned and deliberately executed. As the chief of the Germany Military Economic Staff stated:

History will know only a few examples of cases where a country has directed, even in peacetime, all its economic forces deliberately and systematically toward the requirements of war, as Germany was compelled to do in the period between the two world wars.

(From: W Shirer. *The Rise and Fall of the Third Reich.*)

The rights of workers were deliberately destroyed. The trade unions were replaced by the state-controlled Nazi Labour Front which included all involved in the economy – all workers, members of the professions and employers. All officials had to be members of the party. Its stated aim was not to protect the interests of the workers but 'to create a true

▼ **Source N** Economic planning and reality.
Figures from the Four Year Plan, launched in 1936
(From: J Laver. *Nazi Germany 1933–1945.*)

Commodity	Output (thousand tons)			Plan target
	1936	1938	1942	
Oil	1,790	2,340	6,260	13,830
Aluminium	98	166	260	273
Buna rubber	0,7	5	96	120
Nitrogen	770	914	930	1,040
Explosives	18	45	300	323
Powder	20	26	150	217
Steel	19,216	22,656	20,480	24,000
Iron ore	2,255	3,360	4,137	5,549
Brown coal	161,382	194,985	245,918	240,500
Hard coal	158,400	186,186	166,059	213,000

social and productive community of all Germans. Its task is to see that every individual should be able ... to perform the maximum of work' (Shirer, 327).

While unemployment figures declined, wage restrictions were imposed and, in reality, the real wages of workers declined. Taxes were increased and workers, like everyone else, were expected to make contributions to the party funds. Various government decrees imposed severe restrictions on the freedom of movement of workers from one job to another. A 'workbook' was introduced in 1935 which kept a record of a worker's skills and employment. In 1938, labour conscription was introduced whereby a worker could be sent anywhere by the state. Strikes had of course been forbidden very early under Nazi rule, and later workers could be fined or imprisoned if they were absent from work without special cause.

The agricultural sector played a very significant role in the Nazi plan. It was necessary to make Germany entirely self-sufficient in food. Politically, the Nazis had relied on the support of the German peasants and small farmers who had suffered badly during the Great Depression. Nazi promises of land reform did not materialise as there was too much political risk if they attempted land redistribution by breaking up the estates of the traditional wealthy land owning class, but their economic programme went some way towards relieving the poverty of the small farmers by increasing the prices of some agricultural products. As in industry, and more successfully, the state attempted to take control of all aspects of agricultural production, marketing and processing. Laws were passed forbidding the division or sale of small farms, tying farmers to the land, and agricultural workers were forbidden to leave the land and look for work in the cities. Despite all these measures the state was never able to attain its goals of complete self-sufficiency in food production – the conquest of other countries and the forced requisitioning of agricultural products for German needs enabled them to survive the war years.

Activities . . . .
Consider the table in Source N. Did the Nazis achieve their economic production goals? Justify your answer with specific examples.

. . . .

How did the Nazis win over business and labour?
The following measures were instituted with regard to business and labour:
- Businessmen made substantial profits, particularly those owning heavy industry.

- There were no strikes, and wage restrictions were imposed.
- There was no attempt to nationalise industry in spite of heavy bureaucratic attempts to gear production to meet state needs.
- A Nazi state organisation called Kraft durch Freude (Strength through Joy) was set up, which controlled all social, sport and recreational groups in Germany. It organised very cheap holidays and cruises for workers and cheap tickets for cultural events. Over one million workers belonged to this organisation, and believed that they benefited directly, although the organisation was mainly funded by the workers themselves through membership fees.
- The Nazi propaganda machine emphasised German nationalism and patriotism. People were persuaded to put aside their individual interests and instead to work towards the rebuilding of Germany.

Activities . . . .
Consider the factors above and decide which group would benefit from them.

. . . .

The role of propaganda in Nazi Germany
The Nazi Party would not have been able to transform the society to the extent that it did by the use of terror alone. While individual rights were completely eroded, the Nazis had to offer material and psychological compensations to replace them. Effective propaganda was one of the main weapons used by the Nazis to win and maintain the support of the German people. As you saw in Chapter 2, propaganda is publicity that is always biased and is sometimes untruthful, and it is used to make people think in a certain way about something. Nazi Germany is regarded as the first modern state to use available technological means to spread its doctrines to the people. Dr Goebbels was appointed minister of propaganda and a Reich Chamber of Culture was established in 1933. Its stated purpose was as follows:

In order to pursue a policy of German culture, it is necessary to gather together the creative artists in all spheres into a unified organisation under the leadership of the Reich. The Reich must not only determine the lines of progress, mental and spiritual, but also lead and organize the professions.

(From: W Shirer. *The Rise and Fall of the Third Reich*.)

Propaganda took on many forms including:

- the use of all forms of the media – newspapers, film and the radio in particular. Newspaper editors were told by Goebbel's office what news to print and the tone of editorials. The film industry was forced to follow the directives of the Ministry and radio was directly owned by the state, giving the Nazis complete control.
- massive rallies with a militaristic atmosphere deliberately created;
- censorship, including burning, of any written texts that were considered 'un-German';
- rewriting school and university textbooks;
- modern art works considered 'un-German' were removed from museums.

The consequences of these actions on German society were far-reaching. William Shirer was an American newspaper reporter living in Germany in the 1930s, and on pages 308–9 in his book *The Rise and Fall of the Third Reich* he recorded the observations in Source O about the effect of propaganda on the German people.

▼ *Source O*

Speech by Albert Speer on the role of propaganda in Nazi Germany (at his trial at Nuremberg)

Hitler's dictatorship differed in one fundamental point from all its predecessors in history. His was the first dictatorship in the present period of modern technical develop-

◀ 'All Germany hears the Führer': Adolf Hitler broadcast widely to the German people. Poster from 1936

ment, a dictatorship which made complete use of all technical means in a perfect manner for the domination of its own country.

Through technical devices like the radio and the loudspeaker, eighty million people were deprived of independent thought. It was thereby possible to subject them to the will of one man ...

▼ Source P
The radio as propaganda

I consider radio to be the most modern and the most crucial instrument that exists for influencing the masses. I also believe – one should not say that out loud – that radio will, in the end, replace the press ...

First principle: At all costs avoid being boring. I put that before everything ... You must help to bring forth a nationalist art and culture which is truly appropriate to the pace of modern life and to the mood of the times ... You must use your imagination, an imagination which is based on sure foundations and which employs all means and methods to bring to the ears of the masses the new attitude in a way which is modern, up-to-date, interesting, and appealing; interesting, instructive but not schoolmasterish.

(From instructions by Goebbels to the controllers of German radio, 25 March 1933.)

Women in the Nazi State
As discussed elsewhere, the Nazi Party and the other Fascist parties of Europe projected a strongly masculine image of strength, action and force underpinned by militarism. German society was traditionally deeply patriarchal where the traditional role of women as mothers, wives and homemakers was embedded. As in other countries in the 1920s and 1930s, and again after the Second World War, women were encouraged by all means of propaganda to remain in the home. It was men who needed jobs in the workplace, as according to patriarchal views, men are the breadwinners and heads of families. If unemployment was to be eradicated, it was men who should be given jobs. Instead, women were encouraged to bear as many Aryan children as possible and the more children they had, the more patriotic they were deemed to be.

▼ Source Q
From a report to the Ministry of Justice, 1944

The parents of girls enrolled in the German Girls' League have filed a complaint with the wardship court at Habel-Brandenburg concerning leaders of the League who have intimated to their daughters that they should bear illegitimate children; these leaders have pointed out that in view of the prevailing shortage of men, not every girl could expect to get a husband in future, and that the girls should at least fulfil their task as German women and donate a child to the Führer.

▼ Source R
Hitler speaking on 26 January 1942

I detest women who dabble in politics. And if their dabbling extends to military matters, it becomes utterly unendurable. In no local section of the Party has a woman ever had the right to hold even the smallest post. It has therefore often been said that we were a party of misogynists, who regarded a woman only as a machine for making children, or else as a plaything. That's far from being the case. I attached a lot of importance to women in the field of the training of youth, and that of good works ... Everything that entails combat is exclusively men's business. There are so many other fields in which one must rely upon women. Organising a house, for example.

(From: *Hitler's Table-Talk*.)

Activities
Complete these activities in a small group.
1 Analyse Source O, the speech by Speer (the Nazi minister for armaments and war production), in order to determine his opinion of the consequences of propaganda used by the Nazis.
2 Summarise the Nazi attitude to women and their role in society expressed in Sources Q and R.

Extension activity
Hold a class discussion in which you talk about the role of women in modern society compared to the Nazi perception of the role of women.

Unit 6 The aggressive foreign policies of Germany, Italy and Japan

Unit outcomes

- Assess to what extent Hitler's ambitions and actions played a part in causing the war.
- Assess to what extent the foreign policies of Britain and France, known as appeasement, contributed to the outbreak of the war.
- Analyse how the weakness and inaction of the League of Nations can be seen as a factor.
- Assess the way in which domestic policies and circumstances influenced foreign policies, particularly during the years of economic crisis in the 1930s.

Introduction

The causes of the Second World War require an analysis of a number of factors that played a part in bringing the world to a state of war in 1939. After a period of more than 50 years after the end of the war, we are perhaps in a better position to understand more fully why the war broke out and to avoid simplistic explanations. It is very important to move beyond a simple recall of those events and try to draw connections between them, see patterns, and analyse a number of factors, including causes and consequences. In this way, we will reach a fuller understanding of why the war broke out.

◀ The new frontiers after World War One

KEY
- Former German territory
- Extent of Austro-Hungarian Empire
- Former Russian territory
- Western Thrace to Greece from Bulgaria
- Frontiers in dispute

FINLAND
ESTONIA
LATVIA
DENMARK
LITHUANIA
E. PRUSSIA
GERMANY
POLAND
CZECHOSLOVAKIA
AUSTRIA
HUNGARY
TRANSYLVANIA
TRENTINO
ROMANIA
YUGOSLAVIA
ITALY
BULGARIA
ALBANIA
GREECE

0   200   400 km

Relationships between the major powers in the 1920s

The First World War had a profound effect on the world – not only in terms of the loss of life and material devastation, but also on people's attitude to war as a means of resolving international conflict. The League of Nations, which was formed in 1920, represented the principle of collective security. The assumption was that all governments and nations were committed to preserving the peace. However, while there was some cooperation, there were also tensions and national interests which worked against the sense of collective security. Further, when conflicts arose, governments and the peoples they represented turned away from war as a solution, largely as a result of the lasting effects of the First World War.

There were some attempts at encouraging international cooperation during the 1920s. In Europe, the hostility and desire for revenge felt by the French towards Germany had resulted in the French occupation of the Ruhr industrial area in 1923 when Germany was unable to meet the reparations repayments. This in turn caused a German passive resistance campaign. With a change in the government in France a new policy was adopted which was far more conciliatory, and in Germany Gustav Stresemann shaped a foreign policy that still sought to pursue German grievances, but which aimed at greater cooperation.

The Dawes Plan

This new cooperative attitude was evident in the adoption by France, Britain and Germany of the Dawes Plan, which spread German reparations repayments over a longer period of time. German economic recovery was to be boosted by huge loans, largely funded by American money.

The Treaty of Locarno

The Dawes Plan led in turn to closer cooperation. In 1925 Germany signed the Treaty of Locarno with France, Britain, Belgium and Italy. This treaty formally recognised German acceptance of the changes made in the Treaty of Versailles to its western borders, thereby guaranteeing its acceptance of the loss of Alsace-Lorraine to France and smaller territories to Belgium.

However, no guarantees were given by Germany as far as its former eastern territories were concerned. Germans would not accept the permanent loss of that land, particularly to Poland. Significantly, Britain and France chose to support the agreement over the western boundaries, but not in the east. This was essentially a European agreement, rather than an international one. The mood of conciliation went further with the acceptance of Germany as a member of the League of Nations in 1926. This meant that of the major powers, the United States and the Soviet Union still remained outside the League.

Activities . . . .

1 Briefly summarise how the attitude of the major powers changed towards Germany between 1919 and 1926.
2 Why do you think there was this change in attitude?

. . . .

International cooperation and disarmament efforts

The period of growing optimism in international cooperation in the 1920s was further enhanced by the signing of the Pact of Paris or Kellogg-Briand Pact in 1929 by fifteen nations including the United States. This agreement was an effort by the major powers to outlaw war as a means of solving conflict.

There were also efforts to achieve one of the main goals of the League – that of general world disarmament, particularly after Germany had been forced to disarm under the Treaty of Versailles. These efforts proved to be extremely difficult: it was very hard to match up individual nations' interest in their own security with a sense of collective responsibility in the case of some conflict erupting. The anti-war mood of the people made it very difficult for a government to commit its troops to some foreign war in the name of international security. The French, in particular, sensitive to their own security needs against Germany, refused to disarm unless they were given firm guarantees of assistance from Britain if the need arose. The League's Disarmament Commission presented a compromise draft statement of principles in 1930 which did little to promote real disarmament. The World Disarmament Conference was held in 1932. By this time, there was little chance of any real agreement on disarmament. The world was facing an economic crisis, countries looked after their own interests first and aggressive, militaristic groups began to challenge the status quo, particularly in Italy, Japan and Germany.

International relations in the 1930s

International relations in the 1930s were marked, on the one hand, by the rise of aggressive nationalist governments bent on increasing the power of their countries and, on the other hand, by the conciliatory foreign policies of those countries which may have prevented them. The League of Nations as a collective force played less and less of a role through the 1930s, as individual countries began to put their own interests first. Historians have long debated the extent to which the failure of collective security and the policy of appeasement adopted by individual countries towards aggressors contributed to the outbreak of the Second World War in 1939. What is undisputed is the guilt of those powers that chose aggressive foreign policies as a means of achieving their goals.

Did Hitler plan for war from the beginning?

▼ Source A

Herman Rauschning, one of the early Nazi leaders, wrote this fragment of a conversation with Hitler early in 1934

> 'Do you seriously intend to fight the West?' I asked.
>
> He stopped and looked at me.
>
> 'What else do you think we're arming for?' he retorted ... 'We must proceed step by step, so that no one will impede our advance. How to do this I don't yet know. But that it will be done is guaranteed by Britain's lack of firmness and France's internal disunity.'

▼ Source B

Speech in the Reichstag (German Parliament) by Adolf Hitler, 7 March 1936

> We proclaim now more than ever before our wish to further the cause of understanding between the nations of Europe ... In Europe we have no territorial claims to put forward.

Activities

Read Sources A and B to reach a conclusion about whether Hitler planned war from the beginning. Write a paragraph justifying your answer.

Hitler's ambitions

Long before the Nazis came to power, their goals for Germany had been clearly set out in their 25-point party programme in 1920. Included in the points were the following:

- 'We demand the union of all Germans to form

a Greater Germany on the basis of the right of the self-determination enjoyed by all nations.'
- 'We demand the equality of rights for the German people in its [sic] dealings with other nations, and the abolition of the peace treaties of Versailles and St. Germain'
- 'We demand land and territory for the nourishment of our people and for the settlement of our superfluous population.'

In *Mein Kampf* Hitler expressed his hatred of the Treaty of Versailles and his ambitions for Germany were clearly set out. What is still debated is not what Hitler wanted to do, but whether he deliberately planned for war or whether he was an opportunist who gambled with the other powers' reactions and in the end, stumbled into a war for which he was not sufficiently prepared.

Hitler's efforts to break 'the shackles of Versailles'

When Hitler came to power in 1933, Germany was fairly tightly bound by the restrictions of Versailles. Unification with Austria was forbidden, there were severe restrictions on German armaments and none of the land taken away at Versailles had been recovered. At the same time, however, Germany was no longer isolated – it was a major member of the League of Nations although the French and, to some extent, the Italians, still viewed Germany with some suspicion. The British tended to think that the Treaty of Versailles had been too harsh and were prepared to accommodate the Germans.

Hitler instead chose to go it alone. In 1933, Germany walked out of the Disarmament Conference, after a French refusal to allow them to have equality of armaments. Hitler could legitimately claim that as the other powers refused to disarm, Germany was being victimised. Soon after, he withdrew Germany from the League of Nations. This meant that Germany was no longer bound by the principles of the League and could follow a foreign policy without interference.

During his first two years in power, Hitler secretly speeded up the rearmament of Germany, a process he had started in the 1920s. During 1934, the three branches of the armed forces – the army, navy and airforce – were ordered to begin rebuilding as quickly as possible in secret. Armament manufacturers also began production. Researchers began developing synthetic oil, gasoline and rubber.

Closer alliances with any other European powers at this stage were delayed when

Austrian Nazis assassinated the Austrian Chancellor Dr Dolfuss in July 1934. Although the new Austrian Chancellor Dr Schuschnigg restored order, there was a considerable outcry from the British and French governments. Mussolini went so far as to mass troops on the Austro-Italian border as a warning against a possible German invasion of Austria. Hitler protested his innocence, but the event served as an indication of possible hostile reaction in the future to any other attempts at revision of the terms of Versailles. The British, French and Italians held discussions forming a vague joint strategy to counteract any future attempt by Germany to revise Versailles, but this was not to last for long.

Reincorporation of the Saar, 1935

Hitler continued with his plans. In January 1935, the German population of the Saar region, use of which had been given to France for fifteen years, voted overwhelmingly in a referendum for re-inclusion in Germany. Although provision was made for this in the Treaty of Versailles, the Nazi propaganda machine portrayed it as a huge victory.

Open rearmament, 1935

By March 1935, Hitler felt confident enough to announce that Germany had a military airforce, something that was widely known anyway. He was testing the reaction of the British and French. France immediately announced that military service would be extended. This gave Hitler the diplomatic excuse he wanted. On 9 March 1935, he announced that he was introducing military conscription in order to bring the German army up to 550 000 men. But this, he argued, was only in response to the implied threats of Germany's neighbours. Goebbels, the minister of propaganda, immediately organised a triumphant parade that symbolised the end of Versailles and restored German pride and honour. At the same time, the League of Nations set up a committee to deal with any future actions but took no practical steps to stop Germany. The major European powers failed to come up with any united challenge, particularly as the British were not prepared to take any action. Hitler used a **diplomatic ploy** to soften any adverse foreign reaction by tying German rearmament to promises of peace, renouncing all claims to Alsace-Lorraine and guaranteeing the territorial integrity of Poland and Austria. This was to be a favoured tactic in the future which seemed to get the results he wanted.

With their security beginning to crumble again, in May 1935 the French signed mutual assistance agreements with the Soviet Union and Czechoslovakia in the event of any attack from Germany.

New words

diplomatic involving diplomacy – the process of communication between foreign countries
ploy a clever manoeuvre to gain advantage

The Anglo-German Naval Agreement 1935

Hitler was now in a position to break open any close cooperation between the major powers which may have opposed him. He presented Britain with a non-negotiable offer to rebuild the German navy to within 35 per cent of the British navy. The British not only accepted the offer but agreed to parity (equal numbers) of submarines. The agreement was signed on 18 June 1935.

This agreement was highly significant in terms of the future of peace in Europe. Not only had Hitler ensured the formal acceptance of rearmament by a major power, but he had also destroyed the possibility of a potentially harmful alliance against Germany. The French and Italians were horrified at Britain's decision. The Russians, having been admitted to the League in 1934, were equally upset. The principle of collective security was overthrown. One of the major forces of the League, Britain, had collaborated in the destruction of one of the main clauses of the Treaty of Versailles in order to ensure its own continued naval dominance.

The Italian invasion of Abyssinia 1935–36

The possibility of further European collective security collapsed with the Italian invasion of Abyssinia (now Ethiopia) in October 1935. While Britain was prepared to concede to Hitler's demands, Italian aggression was widely condemned. Mussolini had started a policy of Italian expansion, demanding an empire such as that still owned by Britain and France. After a particularly brutal campaign of bombing, destruction and the use of poison gas, the Italians entered Addis Ababa and formally annexed Abyssinia on 9 May 1936.

International reaction

The members of the League of Nations did condemn the aggression of one of its leading members, and took the step of imposing economic sanctions on Italy, while attempting to mediate. However, the measure was insufficient. The only effective steps would have been to close the Suez Canal to Italian shipping and to impose an oil embargo on Italy, but the British and the French were reluctant to support this. Issues of European security overrode international interests or those of the Abyssinian people. Neither power wanted to drive Mussolini into Hitler's arms through oil sanctions, or to run the risk of Italian aggression against them.

The failure of the League and its principle of collective security, largely as a result of the refusal of Britain and France to support effective actions, was very significant. The status of the League was destroyed as a peace-keeping instrument. Another European power had defied the League. Italy showed further contempt when it withdrew from the League in December 1937. Equally significant was the effect on Hitler. Not only was Italy likely to be open to a closer relationship, but the ineffectual response of Britain and France encouraged Hitler in his ambitions.

Activities ....
1 What do you understand by the term 'collective security'?
2 Why was the League of Nations unable to effectively pursue a policy of collective security? Consider the following factors in answering this question:
   a membership of the League particularly in the 1930s;
   b disunity between member states;
   c economic conditions.

....

The remilitarisation of the Rhineland 1936

Because he had been secretly assured of Mussolini's neutrality if he took any actions to break the Locarno Treaty, Hitler was encouraged to strengthen Germany's western frontier with France. In spite of his own worries and the concerns of the German generals Hitler ordered the military occupation of the Rhineland, which was completely forbidden by the Treaty of Versailles. The troops were moved into the region on 7 March 1936. Hitler was unsure of the reaction of the French and the British, and the German generals were prepared to withdraw the troops at the first sign of resistance. This action has been described as 'perhaps the biggest gamble of his career' (D Thomson. *Europe Since Napoleon*).

The consequences of the reoccupation were significant. First, it strengthened Germany's military position greatly. It put German troops right on the border with France, and enabled the Germans to build a line of strong fortifications to protect Germany from possible French attack. Significantly, it cut France off from its eastern dependants, particularly Czechoslovakia, which was now made much more vulnerable. It was an outright rejection of the Versailles and the Locarno treaties.

Secondly, Hitler's prestige at home was greatly enhanced and he silenced his more cautious military critics. In a referendum late that month 98,8 per cent of the German electorate voted in his favour.

Thirdly, it exposed the real differences in approach towards Germany between Britain and France. While the French requested British support for a countermove, the British believed that this action did not threaten peace. Their inaction encouraged Hitler and exposed their unreliability to the now vulnerable countries of eastern Europe. Western security was now under threat. The Belgium government, who had signed the Locarno Treaty now backed down from its commitment to European security and declared itself neutral.

Activities ....
Consider the major events in Europe between 1933 and 1936.
1 Draw a timeline showing the aggressive actions by Mussolini and Hitler.
2 Draw two columns. In the first write down the major events in their chronological order. In the second, carefully draw up a list of the consequences or effects of each action.

....

Hitler's alliances

One of the biggest obstacles facing Hitler in his earlier years was the relative isolation of Germany and the seemingly close ties between the major European powers. This was shown in the concerted reaction against him in 1934. By 1936, the situation had changed. Mussolini was increasingly alienated from the other European powers. Japan had withdrawn from the League over the refusal to sanction its conquest of the Chinese territory Manchuria. Hitler had made some overtures to Mussolini, but his opportunity for establishing closer ties came with the outbreak of the Spanish civil war in 1936. Both Mussolini and Hitler offered support to the Fascist leader, General Franco. Mussolini sent 70 000 troops while Hitler's support was essentially restricted to advisers, technicians and some military hardware.

While Hitler continued to hope for stronger ties with Britain, he actively pursued Mussolini. This paid off in the signing of the October Protocol in 1936, which was a secret document between the two countries outlining joint foreign policy. This agreement became known as the Rome-Berlin Axis – a phrase first coined by Mussolini when he said that the two countries were becoming 'an axis around which all those European states which are animated by a desire for collaboration and peace may work together'.

In 1937, the links between the two Fascist leaders were cemented when Hitler invited Mussolini to Berlin. There Mussolini enjoyed a huge welcome with parades involving a million spectators and displays of German military might. He returned to Italy very impressed. Hitler was more assured of Mussolini's neutrality if Hitler made any moves on Austria.

Hitler also looked for links with Japan. On 25 November 1936, an Anti-Comintern Pact was signed between Japan and Germany. It was presented as a common front against 'Communist world conspiracy'. However, it did contain a secret clause which bound the new allies more closely together. They agreed that neither would sign a treaty with the Soviet Union and that they would come to each other's aid if attacked by Russia. The Pact was soon joined by Mussolini.

What had Hitler achieved by the end of 1936?

By the end of 1936, Hitler had achieved most of his initial plans. He had overturned many of the hated clauses of the Treaty of Versailles, including rearmament and reoccupation of the Rhineland. He had formed closer ties with countries equally concerned with aggressive expansionism. He had exposed the divisions between the Western powers and the ineffectiveness of the League of Nations. For those historians who claim that Hitler was intent on war from the start, Hitler's actions between 1933 and 1936 can be interpreted as a deliberate preparation for war. Others argue that Hitler took advantage of each opportunity that arose to further his ambitions for Germany and that he did not have a master plan.

Hitler's actions 1938–39

In the years 1938 and 1939, Hitler started on a bolder course of aggressive action in his quest to create a Greater Germany.

The Anschluss with Austria (unification)

On 12 and 13 March 1938, Hitler ordered the invasion of Austria in his efforts to unite all Germans. This aim had been explicitly stated on the first page of *Mein Kampf*. In 1936 Hitler and the Austrian Chancellor had met and reached an agreement whereby Austria would follow a friendly policy towards Germany, while Hitler promised to respect the independence of Austria. In January 1938, there had been an attempted *coup d'état* by Austrian Nazis. The Austrian state banned the party. Hitler ordered Dr Schuschnigg to Germany and put a number of ultimatums to him. Included in these was the order to appoint the Austrian Nazi leader Seyss-Inquart to the cabinet position of minister of public security and to unban the Nazi Party. This was equivalent to interference in the political independence of Austria. Dr Schuschnigg attempted to bypass Hitler by calling for a referendum on the issue of Austrian independence. Hitler ordered the Nazi Party in Germany to create a situation of instability which would give Hitler the excuse to move into Austria. Schuschnigg now backed down and handed over the chancellorship to Seyss-Inquart. The new Nazi chancellor immediately called for assistance from Germany to restore law and order and the German troops marched in.

This improved Hitler's position greatly. He added seven million German-speaking Austrians to Germany, which acquired the Austrian army, mines, industries and the Austrian National Bank. Anschluss also benefited Germany strategically. Germany now had direct access to Italy, Hungary and Yugoslavia, and it surrounded Czechoslovakia on three sides. Hitler's prestige was again greatly enhanced inside Germany and abroad. A plebiscite (referendum) was held in Austria and Germany on the issue of Anschluss – 99,73 per cent of Austrians and 99,03 per cent of Germans voted in favour of Hitler's coup.

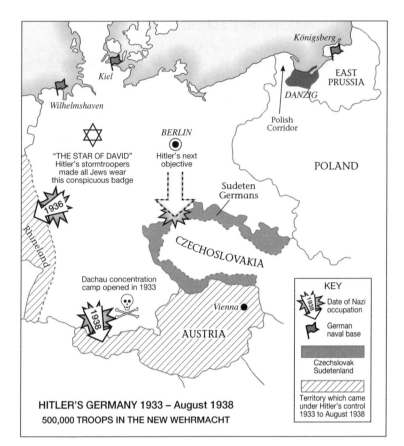

◀ **Source C**
Hitler's Germany 1933–
August 1938
(Adapted from: *Map
History of the Modern
World.*)

Königsberg

Kiel

EAST
PRUSSIA

Wilhelmshaven

DANZIG

Polish
Corridor

BERLIN
◉
Hitler's next
objective

POLAND

"THE STAR OF DAVID"
Hitler's stormtroopers
made all Jews wear
this conspicuous badge

Sudeten
Germans

1936

Rhineland

CZECHOSLOVAKIA

Dachau concentration
camp opened in 1933

Vienna ●

1938

AUSTRIA

KEY

1938 Date of Nazi
occupation

German
naval base

Czechslovak
Sudetenland

Territory which came
under Hitler's control
1933 to August 1938

HITLER'S GERMANY 1933 – August 1938

500,000 TROOPS IN THE NEW WEHRMACHT

Activities ....

1 What are the different events depicted in Source C?
2 Why do you think Hitler was able to form alliances
   with countries like Italy and Japan?
3 Account for the lack of reaction on the part of countries like Britain and France to Germany's actions.

The reaction of the other powers

Unit outcomes

- Understand the reaction of the major powers to Hitler's openly defiant and aggressive actions.
- Discuss the differences between Hitler's stated intentions and his actual policy towards Czechoslovakia.
- Assess the value of public opinion polls.

Introduction

It is difficult with hindsight to understand the policies followed by the European powers in the late 1930s towards Hitler and the other aggressors. Hitler had invaded the Rhineland, Mussolini Abyssinia, and the Japanese Manchuria in 1932 and mainland China in 1937. Some historians argue that the Western powers were increasingly reluctant to be drawn into a conflict in the Far East while the situation in Europe deteriorated rapidly in 1938 and 1939. Added to this was the failure of the United States, a major power in the Pacific region, to take any active steps to stop Japanese aggression. The colonial powers in the region, Britain and France, did not want to be drawn in themselves. All countries stopped short of sanctions against Japan until it was clear that their own colonial possessions were in jeopardy.

At the same time, the western European powers followed a seemingly contradictory policy in Europe. On the one hand, both Britain and France by 1937 had started large programmes of rearmament. The British navy and airforce were modernised and expanded. Once the Conservative government took over in 1937, with Neville Chamberlain as prime minister, rearmament was speeded up further. France, too, began to strengthen her defences, concentrating on a line of heavily armed fortifications on the border with Germany. This strategy was considered out of date even at the time, because it was not suited to modern mobile land and air warfare.

But, on the other hand, Britain in particular adopted a policy of appeasement towards Hitler and to some extent Mussolini. Neville Chamberlain was regarded as its main supporter, but many conservatives in Britain believed it was the only path to follow. Indeed, many openly supported Hitler, and a Fascist Party was formed under Oswald Moseley. It is clear that the policy of appeasement – giving in to reasonable demands in the desire to secure lasting peace – was supported by the British electorate for much of this period. The underlying assumption was that the Treaty of Versailles had been unjust, that the dictators had legitimate and limited grievances, and that when these were resolved future peace would be ensured.

But the implications for international diplomacy were significant. Appeasement was in conflict with the doctrine of collective security. It completely undermined the Treaty of Versailles and the League of Nations. It meant in practical terms that if Britain actively pursued this policy, there was little likelihood of France acting on its own against Germany, to support its vulnerable allies in eastern Europe.

▼ Source A
For appeasement: British Parliamentary Debates, 9 March 1936

> There is, I am thankful to say, no reason to suppose that the present German action implies a threat of hostilities. The German government speak of their 'unchangeable longing for a real pacification of Europe' and express a willingness to conclude a non-aggression pact with France and Belgium.

▼ Source B
Neville Chamberlain, speaking in Kettering on 2 July 1938

> When I think of those four terrible years and I think of the 7 million young men who were cut off in their prime, the 13 million who were maimed and mutilated, the misery and the suffering of the mothers and fathers, the sons and daughters of those who were killed, and the wounded, then I am bound to say ... in war ... there are no winners, but all are losers. It is those thoughts which have made me ... strain every nerve to avoid a repetition of the Great War in Europe.

▼ Source C

Lloyd George, former British prime minister, after a visit to Hitler's Germany in 1936

He has achieved a marvellous change in the spirit of the people, in their attitude to each other and in their economic and social outlook. He is also securing them against the constant dread of starvation, which is one of the worst memories of the last years of war and the first years of peace.

Activities ·······························

1 Do you have any reasons to doubt the German government's 'longing for a real pacification of Europe' in Source A?
2 What are the two different perspectives being expressed in Sources B and C?
3 How can you account for the differences?

·······························

The Czechoslovakian crisis 1938–39

Czechoslovakia was a democratic republic created by the Treaty of Versailles. The country was populated by groups of Czechs and Slovaks as well as a number of minority groups such as Germans, Magyars, Ruthenes and Slavs. An atmosphere of tension could be felt in the country by the late 1930s. Each of the minority groups was wanting self-government, the strongest of them being the Germans. The Sudetenland, an area of Czechoslovakia which bordered on Germany, was mainly inhabited by people of German descent. By 1938 there were approximately 3,5 million Germans in the area. The nationalist hopes of this group of Germans, as well as other minority groups, were strongly encouraged by the Czechoslovakian Nazi Party which had risen to prominence during the 1920s under the leadership of Konrad Henlein. Indeed, the major aim of the Nazi Party in Czechoslovakia was to obtain self-government and self-determination for the German people in the Sudetenland. Henlein was strongly influenced by the Nazi leadership within Germany itself to create a situation whereby the demands of the party would increase the tension in Czechoslovakia, thereby enabling Hitler to implement his long-term plan to occupy the republic.

By 1938 each of the minority groups living in Czechoslovakia was involved in an attempt at self-determination. This was the ideal climate for Hitler to start making the demands which would help in the achievement of his long-term goals. German troops stationed in Austria were massed along the Czechoslovakian border. An intense propaganda campaign was started by the Nazi Party to convince the world that these measures had been taken with the sole purpose of ensuring justice for the German minority in Czechoslovakia. The Czechoslovakian government felt threatened by these strategic actions and ordered the mobilisation of national troops. The government was allied with the French and Russian governments. They thought that these two nations would come to the aid of Czechoslovakia and protect the nation from Nazi-directed German aggression. However, this reliance on the allies had little basis as both France and Russia did not want to antagonise Germany who, after unification with Austria and intensive military preparations, appeared to be a formidable enemy.

Those in power in Great Britain, as represented by Neville Chamberlain, were uneasy with the prospect of war in central Europe. Chamberlain was determined to prevent the outbreak of another European war and his policy of appeasement reinforced this aim. He believed in the power of negotiation and felt that the appeasement of Hitler would result in lasting peace for Europe which Hitler would feel compelled not to break.

On 1 September 1938, Chamberlain went to Berchtesgaden where Hitler presented him with a demand for the secession (handing over) of the Sudetenland to Germany. Chamberlain returned to Britain to consult with his cabinet and the French leadership over these demands and to determine a course of action for Britain and France. The result was an agreement between Great Britain and France which allowed all areas in Czechoslovakia with populations composed of more than half German-speaking residents to be ceded to Germany. Czechoslovakia's new frontiers would receive an international guarantee against any further aggression or moves toward occupation. With no other viable alternatives, the Czechoslovakian government felt compelled to accept the Anglo-French agreement. France and Russia had earlier undertaken a commitment to protect Czechoslovakia and the other eastern states from any German aggression, but because the British were pursuing such a strong appeasement line it was virtually impossible for the French to act alone or with the Russians.

Chamberlain returned to Germany on 22

September to Bad Godesberg on the Rhine, where he presented Hitler with the terms of the agreement. Hitler responded with further demands for the immediate secession of all German areas in Czechoslovakia and the Sudetenland by 1 October 1938. This ultimatum was to take effect in a little more than a week after Chamberlain's return to Germany. For Czechoslovakia to comply with these demands was impossible as there had not been sufficient time to position troops against further German aggression or to withdraw Czechoslovakians from the areas to be ceded. War seemed inevitable as Czechoslovakia and France mobilised their troops while the British navy and airforce were prepared for the possibility of war.

The Munich Conference

A meeting was hastily arranged in Munich by Chamberlain and Mussolini between the four European senior powers: Britain, France, Germany and Italy, in an attempt to find a peaceful solution to the crisis. This was the stated aim of the delegates but Hitler's actions thereafter seemed to indicate that his goals were anything but peaceful. The conference was attended by Chamberlain, Daladie, Hitler and Mussolini. Both Czechoslovakia and its ally, Russia, were excluded from the conference. Stalin was threatened by this exclusion, fearing a conspiracy to enforce German domination of Europe. The Munich agreement provided for the immediate transfer to Germany of all predominantly German areas in

◀ Source D
Czechoslovakia in 1938

Activities ....
Examine Source D, the detailed map of Czechoslovakia.
1 Hold a group discussion to help you list as many reasons as you can think of why Hitler wished to expand into Czechoslovakian territory.
2 How would Czechoslovakia be affected by the loss of the Sudetenland? Give examples to support your answer.
....

Czechoslovakia and for referendums to be held in other areas to determine the majority preference for government. An international commission was established to decide the borders of the two nations. Britain and France offered a guarantee to Czechoslovakia that its new frontiers would not be subjected to further German aggression. In October 1938 German troops marched to occupy the Sudetenland and all predominantly German areas.

This occupation of Czechoslovakian land was a substantial tactical victory for Hitler. Germany had gained Czechoslovakian natural defences through the extension of its frontiers, land that was rich in minerals and industrial activity, as well as approximately one million Czechoslovakians who lived among the Germans.

After the Munich Conference and the signing of an Anglo-German agreement which affirmed the British and German preference for the peaceful resolution of conflict, Chamberlain returned to Britain and made his infamous statement, waving the agreement in jubilation while walking down the runway: 'I believe it is peace for our time' (*Illustrated London News* 8 October 1938. In J Brooman. *The Era of the Second World War.*). Chamberlain was convinced of the success of his appeasement policy and was confident that another European war had been successfully averted.

▼ *Source E*

Street interviews recorded by Mass Observation in London on 20 September 1938

[Man, age 70] I think he [Chamberlain]'s doing wrong ... Why shouldn't the Czechs fight for their country? Why should we allow a bully like Hitler to dominate Europe? Let's fight him and finish it.

[Bus conductor, age 30] What the hell's he got the right to go over there and do a dirty trick like that. It'll have the whole world against us now. Who'll trust us?

[Woman, age 32] It's a low-down dirty deal. It gives lots of them Czechs over to Hitler.

(From: J Brooman. *The Era of the Second World War.*)

◀ *Source F*

Results of public opinion polls in Britain

(From: J Brooman. *The Era of the Second World War.*)

	Result	
March 1938 Should Britain promise assistance to Czechoslovakia if Germany acts as it did towards Austria?	Yes No No opinion	33% 43% 24%
October 1938 Hitler says he has 'No more territorial ambitions in Europe'. Do you believe him?	Yes No	7% 93%
February 1939 Which of these statements comes nearest to representing your view of Mr Chamberlain's policy of appeasement: 1 It is a policy which will ultimately lead to a lasting peace in Europe 2 It will keep us out of war until we have time to rearm 3 It is bringing war nearer by whetting the appetites of the dictators No opinion		28% 46% 24% 2%
April 1939 Is the British Government right in following a policy of giving guarantees to preserve the independence of small European nations?	Yes No	83% 17%

Activities ....

Carefully examine Sources E and F which deal with public opinion.

1 Account for the changing attitude of the British public towards the appeasement of Germany between March 1938 and October 1938.

2 What evidence is there of a shifting attitude towards war against Germany? Give possible reasons for these shifts.

3 Are public opinion polls necessarily accurate? Give reasons for your answers.

....

The German invasion of Czechoslovakia, March 1939

Hitler stated on 28 May 1938 that it was his 'unalterable decision to smash Czechoslovakia by military action in the near future'. The country's Skoda armaments and gold were highly desirable assets for the Germany of Hitler's dream. German troops occupying the Sudetenland were reinforced and readied for military action. German preparation for the invasion of

Czechoslovakia included a widespread press campaign. Nazi-controlled publications were used to spread propaganda which asserted that Sudetenland Germans had suffered under Czechoslovakian rule. The Czechoslovakian government was ordered to align its official policies with those of Germany. For example, anti-Semitism was encouraged and Czechoslovakia was pressured to leave the League of Nations and transfer some of its gold reserves to Germany. Hitler implied that agreeing to these demands would ensure German respect for the independence of Czechoslovakia, and most of the demands were agreed to.

In early 1939 a Slovak rebellion, encouraged by Hitler, resulted in the declaration of Slovakian independence. This, in turn, enabled Hitler to offer German protection to the Czech states of Bohemia and Moravia although Czechoslovakia was effectively ordered to accept this protection. A meeting in Berlin with the Czechoslovakian premier, Hacha, who argued for autonomy, did little to dissuade Hitler. His aggressive programme of European occupation was set in motion when on 15 March 1939, troops marched in to occupy Bohemia and Moravia with the new state of Slovakia being assigned German protectorate status.

Russia, Britain, France and the United States all protested vigorously against German occupation as it became clear that Hitler's promises of halted aggression had been false. The Anglo-German agreement and those agreements established at the Munich Conference had been broken.

Britain felt the consequences of Hitler's apparent turnaround strongly because of the obvious failure of the appeasement policy. Foreign policy was now altered to resistance to aggression. It was felt that Hitler's expansionist policies could no longer be tolerated now that his motives had been so clearly exposed. This new policy was implemented too late for Czechoslovakia whose independence was now gone. Hitler put it succinctly on the night of the German march on Prague: 'Czechoslovakia has herewith ceased to exist.'

Hitler's secret planning and military manoeuvres for the expansion of Germany had now been exposed. It was recognised that Hitler intended to occupy central Europe in its entirety. The secrecy surrounding his intentions was gone and the cautious German foreign policy and talk of peace had become outright aggression which made the reality of war probable.

Unit 8 The outbreak of the Second World War in 1939 in Europe

Unit outcomes

- Analyse Hitler's unfolding plan for war in Europe.
- Explain the involvement of Britain and France in the war.

The road to war from March to September 1939

Hitler's plan for the total occupation of Europe made Poland the obvious next target for his aggression. Germany resented Poland because of the 1919 settlement at Versailles which had ceded a large portion of Eastern Prussia to Polish borders. Danzig, the capital of this region, had been made a free city allowing Poland coastal access. Danzig was also inhabited by a large German population. This all provided an obvious angle for anti-Polish propaganda, similar to the anti-Czechoslovakian propaganda the Nazis had previously employed and which had locally justified that occupation.

Hitler's long-term plan was expansion into Russia. Poland was essentially a gateway to the Soviet Union and a successful Polish occupation would greatly enhance the chances in Russia, both strategically and in terms of number of forces.

During the last few months of 1938 a meeting between German and Polish diplomats had been held in Berlin at which Germany had demanded the return of Danzig and the Polish corridor in return for compensation in Russia. However, by March 1939 the Polish ambassador decided that Germany's demands were unacceptable. In the same month Chamberlain announced that 'in the event of any action that clearly threatened Polish independence ... Her Majesty's government would feel themselves bound at once to lend the Polish government all support in their power' (D Thomson. *Europe since Napoleon.*). This move by the British was fully supported by the French. In April, for the first time in her history, Britain introduced compulsory military service in peacetime. Clearly appeasement for the British and French was now at an end.

This strong and clear opposition to Hitler angered him greatly. The propaganda campaign in Poland became more intense while Germany severed all diplomatic negotiations with Poland. On 28 April 1939 Hitler made a widely broadcast speech in which he denounced both the 1935 Anglo-German Naval Agreement and the 1934 German-Polish Agreement. He seized the port of Memel from Lithuania. Mussolini, not to be left behind, invaded Albania, also violating several treaties. In May 1939 Hitler and Mussolini converted the Axis into a formal military alliance, known as the 'Pact of Steel'.

German-Soviet Agreement: The Non-Aggression Pact

Although Hitler had always been vehemently anti-communist, he recognised the benefits of an alliance with Russia. He believed that war with western Europe was inevitable and he wanted at all costs to avoid war on two fronts. A pact with Russia would also allow expansion in the east. In May 1939 Molotov became the new Russian foreign minister. He signed the treaty with Germany for many reasons: Russia was fearful of Nazi Germany and Stalin was aware of Hitler's long-term plan to expand eastwards. Stalin also felt that Poland would be an effective buffer zone between Germany and Russia. His overriding fear was that Germany would align with the capitalist West and Fascist Italy. Stalin also wanted to buy time to prepare Russia for what he believed would be an unavoidable confrontation with Germany.

Consequently, on 23 August 1939, Molotov and Stalin met with the German Foreign Minister Ribbentrop and the Molotov-Ribbentrop Non-Aggression Pact was signed between Germany and Russia. It stated that in the event of war, Russia would remain neutral and occupy East Poland, Estonia and Latvia, while Germany would occupy Lithuania and the rest of Poland. It also specified that Germany and Russia would not go to war with each other for ten years. This pact was a great setback for Britain and France and soon afterwards, on 25 August, they both signed an agreement with Poland which stated unconditionally that they would support Poland with military force if required.

Hitler then ordered the Polish government to send a delegation to Berlin within 24 hours in the hope of forcing the Poles to eventually agree to his demands. But the Polish government, recalling the fates of Austria and Czechoslovakia, refused the order.

The invasion of Poland

Meanwhile, throughout the summer months, Germany had been making large-scale military preparations, increasing its army, navy and airforce considerably. With this organised, Hitler was ready to launch his attack on Poland. Early on the morning of 1 September 1939, Danzig harbour was invaded and the German troops attacked.

War between the major powers

Britain responded to Hitler's invasion of Poland with a declaration of war on Sunday 3 September 1939, followed by France. The members of the British Commonwealth, including South Africa, also declared war. In May 1940, Neville Chamberlain was forced to resign and was replaced by Winston Churchill. During this period, the war was confined to Europe and by June 1940, Britain faced the power of the German military force on its own. Other arenas emerged with the Italian and later German aggression in North Africa. In a surprise offensive in June 1941, Hitler launched the so-called 'Operation Barbarossa' on Russia. This now brought the Soviet Union into an unlikely alliance with the British. Communists throughout the world threw their weight behind the war effort and played a major part in the resistance movement in occupied countries.

Although the United States had declared its neutral position in the 1930s, as the war progressed, it showed clearly its increasing material support for the Allies. Its 'cash and carry' policy and then its Lend-Lease Act, passed by Congress in March 1941, permitted President Roosevelt to put American resources at the disposal of any state which he considered to be important for the security of the United States. In August 1941 President Roosevelt and Winston Churchill met on a battleship in the Atlantic and drew up an agreement that became known as 'the Atlantic Charter'. This was an attempt to draw up post-war peace aims. It marked an American commitment to a future peace even before it had formally entered the war.

Activity ....

In small groups develop essay plans to answer the following questions.
1 Ulrich von Hassell maintains that 'the decisive turning point toward war was the occupation of Prague. All preceding actions ... the world had accepted'. Discuss.
2 'Peace at any price.' To what extent did this approach characterise the Anglo-French attitude towards Hitler's Germany up to the outbreak of the Second World War?

....

Unit 9 — The entry of Russia, Japan and the United States – global war

Unit outcomes

- Explain how the war escalated to a global scale.
- Understand the reasons for the Japanese attack on Pearl Harbour and the American retaliation.
- Explain the consequences of the Second World War.

The entry of the United States and Japan into the war, December 1941

Since 1937 the Japanese army had been on the offensive in China, and by November 1938 the Japanese controlled most of China's coastline. The outbreak of war in Europe and the fall of France and Holland offered new opportunities for Japanese expansion in Indo-China. In September 1940, Japan cemented its alliance with Germany and Italy with the Tripartite Pact. This agreement recognised Japanese leadership in Asia. However, the United States posed a serious threat to these ambitions. The Americans had done nothing to oppose Japanese expansion in China, but became increasingly concerned at the Japanese advance into South-East Asia which threatened their own position.

In 1940, the United States Pacific fleet was moved from California to Pearl Harbour on Hawaii. This was followed by an embargo (ban) on the sale of aviation fuel to Japan in June, and a ban on the export of iron and steel to Japan in November 1940. In June 1941 the Americans went further by freezing all Japanese assets in the United States and banning all trade between the two countries. This move seriously threatened the Japanese war effort and its economy.

This put the Japanese into a dilemma: negotiation or war. The Japanese prime minister favoured negotiation but he was defeated in December 1941 and replaced by General Tojo. This effectively meant a military dictatorship in Japan. The American insistence on a Japanese withdrawal from China and South-East Asia as a condition for normalising relations partly helped to persuade the Japanese military government that war was inevitable. It was their view that the best chance in such a war for Japan was a sudden strike against the United States. In conference with the Japanese emperor, the decision to launch an attack was taken on 1 December 1941. On 7 December, the Japanese airforce launched a surprise attack on the American fleet in Pearl Harbour. It was this action that brought the United States into the Second World War on the side of the Allies. On 11 December 1941, Germany and Italy declared war on the United States.

The end of the Second World War and its consequences

The war in Europe ended with the unconditional surrender of Germany in May 1945, and in the Far East in August 1945 with the unconditional surrender of Japan.

The Second World War had profound consequences for the world. Not only were there huge losses of civilian life and destruction of property, but the modern war machinery and the dropping of the atomic bomb by the United States had serious psychological consequences. For the first time people experienced the consequences of weapons of mass destruction.

Added to this, only two countries emerged at the end of the war with their power increased: the United States and the Soviet Union. Europe lay in tatters and became the ideological battleground for the superpowers in the period of increasing tension between them that marked much of the post-war decades. Europe became divided as two new armed camps developed. Many overseas nations who had lived under imperial domination as colonies used the post-war period to push for their independence.

The United Nations Organisation was established in 1945 out of the remnants of the old League of Nations to deal with the challenges of a world peace. One of the biggest problems that had to be faced was the refugee problem and the plight of the homeless.

There was also the issue of how to deal with those who were regarded as guilty of causing the war and the horrific deliberate slaughter of millions of people. War Crimes Tribunals were established and the world came to hear of the mass extermination of millions of Europeans, in particular, the European Jews and other minority groups. However, out of the war and with the establishment of the United Nations came the Declaration of Human Rights and a genuine desire to promote this ideal by many in the post-war world.

◀ **Source A**
Hiroshima after the
atomic bomb, 1945

▼ **Source B**

Some contemporary views towards the atomic weapons

'Mission successful.' – Colonel Paul W Tibbets Jr., pilot, Enola Gay, 1945.

'My God! What have we done?' – Captain Robert A Lewis, Enola Gay co-pilot.

'Seldom, if ever, has a war ended leaving the victors with such a sense of uncertainty and fear, with such a realisation that the future is obscure, and that survival is not assured.' – Broadcaster Edward R Murrow, 1945.

'In an instant, without warning, the present had become the unthinkable future.' – Time magazine, 1945.

'The atomic bomb has changed everything except the nature of man.' – Albert Einstein, 1945.

'This revelation of the secrets of nature, long mercifully withheld from man, should arouse the most solemn reflections in the mind and conscience of every human being capable of comprehension.' – Winston Churchill, 1945.

'For all we know, we have created a Frankenstein.' – HV Kaltenborn, dean of radio news commentators, 1945.

'In that terrible flash 16 100 km away, men here have seen not only the fate of Japan, but have glimpsed the future of America.' – James Reston, The New York Times, 1945.

'The world has virtually accepted the inevitability of another war.' – Saturday Review *editor Norman Cousins, December 1948.*

'An arms race unprecedented in the history of the world is driving us madly toward destruction. People are trembling because they feel we are on the verge of a third world war, a war which could sweep civilization back into the Middle Ages.' – The Reverend Billy Graham, presiding at a tent revival in Los Angeles, 1949.

'There are no longer problems of the spirit. There is only the question, "When will I be blown up?"' – William Faulkner, accepting the Nobel Prize, 1950.

(Compiled by SAPA-AP *Daily News* 29 July 1995, 17.)

Activities ·······································

1 a Summarise what the feelings of different people are in Source B.
   b What do these reactions tell you?
   c Write your own comment about the war similar to those in Source B.
2 a Look closely at Sources A and C and describe what you see.
   b How does it make you feel?
3 Study Source D.
   a Which world war cost the most number of lives?
   b Why do you think this war caused so many more people to be killed?

··

The entry of Russia, Japan and the United States – global war **139**

© The Hulton Getty Collection

◀ **Source C**
The German city of
Cologne, following Allied
bombing

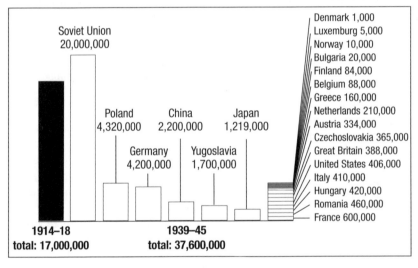

Soviet Union
20,000,000

Poland
4,320,000

China
2,200,000

Japan
1,219,000

Germany
4,200,000

Yugoslavia
1,700,000

Denmark 1,000
Luxemburg 5,000
Norway 10,000
Bulgaria 20,000
Finland 84,000
Belgium 88,000
Greece 160,000
Netherlands 210,000
Austria 334,000
Czechoslovakia 365,000
Great Britain 388,000
United States 406,000
Italy 410,000
Hungary 420,000
Romania 460,000
France 600,000

1914–18
total: 17,000,000

1939–45
total: 37,600,000

◀ **Source D**
Estimate of the
number of people
killed in the war
(includes both
military and civilian
personnel)

Extension activity ·······························

Do some research to find out more about the dropping of
the atomic bombs on Japan. Consider factors like:
- when the decision was taken to drop the bombs and
  by whom;
- what the effects of these bombs were on the Japanese
  and American people;
- what you can conclude about the use of atomic bombs
  in a situation of war.

···

CHAPTER ASSESSMENT

In small groups develop detailed essay plans for each of these questions. Refer back to the section on essay writing on pages 41 to 42 to help you. Then choose one of the essay topics and write an essay which your teacher will use for assessment purposes. Each person in your group must write on a different topic.

1 Discuss the factors that contributed towards the collapse of democracy in Germany, Italy and Japan and explain how these contributed to the establishment of Fascist and militarist governments in these countries.

2 'Hitler was a superb strategist and opportunist who made the most of the weakness of the major powers. However, the declaration of war over Poland caught him by surprise.'
Assess the validity of this statement in the light of events between 1932 and 1939.

3 Analyse the extent to which Hitler used military force and the threat of military force to carry out his foreign policy aims between 1933 and 1939 with the occupation of Czechoslovakia.

4 'The appeasers must bear great responsibility for the outbreak of the Second World War.'
Critically discuss this view.

5 'By supporting the Allies between 1935 and 1941, the USA voluntarily became more involved in the Second World War, but her final involvement was forced by the Japanese.'
Discuss this statement. (You can also refer back to Unit 5 of Chapter 2 for more information on US foreign policy during this period.)

Further reading

Josh Brooman. *A Sense of History: The Era of the Second World War*. Harlow, Essex: Longman, 1993.

Jacob P Britts. *'Doing History': A Practical Guide to Improving Your History Skills*. Cape Town: Maskew Miller Longman, 1993.

Stuart Hood and Litza Jansz. *Fascism for beginners*. Cambridge: Icon Books, 1993.

William I Shirer. *The Rise and Fall of the Third Reich*. London: Pan, 1963.

David Thomson. *Europe since Napoleon*. Harlow, Essex: Longman, 1957.

The Cold War (1945–91)

chapter **4**

contents

chapter outcomes

Knowledge outcomes

As you work through this chapter you will be able to:

- describe the development of the Cold War between 1945 and 1991;
- explain the different phases of the Cold War;
- identify crucial issues and turning-points;
- show the influence of personalities on events.

concepts and skills outcomes

As you work through this chapter you will learn about and apply skills and concepts such as how to:

- analyse, organise and critically evaluate sources;
- work effectively in a group;
- show empathy for people in the past;
- use effective research methods and solve problems;
- organise and communicate the results of historical study.

value outcomes

As you work through this chapter you will get the chance to think about:

- the morality of a mutually destructive arms race;
- the contrast between a democratic and a totalitarian society;
- how perceptions are sometimes more important than facts.

Timeline

		UNITED STATES PRESIDENTS	SOVIET LEADERS
END OF WW2 1945	1945	ROOSEVELT	
Coming of the Cold War		*Death of Roosevelt*	
1947			STALIN
Testing of containment		TRUMAN	
	1950		
1953	1953		
Coexistence and crises		*Death of Stalin*	
		EISENHOWER	
	1960		MALENKOV
		KENNEDY	
	1963		KHRUSHCHEV
1969		*Kennedy assassinated*	
Détente	1970	JOHNSON	BREZHNEV
	1974	NIXON	
1979		*Nixon resigns*	
The second Cold War		FORD	
	1980		BREZHNEV
1985		CARTER	ANDROPOV
The end of the Cold War		REAGAN	CHERNENKO
		BUSH	GORBACHEV
	1990		
1991		*Gorbachev resigns*	

This chapter covers Specific Outcomes 2, 4, 5, 7 and 9 of the Human and Social Sciences learning area.

Unit 1

The coming of the Cold War (1945–47)

Unit outcomes

- Give a definition of the Cold War.
- Analyse the Soviet and US views of the 1945 world.
- Describe the Soviet take-over of Eastern Europe.
- Explain the causes of the change in the US policy.
- Interpret historical sources.
- Understand and analyse an empathetic picture.

Background

On 3 April 1945 Adolf Hitler sat among the ruins of Berlin and contemplated the future of Europe and the world. He concluded that:

> with the defeat of the Third Reich and the emergence of the Asiatic, the African and perhaps the South American nationalisms, there will remain in the world only two great powers capable of confronting each other – the United States of America and Soviet Russia. The laws of history and geography will compel these two powers to a trial of strength.

So, within a few days of his suicide, the Führer predicted the war between two of his enemies – the war which was to last for the next 45 years.

The collapse of Germany and Japan created a vacuum both in Europe and in the East. The vital question was: who was going to fill it?

Defining a Cold War

What exactly is meant by the phrase 'Cold War' as it was used in the period after 1945? Let us analyse the opinions of three recent historians.

▼ Source A

The term COLD was used in a double and indeed contradictory sense: first, it meant that relations between east and west were cold, frozen, paralysed, frosted, i.e. were not warm; but secondly, it meant that although relations were bad and warlike, they were restrained to the extent of not having reached the stage of 'hot' war.

Considering their opposites makes the distinction clearer; in the first case, the opposite of cold war is thaw; in the second, it is all-out or hot war.

(From: F Halliday. *The Making of the Second Cold War.*)

▼ Source B

Relations between the Western powers and the communist states of the East were relations of constant manoeuvre for advantage and almost incessant hostility.

(From: D Thomson. *Europe Since Napoleon.*)

▼ Source C

The Cold War would be fought with economic and propaganda weapons; with diplomacy and limited war. Always, however, the contestants would draw back from a final conflict for in the Atomic Age, if the war became 'hot', it could result only in mutual destruction.

(From: P Hastings. *The Cold War (1945–1969).*)

Activities

- 1 Describe in your own words the two meanings of the word 'cold'.
- 2 Why did the Cold War never become a 'hot' war between East and West?
- 3 Study Sources A, B and C and list five characteristics of the Cold War.

The world in 1945: The Soviet view

As they analysed the post-war world, Stalin and his advisers were deeply conscious of three important factors.

1 There was a basic conflict with the USA over ideology. The USSR was a socialist one-party state based on the rule of the working class, while the USA was a liberal democracy where private capitalism and the pursuit of business profit flourished.

2 There was a history of Western opposition to the USSR.

- Russia had been repeatedly invaded by the West: in 1812 (Napoleon); in 1854 (France and Britain into the Crimea); in 1914 (Germany); in 1919–20 (the Western Powers in the civil war against the first Bolshevik state); in 1941 (Hitler).
- In the 1930s and during the Second World War, Western policy seemed to be directed against Russia. For example:
  a In 1938 Russia had been excluded from the Munich agreement when it looked as if Hitler's expansion was being turned to the East.
  b In spite of Russian appeals, the Allies had delayed the opening of a second front in France until 1944. It seemed as if they were leaving Russia and Germany to mutually exhaust themselves.
  c The Russians had a continual fear that the Western powers would make a separate peace with Germany – as they had done with Italy.
  d Russia had been excluded from information about the Western development of the atomic bomb.

3 The USSR had only just escaped military disaster – but the cost had been enormous. About 20 million Russians had died. In the territory occupied by the Germans about 70 000 villages, 654 000 kilometres of railway track and half of all the railway bridges had been destroyed. Agriculture had been disrupted and in 1945 production was about 60 per cent of that in 1940; steel output had reached 12,3 million tons compared with 18,3 million tons in 1940. Admittedly, the Red Army numbered about 11 million personnel, but against that, the US forces alone had about 12 million – and the Americans had the atomic bomb. In this situation, rebuilding the Soviet economy had to be a first priority, so assistance from the West and reparations from ex-enemy countries would be valuable.

The USSR's tactics

Looking back, we can list Soviet foreign policy tactics under three headings:

1 All resources and forces had to be mobilised to halt and turn back the march of American capitalism, but to stop short at endangering the security of the Soviet Union. The support of communists, socialists, radicals and capitalists who were also nationalists was to be enlisted;

2 Soviet sources of strength, such as the Red Army and Soviet control of foreign communist parties, were to be utilised to the very limit so as to defend Soviet security interests and, wherever possible, expand Soviet influence;

3 Great care was to be taken, given the different levels of influence the Soviet Union enjoyed in eastern and south-eastern Europe, Germany and western and southern Europe, not to provoke the United States unnecessarily.

(From: M McCauley. *The Origins of the Cold War.*)

The expansion of communist control in Eastern Europe

When fighting in Europe ended in May 1945, the USSR had already added 24 million people to the Soviet Union, with the conquest of the Baltic States, Eastern Poland, Bessarabia, parts of Finland and East Prussia. The Red Army was also occupying Czechoslovakia, Bulgaria, Hungary, Rumania, Albania, Austria and the eastern portion of Germany. Only in Yugoslavia and Greece was the 'red tide' stopped.

In the next three years communist-controlled governments were gradually set up in all of these states. At first, in the liberated countries 'popular front' governments were established: all democratic elements in the populations were to be represented and there were to be free elections. Communist parties were popular since communists had often been leaders in the resistance against the Nazis. During this initial phase, all pro-Nazi and anti-Soviet elements were removed from public life and, with backing from the Red Army, key positions in the government taken over, for example, control of defence, police and propaganda. The next stage of the take-over process came with the formation of coalition governments dominated by the Communist Party. Peasant parties and middle-class liberal parties were driven into opposition, which became increasingly difficult with press censorship. One by one, non-communist leaders were discredited and eliminated, for example, Jan Masaryk in Czechoslovakia. A key factor in this whole process was the Red Army. By the end of 1948, Stalin had turned the countries of eastern Europe into satellites of Russia.

Activities . . . .

Carefully consult Source D and then complete the activities below.

1 Which areas were seized by Russia in 1945?
2 Which states had become communist by 1949?
3 What comments can you make about the rate at which Russia was expanding?

. . . .

The division of Europe

(Adapted from: P Hastings. *The Cold War (1945–1969).*)

KEY

Territory seized by
Russia 1945

States which had
become Communist
by 1949

The Iron Curtain

0   200   400 km

FINLAND

KARELIA

SWEDEN

Leningrad

ESTONIA

LATVIA

DENMARK

To Russia 1945

LITHUANIA

EAST
PRUSSIA

Danzig

Minsk

Stettin

Bremen

Berlin

British
Zone

GERMANY

Russian
Zone

POLAND

To Poland 1945

Warsaw

EASTERN
POLAND

USSR

NETHERLANDS

R. Rhine

Bonn

BELGIUM

American
Zone

Prague

Lublin

CZECHOSLOVAKIA

To Russia 1945

EUPEN &
MALMEDY

Nuremberg

R. Danube

Vienna

A.Z.   R.Z.

AUSTRIA

SWITZERLAND

F.Z.   B.Z.

Budapest

HUNGARY

BUKHOVINA

BESSARABIA

ROMANIA

FRANCE

Bucharest

YUGOSLAVIA

Belgrade

R. Danube

BLACK
SEA

Marseilles

BULGARIA

Sofia

ITALY

ALBANIA

Bosphorus

Salonika

Dardanelles

GREECE

TURKEY

MEDITERRANEAN SEA

Athens

The coming of the Cold War (1945–47) **145**

Poland – a case study

Poland, the largest of the eastern European states, was of great interest to the major powers. Britain and France had gone to war over Poland in September 1939, and Polish soldiers and airmen had made a significant contribution to British military efforts. Churchill, in particular, considered that post-war Poland should be independent and should regain its lost territories. In the USA, a solid block of Polish voters was an important factor in congressional and presidential elections. For Stalin, Poland was 'the essential prize'. Invaders of Russia had usually come through Poland and, with his focus on security, Stalin was determined that an anti-communist government would not be allowed in Poland, and that Russia would retain land in eastern Poland which she had occupied in 1939 and regained during the fighting in 1944.

When the London Poles demanded an explanation, Stalin broke off relations with them and in July 1944, set up a rival Polish government. This was the Polish Committee of National Liberation or Lublin Committee which was dominated by communists.

Further tension was caused by the Warsaw Uprising in August 1944. With the Red Army no more than six miles away, the Warsaw Home Army rose against the Germans. However, the Russians refused to help them and the Germans killed about 300 000 Poles and destroyed the city of Warsaw. If the rising had been successful, Stalin would have been faced by a well-organised group of non-communist Poles, supported by the London committee.

In January 1945, Russia recognised the Lublin Committee as the legal government of Poland.

◀ Map of Poland: Europe after Hitler (Adapted from: BJ Elliott: *Western Europe after Hitler.*)

Rival governments

Some Poles had escaped the Nazi occupation of Poland in 1939 and settled in London, where they set up a provisional government. These were known as the London Poles and were supported by Britain and the USA. Relations between the London Poles and the Russians worsened in April 1943, when the German army revealed that it had discovered a mass grave in the Katyn Forest: these were the remains of some 10 000 Polish officers from the Polish army who, it was believed, had been captured by the Russians in 1939. It appears likely that the Russians were responsible, although it has not been finally proven.

Conference decisions

At the Teheran conference (1943), Britain and the USA agreed that Russia should retain most of eastern Poland after the war. Poland was to be compensated by taking over German territory up to the Oder and Neisse Rivers – known as the Oder-Neisse Line. However, there was no agreement about a new Polish government.

At the Yalta Conference (February 1945), Russia agreed that some London Poles would join the Lublin Committee.

By the Potsdam Conference (July–August 1945), the Russians had accepted Mikolajczyk, the leader of the London Poles, as vice-president of the Polish government. It was agreed that there would be free elections.

Post-war developments

Mikolajczyk was given the post of minister of agriculture as well as that of vice-president, but most posts were held by communists. He was elected as leader of the Peasant Party but such was the pressure of censorship, suppression and intimidation, that, within eighteen months, he was forced to flee. Despite protests from the British and the Americans, a constitution on Soviet lines was adopted in February 1947. The Red Army destroyed nationalist guerrilla forces.

Activities ....
Discuss the following questions in groups.
1 Summarise the details of Russian policy towards Poland.
2 To what extent can Russian policy towards Poland be justified?

The world in 1945: The American view

President Roosevelt and the American government did not aim at establishing a post-war balance of power in Europe to safeguard the United States. Instead, they expected this security to stem from mutual Russian–American goodwill. This expectation of a post-war 'era of good feeling' between the Soviet Union and the United States was characteristic of American thinking which hoped that the friendly relations and mutual respect which American leaders believed had matured during the war, would preserve the common outlook and purposes, and guarantee an enduring peace.

From early in 1942, the American government proclaimed the principle that no final decisions on matters of post-war frontiers or systems of government should be made until the end of the war. President Roosevelt campaigned both at home and abroad on behalf of the United Nations Organisation (UNO). He and other Americans were convinced that they were winning over the Russians to the American dream of a world legal and moral order.

Roosevelt saw himself as a mediator between Stalin and Churchill and was sure that he could handle the Russians. However, Roosevelt died on 12 April 1945. The tragedy was that he was not given the opportunity to deal with the Russians immediately after the end of the war in Europe. Truman, the new president, had great courage, but he lacked the prestige and experience of Roosevelt.

Activities ....
1 Do you believe that if Roosevelt had been alive the Cold War would not have happened? Justify your answer.
2 How did Roosevelt die? Do some research to find out the answer to this question.
....

1945: The turning point

Timeline	
February	Yalta Conference
12 April	Death of Roosevelt; Truman becomes president
April–June	San Francisco Conference – Charter of the UNO drafted and signed (26 June)
8 May	Germany surrenders
16 July	First test of the US A-bomb
July–2 August	Potsdam Conference
6 August	Hiroshima
9 August	Nagasaki
15 August	Japan surrenders

The Yalta Conference

As their armies closed on Nazi Germany, Roosevelt, Stalin and Churchill met at Yalta, in the Russian Crimea, in February 1945.

Several important decisions were made at the Yalta Conference.
1 Final agreement was reached upon how best to end the war against Hitler.
2 Arrangements were made to divide Germany after the end of the fighting, into a number of zones, each of which would be occupied by the forces of one of the Allies. Berlin would be similarly divided into sectors.
3 Stalin agreed that within two to three months of the defeat of Hitler, the Soviet Union would declare war on Japan.
4 The peoples of the countries which were being freed from Hitler's grasp were promised that they would be given the chance to choose for themselves the kind of government they wanted.

© Imperial War Museum

5 Roosevelt and Churchill reluctantly agreed that the frontiers of Poland should be moved so that Russia would gain some of eastern Poland; the Poles would be compensated by some of eastern Germany. A new provisional government would be set up in Poland.

6 Agreement was reached on voting rights and other matters relating to the United Nations Organisation, and it was agreed that a conference should be held in San Francisco in April, to settle the final details.

◀ The division of Germany and Poland (Adapted from: H Ward. *World Powers in the Twentieth Century*.)

The Potsdam Conference (July–August 1945)

When the conference delegates assembled at the East German town of Potsdam, the attitudes of the American leaders had begun to change, as several underlying circumstances had changed.

- After Roosevelt's death Harry Truman had become president of the USA. He was inexperienced and ill-informed about foreign affairs and, initially at least, he had to rely on his foreign policy advisers. However, he learned quickly and he decided to be decisive and less tolerant with the Russians. At a stormy meeting with Molotov, the Russian foreign minister, on 23 April he bluntly accused the Russians of failing to live up to the Yalta Agreement on Poland, particularly over the restructuring of the provisional government and the proposal to move the western boundary of the country. He told Molotov that this message had to be delivered to Stalin immediately. Molotov protested: 'I have never been talked to like that in my life.'
- By the beginning of May, Truman had been briefed about the development of the atomic bomb. Although it was not tested until 16 July, it seemed likely that the bomb would work. If so, the Russians would not be required for the war against Japan. Also, the bomb would be a powerful lever in negotiations about post-war Germany.
- The war against Germany was over. Germany surrendered on 8 May 1945.
- During the early months of 1945 an increasing number of American politicians and generals had contact with the Russians. Many of them were appalled at what they saw. General George Patton described some Soviet officers as Mongolian bandits. The progress of the Russian take-over of eastern Europe alarmed American politicians. One leader wrote: '[we must end] this appeasement of the Reds before it is too late'.

Through Russian eyes, the change in the American attitude was alarming. Several further developments increased this alarm.

- Immediately after the German surrender, Truman stopped the shipment of Lend-Lease supplies to Russia and Britain. However, shipments were resumed temporarily after complaints from Moscow and London.
- The Russians had asked for a credit of several billion dollars to assist their post-war reconstruction, but the Americans delayed in granting this.
- Although Stalin knew about the atomic bomb development through Russian spies, he resented that the Americans had not been open about this.

The United Nations Organisation

The UNO was to be the new international organisation. The UN Charter was finally signed on 26 June 1945 after a conference in San Francisco in April.

About 50 countries became members. In the General Assembly of the UN, each member country was to be represented and would have one vote (it was agreed that two of the Soviet republics would have a separate vote). However, the great powers did not want small countries to have an equal say in world affairs, so much of the real power was given to the Security Council.

The USA, together with Britain, France, the Soviet Union and nationalist China, became the five permanent members of the Security Council. The Security Council had the right to use force to deal with threats to world peace. In addition, each of the permanent members had the right to veto – or block – decision-making.

A permanent home for the UNO was found in New York.

Some critics doubted if the great powers – with their different interests and priorities – would be able to act together. By the end of 1949, the Soviet Union had used the veto in the Security Council 43 times.

▼ **Source F** The structure of the UNO
(From: BBC. *Twentieth Century History.*)

UN Assembly
- comprises all members
- voting, two-thirds majority to carry a resolution

UN Security Council
- comprised 11 members (1949); 15 (today)
- 5 permanent members with powers of veto (USA, UK, France, USSR, Nationalist China)
- 6 non-permanent members elected by General Assembly for term of two years

Activities
1. Describe the structure of the United Nations Organisation, as shown in Source F.
2. Study the cartoon in Source G.
   a Who are the political leaders shown in the cartoon?
   b Suggest a date for this cartoon.

UNITED NATIONS CLUB

RULE: All players to play together, but not so as to cramp any player's style. (That would be unrealistic)

"A FINE TEAM — BUT COULD DO WITH A DASH OF UNITY...."

© Solo Syndication

◀*Source G*
The United Nations club – cartoon by David Low
(From: GA Smith. *The USA as a World Power.*)

c Explain the cartoonist's viewpoint. Is it optimistic or pessimistic about the future of the UNO? Give reasons for your answer.

· ·

When the conference met the atmosphere was far from friendly. Churchill had been defeated in the British General Election and in the middle of the conference, he was replaced by Clement Attlee, the new Labour prime minister. So, of the Big Three who had met at Yalta in February, only Stalin remained.

In the business sessions, some compromises were reached:

- further arrangements were made for the occupation of Germany;
- the USSR reduced its demands for reparations from Germany, even though this was a vital matter for Stalin in view of the

end of Lend-Lease and denial of American credit;
- the West agreed to the Polish take-over of ex-German territory.

During the conference, Truman casually mentioned to Stalin that the USA had successfully tested an atomic bomb. This drew little reaction from Stalin, who already knew about atomic research developments from information provided by Russian spies. However, an immediate message was sent back to Moscow to accelerate work on the Soviet bomb project.

Various problematic issues were left open on the understanding that they would be handled by the council of foreign ministers who were to meet regularly in the future. However, the first meeting of this council in late September 1945 ended with nothing being resolved.

© Keystone Pressedienst

◀*Source H*
The leaders at the Potsdam Conference
(From: P Lane. *The USA in the Twentieth Century.*)

Study Source E and Source H (on pages 148 and 150) – the photographs of the leaders at the two conferences.

1 Identify the leaders in the two photographs of the conferences and indicate which country they represent.
2 Explain the changes in the British and American leadership. What were the effects of these changes?
3 Name the eastern European country whose new boundaries caused great discussion at the first conference. What was the final decision?
4 Briefly describe the arrangements made for Germany at the end of the war.

···

Extension activity ···························
Put yourself in the position of the Russian leader. In your own words, write a secret letter to the Supreme Soviet, giving the reasons for your policy at the two conferences.

···

Containment

During 1945, American policy towards Soviet Russia changed. American officials and particularly the new president, Harry Truman, became convinced that Stalin was determined to expand as far and as fast as the Red Army would permit. The take-over of eastern Europe and new Russian demands for territory in Iran gave evidence of this expansion. In a strongly-worded document written in January 1946, Truman concluded that he was 'tired of babying the Soviets'.

In February 1946, Truman's suspicions seemed to be confirmed by the famous 'Long Telegram' from George Kennan, a leading Soviet expert and at that time, the official in charge of the US embassy in Moscow.

▼ *Source I* The Russian Bear
(From: Fisher and Williams. *Past into Present.*)

▼ *Source J*
Kennan's Long Telegram is one of the most important documents of the post-war era and was the decisive factor in convincing Truman to change to a firm policy towards the USSR.

The suspiciousness and aggressiveness of the Soviet leadership stemmed, according to Kennan, from 'basic inner Russian necessities' and not from any 'objective analysis of [the] situation beyond Russia's borders'. He pointed out that the root cause of the Kremlin's 'neurotic view of world affairs' was the traditional and instinctive Russian sense of insecurity. This led Soviet leaders to go over to the offensive 'in patient but deadly struggle for total destruction [of] rival power, never in compacts or compromises with it'.

American concessions would not affect official Soviet aggressiveness.

We have here a political force committed fanatically to the belief that with US there can be no permanent modus vivendi, *that it is desirable and necessary that the internal harmony of our society be disrupted, our traditional way of life destroyed, the international authority of our state be broken if Soviet power is to be secure.*

The Soviets would do all in their power to strengthen the socialist bloc and weaken the capitalist countries. Aided by communist parties directed by an underground general staff of world proportions and secretly co-ordinated from Moscow, they would seek to undermine the stronger Western powers and to topple all those governments from Turkey to Switzerland and Great Britain, which resisted Soviet demands. The Western nations must therefore draw together in a more cohesive bloc, led by the USA.
(From: M McCauley. *The Origins of the Cold War.*)

▼ *Source K*
Churchill sounded a warning in a speech at Fulton, Missouri, in March 1946. He identified an 'iron curtain across Europe'.

From Stettin on the Baltic, to Trieste on the Adriatic, an iron curtain has descended across the continent. Behind that line, lie all the capitals of the ancient states of Central and Eastern Europe ... The Communist Parties which are very small in all these Eastern states of Europe, have been raised to power far beyond their numbers and are seeking everywhere to obtain totalitarian control ...

Whatever conclusions may be drawn from these facts – and facts they are – this is certainly not the liberated Europe we fought to build up. Nor is it one which contains the essentials of permanent peace.

(From: M McCauley. *The Origins of the Cold War*.)

▲ Winston Churchill

▼ *Source L*
Later in March 1946, Stalin replied to Churchill, calling him a 'warmonger' and claiming that Russia needed security

The following circumstances should not be forgotten. The Germans made their invasion of the USSR through Finland, Poland, Rumania, Bulgaria and Hungary. The Germans were able to make their invasion through these countries because, at the time, governments hostile to the Soviet Union existed in these countries. As a result of the German invasion the Soviet Union has lost irretrievably in the fighting against the Germans, and also through the German occupation and the deportation of Soviet citizens to German servitude, a total of about seven million people. In other words, the Soviet Union's loss of life has been several times greater than that of Britain and the United States of America put together. Possibly in some quarter an inclination is felt to forget about these colossal sacrifices of the Soviet people which secured the liberation of Europe from the Hitlerite yoke. But the Soviet Union cannot forget about them. And so what can there be surprising about the fact that the Soviet Union, anxious for its future safety, is trying to see to it that governments loyal in their attitude to the Soviet Union should exist in these countries? How can anyone, who has not taken leave of his senses, describe these peaceful aspirations of the Soviet Union as expansionist tendencies on the part of our state?

(From: M McCauley. *The Origins of the Cold War*.)

▼ *Source M*
The doctrine of containment
Containment, as the basis of American policy, was described in an article written later by George Kennan

It is clear that the main element of any United States policy towards the Soviet Union must be that of a longterm, patient but firm and vigilant containment of Russian expansive tendencies ... It is clear that the United States cannot expect in the foreseeable future to enjoy political intimacy with the Soviet regime. It must continue to regard the Soviet Union as a rival, not a partner, in the political arena. It must continue to expect that Soviet policies will reflect no abstract love of peace and stability, no real faith in the possibility of a permanent happy coexistence of the Socialist and Capitalist worlds, but rather a cautious, persistent pressure towards the disruption and weakening of all rival influence and rival power.

(From: M McCauley. *The Origins of the Cold War*.)

Activities
1 Who was George Kennan?
2 a How does Kennan describe the philosophy of the Russians and their basic aims in Sources J and M?
  b To what extent is this confirmed by Stalin in Source L?
3 Describe the response which Kennan recommends to the American policy makers in Source M.
4 a What was the 'iron curtain' as described by Churchill in Source K?
  b What official position did Churchill hold at this time?
5 Summarise Stalin's reply (Source L) to Churchill's accusation.

The Truman Doctrine and Marshall Aid

The implementation of the doctrine of containment became clear in 1947.

The Truman Doctrine
When British troops arrived in Greece in 1944, they found a civil war in progress between the communists and those who supported the king. The British restored the king, but in 1946 the Greek communists again rebelled and this time they were supported by the neighbouring communist governments.

Turkey was threatened by the Soviet claim to control the Straits at the entrance to the Black Sea.

The winter of 1946–47 was a severe one and brought complete economic dislocation to the countries of western Europe. Britain was badly affected and on 21 February 1947, the British government informed the USA that it could no longer afford to provide economic and military aid to the anti-communist forces in Greece and Turkey.

The USA responded quickly and in a speech to Congress on 12 March 1947, the president announced what was to become known as the Truman Doctrine: $400 million was to be sent immediately to support Greece and Turkey, but equally important, the USA pledged to assist any country which was threatened by communism. Thus the Truman Doctrine became the cornerstone of US policy – the containment of communism (see Source M above).

The USA was committed to being the world's policeman and the American people were called on to take up this mission.

© INPRA

▲ Harry S. Truman

▼ *Source N*

Speech by President Truman, 12 March 1947

At the present moment in world history, nearly every nation must choose between alternative ways of life. The choice is too often not a free one.

One way of life is based upon the will of the majority, and is distinguished by free institutions, representative government, free elections, guarantees of individual liberty, freedom of speech and religion, and freedom from political oppression.

The second way of life is based upon the will of a minority forcibly imposed on a majority. It relies upon terror and oppression, a controlled press and radio, fixed elections, and the suppression of personal freedoms.

I believe that it must be the policy of the United States to support free peoples who are resisting attempted subjugation by armed minorities or by outside pressures.

I believe that we must assist free peoples to work out their own destinies in their own way ...

The seeds of totalitarian regimes are nurtured by misery and want. They spread and grow in the evil soil of poverty and strife. They reach their full growth when the hope of a people for a better life has died.

We must keep that hope alive.

The free peoples of the world look to us for support in maintaining their freedoms.

(From: J Vick. *Modern America*)

Activities ....

1 Summarise the main points of Truman's speech in Source N.
2 Do you agree with Truman's point that the US is responsible for maintaining freedom in the world?

The Marshall Plan

Truman believed that communism could best be resisted by providing economic aid. So, on 5 June 1947, Secretary of State George Marshall put forward a plan to give billions of dollars of aid to Europe.

Our policy is directed not against any country or doctrine but against hunger, poverty, desperation and chaos. Its purpose should be the revival of a working economy in the world so as to permit the emergence of political and social conditions in which free institutions can exist ...

Britain and France quickly accepted the offer and began to prepare what was to become a 16-nation Organisation for European Economic Cooperation (OEEC), which was formally launched in June 1948. This organisation was granted $22 400 billion over the next four years.

The scheme was offered to Russia and the eastern European countries as well. But Stalin refused the offer, viewing the plan as an attempt by the USA to take economic control of Europe. The satellite governments of eastern Europe were ordered to do the same. (See Empathy exercise on page 154 to 155.)

▼ Source O

'Come on Sam – it's up to us again' (July 1947)

▼ Source P

Progress in countries receiving Marshall Aid
(From: H Mills. *Twentieth Century World History in Focus.*)

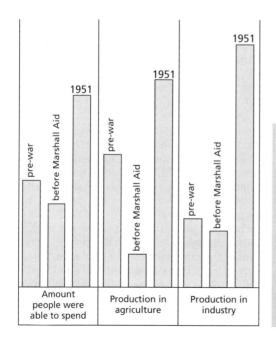

| Amount people were able to spend | Production in agriculture | Production in industry |

Activities

1 What is the attitude of the cartoonist in Source O? Give reasons for your answer.

2 a Summarise the information given to you in the bar graph in Source P.

  b Based on this graph, do you think that the Marshall Plan was a success?

3 Compare and contrast the policies of President Roosevelt and President Truman towards the Russians.

4 The Truman Doctrine has been called the beginning of the Cold War. Argue a case for or against this viewpoint.

The Cominform

The Cominform was the Soviet response to the Marshall Plan. At a meeting in Poland in October 1947, the communist leaders of the eastern European countries set up the Communist Information Bureau. One function of this body was to ensure that the 'Socialist camp' should speak with one voice – the voice of Moscow.

In 1949, the Council for Mutual Economic Assistance (COMECON) was established to bring the communist states together economically.

The take-over of Czechoslovakia (February 1948)

Up to 1948, a democratically elected coalition government under a communist prime minister had survived. But the communists were losing support and helped by internal strikes and the presence of Russian troops in neighbouring Austria, they took control by force. President Benes resigned and the respected Foreign Minister, Jan Masaryk, died in suspicious circumstances. The Western world was shocked.

Understanding historical skills and concepts

Empathy

Empathy has been defined as the ability to understand the motives, feelings, problems, beliefs and values of people in the past. The creation of empathy requires the ability:

- to put yourself in the position of other people in a given historical situation although not necessarily agreeing or sympathising with them;
- to appreciate that people in the past were real and had feelings;
- to recognise that there were different and often opposing viewpoints in the past;

- to acquire the 'feel of the times' in a past situation;
- to enter a historical situation through focusing your imagination on the evidence relating to particular events and issues.

Three aspects are vital to developing empathy:

- understanding the individual's views and attitudes;
- appreciating the circumstances of the times;
- using historical evidence.

Empathy exercises frequently ask you to write diaries, speeches or letters which could have been written in the past. Groupwork such as drama, role-play, simulation and debate can also develop your skills of empathy.

Empathy is important in developing historical understanding:

it attempts to get to grips with the strangeness of much of the past and it helps to create a habit of mind in which strangeness or difference is not dismissed as stupid, but is approached with openness and with a desire to collect evidence and improve understanding (Southern Regional Examinations Board pamphlet, UK 1986).

Activities

Study the text of Source Q, a short speech written by a learner in a recent Grade 12 exam. In the speech the learner creates an empathetic view of Stalin explaining why he has decided not to participate in the Marshall Plan.
1 List the reasons which 'Stalin' gives for this viewpoint, and contrast these with the viewpoint of the USA on this issue.
2 Pick out three ways in which this speech shows empathy.

▼ Source Q

My people, I, Stalin of Russia have decided not to accept the Marshall Plan in your interests. America has proposed this plan, seemingly with the aim of beating poverty and chaos in Europe. This, however, is a cover-up for their real reasons. For who would just give so much away if they had no ulterior motives? They want to give money to countries and the countries will be expected to give cooperation with the USA and will be expected to provide military bases in their lands in return – this will add to the ever-increasing encirclement of Russia. I would never let this foul disease,

this kowtowing to the USA enter our motherland. They intend to revive Germany – our age-old enemy, so that once again she would be able to attack us and kill our people. No! I will not partake of a proposal which would lead to that. It is an attempt to replace political with economic imperialism and to build up a buffer zone in an attempt to contain us. She will use German heavy industry as a base for American expansion in Europe – I will not tolerate this hypocrisy and we, as a nation will protect our independence, our way of life, our territory and our people at all cost. We will not take this offer as we are strong enough to ensure our own economic improvement and do not need any help from our enemies, help that will destroy us and our security.

Who caused the Cold War? A historical debate

The views of historians about the origins of the Cold War are usually divided into three interpretations.
1 The traditional or conventional view. This suggests that after 1945, Stalin set out to conquer the world and the West was forced to defend itself.
2 The revisionist view. This argues that Stalin was not interested in world conquest but in the safety of his own country. American policies were not defensive but provocative in trying to establish American domination throughout the world.
3 The post-revisionist view. This is the most recent interpretation and argues that both sides were to blame and that perhaps misunderstanding was a dominant cause.

In studying the events of the period, learners should be aware of this debate and come to their own conclusions.

Activities

Study Sources R and S – extracts from writings by two historians – and then complete these activities.
1 Analyse the text under these headings, giving the elements of each interpretation:
Traditional view:
Revisionist view:
Post-revisionist view:
Effect of the problem areas:
- Roosevelt followed by Truman
- Poland
- Germany.
2 Summarise your conclusion.

▼ Source R

American revisionist historians have put the blame on their own side, on the determination to consolidate and extend US economic dominance, or at least on the distinct change of policy that came with Truman's inheritance of the White House. Recent scholars have pinned the responsibility squarely on Stalin and his imperial ambitions. Neither answer is persuasive. Leaders of great powers, amid wars and negotiations and the constant press of events, are seldom able to devise a coherent plan, or to apply it.

The Soviet Union had an ideology which gave the capitalist West ample cause to be nervous, and Russia had a history which mandated a suspicion of its neighbours. The tensions in their relations might have been eased, as President Roosevelt had believed, by American goodwill. But Roosevelt died, and Truman had to prove himself fit to fill those giant shoes. Truman took the best advice on offer, and the bulk of his cabinet, his diplomats and his Soviet experts, urged him to be firm. It is just possible, had Roosevelt lived, and had there been no stricken Europe between them, no western European allies still festooned in embarrassing colonial entanglements, and in a most prickly pride, that the Cold War might not have got under way. But Roosevelt was dead, the Americans had the monopoly of the bomb, and Europe sprawled between the victors, to be occupied, rescued or fought over.

The real culprit was the dreadful logic faced by both sides when they confronted the problem of what was to be done with defeated Germany. The dilemma was plain: to ensure that it could not start a third European War, but also to treat it fairly enough, so that German resentment would not explode dangerously in the future, as it had done after the Treaty of Versailles in 1919. For Stalin that meant occupation, and a defensive zone for the Soviet Union throughout eastern Europe. For the West it mean de-Nazification, free enterprise and stable democratic institutions, with the emphasis often on the stability rather than

the democracy. But the problem of Germany, where both sides were prepared to be ruthless, led inevitably to the problem of Poland, where the West was touched by honour and sentiment and by domestic political considerations.

Roosevelt's admirable hopes for a post-war settlement based on the wartime Grand Alliance depended upon the maintenance of trust, which withered in the bitter disputes over Poland in the summer between the conferences of Yalta and Potsdam. But Germany and Poland were only the most dramatic aspects of the much larger problem of Europe. Unconditional surrender meant Germany laid waste, Britain exhausted, France and Italy demoralised, and the whole continent of Europe prostrate.

Only Russia and the United States were in a position even to begin to grapple with the challenge. Neither one, it was soon clear, was prepared to let the other impose their different solutions: Sovietisation on the one hand, and the Marshall Plan on the other. Europe's age-old question of the balance of power blended swiftly into the ideological struggle between capitalism and communism. The two incompatible approaches to the problem of Europe were to become the competing visions of the wider struggle between the two mutually uncomprehending camps.

(Adapted from: M Walker. *The Cold War.*)

▼ Source S

You don't really need to decide whether Stalin **did** intend to conquer the world in 1945; what matters is the fact that many people in the West **thought** he did – or were persuaded to think so – and were ready to support the West's policies of counter-attack. In other words, what actually happened was less important than what people **thought** had happened, and (as in all wars!) actions by one side which may have been genuinely defensive, looked aggressive to the other.

(From: H Ward. *World Powers in the Twentieth Century.*)

The testing of containment (1947–53)

Unit outcomes

- Explain how the US policy of containment was tested both in Europe (in detail) and Asia (in outline).
- Describe the clash over post-war arrangements in Germany and the events of the Berlin Blockade.
- Assess the rival viewpoints over Berlin and evaluate the options open to the West.
- Recognise the importance of the Korean War.
- Evaluate the state of the Cold War at the death of Stalin (1953).
- Interpret historical sources.
- Create an empathetic picture of life in Berlin during the blockade.

Germany and the Cold War

Timeline		
1945	February	Yalta Conference
	July–August	Potsdam Conference
1946		US and Britain stop deliveries of reparations to Russian zone
1947	January	Bizonia: union of American and British zones
1948	June	Currency reform in West Germany; Berlin Blockade and Berlin airlift begin
1949	May	Berlin Blockade and airlift end
	July	First Russian atomic bomb explodes
	September	Federal Republic of Germany
	October	German Democratic Republic
1953		Death of Stalin
1955	May	Federal Republic of Germany a member of NATO
1956	January	German Democratic Republic a member of Warsaw Pact
1961		Berlin Crisis and building of the Berlin Wall

Introduction

At the end of the war, the Western Allies were determined that Germany would never again be a threat to peace. The country was to be divided into zones of occupation between the USA, Britain, Russia and France. Control would be in the hands of the Allied Control Council, consisting of the four military governors of the occupied zones. Berlin would be similarly divided into four and control here would be by the Allied Kommandatura. Germany would become a political unit and would be treated as an economic unit. France, however, was opposed to a centralised Germany which she saw as a threat to her security.

Reparations

It was agreed at Yalta that Germany would pay reparations, the bulk of which would go to Russia. The Russians claimed $10 000 million, and although the Allies accepted the principle, they did not accept the amount. It was agreed at Potsdam that the USSR could take reparations from her own zone of occupation, and also that she should receive from the Western zones 25 per cent of all machinery and industrial plant that was unnecessary for Germany's peacetime economy. In return, the USSR would send from her zone to the Western zones food, coal and raw materials to the value of 60 per cent of what she received from the West.

These were the plans, but the reality was different. The Americans and British found that their zones could not produce sufficient food to support their people. Between 1945 and 1947, the British and Americans had to import food to the value of $700 million per year. At the same time, they still had to send reparations to the Russians. By 1946, the Russians were holding up their counter-deliveries of food and raw materials.

In the spring of 1946, the Americans and British stopped deliveries to the Russians, and in September, the Americans made a proposal to unify the economy of the American zone with any or all of the other zones. Only the British accepted and on 1 January 1947, the two zones merged into Bizonia. The French also joined in mid-1948.

The American plan had been to run Germany as one economic unit, but instead the country had become divided economically between West and East. It was not long before the Western Allies began to draw up a constitution for their half of Germany; so obviously they were planning to make West Germany an independent state. This alarmed the Russians who did not want a strong, rich German state in the West. They wanted to dominate Germany by keeping her poor.

The Berlin Blockade

As you can see from Source A, Berlin was not on the border between East and West, it was right in the heart of the Soviet occupation zone of East Germany and was similarly divided into four sectors like the rest of Germany. The Russians decided to try to force the Allies out of Berlin – which one Russian leader described as 'a bone stuck in the throat'.

Soviet action was triggered by the American decision to introduce a new currency – the Deutsche Mark – into West Germany and West Berlin. This would promote economic recovery and curb inflation and the black market.

In April 1948, the Russians had begun to impose restrictions on road and rail links between West Berlin and the Western zones. But after the introduction of the new Western currency in June, the Soviets cut all rail, road and canal links to West Berlin (24 June). West Berlin was now isolated about 200 km inside Soviet-occupied territory. The Russians also hurried to introduce their own currency reform.

The Western Allies had three options: they could try to break the blockade by force, send-ing military convoys from West Germany to West Berlin; they could pull out of West Berlin and abandon the city to the Russians; or they could try to overcome the blockade by moving supplies in by air. The third option was adopted.

The Berlin airlift

The Western Allies mounted a massive effort. The initial estimate was that 4 500 tons of supplies would be required every day, and round-the-clock flying would be necessary.

Transport aircraft were drawn from all over the world and by December 1948, 4 500 tons were being flown in daily. Planes arrived at and left Berlin every 30 seconds. By March 1949, the figure was up to 8 000 tons a day and on 9 May 1949, the Russians called off the blockade.

During the summer of 1948 the Americans and British imposed a counter-blockade on goods going from the Western zones to the Eastern zone. As East Germany was dependent on the West for its supplies of coal and steel, by early 1949 the East German economy was virtually at a standstill.

Results of the blockade

'The Berlin Blockade was a deliberate attack on the Western position in Germany and on the American commitment to Europe' (P Windsor. *History of Berlin*. 1963). But Stalin had obviously miscalculated, and the success of the airlift was a major defeat for him. It was now clear that there was going to be no agreement between America and Russia. In April 1949, President Truman had set up the North Atlantic Treaty Organisation (NATO), a defensive military

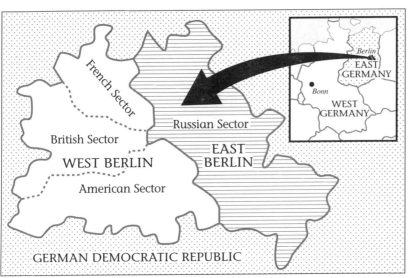

alliance of twelve countries directed against Russia. The first commander-in-chief was General Eisenhower and headquarters were set up in Paris. Membership of NATO committed the USA to war in advance and swept away the principles of the Monroe Doctrine. American rearmament budgets were increased considerably. Truman's policy of containment had been tested in Berlin, and NATO became an important instrument in carrying the policy further.

The Russian response came a few years later, with the formation, in 1955, of the Warsaw Pact, a military alliance of communist states. Europe was now divided into two armed camps. In July 1949, the Russians had exploded their first atomic bomb.

In another way, too, the Berlin blockade hardened the rival positions in the Cold War – it accelerated the creation of two separate German states. In May 1949, the three Western zones of Germany became the German Federal Republic with Bonn as its capital and Konrad Adenauer as the first chancellor. In October 1949, the Soviet zone became the German Democratic Republic.

No peace treaty with Germany was signed. The Soviets refused to recognise the existence of West Germany and the West refused to recognise East Germany. In this way, America and Russia acknowledged their failure to solve the German problem. Their fears had led to a divided Germany and a divided Berlin – a compromise of sorts had been reached.

▼ Source B

The new currency made necessary the permanent division of Germany. The worthless old marks flooded into the Soviet zone. The Soviet Military Governor had to take emergency measures to protect eastern Germany. To keep out speculators who were making profits out of the currency situation, some barriers were set up on the lines of communication between Berlin and the western zones.

(Adapted from: 'Soviet Foreign Policy', an article written by Ilya S Kremer from a British Magazine in 1968.)

▼ Source C

The Soviet authorities were ready to provide food and fuel for the population of the whole of Berlin, but the Western occupying powers deprived the inhabitants of West Berlin of the possibility of obtaining any help from Eastern Germany and tried to represent the situation thus created as a blockade ... The USA organised a so-called 'airlift' to supply West Berlin by air ... This stunt served the purpose of propaganda and

was also bound to intensify the Cold War.

(Statement in a Russian newspaper, September 1949.)

▼ Source D

On 3 July 1948, Marshal Sokolovsky said that the 'technical difficulties' (in Berlin) would continue until the West had abandoned its plans for a West German government.

(Extract from a school textbook, published in 1976.)

▼ Source E

When Berlin falls, Western Germany will be next.

(General Lucius Clay, US Commander in Berlin – 1948.)

▼ Source F

The Berlin Blockade is a move to test our capacity and will to resist. This action and their previous attempts to take over Greece and Turkey were part of a Russian plan to probe for soft spots in the Western Allies' position all around their own perimeter.

(President Truman of the USA.)

▼ Source G Hopeful youngsters in West Berlin wait for a shower of gifts

© Press and Information office of the Federal Republic of Germany, Bonn

▼ Source H
The most important clause of the Atlantic Pact

The parties agree that an armed attack against one or more of them in Europe or North America shall be considered an attack against them all.

◄*Source I*
Unintentional cupid
(*Baltimore Sun*, July
1949)
(From: GA Smith. *The
USA as a World
Power.*)

Activities ·····························

1 What arrangements were made at Yalta and Potsdam for the treatment of Germany at the end of the Second World War?
2 Explain the plan about reparations and how this was to be fitted into the treatment of Germany as one economic unit.
3 Analyse and explain the Soviet viewpoint expressed in Source B.
4 What was the real Soviet reason for the blockade?
5 The Western Allies had three options in the face of the Russian blockade. Use the suggested problem-solving approach (on this page) and evaluate the advantages and drawbacks of each of these options.
6 Use the sources to describe and contrast the US view of why the airlift was necessary, with the official Russian view.
7 Put yourself in the position of one of the spectators shown in the photograph (Source G). Describe a day in your life during January 1949.
8 Study Source I. Identify four members of the group. Explain the viewpoint of the American cartoonist and how he sees the Russians.
9 Explain the importance of the Atlantic Pact (Source H).
10 The hardening of the Cold War. Write a short note on each of these developments explaining their general aim and how they are linked together.

AMERICAN ACTION	SOVIET RESPONSE
Truman Doctrine (1947)	Cominform (1947)
Marshall Plan (1947)	Comecon (1949)
NATO (1949)	Warsaw Pact (1955)

11 As a class, discuss how the Berlin Blockade and its aftermath caused a new low freezing-point in the Cold War.

·····························

Understanding historical skills and concepts

Problem-solving

The development of problem-solving techniques is an important skill which will be useful for you in many areas of your life.

An organised approach to problem-solving is necessary and you can practise it in your study of Human and Social Sciences. The following method is suggested.

1 Identify the problem or problems. State the problem in your own words.
2 Decide on your aims, goals and objectives and those of other people involved. These should be short-term and long-term objectives, and might require an analysis of why these objectives have been chosen.
3 Gather information about the problem(s). This may involve measuring, interviewing, analysing documents, using questionnaires and surveys.
4 Analyse the context, components and causes of the problem(s). All relevant factors should be considered, analysed and evaluated. Different perspectives should be studied and discussed.

5 Consider alternative solutions. In how many ways could this problem be solved? What would be the consequences and any possible reaction, both for you and for society in general?
6 Decide on the best solution.
7 Implement the solution. What is the best way to take action? What should be done first: what are the priorities? Check the progress of the action.
8 Evaluate your progress. Was the problem solved? What could be done better? What can be learned from this experience? Should there be any sequel or follow-up?
9 Record and communicate. The details of the problem-solving process should be recorded and the results communicated to all interested parties.

This framework is, of course, flexible and may be adapted to fit particular situations.

Activities ....
Use the given problem-solving method to prepare a presentation on:
1 access to Berlin in June 1948;
2 the placing of Russian missiles in Cuba (October 1962).
You will find some information on the Cuban missile crisis on pages 174–175, but you should also use books from your school or local library.
....

Containment in the East

In April 1949, when the North Atlantic Treaty was signed, and with the end of the Berlin blockade in May, the American government could be pleased about the world situation. The march of Russian communism in Europe seemed to have been contained by the Truman Doctrine and NATO.

However, a few months later, the view did not seem so favourable. In August 1949 the USSR exploded its first atomic bomb and on 1 October, the People's Republic of China was proclaimed. China had been 'lost' to the communists led by Mao Zedong.

China

Americans had always had special regard for China: missionaries had been sent there during the nineteenth century and schools set up, and America had wanted to prevent the break-up of China into European spheres of interest. A myth started to grow: 'America helped the Chinese, in return the Chinese loved the Americans!'

A civil war had broken out in China in 1927 when nationalist forces under Chian Kai-shek tried to destroy the Chinese communists. The war ebbed and flowed until 1937, when both sides agreed to a truce so that they could concentrate on the war against Japan. However, civil war was always likely to break out again when Japan was defeated.

During the Second World War, the Americans flew in millions of dollars worth of weapons and supplies to help China fight against Japan. Towards the end of the war, American officials tried to negotiate a lasting settlement between the two groups, but the two leaders failed to reach agreement.

In December 1945, Truman recognised Chiang's nationalists as the legal government of China and the Americans provided assistance with supplies and money, and even the support of some US marines (who did not take part in the fighting).

By 1948–49, it became clear that, in spite of American aid, the communists were winning control of China. There was nothing that the American government could do about it. A letter from the secretary of state to President Truman (see Source K) explained the situation.

▼ ***Source J*** East Asia in 1955
(Adapted from: GA Smith. *The USA as a World Power.*)

▼ Source K

The leaders of the Kuomintang had proved incapable of meeting the crisis confronting them, its troops had lost the will to fight, and its Government had lost popular support. The Communists, on the other hand, through a ruthless discipline and fanatical zeal, attempted to sell themselves as guardians and liberators of the people ... the only alternative open to the United States was full-scale intervention in [sic] behalf of a Government which had lost the confidence of its own troops and its own people ...

The unfortunate but inescapable fact is that the ominous result of the civil war in China was beyond the control of the government of the United States ...

(Extract from a letter from Dean Acheson to President Truman, 30 July 1949, dealing with US/Chinese relationships from 1944–49.)

In October 1949, Chiang and his defeated army escaped to the island of Formosa (now known as Taiwan) and Mao became leader of the communist People's Republic of China.

In January 1950, Mao visited Stalin in Moscow and a treaty of assistance was signed. This seemed to confirm the view held by many Americans that the Chinese revolution was a front for Russian action.

Activities

1 Study Source J – the map of East Asia. Identify China, Japan, Formosa, Vietnam and the USSR.
2 Why was the 'loss' of China such a blow for the Americans?
3 What reasons does the US secretary of state give for this 'loss' of China (Source K)?

NSC 68

In the same month (January 1950), Truman asked his National Security Council for a wide-ranging review of all of America's foreign and defence policy in the light of the loss of China and the Soviet possession of an atomic bomb. In April 1950, the Council presented its report in Paper No. 68 (known as NSC 68). The report saw recent developments as one global theme: the rising strength of Russia. It foresaw an 'indefinite period of tension and danger' and considered that America must be ready to meet each challenge promptly. NSC 68 pointed out that containment required superior military

strength; and now that the USSR had the atomic bomb, the USA must embark on massive conventional rearmament. The estimated yearly cost of this policy to the USA would be $35 to $50 billion.

President Truman was not completely convinced by NSC 68 and he knew that the US Congress would not approve such huge military expenditure.

Then, on 25 June 1950, communist troops from North Korea invaded the democratic republic of South Korea.

Activities

Explain the relationship between NSC 68 and the policy of containment.

The Korean War

President Truman reacted immediately. He ordered US forces to give sea and air cover to the South Koreans and he sent a strong fleet to patrol the straits between Taiwan and mainland China. He organised the United Nations Security Council to give assistance to the South Koreans.

For Truman, this was confirmation of the views put forward in NSC 68, that is, there was a huge Moscow-directed communist conspiracy to take over the world. This threat had to be contained.

The crucial moment of the war came early in 1951. Chinese troops had come to the assistance of the North Koreans in December 1950, and within a few months, they were driving into South Korea. General MacArthur, the UN military commander, wanted to extend the war against China, which would probably have meant the use of the atomic bomb. But President Truman rejected this option and in April 1951, he relieved MacArthur of his command. The Korean War remained a limited war – limited in area and limited to non-nuclear weapons. Eventually, in 1953, an armistice was arranged.

In addition to the huge number of casualties on both sides, the effect of the Korean War was important. Truman was now convinced that the NSC 68 policy was correct. He persuaded Congress to grant a huge military budget and the USA began a large rearmament programme. The remilitarisation of Germany and Japan was promoted, and the USA would give aid to any anti-communist government anywhere. The adoption of NSC 68 reinforced the Truman Doctrine as the basis of the policy of containment throughout the world.

Indo-China

South of Korea, in Indo-China (or Vietnam) another war had been going on against the communists since 1946. At the end of the Second World War, the French had returned to reclaim their former colony of Indo-China. They soon became involved in a guerrilla war against the local communists led by Ho Chi Minh. By 1950, the USA was providing financial support to the French, but they were not yet involved militarily.

McCarthyism

To persuade Congress to approve his policy of containment, President Truman had highlighted the dangers of communism and how communist traitors had undermined and weakened governments – various spies had been uncovered both in Britain and the USA. By the early 1950s, this had become a 'witchhunt' against individuals in the US government. The hunt was led by Senator Joe McCarthy and the setbacks in China and Korea gave him his chance. McCarthy exercised considerable influence through his manipulation of the press and television. His criticisms damaged the Truman government and contributed to the Republican victory in the 1952 presidential elections. McCarthy's activities were closed down in 1954, and he died in 1957.

The death of Stalin

Stalin died on 5 March 1953. In the few months before his death, evidence suggests that he was preparing the Soviet Union for a great war with the USA. The main theme of the Communist Party Congress in October 1952 was that war was inevitable. Late in 1952, a plot of Jewish doctors was uncovered: they were to be purged and this would be the provocation for the struggle against the USA. With the excuse that he was ridding the Soviet Union of Western influence, Stalin made threats against the lives of other leaders such as Molotov, Malenkov, Khrushchev and even Beria.

▼ *Source L*
Edvard Radzinsky writes in his biography of Stalin, published in 1996

Like all previous victims, Beria was required to complete the work entrusted to him before his removal. He was more immediately relevant to the Great Dream than anyone else.

The new, more powerful nuclear bomb had been tested under Beria's supervision in 1951. Now, in 1953, his scientists had created a new weapon of unprecedented power. The transportable hydrogen bomb was shortly to be tested. Its yield was expected to be twenty times that of the bomb dropped on Hiroshima. There was nothing else like it in the world. The Boss [Stalin] alone possessed such a weapon. (The bomb would not be tested till August 1953, some months after his death.)

Before this new weapon became available, Stalin had ordered Beria to complete Moscow's rocket defences. It had been decided at the end of the forties to surround Moscow with special formations armed with enough ballistic missiles to shoot down any plane flying toward the city. Two gigantic concrete rings were built, with anti-aircraft rocket installations at intervals around them. The Boss insisted that this work should be carried out in feverish haste. The work was done by the experienced construction workers available to Beria's department. There were six hundred rockets to each placement. Twenty rockets could be launched simultaneously. Radar stations traced the targets, rockets soared ... But co-ordination was unsatisfactory. The Boss told Beria to hurry up. The engineers were housed in barracks. Beria summoned the chief designer and told him that the system must be made to work – or else.

It began to work. By early 1953, the Boss knew that Moscow would soon be looking at the West from behind a picket fence of rockets.

Everything was ready: the superweapon and the most powerful army in the world, which had not yet forgotten the art of killing. It had not been idle talk when Stalin said to Molotov soon after the war: 'The First World War delivered one country from capitalist slavery, the Second has created the socialist system, and the Third will finish imperialism for ever.' In 'in-depth language' this meant: 'We shall start a war and we shall finish it.' The Great Dream, bequeathed to him by the God Lenin, would come true.

▲ Stalin and other Soviet leaders, Moscow, August 1945
(From: E Radzinsky. *Stalin.*)

Activities

Study Source L.

1 To what extent do Stalin's plans for 1953 agree with his policies towards the West since 1945?

2 Explain why or why not you would consider the source to be reliable (trustworthy).

Before these events could happen Stalin died of what was called a 'haemorrhage of the brain', perhaps this had been encouraged by his intended victims. His death marked the end of the first stage of the Cold War. New leaders took over in the Soviet Union, and already in January 1953, Dwight Eisenhower had replaced Truman as president of the USA. In 1953, another phase of the Cold War was about to begin.

Lack of space has prevented fuller treatment of the civil war in China and the Korean War. For further details learners should consult the references in the further reading section on page 188.

Coexistence and crises (1953–69)

Unit outcomes

- Describe the development of nuclear weapons.
- Contrast the policies of the American and Russian leaders.
- Explain the revolts in the Russian satellites.
- Analyse the dangerous situations in Berlin (1961) and Cuba (1962).
- Interpret historical sources.
- Apply the problem-solving model to the Cuban situation.

Introduction

By 1953, the first stage of the Cold War had been completed. The wartime leaders, Truman in America and Stalin in Russia, had implemented their rival policies and had now passed from the scene.

In the years that followed, later leaders of the two superpowers adopted different policies as circumstances changed. It will not be possible for us to study the details of the many events up to the resignation of Mikhail Gorbachev in 1991 – when it could be said that the Cold War ended. What we shall do is consider the differing policies in general within a chronological framework; and several important crises will be studied in greater depth.

The nuclear armaments race

From the beginning of the Cold War the development of nuclear weapons was a constant factor in the clash between the superpowers.

At the Potsdam Conference in July 1945, President Truman had told Stalin about the successful testing of an atomic bomb, and bombs were dropped on the Japanese cities of Hiroshima and Nagasaki in August. Stalin accepted the nuclear challenge and over the next ten years the Soviet Union quickly caught up with America (see Source A).

In the first few years after 1945, America had a huge nuclear superiority and was not vulnerable to a possible nuclear attack from the USSR. The USSR had many more ground forces. However, on 4 October 1957, the Americans had

a great shock when the USSR launched Sputnik, the world's first space satellite. Sputnik I was very small – only 60 centimetres in diameter – but one month later, the Russians launched Sputnik II which was bigger and carried a black and white dog called Laika (see Source C). The launch of this space satellite meant that the Russians had the capacity to fire a rocket across continents – a rocket which could easily carry a nuclear bomb. The USA had lost its invulnerability.

In 1958, the USA created the National Aeronautics and Space Administration (NASA) to promote the development of rocket technology, and the first US space satellite was launched in the same year.

As rocket technology improved and the number of nuclear weapons increased (see Source B for the situation in 1962), it became clear to the politicians on both sides of the Cold War, that a nuclear war would lead to the destruction of human society – to what was called Mutual Assured Destruction (MAD). So national defence came to be based on deterring potential aggression, and making sure that any confrontation between the superpowers did not develop into a real all-out shooting war.

Later developments were agreements to limit the spread of nuclear weapons, for example, the SALT treaties and popular campaigns for nuclear disarmament.

Activities

1 Study Source A and describe how the USSR was at first inferior in weapons to the USA and then, for a short time, superior.

2 a Explain the message in Source C.
  b How has this situation arisen and in what way was it important?
  c Do you consider the cartoon to be biased? If so, in what way?

3 List the advantages in weapons which each side had in 1962 (Source B). Find out why 1962 was a significant year.

4 Explain the MAD concept and what it meant for the policies of the superpowers.

5 Describe the explosion and effects of a hydrogen bomb (Sources D and E).

▼ *Source A* The balance of terror

UNITED STATES	
1945–9	American monopoly of nuclear weapons: United States could strike into heart of USSR by using bombers based on borders of Soviet Union
1947	670 000 men in armed forces
1949	Stockpile 100+ atomic weapons
1952	First H-bomb exploded
1953	1 000+ atomic and hydrogen weapons
1955	1 300+ bombers capable of delivering nuclear weapons to USSR
1957	–
1958	Space satellite + ICBM
1960	Submarine launched ballistic missile (SLBM)
1961	–
1962	First man in space
1968	–

SOVIET UNION	
1945–9	To counter the American threat large Soviet armies were kept in satellite countries
1947	2,8 million men in armed forces
1949	First Soviet atomic weapons test
1952	–
1953	First Soviet H-bomb exploded; 100–200 nuclear weapons; (bombers incapable of reaching USA)
1955	350+ bombers capable of delivering nuclear weapons to USA
1957	Space satellite showed rocket power to carry intercontinental ballistic missile (ICBM)
1958	–
1960	–
1961	First man in space
1962	–
1968	Submarine-launched ballistic missile

	USA	USSR
ICBM	450	76
MRBM	250	700
Bombers	2 260	1 600
Tanks	16 000	38 000
Submarines:		
nuclear	32	12
conventional	260	495
Cruisers:	66	30
escorts	1 107	189
Battleships and carriers	76	nil

▼ **Source C** Dog daze (*St. Louis Dispatch*, 1957)
(From: GA Smith. *The USA as a World Power.*)

◀**Source D**
Nuclear bomb test

▼ **Source E**
The first hydrogen bomb

America exploded the first hydrogen bomb on 1 November 1952 at Eniwetok Atoll in the Pacific. As the bomb exploded flames 2 miles wide and 5 miles high shot into the air. A pillar of smoke rose for 25 miles and a mushroom cloud formed a hundred miles long. The test island disappeared leaving a hole in the ocean bed 175 feet deep and a mile in diameter. Experts estimated that in a modern city the blast would cover an area of 300 square miles. A war with such bombs would destroy civilisation.
(From: J Vick. *Modern America.*)

American policy

In the presidential election in November 1952, the Republican, Dwight Eisenhower, won a massive victory and he took office in January 1953. During the election the Truman government was attacked as being 'soft' on communism and the new Secretary of State, John Foster Dulles, was determined to use US power more aggressively.

He considered that the policy of containment was not enough.

▼ Source F

John Foster Dulles testifies to the Senate Committee on Foreign Relations, 15 January 1953

We shall never have a secure peace or a happy world so long as Soviet Communism dominates one-third of all the peoples that there are, and is in the process of trying at least to extend its rule to many others ...

Therefore, we must always have in mind the liberation of these captive peoples ... a policy [of containment] is bound to fail because a purely defensive policy never wins against an aggressive policy. If our only policy is to stay where we are, we will be driven back.

(From: GA Smith. *The USA as a World Power*.)

Dulles favoured a policy of 'brinkmanship', that is, being ready to go right to the brink of war in disputes with the enemy. In 1956 he stated: 'The ability to get to the verge without getting into the war is the necessary art. If you cannot master it, you inevitably get into war. If you try to run away from it, if you are scared to go to the brink, you are lost.'

This policy seemed to have dangers especially as Dulles talked of the 'deterrent of massive retaliatory power' – implying that nuclear bombs could be used.

The suggestion that Eisenhower was considering the nuclear option in Korea seemed to focus the peace talks and an armistice was concluded in July 1953. However, the USA refused to be drawn into the war in Indo-China (Vietnam) when the French suffered a major defeat at Dien Bien Phu in May 1954.

Dulles set out to strengthen the containment of the Communist Bloc by forming alliances of the states around it. NATO was already in place and in September 1954, the South-East Asia Treaty Organisation (SEATO) was formed in the East. The Baghdad Pact was signed in February 1955, to cover the Middle East.

However, the nuclear threat was growing – the first Soviet H-bomb had been tested in 1953 – and the American leaders were pleased to attend a Summit Conference at Geneva in October 1955. There was talk of the 'Geneva Spirit' and the end of the Cold War. The new Russian leaders were also prepared to talk for they had their own problems.

▼ Source G Don't be afraid ... I can always pull you back (*Washington Post*, 1955)

(From: GA Smith. *The USA as a World Power*.)

Russian policy

After the death of Stalin in March 1953, a collective leadership was set up; Georgi Malenkov became prime minister and Nikita Khrushchev the secretary of the Russian Communist Party. Beria, head of the secret police, was shot by his colleagues in June 1953. In February 1955, Malenkov resigned and Bulganin became prime minister.

At the Party Congress in February 1956, Khrushchev astonished both the communist and non-communist worlds. He bitterly denounced Stalin as a brutal dictator who had set up a 'personality cult' to get everyone to say how wonderful he was. Khrushchev recognised the nuclear alternative and proposed that the communist countries should 'coexist' peacefully with the West. Khrushchev said:

The principle of peaceful coexistence is gaining ever wider international recognition ... And this is natural, for in present conditions there is no other way out. Indeed there are only two ways: either peaceful coexistence or the most destructive war in history. There is no third way.

Thirdly, he talked of 'different roads to Socialism' implying that a socialist state need not be an exact model of the Soviet state, that is, achieved by violent revolution. The road to power could be a parliamentary one.

Activities

1 Explain in your own words how Dulles' policies differed from those of Truman.
2 a Describe how the cartoon in Source G illustrates one of the policies of John Foster Dulles.
  b What is the danger of this policy?
3 a What were the three aspects of Khrushchev's speech in 1956?
  b In what ways was the speech revolutionary?

The satellites revolt

Khrushchev's aim seems to have been to unite the communist world under Russian leadership and to overcome objections to Stalin's brand of leadership.

Even before 1956, there had been indications of the new Russian approach. In 1953, there were demonstrations in Czechoslovakia which were suppressed by local police. In June 1953, workers in **East Germany** were told that they must produce more, in longer hours, for a 10 per cent pay cut. Building workers in East Berlin went on strike and were soon joined by other workers.

Demonstrating crowds filled the streets both in East Berlin and in other East German cities. Russian troops were called in to restore order. A curfew and martial law were declared and there were reports of arrests and executions by the Russian authorities. One result was an increase in East Germans seeking refuge in the West – about 300 000 in 1953 alone. However, the Russians announced considerable economic concessions to East Germany: the new measures which had triggered the unrest were withdrawn; reparations to Russia were cancelled; industries confiscated by Russia after the war were returned and Soviet occupation costs reduced. In March 1954, Russia recognised East Germany as an independent state.

In **Yugoslavia,** the communist leader Marshal Tito had led liberation from the Nazis in 1945. He had declared himself neutral in the Cold War and had refused to become a satellite of the Soviet Union. Stalin had used propaganda and threats against him, but had drawn back from direct military action. In 1951, the Western Allies had given Tito a 50 million pound loan to buy arms. Now, in May 1955, Khrushchev and Bulganin visited Yugoslavia to make peace with

Tito. Tito refused to come into the Soviet bloc and Khrushchev admitted that in the original dispute the Soviet Union had been wrong. It looked as if a national approach to communism was permissible.

The **Poles** were delighted with Khrushchev's 1956 speech. They wanted better living conditions and also less control by the Russians. This seemed an appropriate moment to demand these concessions. In July 1956, unrest broke out in the city of Poznan and there were demonstrations in other Polish cities. Gomulka (who had been imprisoned under Stalin) became first secretary and senior Stalin-appointed officials were dismissed. The Russians were alarmed and Khrushchev, Bulganin and Zhukov flew to Warsaw to hold talks with Polish leaders.

These talks were extremely tense and the use of force was threatened on both sides. The Poles had no intention of taking the country out of the Soviet bloc and finally Khrushchev accepted a form of national communism in Poland with much less Soviet control. In a way, Khrushchev had succeeded because Poland remained a member of the Warsaw Pact. Later in 1956, the Gomulka government supported Russian intervention in Hungary and in 1968 assisted with the suppression in Czechoslovakia.

In 1956, the revolt in **Hungary** was a test of the policies of both the USA and the USSR. Here was Dulles' chance to roll back communism and liberate people from communist rule; here was Khrushchev's chance to put into practice the principle he had proclaimed in his speech to the Party Congress.

In the time of Stalin, Hungary had been ruled by CP Rakosi. He used the secret police ruthlessly and the economy was geared to satisfying the demands of East Germany and Russia. In many ways, Hungary became a Russian colony. When Stalin died, Rakosi resigned to be replaced as prime minister by the moderate Imre Nagy. Nagy introduced some economic reforms and became popular with the Hungarian people. However, in 1955, Khrushchev brought back the tougher Rakosi who re-instituted his previous methods. This aroused demonstrations and strikes: there was fighting between Hungarian civilians and Russian troops and demands for the return of Nagy as prime minister. A new national government, headed by Nagy, was formed and it seemed – on the model of Poland – that Russia was prepared to accept a lessening of her influence in the country; the Red Army began to withdraw. However, Nagy was not able to control the demands of Hungarian nationalism for a multi-party democracy, the neutrality of Hungary and withdrawal from the Warsaw Pact.

Khrushchev was not prepared to accept this and, in early November, the Red Army came back in massive strength. The Hungarians appealed to the West for help, but the USA, Britain and France were involved in the Suez Crisis. President Eisenhower was in the middle of a presidential election; and anyway, what could the West do apart from considering the nuclear option? The aggressive bluff of Secretary of State Dulles had been called and the Hungarians were left to their fate. The Hungarian people resisted the tanks and the infantry of the Red Army and the fighting was savage (about 25 000 Hungarians were killed). By 14 November it was all over: a new pro-Russian government was put in power. Nagy was arrested and later shot.

Khrushchev accepted the reforms in Poland because she stayed loyal to Russia. But he was not prepared to accept Hungary's withdrawal from the communist bloc, nor were free elections possible because this would mean the end of communism. If Hungary was allowed to withdraw, other East European states would want to follow. The United Nations condemned the Soviet actions, and Eisenhower wrote a strong protest to Bulganin, but these actions were ignored by the Russian leaders. It was clear that the West would not risk a nuclear war to assist the 'liberation' of the peoples of East Europe.

Czechoslovakia (1968)

Twelve years after the suppression of Hungary, a similar situation arose in Czechoslovakia. Economic problems provoked popular unrest and in 1968 a new leader, Alexander Dubček, was appointed. He introduced liberal reforms but he emphasised that he was not going to take Czechoslovakia out of the Warsaw Pact, although he wanted the country to be free to sort out its own problems. Brezhnev, who had become the Russian leader after Khrushchev, accepted this at first. But he became alarmed when Tito and the Rumanian leader visited Dubček in Prague. Russian troops were sent into Czechoslovakia. Dubček was arrested and a new conservative government was set up. Czechoslovakia had gone the way of Hungary. In spite of Western protests Brezhnev justified his action by what became known as the Brezhnev Doctrine:

When internal and external forces hostile to Socialism attempt to turn the develop-ment of any Socialist country in the direction of the capitalist system, when a threat arises to the cause of Socialism in that country, a threat to the security of the Socialist Commonwealth as a whole – it already becomes not only a problem for the people of that country but also a general problem, the concern of all Socialist countries.

▼ **Source H**
Eyewitness in Hungary, 1956

According to a Vienna eyewitness, Budapest demonstrators eventually succeeded in removing the 24-feet-high (7-metre-high) statue of Stalin from its pedestal. Earlier attempts last night to remove it with the aid of winches and chains had failed. In the early hours of today, demonstrators procured blow-lamps and burned through the base of the statue, and amid a great shout of joy, sent the statue tumbling to the ground.

The eyewitness was impressed with the 'demonstratively passive attitude' adopted by the Hungarian police and troops. Unless demonstrators were armed and threatening, the police and troops ignored them. Many soldiers had removed the communist emblems from their caps.

▼ **Source I** Marshall Tito: the rebellious duckling

▼ **Source J** The Russians arrive in Czechoslovakia (1968)

"Of course, Mr Dubeck, we've had to bring a few lady stenographers, one or two secretaries and some tea boys ..."

Activities

1 Study the events of each of the satellite revolts: each country had one basic demand. What was it?

2 Describe and explain the outcome of the revolt in each country.

3 In your own words, explain the Brezhnev Doctrine.

4 Read Source H and then answer the following.

   a Why did the demonstrators want to remove the statue of Stalin?

   b Explain the attitude of the police and troops.

   c Explain if and why you would consider this source to be reliable.

5 Study Source I.

   a Give names to the various figures, including at least two of the chickens.

   b Suggest a date for this cartoon.

   c Explain the cartoonist's message referring to features in the cartoon.

6 Study Source J.

   a Who was Mr Dubček?

   b Name two of the figures in the column of Russians.

   c Explain the cartoonist's message referring to features in the cartoon.

   d Is this source biased in any way? Explain your answer.

The Berlin crisis: a case study

In the years after 1956, Khrushchev held firm to his policy of 'peaceful coexistence' as the only alternative to the catastrophe of a nuclear war with the USA. Yet he was not prepared to concede any advantages to the West. In 1959, he visited the USA and had a friendly and successful meeting with President Eisenhower at Camp David; yet he walked out of the Paris summit in 1960 after the American U2 spy plane had been shot down.

The 1957 Sputnik triumph seemed to give Khrushchev great confidence and combined with other reasons – as summarised by Walker in Source K – he was prepared to probe the limits of the brinkmanship of John Foster Dulles (who died in 1959). So, two very dangerous crises in the nuclear relationship came over Berlin and Cuba.

▼ **Source K**

Khrushchev's Berlin campaign was seen by ... President Kennedy's national security adviser, McGeorge Bundy, as a logical result of the Sputnik event. For the White House, the Berlin crisis was: 'A Soviet exercise in atomic diplomacy ... an effort to use a new appearance of Soviet nuclear strength to force changes in the centre of Europe.' It was the first deliberate nuclear challenge by the Kremlin, a foray into the world of risk and what Dulles had labelled brinkmanship. A complexity of motives were at work here: the pride of the Soviet military; the Kremlin's determination to be seen to command American respect; the temptation to test the depth of American resolve, and the cohesion of the NATO alliance, by some nuclear pressure. A final factor may have been Krushchev's own internal jostling with political rivals and constituencies, in the Soviet Union and perhaps in China.

(From: M Walker. *The Cold War.*)

Khrushchev provoked a Berlin crisis in late 1958 by threatening to sign a separate peace treaty with East Germany and hand over the access routes to West Berlin. This might well result in a blockade situation similar to that in 1948. He repeated this threat at his summit meeting with the new US president in June 1961. No agreement was reached.

The Berlin Wall

Follow the story by studying the sources.

▼ *Source L*
East German refugees crossing via West Berlin or across the West German border

1949	129 245
1950	197 782
1951	165 648
1952	182 393
1953	331 390
1954	184 198
1955	252 870
1956	279 189
1957	261 622
1958	204 092
1959	143 917
1960	199 188
1961	207 026
1962	21 356
1963	42 632
1964	41 876

- The total East German population in 1949 was 17 500 000.
- Between 1949 and 30 June 1961, a total of 2 600 000 refugees left East Germany via West Berlin or across the West German border.
- About 40 000 of those who left were skilled professional. Also 30 000 students.

(From: H Mills. *Twentieth Century World History in Focus*.)

▼ *Source M*
The drain of workers was creating a simply disastrous situation in the DDR [East Germany] ... If things had continued like this much longer, I don't know what would have happened.

(From: Khrushchev. *Khrushchev Remembers*.
In Nichol and Lang. *Modern World History GCSE*.)

▼ *Source N*
[West Berlin had] elegant shops flaunting the latest fashions and chic travel goods [and cafés where] the finest ice-cream sundaes ... were to be had and ... lush slabs of hazelnut Torte [cake] capped with outsized dollops of snow, outrageously rich Schlagsahne [whipped cream].

(From: Norman Gelb. *The Berlin Wall*.)

▼ *Source O*
[In East Berlin] I walked past the open door of a greengrocer's shop and saw a queue of about twenty-five people ... I faithfully joined the queue to find ... that I had been waiting for twenty minutes for ... potatoes! ... Meat is rather limited ... Butter at the moment is rationed to half a pound per head per week ... Often too in the summer months, butter and milk are 'off' before you have them home, as very few shops have refrigerators.

(From: Norman Gelb. *The Berlin Wall*.)

▼ *Source P*
Walter Ulbricht, President of East Germany, wanted to keep these people out of East Germany

... counter-revolutionary filth, spies and diversionists, speculators and traffickers, inhuman beings, prostitutes and corrupted teddy boys ...

On 13 August 1961, the East Germans began to build a wall to seal off the two sectors of the city.

▼ Map of the Berlin Wall

Activities

1 Why did Khrushchev provoke a crisis in Berlin?
Summarise Source K.

2 What percentage of the population of East Germany
fled to the West between 1949 and 1961? (Source L)

3 Use Sources Q and R to put yourself in the situation of
one of the East or West German people. Write a short
paragraph describing your feelings.

4 How did Walter Ulbricht justify the building of the
Wall? (Source P)

5 Divide the class into small groups to discuss Source S.
Each group should produce two newspaper headlines
for an article to go with the photograph:
a one for a West Berlin newspaper;
b and the other for an East Berlin newspaper.
Also discuss the reliability of the photograph.

6 Find out what President Kennedy meant when he said:
'Ich bin ein Berliner.'

▼ *Source S*

East German guards recovering the body of a young man shot dead while trying to escape to the West

The Cuban missile crisis (1962): nearly a 'hot' war

The greatest threat to peace came in 1962 in Cuba. For many years, Cuba had been a US protectorate, but in 1959 there was a revolution and the communists, led by Fidel Castro, took over. Castro confiscated land and seized American-owned properties. The USA reacted by freezing Cuban assets in the USA and refusing to buy Cuba's sugar crops. Meanwhile, the USSR provided economic support for Castro's government. It seemed as if the USA would have a communist neighbour.

The Bay of Pigs

In 1961 the US government backed an attempt by Cuban exiles to overthrow the Castro government. The invaders were to land at the Bay of Pigs. The raid failed disastrously and the reputation of US President Kennedy suffered.

Soviet missiles in Cuba

In October 1962, aerial photographs showed that missile launching pads were being built by the Russians in Cuba. Once the missiles were installed, almost every US city would be within range.

In a television broadcast, President Kennedy made it clear that the missiles had to go (Source U). But how could this be done? Kennedy had various options and after long discussions with his advisers, he decided to impose a naval blockade or quarantine to prevent Russian ships from reaching Cuba with missiles. At the same time, he negotiated with Khrushchev for the removal of the missiles from Cuba.

After ten days of tension and dramatic exchanges between Kennedy and Khrushchev, the Russians backed down and removed the missiles from Cuba. Kennedy lifted the quarantine and promised not to invade Cuba in future. He also promised privately to remove US missiles from Turkey on the border of the USSR.

Results

The Cuban crisis was the closest that the USA and USSR have come to making the Cold War into a 'hot' war. They went to the 'brink' and then pulled back.

Both leaders recognised how close they had come to a nuclear war, and in the following years measures were taken to prevent such a situation arising again. In 1963, a special telephone link – the so-called 'hot line' – was set up between Washington and Moscow so that the leaders could talk to each other in times of crisis. Also in 1963, a ban on nuclear testing in the atmosphere and under water was introduced. It was not until 1968 that a **non-proliferation treaty** on nuclear weapons was signed.

New words

non-proliferation treaty a treaty to prevent an increase in the numbers of nuclear weapons

▼ *Source T*

Then I had the idea of installing missiles in Cuba without letting the United States find out they were there until it was too late to do anything about them. The installation of our missiles would, I thought, restrain the US from hasty military action against Castro's government ... The Americans had surrounded our country with military bases ... and now they would learn just what it feels like to have enemy missiles pointing at you.

(From: Khrushchev. *Khrushchev Remembers*. In Nichol and Lang. *Modern World History GCSE*.)

Speech by President Kennedy, 22 October 1962

The 1930s taught us a clear lesson: aggressive conduct, if allowed to grow unchecked and unchallenged, ultimately leads to war. This nation is opposed to war. We are also true to our word. Our unswerving objective, therefore, must also be to prevent the use of these missiles against this or any other country and to secure their withdrawal or elimination from the western atmosphere.

(From: Nichol and Lang. *Modern World History GCSE.*)

Activities

1 What were Khrushchev's aims in planning to install missiles in Cuba as described in Source T?
2 Why did Kennedy take such strong action? (See Sources U and V.)

Extension activity

'We were eyeball to eyeball and the other fellow just blinked.'

To what extent do you agree with this statement about the Cuban crisis by an American official? Write a short essay in which you discuss how close the US and USSR came to a 'hot' war.

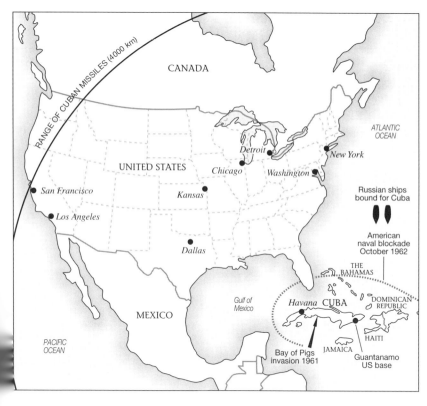

◀ **Source V**

Map of Cuba and the USA (Adapted from: Nichol and Lang. *Modern World History GCSE.*)

Détente (1969–79)

Unit outcomes

- Analyse the meaning and reasons for détente.
- Contrast examples of détente and examples of the Cold War.
- Interpret visual and written sources.
- Give an empathetic picture.

What was détente?

Détente is a French word which means 'easing of tension'. Applied to the Cold War, it meant a backing away from the confrontation of the previous 25 years.

	DÉTENTE 1969–1979					
	CHRONOLOGY					
	Leaders		**Conferences/ Meetings**	**Nuclear Developments**	**Crises**	**Other events**
Year	**USA**	**USSR**				
1969	Nixon	Brezhnev (since 1964)			USSR-China Border clashes	
1970						
1971			Kissinger to China			China admitted to UNO; Nixon's economic package
1972			Nixon to China; Nixon to USSR; Berlin Agreement	Salt I Biological Warfare Treaty		
1973			Vietnam Peace Treaty (Paris); Brezhnev to USA	H-Bomb Test (China)	Yom-Kippur War (Middle East)	Oil Crisis
1974	Ford		Nixon to USSR			Watergate Scandal (Nixon resigned)
1975			Helsinki Agreement; Ford to China		Angola	Saigon occupied by Viet Cong; Agreement on US grain sales to USSR
1976						Death of Mao Zedong (China)
1977	Carter					
1978			Camp David Agreement (Middle East)	Salt II		
1979					USSR invaded Afghanistan	Shah of Iran overthrown; US Hostage Crisis (Iran)

▼ Source A

President Nixon: Inaugural address, January 1969

After a period of confrontation, we are entering an era of negotiation. Let all nations know that during this Administration, our lines of communication are open ... With those who are willing to join, let us cooperate to reduce the burden of arms to strengthen the structure of peace.

(From: M Walker. *The Cold War.*)

▼ Source B

President Nixon, 1973

Détente does not mean the end of danger ... it is not the same thing as lasting peace.

(From: M Walker. *The Cold War.*)

▼ Source C

Comments by Henry Kissinger, American Secretary of State, 1974

Détente is a process of managing relations with a country that could become hostile in order to preserve the peace while maintaining our vital interests.

(From: Nichol and Lang. *Modern World History GCSE.*)

▼ Source D

Leonid Brezhnev, Soviet leader, 1973

During détente the struggle between the Soviet and American systems in the form of economics, politics and beliefs will be continued. But we shall make sure that this struggle takes place in a way which does not threaten wars, dangerous conflict and an uncontrolled arms race.

(From: Nichol and Lang. *Modern World History GCSE.*)

Activities ⋯⋯⋯⋯⋯⋯⋯⋯⋯

1 Work out a short definition of détente using Sources A, B, C and D.
2 What are some of the differences in the meanings of 'détente' as given in Sources A to D?
3 Why are these differences important?

⋯⋯⋯⋯⋯⋯⋯⋯⋯⋯⋯⋯⋯⋯⋯⋯⋯

Why détente?

There were several reason why the superpowers saw that a lessening of tension would be to their advantage.

First, there was the ever-present threat of nuclear war. The USA had come to recognise the strength of the USSR both in nuclear and conventional arms; and the Cuban crisis had shown the danger of a confrontation. There was also the huge cost of the arms race.

The split between Russia and China was a major factor. Since 1950, American hostility had kept China isolated. Mao Zedong disagreed strongly with the Soviet government on ideological matters and the USSR had withdrawn its aid to China in 1960. In 1969 there were heavy military clashes along the common border and at one stage, the Russians were said to be considering a **pre-emptive** nuclear strike against the Chinese nuclear research plants – the Chinese successfully tested an H-bomb in 1973. As the Korean and Vietnam war raged on her doorstep, China was concerned about American intentions, particularly over the possible use of nuclear weapons. Also, China did not want to be the odd one out in a group with America and Russia.

Then there was the economic argument. In spite of her huge wealth, America had overstretched her finances in the Vietnam war. The billions of dollars which she had spent on weapons could be better used elsewhere. In 1971, Nixon introduced a radical change in US economic policy (see Source H). The outcome of the Vietnam war was a huge blow to American self-confidence and she was no longer prepared to act as the world's policeman. Both Russia and China were anxious to develop stronger trading links with the West.

Various aspects of détente are described in the sources which follow; study these carefully before you attempt the activities.

New words

pre-emptive to disable a threatening enemy by an unexpected attack

The end in Vietnam

▼ Source E Peace with honour (*The Observer*, 6 April 1975)

(From: GA Smith. *The USA as a World Power.*)

'Greetings, French Liberators!'

'Greetings, Nationalist Liberators!'

'Greetings, Viet Cong Liberators!'

'Greetings, American Liberators!'

'Greetings, Government Liberators!'

'Greetings, North Vietnamese Liberators!'

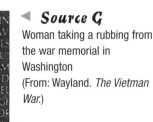

◀ *Source F*
Views of the Vietnamese people (*Denver Post*, 1972)
(From: GA Smith. *The USA as a World Power.*)

◀ *Source G*
Woman taking a rubbing from the war memorial in Washington
(From: Wayland. *The Vietman War.*)

▼ *Source H*

Nixon's economic package (August 1971)

> *Nixon unveiled a stunning package, a dramatic extension of state powers over the economy which – after a decade of dominant free-market theories – seem very sweeping. He imposed a freeze on wages, on prices, and a tax on all imports and effectively took the United States off the gold standard and the world off the dollar standard, by finally closing the gold window. The USA would no longer make gold available for dollars to other countries' central banks.*

(From: M Walker. *The Cold War.*)

Attitudes towards détente

▼ *Source I*

Leonid Brezhnev and détente (1974)

(From: Nichol and Lang. *Modern World History GCSE.*)

▼ *Source J*

A British view of détente (1976)

(From: H Ward. *World Powers in the Twentieth Century.*)

3 Comment critically on one of the Sources E, F or G, explaining how each source shows the suffering of one group of participants.

4 Explain the meaning of Nixon's economic package in Source H. Your teacher will help you with this.

5 Find out why President Nixon resigned.

6 From the chronology table at the beginning of this unit, find four events which show the spirit of détente and four events which show that the Cold War continued.

7 Put yourself in the position of the Soviet leader, Leonid Brezhnev, and explain your involvement in two of the events you have selected in question 6.

Activities • • • • • • • • • • • • • • • •

Attempt these activities in small groups. Further research may be necessary.

1 a Explain the meaning of the cartoon (Source I).
   b Is the cartoonist's viewpoint in favour of or against détente?

2 a Identify the two figures in Source J.
   b Explain the cartoonist's viewpoint and show if it is in favour of the Americans.

Extension activity • • • • • • • • • • • • • • • •

Do some research to find out about the role played by the USA and the USSR in either the Yom Kippur war in the Middle East (1973) or the war in Angola (1975).

The second Cold War (1979–85)

Unit outcomes

- Explain the reasons for the death of détente.
- Describe President Reagan's attitudes and actions.
- Evaluate the practicality of the 'Star Wars' project.
- Interpret historical sources.

The death of détente

Détente had been marked by a retreat from an all-out arms race and a search for an agreed level of armament – although not by any great disarmament. Détente involved agreement on Europe and on Third World conflicts. There were summits, conferences and visits by heads

THE SECOND COLD WAR (1979–1985) CHRONOLOGY						
	Leaders					
Year	**USA**	**USSR**	**Conferences/ Treaties**	**Nuclear/Space Developments**	**Crises**	**Other events**
1979	Carter (from 1977)	Brezhnev (from 1964)			Afghanistan: Soviet Invasion; US hostages (Iran)	Iran: Shah overthrown; Margaret Thatcher: British Prime Minister
1980				SALT II Agreement not accepted by US Senate		US hostages rescue attempt failed; Iraq invades Iran
1981	Reagan					Unrest in Poland: Martial Law declared; US hostages released (January)
1982		Andropov		START Talks began		Death of Brezhnev (November); Israel invades Lebanon (Middle East); Britain/Argentina at war over Falkland Islands
1983				US "Star Wars" project (SDI) announced	Korean airliner shot down (September); Nuclear alert (November)	US Marines occupied Grenada (Central America); Marine barracks bombed in Lebanon
1984		Chernenko				Death of Andropov
1985	Reagan					

of state, and altogether more tolerance of the rival viewpoints of the USA and USSR.

Yet, even by the middle of President Carter's term of office, there were signs of a hardening of attitude by the US government. Brezhnev seemed to be increasing defence spending in the Soviet Union – the new multi-warhead SS-20 missile was deployed in 1977, the Soviets were selling arms to Iraq and Syria, as well as giving support to the Palestine Liberation Organisation (PLO) and to Cuban involvement in Angola.

The Soviet invasion of Afghanistan was a decisive factor in influencing the US Senate against the SALT II treaty, while the Iran hostage crisis, with the failure of the rescue attempt, was a great humiliation for the USA.

Features of the new Cold War

- An increased emphasis by both sides on the likelihood of war and the need for military preparedness.
- A cooling in relations between the two powers shown by a lack of progress in the arms control talks. The USSR was accused of backing international terrorism.
- A wave of revolutions in Third World states – for this, the USA blamed the USSR.

◀ *Source A*

A cartoon from 1980
(From: GA Smith. *The USA as a World Power.*)

- Greater control of opponents of the government, both in the USA and the USSR, for example, huge reduction in the Jewish emigration quota from the USSR, martial law in Poland, **curbing** of trade union activities in the USA.

▼ *Source B*

Speech by President Reagan, January 1981

I know of no leader of the Soviet Union since the revolution, and including the present leadership, that has not more than once repeated in the various Communist congresses they hold, their determination that their goal must be the promotion of world revolution and a one-world Socialist or Communist state ... the only morality they recognise is what will further their cause, meaning they reserve unto themselves the right to commit any crime, to lie, to cheat, in order to attain that.

(From: M Walker. *The Cold War.*)

Activities

1 What event do you think Source A is referring to?
2 What message is the cartoonist trying to convey?

In January 1980, President Carter announced new registration of young men for the draft into the armed forces, as well as a 5 per cent increase in the country's defence budget. He announced that 'an attempt by any outside force to gain control of the Persian Gulf region would be regarded as an assault on the vital interests of the USA and such an assault would be repelled by any means necessary, including military force' – strong words.

As the 1980s began, the new President Reagan in Washington and Prime Minister Thatcher in London resolved to rebuild the West's defences, to overcome **defeatism** and move back the Soviet advances of the previous decade.

Speech by President Reagan, 1983

[It is important not] to ignore the facts of history and the aggressive impulses of an evil Empire, to simply call the arms race a giant misunderstanding and thereby remove yourself from the struggle between right and wrong and good and evil.

(From: M Walker. *The Cold War.*)

▼ *Source D*

Reagan's 'secret' plan

Reagan's re-armament programme was a classic example of Keynesian deficit-spending, public investment to lift the economy out of recession. It certainly achieved that result, and the Reagan economic boom of the mid- and later 1980s was a triumphant endorsement of Keynes's economic theories. The recession after 1989 points, however, to the folly of public investment in the economically fruitless field of weapons. A similar pumping of an extra $100 billion a year of public investment into education and infrastructure might have shown a greater economic return. But that was not the point. Reagan's rearmament was an investment in national security. It was also the test of Reagan's private conviction that the United States could afford an arms race, while the Soviet Union could not. The Soviet Union would either have to renounce the arms race, or bankrupt itself into collapse in the vain effort to keep up. 'I think there is every indication and every

reason to believe that the Soviet Union cannot increase its production of arms.'

(From: M Walker. *The Cold War.*)

▼ *Source E*

Nuclear Defence: The 'Star Wars' project

In March 1983, President Reagan announced a new ambitious weapons programme – the 'Star Wars' project. Its official name was the Strategic Defence Initiative (SDI) and the aim was to protect the USA from a Soviet nuclear attack. The basic idea was to set up a giant shield in space and use weapons like laser to shoot down any Soviet missiles before they could reach the United States.

(Adapted from: GA Smith. *The USA as a World Power.*)

▼ *Source G*

Nuclear attack alert, November 1983

(a) The world situation is now slipping towards a very dangerous precipice.'

(Soviet Foreign Minister Gromyko, September 1983)

(b) '... the KGB suspected that an imminent NATO exercise, Able Archer 83, could be the occasion for a full-scale nuclear strike against the Soviet Union: ... [the exercise] was designed to practise command coordination for nuclear-release procedures.'

(c) 'The Soviets went on to heightened alert too, with ... nuclear capable aircraft being placed on stand-by ...'

(From: M Walker. *The Cold War.*)

▲ *Source F* 'Cowboy' Reagan (1985) (From: GA Smith. *The USA as a World Power.*)

▼ *Source I*

The effect of a ten megaton nuclear bomb
(Adapted from: H Mills. *Twentieth Century World History in Focus.*)

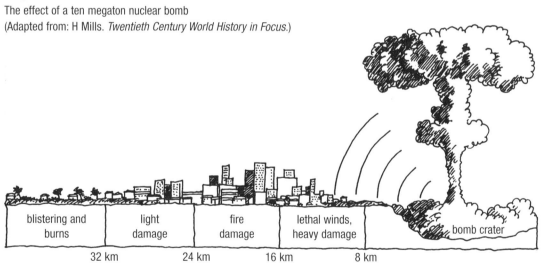

blistering and burns	light damage	fire damage	lethal winds, heavy damage	bomb crater
32 km	24 km	16 km	8 km	

Activities

1 In a sentence, summarise President Reagan's view of the Soviet Union using Sources B and C.
2 What were the three aims of Reagan's rearmament programme? (Source D)
3 After a group discussion, draw a diagram to show how Reagan's 'Star Wars' project might work.
4 Explain the viewpoint of the cartoonist in Source F.

5 Study the Chronology Table of events and explain why the USSR expected a pre-emptive nuclear attack in November 1983.
6 Explain the cartoonist's message in Source H.
7 Describe the effects of a nuclear bomb as shown in Source I.

Unit outcomes

- Describe the actions and explain the importance of Mikhail Gorbachev, the new Soviet leader.
- Discuss the final stages of the nuclear arms race.
- Select and analyse the reasons for the end of the Cold War.
- Interpret historical sources – both visual and written.

A new leader

In 1984 Mikhail Gorbachev began to emerge as the new leader of the Soviet Union. He became acting general secretary while the elderly Chernenko was recovering from illness, and after Chernenko's death, Gorbachev became general secretary in March 1985. He was in his mid-50s and had been actively involved in a recent debate

THE END OF THE COLD WAR (1985–1991) CHRONOLOGY						
	Leaders					
Year	USA	USSR	Conferences/ Treaties	Nuclear/Space Developments	Crises	Other events
1985	Reagan (from 1981)	Gorbachev (from March)	Geneva (October)			
1986			Reykjavik (October)			US planes bombed Libya; US space rocket disaster (Jan); Chernobyl reactor fire, USSR (April)
1987			Washington (December); Gorbachev visited USA	Intermediate Range Nuclear Force (INF) Treaty		
1988			Moscow (May); Gorbachev speech to UNO (December)			Peace between Iraq and Iran
1989	Bush		Gorbachev visited China; Malta (December)			Berlin Wall fell (November); Soviet troops withdrew from Afghanistan; Massacre in Tiananmen Square (Beijing)
1990			Economic Summit – Houston, Texas		Iraq invaded Kuwait	
1991		Yeltsin		START Treaty signed in Moscow	Gulf War	Gorbachev resigned as Soviet President (December)

among academics and government officials about the rigidity of Soviet policies in general, which were causing the Soviet Union and the whole communist system to experience serious problems. There were two crucial **imperatives** towards change: the first was the nuclear arms race, and the second was the Soviet economy. In a series of summit meetings with US Presidents Reagan and Bush over the next six years, Gorbachev negotiated the end of the Cold War.

New words
imperatives urgent reasons

The nuclear arms race

The Soviets were alarmed by Reagan's Star Wars project, and they had been alarmed by how close they had been to a nuclear confrontation with the USA in November 1983. Foreign Minister Gromyko complained in January 1984, that 'new missiles, bombers and aircraft carriers are being churned out (by the Americans) who are thinking in terms of war'.

Two events in early 1986 suggested that the human race might destroy itself by accident: in January a US space rocket exploded at launch killing the seven astronauts on board; 'a massive malfunction' according to one commentator. In April a nuclear reactor at Chernobyl in the Soviet Union blew up and caught fire; radiation was scattered over a wide area (see Source A).

▼ *Source A* Two nuclear/space disasters (May 1986)
(From: GA Smith. *The USA as a World Power.*)

At summit meetings in Geneva (1985) and Reykjavik in Iceland (1986), Gorbachev and Reagan discussed the elimination of whole categories of missiles. This culminated in the Intermediate Range Nuclear Force (INF) Treaty signed in Washington in 1987. This treaty proposed to eliminate missiles within three years in the arsenals of both countries. A Strategic Arms Reduction Treaty (START) was finally signed between Gorbachev and President Bush in 1991.

Political reform

Within the Soviet Union, following the principles of perestroika (restructuring) and glasnost (openness) Gorbachev announced dramatic political reform at the Communist Party Conference in 1988. This included a Soviet version of the American Bill of Rights and a proposal to hold free elections in 1989.

In December 1988, Gorbachev's speech to the United Nations in New York spelt out the end of the Cold War. There were three dramatic features to his address, and any one of them could be seen as a turning-point. In combination, they amounted to a revolution that went far beyond détente, ripping up the post-1945 settlement of Yalta, and trying also to end the ideological conflict that had gripped the world since 1917.

▼ *Source B*
Extracts from Gorbachev's speech
We are entering an era in which progress will be based on the common interests of the whole of humankind. The realisation of this fact demands that the common values

of humanity must be the determining prior-
ity in international politics ... This new
stage requires the freeing of international
relations from ideology ...

Force or the threat of force neither can
nor should be instruments of foreign poli-
cy ... The principle of the freedom of
choice is mandatory. Refusal to recognise
this principle will have serious conse-
quences for world peace. To deny a nation
the freedom of choice, regardless of the
pretext or the verbal guise in which it is
cloaked, is to upset the unstable balance
that has been achieved ... Freedom of
choice is a universal principle. It knows
no exception.

(From: M Walker. *The Cold War.*)

This principle, Gorbachev stressed, applied to 'both the capitalist and socialist system'. This did not only rip up the Brezhnev Doctrine, which had reserved the Soviet right to intervene in Eastern Europe to maintain its authority and the post-Yalta balance of power. It also accepted

that the citizens of eastern European countries had the right to choose their own social and political course and governments, irrespective of Soviet interests. This endorsed not only Dubček's attempt to build, in the Czechoslovakia of the 1960s, a socialism with a human face, but it also accepted the principle of a Czech and Slovak or Polish face without any socialism at all.

The third breakthrough of Gorbachev's speech was to announce: 'A new historic reality: the principle of excessive stockpiling of arms is giving way to the principle of reasonable sufficiency for defence'. This was to withdraw the arms race and, by implication, renounce the attempt to maintain a force powerful enough to maintain the offensive option.

Gorbachev announced a unilateral cut of half a million men from the Soviet army; the withdrawal of Soviet troops from Afghanistan had begun along with negotiations that would lead to the withdrawal of Cuban troops from Angola. The Berlin Wall, a symbol of the Cold War, came crashing down in November 1989. (M Walker. *The Cold War.*)

◀ *Source C*
The Berlin Wall comes down (November 1989) (From: *Hindsight: GCSE Modern History Review.*)

Gorbachev faced great pressure from the conservatives within the communist leadership, but he held to his course in spite of the break-up of the Soviet Union: by 1991 eight of the fifteen republics had declared full independence.

The economy

At the Malta summit in December 1989, Gorbachev was promised American economic assistance. On the expectation of this assistance and Western investment, a group of Soviet economists drew up a plan for a transition to a semi-free market system containing a welfare state, as well as sharp cuts in defence spending. In the West a so-called 'Grand Bargain' was debated. This envisaged some $30 billion a year of Western support in return for sweeping structural changes in the Soviet economy. But after signing the START treaty in Moscow in 1991, Bush flew home without agreeing to economic aid and leaving Gorbachev to face growing opposition of the Old Guard of the Communist Party. In an economic situation of food shortages, growing inflation and unemployment, a coup was attempted in August 1991. Boris Yeltsin emerged as the new leader and Gorbachev resigned as Soviet president in December.

The American sense of achievement at having won the Cold War was overshadowed by the costs of the victory.

▼ *Source D*

Reagan's strategy to crack the Soviet economy forcing it into an arms race it could not sustain had worked. But it worked at dreadful cost. The US economy could not afford it either. The Reagan rearmament programme was financed by budget deficits, which were in turn financed by borrowing foreign capital.

(From: M Walker. *The Cold War*.)

The USA was living on borrowed money. In addition, the USA and Britain had moved into recession, the Japanese stock market was tumbling by 40 per cent and the wealth of West Germany was being devoted to revitalising a reunited East Germany. There was little investment funding for the proposed 'Grand Bargain'.

In 1992 former President Richard Nixon appealed to President Bush for Western support and investment to promote Russian democracy, but it was an unsuccessful appeal. The exhausted America of 1992 lost her opportunity to invest in the building of a vast new market of about 400 million people, who were hungry for capitalism.

▼ *Source E*   The 'suffering taxpayers' (1970)
(From: GA Smith. *The USA as a World Power*.)

▼ *Source F*

The Cold War ended as it had begun, with the death of an empire, and an attempt to keep its name alive through a resort to that same polite fiction which had maintained a Commonwealth long after the British Empire had collapsed through the impoverishment of its homeland. Just as Britain endured to find a new international presence through her special relationship with the USA and her eventual, reluctant absorption into Europe's economic family, the relics of the Soviet Union sought a similar escape to a new future. But Britain had embarked on that course in a period of global economic growth. Russia and her neighbours faced a colder and a sadly meaner world, without even the pomp and parades of the British monarchy to mask reality with fading splendour.

(From: M Walker. *The Cold War*.)

▼ Source G

It is now estimated that, since it began developing the atomic bomb in 1940, the US government spent almost 19 trillion dollars on defence and nuclear weapons; of this figure $5.5 trillion was spent on nuclear weapons.

To put this more simply: for the past 58 years up to the end of the Cold War in 1989, American spending on nuclear weapons has averaged almost $500 every year for each man, woman and child in the country.

(Report of the Brookings Institute, an American think-tank, published in July 1998.)

▼ Source H

Article in *The Natal Witness*, 9 July 1998

After the 1973 Arab-Israeli War, world oil prices quintupled. As the world's second-largest oil producer, the Soviet Union was able to use the increased income from oil exports to create a façade of false prosperity to paper over the failure of the Russian economy. This lasted until 1981 when world oil prices dropped drastically. After that, there followed a desperate, doomed attempt to reform the Soviet economic and political system.

Activities ·····

1 Study the chronology table (1985–91)
   a Where did Gorbachev meet with American Presidents Reagan and Bush in the period 1985 to 1990?
   b Find five examples of how the Cold War was easing in this period.
   c Find four examples which show that aspects of the Cold War were continuing.
2 Explain the cartoonist's viewpoint in Source A.
3 Explain what was achieved by the two treaties reducing nuclear arms (INF and START).
4 Analyse Gorbachev's speech using the text and Source B, summarising the three dramatic features of Soviet policy.
5 Explain the emotion expressed in Source C.
6 Explain the meaning of the 1970 cartoon (Source E) and relate it to the situation in 1991.
7 There were three general reasons for the end of the Cold War:
   • Mikhail Gorbachev became the leader of the Soviet Union.
   • The nuclear arms race.
   • The economies of the USA and the Soviet Union.
     Write a short note on each of these reasons explaining how it affected the Cold War.
8 Study Sources G and H. Write a paragraph explaining the implication of these sources for the US and Soviet economies and the Cold War.

Extension activity ·····

Consider these issues in small groups.
1 In what ways was the end of the Cold War a disappointment, both for the USA and for the Soviet Union?
2 There were two underlying themes in the history of the Cold War between 1945 and 1991. Read back over the pages of this chapter and try to isolate these themes.

CHAPTER ASSESSMENT

In small groups write essay plans for the following topics. Then choose one of the topics and complete an essay on it. Remember that the learners in your group should complete different essays.

1 'The Truman Doctrine marked the beginning of the Cold War.' Discuss this statement.
2 It can be said that Berlin was a flashpoint of the Cold War. In the light of events between 1945 and 1961 explain whether this viewpoint is valid or not.
3 'The most outstanding characteristic of the course of the Cold War was the formation of the rival defence organisations of Nato (1949) and the Warsaw Pact (1955).'
   Discuss this statement by referring to the formation, functions, member countries and the significance of these two defence organisations.
4 'Contrary to Russian communist propaganda of the Cold War era, many satellite states were dissatisfied with Russian domination.'
   Discuss this statement in the light of the uprisings in Poland and Hungary in 1956 and Czechoslovakia in 1968.
5 Analyse the role of US President Ronald Reagan in ending the Cold War.

Further reading

This is a small selection from the large number of books available. The title by Martin Walker is particularly recommended.

C Bown and PJ Mooney. *Cold War to Détente.* London: Heinemann, 1976.

P Hastings. *The Cold War (1945–1969).* London: Ernest Benn, 1969.

W Lafeber. *America, Russia and the Cold War (1945–1975).* New York: John Wiley, 1976.

M McCauley. *The Origins of the Cold War.* Harlow, Essex: Longman, 1983.

H Mills. *Twentieth Century World History in Focus.* Basingstoke: Macmillan, 1984.

GA Smith. *The USA as a World Power.* York, England: Longman, 1989.

J Vick. *Modern America.* University Tutorial Press, 1985.

M Walker. *The Cold War.* Slough, England: Vintage, 1994.

Decolonisation and independent Africa

chapter 5

Contents

Chapter outcomes

Knowledge outcomes

As you work through this chapter you will be able to:
- understand the causes of decolonisation;
- outline the external and internal forces leading to decolonisation;
- establish patterns of decolonisation;
- know the political changes following independence;
- appreciate the cultural changes in post-colonial Africa;
- understand the roots of the economic crises;
- understand important concepts such as decolonisation, nationalism, Pan-Africanism, liberation wars, settler colonialism, dictatorship, one-party state, democracy, debt crises and economic development.

Concepts and skills outcomes

As you work through this chapter you will learn about and apply skills and concepts such as how to:
- define and explain historical problems;
- make generalisations based on evidence;
- identify cause and effect;
- empathise with others;
- judge information and identify assumptions;
- solve problems and draw conclusions;
- predict outcomes.

Value outcomes

As you work through this chapter you will get the chance to think about:
- the ethical problems and questions that colonialism raises;
- whether colonialism can be blamed for many of Africa's problems;
- how well Africa is coping with the challenges of independence.

Timeline

1922	1921 Formation of the Congress of British West Africa
	1922 Self-government in Egypt
	1929 Women's War in Nigeria
	Founding of the Tanganyika African Association
1930	Wall Street Crash and the Great Depression
	1935 Italian invasion of Ethiopia
1940	1944 Atlantic Charter
	Brazzaville Conference
	1945 Formation of the United Nations Organisation
	Fifth Pan-Africanist Congress, London
	1946 Formation of the United Gold Coast Convention
	1948 Nkrumah forms Convention People's Party
1950	1951 Libya's independence
	1956 Independence for Morocco, Sudan and Tunisia
	1957 Ghana attains independence
	1958 Independence referendum in French colonies
	All African People's Conference, Ghana
	1959 France withdraws support for Guinea
1960	1960 France grants independence to its colonies
	Crisis in the Congo – Leopoldville
	Nationalist uprisings in Angola, Mozambique and South Africa
	1963 Founding of the Organisation for African Unity (OAU)
	1964 Ghana becomes single-party state
	1965 Mobutu becomes president of Zaire
	1966 Military coups in Benin, Togo, Upper –67 Volta, Burkina Faso, Central African Republic, Ghana, Nigeria
1970	1971 Idi Amin seizes power in Uganda
	1974 Collapse of Portuguese colonialism
	1975 Founding of the Economic Community of West Africa
	1976 Soweto students' uprisings in South Africa
	1977 Attempted overthrow of Benin by white mercenaries
1980	1980 Formation of Southern African Development Community
1990	1994 Inauguration of democratically elected government in South Africa
	1997 Liberia adopts a democratic system of government

This chapter covers Specific Outcomes 1, 2, 3, 8 and 9 of the Human and Social Sciences learning area.

The drama of independence

Unit outcomes

- Appreciate the excitement caused by independence.
- Develop a sense of how people felt (empathy).
- Explore and evaluate a variety of historical sources.
- Develop writing and map-reading skills.
- Increase your vocabulary through learning new concepts and words.

Introduction

This chapter explores various themes including the destruction of European colonial rule in Africa, the attainment of independence, and the attempts by new independent African states to create new post-colonial societies and deal with the many challenges arising from this process.

Unit 1 captures the excitement accompanying the moment of independence. The struggle against colonial rule and the attainment of independence by Africans was a major achievement of the human spirit. The moment of independence across the continent was accompanied by optimism and great expectations. The history of what happened to these expectations and hopes is the story that unfolds in the following pages.

During the liberation of Africa, nationalist leaders struggled against European colonial officials. After the Second World War African nationalists aimed to seize power in each colony and create modern states, but the **metropolitan statesmen** had different plans for Africa. Britain hoped to hand over power very gradually to friendly successor states, France and Portugal planned to create close ties with the colonies, while Belgium did not outline any plans for the future of her colonies.

The material presented in this chapter introduces various points of view with regard to African liberation. However, the central focus is on African nationalism, because it gives Africans more responsibility in the struggle for independence. The sources which follow show that the excitement accompanying independence celebrations and the challenges following independence are historical events in which Africans were not mere victims but were also actors responsible for the failures and successes.

Reliving independence

▼ *Source A*

The hour of triumph
Tuesday 18th September [1956]

I had previously arranged with the Speaker that since I had an important announcement to make, he would permit me to take the floor as soon as I stood up.

As soon as the hands of the clock reached twelve I stood up. 'Mr Speaker' I said, 'with your permission I should like to make a statement'. I then proceeded to read the **dispatch** *from the* **Secretary of State***.*

'I now have the honour to inform you that **Her Majesty's Government** *will at first available opportunity introduce into the United Kingdom Parliament a Bill to accord Independence to the Gold Coast and, subject to Parliamentary approval, Her Majesty's Government intends full Independence should come about on the 6th March 1957'.*

The whole of the Assembly was for a few seconds dumb-founded. Then all at once the almost sacred silence was broken by ear-splitting cheers, cheers that must have been unprecedented in the Assembly.

The whole country was celebrating. That evening a friend of mine arrived from Kumasi and excitedly related to me how the news had been received there. 'Kwame' he said 'you should really have been there! As sure as I am standing here, Kwame, the supporters of the NLM were more wild with excitement than even the "CPP-ist". Many of them, not content with a single "Freedom" salute, raised both hands in the air as they yelled "Freedom!".'

(From: Kwame Nkrumah. *Ghana: the Autobiography of Kwame Nkrumah*.)

▼ President Kwame Nkrumah of Ghana

▼ Source B
Uhuru! Uhuru! In Kenya

Kenya regained her Uhuru from the British on 12 December 1963. A minute before midnight, lights were put out at the Nairobi stadium so that the people from all over the country and the world who had gathered there for the midnight ceremony were swallowed by the darkness. In the dark the **Union Jack** *was quickly lowered. When the next lights came on the Kenyan flag was flying and fluttering, and waving in the air. The police band played the new National Anthem and the crowd cheered continuously when they saw the flag was black, and red and green. The cheering sounded like one intense cracking of many trees, falling on the thick mud of the stadium.*

(From: Ngugi Wa Thiongo. *A Grain of Wheat*.)

▼ Source C
New York Times, 12 December 1963
Joyful Kenya Gets Independence From Britain
London Frees Final Colonial Holding in East Africa – Seat in UN Assured
By Robert Conley
Special to the New York Times

NAIROBI, Kenya, Thursday Dec. 12 – Kenya emerged today as Africa's newest independent state.

***Jubilation** swept through the new country.*

With Britain's Union Jack replaced by the black, red, and green flag of the new state, political power in Britain's last East African colonial holding slipped from the grasp of its 55,759 whites and was taken up by 8,365, 942 Africans.

Activities

1 What are the different types of historical sources on this page?
2 Imagine that you are a journalist at the national assembly when Kwame Nkrumah announced the date of independence (Source A). Write a short report on the occasion for your newspaper.
3 Imagine you were one of the Kenyans in the Nairobi stadium in Source B.
  a What feelings did you have towards the leaders like Jomo Kenyatta?
  b What were you hoping for from independence?

New and old: the changing map of Africa

Decolonisation was the **mirror image** of colonialism. It took almost 30 years for the colonial powers to finalise the colonial boundaries and their way of ruling. For almost 80 years Europeans ruled without going to war over the boundaries of their colonies. Despite this apparent stability, it took only a short period from 1945 to 1960 to break up the **colonial empire** leading to the emergence of independent African states. Although the colonial bound-

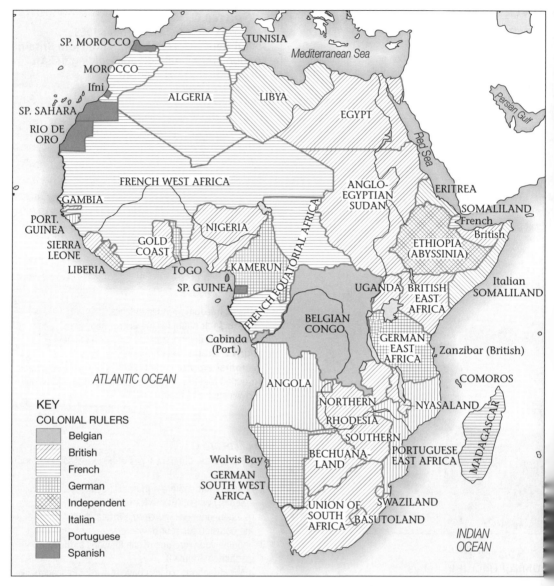

KEY

COLONIAL RULERS

- Belgian
- British
- French
- German
- Independent
- Italian
- Portuguese
- Spanish

▲ *Source D* Colonial rule in Africa

aries had been artificially imposed by the colonial powers, the emerging African states took them as given, and the struggle for independence took place within the colonial boundaries.

Despite the excitement and expectations that greeted the coming of independence, the new order could not be separated from the old colonial powers. The colonial capitals now became the centres of new governments, the colonial governors' residences were transformed into presidential houses. The new languages of government business were the colonisers' language. The **bureaucracy** to run the new governments,

the judicial (legal) systems, education, and the security forces still reflected the old colonial order.

In the midst of the celebrations of independence the nations were filled with expectations of change. People hoped to see an improvement in their standards of living, and increased political freedom to restore their dignity which had been eroded by many years of colonialism.

New words

bureaucracy central administration of a government

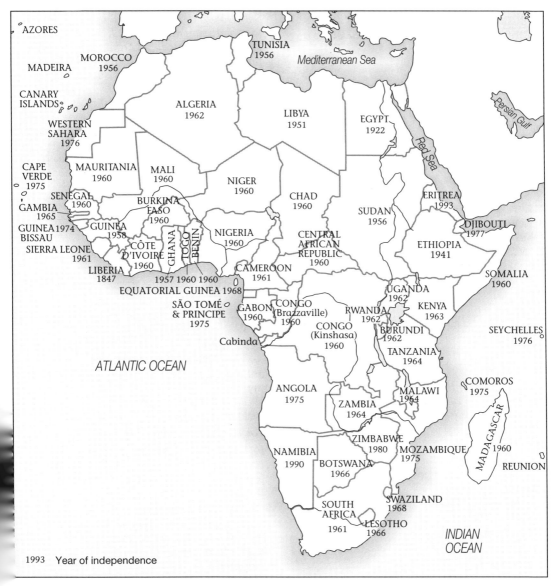

AZORES

TUNISIA
1956

Mediterranean Sea

MOROCCO
1956

MADEIRA

ALGERIA
1962

LIBYA
1951

EGYPT
1922

Persian Gulf

CANARY
ISLANDS

WESTERN
SAHARA
1976

Red Sea

CAPE
VERDE
1975

MAURITANIA
1960

MALI
1960

NIGER
1960

CHAD
1960

ERITREA
1993

SENEGAL
1960

BURKINA
FASO
1960

SUDAN
1956

DJIBOUTI
1977

GAMBIA
1965

GUINEA 1974
BISSAU

GUINEA
1958

NIGERIA
1960

CENTRAL
AFRICAN
REPUBLIC
1960

ETHIOPIA
1941

SIERRA LEONE
1961

CÔTE
D'IVOIRE
1960

GHANA

TOGO

BENIN

LIBERIA
1847

1957 1960 1960

CAMEROON
1961

SOMALIA
1960

EQUATORIAL GUINEA 1968

UGANDA
1962

KENYA
1963

SÃO TOMÉ
& PRINCIPE
1975

GABON
1960

CONGO
(Brazzaville)
1960

RWANDA
1962

SEYCHELLES
1976

Cabinda

CONGO
(Kinshasa)
1960

BURUNDI
1962

TANZANIA
1964

ATLANTIC OCEAN

ANGOLA
1975

ZAMBIA
1964

MALAWI
1964

COMOROS
1975

MADAGASCAR

1960

ZIMBABWE
1980

MOZAMBIQUE
1975

REUNION

NAMIBIA
1990

BOTSWANA
1966

SWAZILAND
1968

SOUTH
AFRICA
1961

LESOTHO
1966

INDIAN
OCEAN

1993   Year of independence

▲ *Source E* Independent Africa

Activities . . . .

1 Look carefully at Source D and answer the questions below.

  a Which one of the colonial powers had the biggest colonial empire?

  b Which one of the colonial powers had the smallest colonial empire?

  c What Portuguese colony is left out on the map?

  d Name one African country that remained independent during the era of colonialism.

2 Look carefully at Source E and answer the questions below.

  a Which countries had obtained independence by 1956?

  b Which countries attained independence between 1957 and 1959?

  c Which countries became independent in 1960 and who were their colonising powers?

  d Name the colonisers and the countries that attained independence in the period 1961 to 1970.

  e Which countries obtained independence after 1970 and who ruled them?

  f Name a country that is a product of the redrawing of the independence boundaries.

. . . .

Extension activity . . . .

With a partner do some research to find the names of the capital cities of the independent African countries, noting those that have changed from the era of colonialism.

. . . .

Attainment of independence or decolonisation? The African experience of the struggle

Sources F, G, and H below were selected to present an Africanist point of view of the attainment of independence. Two of the people mentioned and quoted were famous pan-Africanist nationalists, Kwame Nkrumah and Jomo Kenyatta. Read this section carefully taking note of what the sources mention about the responsibility for independence.

▼ Source F
New York Times, 16 May 1952
New World of Africa's Gold Coast Arises From Ashes of Colonialism
By William S White
Special to the New York Times

Accra, Gold Coast, May 15,

Britain, once ruler of the Gold Coast, is in headlong flight not simply from a long past imperialism; here is being worked out a suicide of colonialism as well. Nowhere else in the world has there been such an experiment as is in progress here.

The natives, after rioting bloodily in 1948 and again in 1950, have had a growing measure of self-government under a native Prime Minister, Kwame Nkrumah (pronounced 'Krooma').

Now they are after absolute independence and their declared design is to throw out the British altogether except in so far as British experts in the science of government may care to remain as paid assistants to a cabinet of Africans.

▼ Source G
Excerpts from Kwame Nkrumah's 'The Motion of Destiny' speech before the House of Assembly on 10 July 1953

The right of a people to decide their own destiny, to make their way in freedom, is not to be measured by the **yardstick** of colour or degree of social development. It is an **unalienable** right of peoples which they are powerless to exercise when forces, stronger than they themselves, by whatever means, for whatever reasons, take this right away from them.

If there is to be a criterion of a people's preparedness for self-government, then I say it is their readiness to assume the responsibility of ruling themselves. For who but a people themselves can say they are prepared? ...

Self-government which we demand, therefore, is the means by which our people can develop their attributes and express their **potentialities** to the full. As long as we remain subject to an alien power, too much of our energies are diverted from **constructive enterprise**. Oppressive forces breed frustration. Imperialism and colonialism are a twofold evil. The theme is expressed in the truism that 'no nation which oppresses another can itself be free'... Imperialism and colonialism are a barrier to true friendship.

New words

yardstick standard of comparison
unalienable that which cannot be taken away
potentialities capabilities
constructive enterprise activities which are important

▼ Source H
New York Times, 23 May 1962
Clanging Oil Drums Punctuate Vote Rallies in Kenya
By Robert Conley
Special to the New York Times

NAIROBI, Kenya, May 22,

Jomo Kenyatta extended his arms, threw back his head and sent the Swahili words 'uhuru, uhuru!' ('freedom, freedom!') booming over the crowd.

Twenty thousand Africans at the election rally shouted and cheered, banging oil drums with stones and hurling the words back at the leader of Kenya African National Union.

Kikuyu women, their heads shaved, jumped up and down, the bells around their waist jingling. They chanted over and over, 'We will not sleep, we will not sleep, we will not sleep until Kenyatta wins!'...

Activities

1 Write a paragraph on what might be an African view of the process leading to independence, noting what they were fighting against, the people who fought and the result of their fighting. Base your paragraph on Sources F, G and H.
2 Look at Sources I to M below reporting on the positions of the colonial powers. Is there a pattern in their position or policy towards African independence?

Metropoles and decolonisation

The sources in this section are taken from newspaper reports of the same era as the sources above, but they show European and Western views on decolonisation. Use these sources to learn more about the positions of the United Nations Organisation, the United States of America, Britain and France, as well as to understand the differences between the countries' decolonisation policies.

▼ Source I

New York Times, 20 June 1945
Charter Holds out Hope to Colonials
Requires responsible Nations to Report to League on Condition of Peoples
By John H Crider
Special to the New York Times

> San Francisco, June 19 – Under the **trusteeship** section of the charter agreed upon last night all the nations of the world having charge of peoples not wholly independent will for the first time in history undertake to report to a world organization on the health and well-being of these peoples.
>
> This part of the trusteeship section, experts point out today, seemed by far the most significant advance represented by the new approach to the problems of dependent peoples. It was hailed as a reflection of how far the world has moved in its attitudes toward such peoples in the last quarter of the century.
>
> Much newer in history, however, is what amounts to a **pledge** on the part of all nations with dependent peoples in whatever category, that they will look after the welfare and aid them toward the goal of self-government, which one official said represented 'a first faltering step toward acceptance of the principle that nations are accountable to civilization for the well-being of dependent peoples'.

> **New words**
>
> **trusteeship** exercise of political control by Britain and France over former German colonies in Africa under the League of Nations
> **pledge** promise
> **Charter amendment** correction of or adding to the Charter
> **imperial preferences** the choices of the colonising power
> **nationalism** patriotic feelings towards one's country (see Unit 2 for further discussion)

▼ Source J

New York Times, 13 December 1945
Welles Denounces 'Imperial System'

> Washington, Feb. 17 (UP) – Former Under-Secretary of State Summer Welles said tonight that the United Nations' General Assembly must face squarely the demand of millions of colonial peoples for freedom and self-government if it were to build a lasting peace.
>
> He said in a broadcast that a new world order based on freedom and justice would not permit the continuance of the 'imperial system' and its 'exploitation of the weak by the strong'.
>
> Mr Welles hailed as 'a step in the right direction' the **Charter amendment** proposed by American delegates that would require Britain, France and other colonial powers to develop, under the UNO's control, self-government and free political institutions within their colonies.

▼ Source K

New York Times, 16 June 1950
Paris to Integrate Colonies in Nation
By Michael Clark
Special to the New York Times

> Paris, May 15 – The political and economic integration of French colonial territories with the French Republic on the basis of **imperial preferences** was defined as France's colonial policy at a meeting of the Overseas High Commissioner in Paris last week.
>
> The French officials were aware that this doctrine, which was announced today, was not in accord with United States encouragement of **nationalism** and independence in colonial areas, as exhibited by Secretary of State Dean Acheson's statement on Indo-China in Paris last Monday.
>
> M Letourneau, who was flanked by the High Commissioners of French West Africa, French Equatorial Africa, the Cameroons and Madagascar, said that the policy of integrating these territories into the republic, provided for by the constitution, had become a basic goal of French colonial policy.

▼ Source L

New York Times, 22 November 1947
End African Conference
London announces Preparations for 'Important Developments'.
Special to the New York Times

LONDON, Nov. 21 – A conference of Governors and Governors designate of British colonies in Africa ended today after meeting in private for two weeks.

A statement issued tonight by the Colonial Office said that there had been discussions on 'many important questions of policy' at a time when 'important political developments have recently taken place or are **impending***'.*

These developments, it said, affect 'the composition of legislative councils, the **central executive machinery of Governments** *and the development of local Government bodies' and 'far reaching plans for economic and social development'.*

▼ Source M

New York Times, 14 November 1953
Policy Clash Seen in Western Africa
Britain's Encouragement of Self-government Is Opposed to French Integration
By Michael Clark
Special to the New York Times

DAKAR, French West Africa, Nov. 6 – The divergent colonial policies of Britain and France in West Africa are expected to make international cooperation increasingly difficult south of the Sahara.

The British territories, especially Nigeria and the Gold Coast, are progressing rapidly toward self-government. Meanwhile French West Africa is being closely integrated with metropolitan France on the basis of a common citizenship and interlocking political institutions.

Activities

In small groups work through Sources I to M and answer the questions below.
1 Who was responsible for working out British and French colonial policy?
2 Where was colonial policy decided?
3 Did African people participate in developing decolonisation policy?
4 Is British and French colonial policy in agreement with the United Nations policy on self-government and independence?

Extension activity

What would you suggest is the United States of America's position on the decolonisation of African colonies? Give reasons for your answer.

Historians' interpretations of decolonisation

Interpretations of the process leading to the independence of African countries have been debated. Until now two views have dominated the debate. First, the historians who focus on the activities taking place in Africa have suggested that Africans won their independence from their colonial masters. Because these historians concentrate on the role of Africans in the process of decolonisation they have earned the label of 'Africanist'. Secondly, the historians who study the imperial policies of the colonial powers argue that the colonial powers planned the process of decolonisation. Because they focus on claims that the process was planned and controlled by imperial powers this view has earned the name of 'imperial school' or 'planned decolonisation'.

However, there is also a third view that takes into consideration the 'Africanist' and 'imperial' views and adds other factors with wider implications. In the section below we briefly outline the features of these schools of thought.

African nationalist view

Nationalist historians share the view of the first generation of political leaders that locates the responsibility for ending colonial rule in African hands. They conclude this by examining African protest movements against colonial rule. Nationalist historians show colonial powers resisting the African demand for self-determination (independence). In order to win independence from the colonial powers Africans organised support from many groups in society. The strategies and the demands made by Africans became their subject of study.

Nationalist historians saw the struggle for independence as leading to nation-building. Political parties were seen as the means to nationhood. These historians initially did not criticise the rise of **one-party state systems**. However, the failure of independence to provide Africans with the liberties they had hoped for led to disappointment and a loss of belief in the benefits of independence. Since then nationalist historians have increasingly turned to the study of **organs of civil society** as the basis for nation-building.

Planned decolonisation

This view places the **initiative** for decolonisation with the British and French colonial offices in the **metropoles**. According to this view, plans to reform colonialism in preparation for granting Africans self-government were started before the Second World War. The point that comes out is that it was not in reaction to African nationalism but it was **proactive**. The plans were prompted by the disillusionment arising from the failure to discharge their **imperial trusteeship** more effectively in the period before 1939.

The post-war 'Development and Welfare plans' and reforms in the colonial administration that allowed for Africans' representation in the Legislative and Executive councils are given as indicators of this policy. The French Brazzaville conference in 1944 which placed representative government on the agenda planned a closer association between the colonies and France. Here we are told that decolonisation was carried out by the 'benevolent colonial state'. The timing and speed of decolonisation was thus all determined by the charitable and helpful colonial masters.

New words

impending about to happen
central executive machinery of government central administration
divergent different
one-party state system a system of government where only one party is legally permitted to exist
organs of civil society social and political organisations which operate outside formal political parties
initiative power or ability to begin something
metropole mother country of a colonising nation
proactive taking a lead before anyone else
imperial trusteeship a belief by the colonising powers that they held the colonies in trustee until Africans were ready to rule themselves

The global view

This view takes both the nationalist and imperial views as essential. It makes two further contributions: first, that neither the nationalist nor the imperial schools are complete by themselves, and secondly, that factors contributing to the process of decolonisation went beyond those suggested by the nationalist and imperial historians. The global view suggests that the role played by the United States and the Soviet Union in their anti-colonialism is important. Other factors worth considering are the Great Depression, the Second World War, the Cold War, and Asian support for African independence. This view examines the interrelatedness of these factors and how they influenced each other in granting independence to African countries.

This view notes British reluctance to decolonise for fear of losing power, prestige and economic strength. Prime Minister Churchill declared in 1942 that he did not become prime minister to preside over the dissolution of the British Empire and this is echoed in De Gaulle's words in 1947 'to lose the French colonial empire would be humiliation that could even cost France its independence'.

Understanding historical skills and concepts

Historical interpretations and generalisations

Historical interpretations

If you look through the many sources used in Unit 1 you will notice that they give very different interpretations of the same events in history, depending on the perspectives of those who are reporting on or evaluating the events. It is an important skill for you to be able to work out the differences between interpretations, and to understand why the events have been interpreted in a specific way.

These are some of the most important questions to ask when you assess different historical interpretations or points of view.

1 What audience is each interpretation addressing?
2 What is the argument for each view?
3 What evidence does each view use for its argument?
4 Is there a purpose for the particular point of view?
5 What are the main ideas in these writings?
6 Are there any philosophies influencing these views?
7 What major historical changes influenced the thinking in this era?

Each one of the questions above provides useful clues that help to assess the point of view of a piece of work. These clues relate to:
1 the audience
2 the purpose
3 the evidence used
4 ideological factors
5 the current ideas in society
6 the author(s)
7 the history around that time.

Making generalisations

Historians often work from a huge body of evidence, and one of the skills they use to sort out data or information is to find general patterns in the data. Making generalisations requires that:

- you find common themes
- you rank the themes starting with the most important and ending with the least important
- you use evidence to establish a trend or pattern.

Activities

These activities on decolonisation are based on all the sources and evidence used in Unit 1. Work together in a group of four to six learners.

1 Sort all the sources in Unit 1 that could be used to write a nationalist history.

2 Find all the articles that present an imperial view of the process of decolonisation.
3 Are there any sources that could be used for the global view on decolonisation?
4 Write down your reasons for choosing the documents that you did for each one of the schools of thought.
5 Why was independence in African countries welcomed with great delight?

Extension activity

Write three paragraphs in which you summarise the main points of:

- nationalist history
- the imperial view
- the global view.

Unit 2 — African nationalism

Unit outcomes

- Learn more about the concept of African nationalism.
- Discuss African grievances against colonial rule.
- Understand the different forms of African resistance to colonialism.
- Discuss the impact of mass political movements against colonialism, with particular reference to the Gold Coast.

What is African nationalism?

African nationalism (hereafter referred to as nationalism) has many definitions, some of which are broad and others narrow. On the one hand, Thomas Hodgkin provides us with a broad definition:

> ... the term nationalism is used in a broad sense to describe any organisation or group that explicitly asserts the rights, claims and aspirations of an African society in opposition to European authority, whatever its institutional form and objectives.

On the other hand, we have Coleman's narrow definition:

> ... the term is used narrowly to describe only those types of organisations which are essentially political, not religious, economic or educational in character and which have as their object the realisation of self-determination or independence for a recognisable African nation.

Both definitions have been criticised. Hodgkin's definition is thought simplistic as it only considers that Africans had one battle to fight – against colonialism. Coleman's definition is viewed as too narrow because it hides the complex relations between political movements. Coleman's definition also tends to suggest that where there were no political parties, there was no nationalism.

It is important to note that Hodgkin's definition is closer to current political analysis of struggles for democracy that focus on the role of **social movements** called **civil society**.

African political thinkers have also attempted to define nationalism. Zimbabwe nationalist writing in 1959 defined African nationalism as follows:

> On examination, the basic ingredients that go to make up the present African nationalism, may be **enumerated** as the African's desire to participate fully in the central government of the country, his desire for economic justice that recognises fully the principle of 'equal pay for equal work' regardless of the colour of the skin, his desire to have full political rights in his own country; his dislike of being treated as a stranger in the land of his birth; his dislike of being treated as means for white man's end; and his dislike for laws of the country that **prescribe** for him a permanent position of inferiority as a human being. It is this exclusive policy of white supremacy that has created a deep dissatisfaction among African peoples.
>
> (From: Sithole. *African nationalism*.)

African nationalism was based on grievances (complaints) against colonial rule. In this way it was different from European nationalism which was based on cultural identity and solidarity. In Africa, nationalism is not the same as **ethnic solidarity** – that is ethnicity. Africanist historians prefer the use of the term ethnicity to 'tribalism' because of the negative undertones associated with it. African nationalism was an intense commitment to the nation and not to the ethnic group. Nationalist leaders held the opinion that organising on an ethnic basis caused divisions, so African nationalism played down the ethnic difference. Regarding one's own ethnic group as the most important was called tribalism – a negative label which suggested being backward and primitive. In contrast, nationalism was seen as a force arising out of their common experiences under colonial rule. It was inclusive.

Activities

1 What are the different definitions of nationalism discussed in the above section?
2 Work out your own definition of nationalism. Write it down in a few lines.
3 What do you understand by 'civil society' or 'social movements'?
4 What do you consider to be the key idea of each one of the definitions looked at?
5 Is Sithole's definition of nationalism easy to fit into the other definitions? Give reasons for your answer.
6 To what extent are definitions of concepts useful to you as a reader?
7 What do you consider to be the greatest achievement of nationalism?
8 What is ethnicity?
9 Is ethnicity a useful or desirable form of identity today?

Extension activity

Hold a class debate in which you discuss whether ethnic identity undermines a national identity.

The benefits of nationalism

Nationalism contributed to African struggles for independence. It was a creative force that broke the ethnic barriers that had been encouraged through the colonial practice of **indirect rule** by traditional rulers. Ongoing and widespread nationalist struggles greatly raised the cost of colonialism which helped to force the colonial powers to concede independence. The liberation of Africa was a major achievement of the nationalist spirit despite the disappointments that followed.

One of the achievements of nationalism was that it provided a broader basis for unity among Africans. African countries are multi-ethnic and the task of bringing together people from so many cultural backgrounds was only achieved through nationalism. This achievement was significant although it had its failures.

The division between rural and urban areas was also bridged by nationalism. Although the interests of the rural and town dwellers may have been different, they all shared the same enemy, colonialism.

Nationalism also brought people from different classes together in their common hatred of colonialism. The leaders of the political movements in Africa were people who had received a Western education. They have often been referred to as the elites. The nationalist movement joined together the elites, the traders, teachers, peasants and the unemployed.

Another area which was unique to the nationalist struggles was the cooperation of men and women. Opposition to colonial rule brought women into active politics, representing their own interests and working together with political movements against colonial rule. Women also provided the leadership of these political movements. In Nigeria, the Aba women's protests against colonial demands are a well-known example. When men were not ready to challenge the colonial officials women taunted them to prove that they were men by doing something.

The tensions caused by nationalism

The nationalist movement also caused conflicts in society. The tensions between the traditional rulers and the nationalist leaders were felt in many societies. The conflict between the new educated elites and the traditional elites centred on who was to lead the people to independence. Under colonial rule the traditional rulers had authority given to them and the educated elites mostly found themselves outside the political arena. With the rise of nationalism the educated had found a way of taking part in the affairs of their countries. But this participation threatened the traditional rulers' political control. In most African countries the chiefs tended to play a negative role in the struggle for independence. In many cases the chiefs wanted their territories to be granted separate independence. This was the situation with the Kakaka of Uganda, and the Litunga of the Lozi. By the 1950s the colonial rulers had come full circle and begun looking to the elites for political leadership. A number of traditional rulers who were considered to stand in the way of independence found themselves removed and exiled from their countries.

Generation conflict between the young and the old was also widespread in the nationalist movement. The young nationalist leaders were more radical than the older people. The younger generation grew impatient with the **gradualist politics** of the older generation. They wanted action and demanded independence now. In the Gold Coast, Kwame Nkrumah, who had joined the United Gold Coast Convention (UGCC) under Danquah in 1946, found their strategy inappropriate. In 1947, following some disagreements, he left the party and formed the Convention People's Party leading Ghana to independence. In Northern Rhodesia, Kenneth Kaunda found Harry Nkumbula's African National Congress to be incompetent. In 1959, together with others, he founded the United National Independence Party that won Zambia's independence in 1964.

African nationalism became a formidable force that could not be stopped. The British prime minister even referred to it as the 'Winds of change sweeping across Africa'. Despite its great achievements, it also created problems that would emerge later in the post-colonial era.

Grievances against colonial rule

The loss of their independence and the accompanying colonial demands made colonialism unacceptable to most if not all Africans. African opposition to foreign European rule lasted throughout the entire colonial period. In the initial period it still took on military aspects until Africans recognised that this was a losing strategy. Examples of military resistance can be found in the Maji Maji Uprisings against German rule in Tanganyika in 1905. Africans wanted to regain their lost independence.

Colonial rule was like a dictatorship. Africans were excluded from participating in the politics of their own countries. Only the chiefs were allowed to rule on behalf of the colonial rulers. Africans had no decision-making powers or representation. Laws affecting African people were made in all-white Legislative Councils. After the Second World War British reforms allowed for an allocated number of elected African representatives in Legislative Councils. In this way, Africans had very little experience in the practice of governing under colonial rule.

The colonial economic policies and practices generated African opposition. **Land alienation**, increased taxation and poor working conditions led to African protests. These ranged from the unorganised and often individual responses of evading tax by running away, to well-organised and successful strikes. On the Northern Rhodesia (Zambian) Copper Belt in 1935, African miners took strike action to indicate their opposition to increased hut tax. The Nigerian market women successfully organised a protest against increased taxation. This event is called 'The Women's War of 1929'.

New words

land alienation removal of land from legitimate owners or users without their consent
universality belonging to all or applying to all

The appropriation (seizure) of land from Africans by the colonial state stirred Africans to organise against it. The removal of African land was practised in East and Southern African colonies for two major reasons. First, to create room for European settlers, and secondly, to help the mining economies of southern Africa to force African men to the mines by taking away their agricultural land. In Nyasaland (Malawi), John Chilembwe, a Baptist pastor, organised an armed uprising in protest against land alienation. In Kenya, African opposition to land alienation found expression in the famous Mau Mau Uprising in the 1950s. However, land alienation was not a major grievance against colonial rule in British and French West Africa.

Labour policies and practices which exploited Africans under colonial rule were the cause of many labour protests in Africa. Labour practices which forced African men, women and children to work on public works without pay were at first practiced by every colonial power. When forced labour was replaced with wage labour it did help to improve conditions for Africans slightly, but the pay remained very low. African responses to the poor working and living conditions ranged from individual's withdrawal of their services to well-organised strikes led by trade unions.

African participation in both the First and Second World Wars led to unhappiness with European rule in Africa. African soldiers saw a contradiction between European principles of the **universality** of humanity and their practices. The early nationalist Baptist pastor, John

Chilembwe, expressed what many Africans felt about the First World War:

> Let the rich, bankers, ..., shopkeepers, farmers, landlords go to war and get shot. Instead the poor Africans who have nothing to own in this present world, who in death became only a long line of widows and orphans in utter want are invited to die for a cause which is not theirs.

The promises of freedom implied in Christianity and democracy inspired Africans living under harsh colonial regimes to fight for these ideals. The undermining of African values led to a new movement in West Africa called 'negritude'. Negritude was a literary movement stressing the importance of African values.

Other factors that contributed to creating conditions in which nationalism thrived included the Great Depression and the Italian invasion of Ethiopia in 1935. These two events increased Africans' disillusionment with what the West could do for Africa. The Great Depression (see Chapter 2) led to unemployment, forced repatriation from the cities and increased taxation.

New words

mutual aid associations activities based on members' support (often in the form of money) for each other in times of need
secular not concerned with religion
federal system of government a system of government in which several states form a unity, but remain independent in internal affairs

Foundations of nationalism

The African search for appropriate ways of challenging European colonial rule led to many different forms and methods of resistance which reflected both the resources at the disposal of African people and their growing political consciousness.

The levels of political organisation and consciousness started with ethnic-based **mutual aid associations**. These associations took various forms. In Kenya the Kikuyu Central Association mobilised people around the issue of land alienation. Welfare associations were the first inter-ethnic organisations to directly challenge colonial rule.

The Tanganyika African Association, founded in 1929, is an example of a welfare association that demanded an African voice in government. In 1953 the Tanganyika African Association was transformed into the Tanganyika African

National Union (TANU), the political party that led Tanganyika to independence.

Opposition to colonial rule was also expressed in religious and other **secular** terms. African Christian leaders who became dissatisfied with mission Christianity broke away and formed their own independent churches. The African independent churches were also called Ethiopian and Zionist churches.

Another important expression of opposition to colonial rule were women's protest movements. In 1929 the Igbo women of Nigeria organised spectacular protests against taxation. This protest has become known as the "Women's War 'Aba riots' of 1929".

However, it is important to stress that workers in colonial Africa were the most important supporters of nationalism. Although African workers were not permitted to form trade unions in British Africa before the end of the Second World War, workers were able to protest against colonial rule through strike action. In 1935 the mine workers in Zambia went on strike against increased taxation. After the Second World War organised labour became a formidable force against colonial rule throughout Africa. It was the workers' strikes of 1948 in the Gold Coast that brought about a series of political crises that led to internal self-government in 1952.

Extension activity

Find out about another example of the African response to colonialism and do some research to write up a profile of the organisation.

Mass political movements

Mass political movements have been called the truly nationalist movements. These movements were called mass movements because of their huge following. They were represented by modern political parties modelled on parties in the West. These movements united Africans across ethnic, class, race and gender divisions against colonial rule. The movements were also called supra-territorial because they were active across a whole country. Egypt had the first mass nationalist movements seeking independence in 1882. While Egypt gained a measure of self-government by 1922, the rest of Africa took a different route.

The first supra-territorial organisations emerged in West Africa. The British allowed some political activities, but in French West Africa only Senegal enjoyed political rights. The Senegalese were allowed to elect an African representative to the French Assembly in Paris. In the rest of the colonies political activities were generally suppressed until after the Second World War. The Portuguese were determined to suppress any political activities among the colonised.

The limited political space given to British West Africa led African educated elites to form the National Congress of British West Africa (NCBWA) in 1921. It had branches in Nigeria, the Gold Coast, Sierra Leone and Gambia. The NCBWA pursued moderate politics whose methods were writing petitions to colonial officials. Its main demand was for increased African representation in the colonies' Legislative Councils. In the inter-war period these moderate politics were challenged by young Nigerians. These Nigerians formed the Youth Movement which asked for autonomy (independence) from Britain. The Youth Movement aimed at uniting Nigerians in a single nation, a united Nigeria. This earned it the description of the first truly nationalist movement.

Territorial nationalism developed after the Second World War. The post-war leaders believed that nationalism was not only about opposition to European control. They knew that nationalism also had to create new nation-states out of the diverse groups of people inhabiting the colonies. The mass political parties formed after the Second World War had to mobilise the people to end colonial rule and also begin to build new nations. For an example of this process we turn to the Gold Coast (Ghana).

Mass politics in the Gold Coast

On 6 March 1957 the Gold Coast became the first sub-Saharan African country to obtain independence through pressing for constitutional reforms. By attaining independence first it provided a model that the British would follow elsewhere in Africa. Ghana's path to independence opens the debate on whether decolonisation was planned or attained through African efforts.

The NCBWA demand that the British increase African representation in the territorial Legislative Councils was eventually answered in the Gold Coast. In 1946 the British introduced a constitution that created an African majority in the Legislative Council. However, the greater number of these representatives were to be nominated by the country's chiefs. As could be expected, the educated Africans found this arrangement unacceptable.

In 1947 JB Danquah, a lawyer and a member of the NCBWA, together with a few others formed the first nationalist party for the Gold Coast, the United Gold Coast Convention

(UGCC). The UGCC wanted the 1946 constitution changed to increase the number of elected rather than nominated Africans in the Legislative Council. Danquah invited a young pan-Africanist, Kwame Nkrumah, to become its secretary and organise the party.

A peaceful demonstration by ex-servicemen protesting against the rising cost of living was met with police brutality. The police actions angered the urban Africans who began rioting in Accra, Kumasi and other towns. The state responded by targeting the only political party, accusing it of being behind the riots. Nkrumah and Danquah and other UGCC leaders were arrested and imprisoned in March 1948 (also see page 204).

'Programme of Positive Action'

Later in 1948 Nkrumah broke away from the UGCC as a result of a disagreement of the tactics to be used in the struggle for independence. He formed the Convention People's Party (CPP). The CPP adopted a radical programme called 'Positive Action' in support of their demand for immediate independence. Its methods were to include strikes, boycotts and mass rallies. In 1948 and 1949 the CPP put the programme in action across the territory.

The colonial governor in the Gold Coast took two drastic measures. First, he arrested Nkrumah and threw him back in prison. The second measure involved bending to pressure to change the constitution. Although the 1946 constitution was changed, it still did not allow an elected majority in the Legislative Council. Despite the leaders being imprisoned, the CPP won a decisive victory in the 1951 elections.

Nkrumah became the leader of a provisional government, and started preparing the Gold Coast for independence. The British hoped to work with Nkrumah in setting up institutions for governing and preparing Africans for eventually taking over control. In 1952 Nkrumah was given the title of prime minister. From this time the CPP negotiated with the British for a constitution that would allow for a Legislative Council that no longer contained special and nominated members. The drive to eliminate the powers of chiefs to nominate representatives to the Legislative Council turned chiefs against the CPP. Other parties challenging the CPP emerged. In 1954 a new constitution that would lead the Gold Coast to independence did not allow for nominated members in the Legislative Council.

The 1956 election, the final and deciding election for the leaders of the new government of independent Ghana, saw the opposition parties grouped together under the demand for a federal system of government. They maintained that a **federal system of government** would give proper balance between the local and national interests. These parties included the Northern People's Party and the Asante-based National Liberation Movement. The Convention People's Party won the election, thereby convincing the British to proclaim the Gold Coast under the new name of Ghana.

New words

statesmen political leaders
illiterate a person who cannot read or write
inmate prisoner

▼ Map showing location of Ghana in Africa and flag of Ghana

KEY

■	Red
□	Yellow
▨	Green
■	Black

▲ The three horizontal stripes in the flag are red, yellow and green. These colours are also found in the Ethiopian flag and have come to signify African unity. The star in the middle is black.
(From: The Diagram Group. *Nations of Africa*.)

Activities

1 Outline the growth of Ghanaian nationalism.
2 Read through the profile of Nkrumah contained in Source A below. What aspects of his life do you think contributed to his success in leading Ghana to independence?
3 What sort of relationship existed between the British colonial officials and the nationalist leaders?
4 Write a few lines giving reasons why you think the CPP was successful in winning independence for Ghana.

Extension activity

In what ways is Source A biased? Use the skills from pages 50–51 to help you with this activity.

▼ Source A

New York Times, 6 March 1957
Independence Leader: Kwame Nkrumah

> *Wednesday, March 6 – The first citizen of Ghana, a cocoa-rich land on the side of the hump of West Africa that became independent today, went to college in Pennsylvania and was voted the 'most interesting' man in his class.*

> *Kwame Nkrumah was the first Negro to become Prime Minister of a British colony. As popular leader of one of European colonies in Africa to gain full independence, he is of interest and concern to* **statesmen** *around the world. The success or failure of Britain's 'experiment' with the Gold Coast colony and Mr Nkrumah's plans for the new state are bound to affect for decades the history of Africa.*

> *Kwame Nkrumah, [was] born in the mud-hut village of Nkrofol in 1909 ... After he completed schooling at a Roman Catholic mission and the country's Achimota College, Kwame Nkrumah was given funds by a diamond prospecting uncle for a trip to the United States. He enrolled at Lincoln University, Oxford, Pa., in 1935, receiving his BA four years later, and later becoming a bachelor of Sacred Theology. He was a philosophy instructor at Lincoln for a while, and earned an MA in anthropology at the University of Pennsylvania.*

> *The young scholar was an active leader of the African Students' Association of America and Canada. Early in his career he began attacking British colonialism. In 1945 he attended the London School of Economics ...*

> *Mr Nkrumah returned to his homeland in 1947 and soon after that the determinative phase of his career really begun. In February, 1948, a British Parliamentary Commission that had been rushed to Accra blamed the colonial regime for denying the Negroes a voice in the government. The upshot was a new constitution. Mr Nkrumah denounced the new charter and demanded 'positive action' – defined as 'strike based on perfect nonviolence'. But the policy did not work. Mr Nkrumah was arrested.*

*Being in prison made Mr Nkrumah a hero and a martyr when the election was held. His Convention People's party got 80% of the votes – cast after elaborate ... education of the **illiterate** natives in the technique of voting – and Mr Nkrumah's first big fight was won.*

*Sir Charles Arden-Clarke, Colonial Governor, freed him and appointed him leader of Government Business with power approximating those of Prime Minister. Later he assumed the title and position of Prime Minister. The Gold Coast prison director resigned, protesting against being put in a position to take orders from a former **inmate**.*

Unit 3
Colonial reforms

Unit outcomes

- Gain an understanding of the colonial policies of the different colonial powers.
- Appreciate the historical forces of change.
- Understand new concepts such as structures of government, self-determination, independence and neo-colonialism.
- Trace trends in the development of policy and learn to evaluate policy statements.

Introduction

This unit traces the changes in French and British decolonisation policy. It also discusses the Portuguese and Belgian positions on decolonisation. In the case of the British and the French, the unit identifies their policy during the course of the Second World War and examines how it changed. Some reasons are given for the changes. This section has policy statements by those involved in making and implementing colonial policy. The role of the superpowers and African nationalism in influencing policy will also be discussed.

The reform of colonial policy

Britain and France realised the need to reform their colonial policies by the time of the Second World War, but Portugal and Belgium were not similarly concerned. British and French colonial reforms had a number of things in common. They both aimed at reforms that would gradually lead to African internal government, but at a pace which they would control. Both colonial powers realised that the levels of colonial economic development in their African colonies were low and needed further massive investments. To address this they came up with Colonial Development plans. These plans were also in the best interests of Britain and France, for they realised after the war that they needed the colonies for their own economic recovery.

The British and French thought of African self-government as lying in the distant future, probably more than a generation away. But, they thought of their Economic and Welfare Development plans as a step towards preparing

Africans for self-government. Investment in higher education would ensure that the leadership would be prepared. Both Britain and France came up with these schemes as the best way of establishing close relationships with the territories with the end of colonialism. However, the two colonial powers chose different strategies for establishing this close relationship. France decided that close integration should be the outcome of decolonisation, while Britain preferred to have an association of independent states in a British Commonwealth. By 1960, both the British and French models of decolonisation had experienced a shift.

New words

right of association legal rights allowing groups of people to meet freely without being stopped by government agents or other individuals

French decolonisation policy

As noted earlier, France had offered African territories close integration with France at the Brazzaville Conference of 1944. The Brazzaville decisions were included in the 1946 French Constitution which made all inhabitants of French Africa automatically become French citizens without a loss of personal status. As soon as the 1946 constitution proclaimed the **right of association**, political parties and trade unions appeared in French Africa. Some of these political parties would work towards changing the policy of close integration.

In 1950 officials were still favouring the policy of close integration with France, but by 1953 a split was evident in the group of African Deputies in Paris.

▼ Source A
New York Times, 23 August 1953

Leopold Sedar Senghor, deputy from Senegal and leader of a group of overseas independents in Paris, wants to revise the French Constitution so as to make France and the French Union a federal entity with equal status for the overseas territories.

By 1957 pressure for constitutional changes had grown to the extent that African deputies were confident to sponsor a motion in the National Assembly in Paris.

▼ *Source B*

New York Times, 3 February 1957

Paris: 2 Feb. – The government defeated attempts in the National Assembly today to provide France's African territories fully fledged self-government.

African deputies, however, won some concessions as the National Assembly agreed to conduct a referendum in the colonies to decide the future of the colonies. The options given were reported as follows.

▼ *Source C*

New York Times, 20 July 1958

Paris, 19 July – France will offer three choices of future status to her overseas territories under the new constitution – continuance as territories, integration with France or membership in a federation.

Voters were given the choice of rejecting or accepting the new constitution. Acceptance meant joining the newly proposed community as fully autonomous states. Rejection meant **secession** from French Union and independence, cutting off French or any assistance.

The election was held on 28 September 1958 and by 29 September results of the polling were in.

New words

secession act of one region withdrawing from the state
neo-colonial one-sided relationship in favour of former colonial power

▼ *Source D*

New York Times, 29 September 1958

Paris, Monday 29 Sept – Incomplete returns from France's overseas territories showed overwhelming acceptance of a federal community with France. Only one territory, that of Guinea in West Africa, appeared thus far to have chosen complete independence.

▼ *Source E*

New York Times, 30 September 1958
Paris cuts ties to French Guinea after no vote

Paris, 29 Sept. – France lost no time today in pushing the West African territory of Guinea out of the French community as a result of its rejection of the constitution yesterday ...

Even before the final returns were in, a note was handed to Sekou Toure, head of the Guinea government, informing him that Guinea was separated from other territories of French West Africa and could no longer expect administrative or financial aid.

By the time France granted independence to its African colonies in 1960, the policy had shifted from one of integration as in the Brazzaville protocol and the 1946 constitution, to a watered-down federation of autonomous states. This was what was proposed by the African deputies and rejected by the National Assembly.

The **neo-colonial** link for francophone Africa (French Africa) included a common currency (the French franc), France's control of the trade and financial policies of the new states, military cooperation involving military bases for French troops, as well as continued French administrative and financial assistance. In many ways France had a firmer control over its former colonies than Britain or Portugal.

Activities

1 Examine the policy statements in Sources A to E and then outline the changes in the French policy of decolonisation.
2 To what extent was this a planned policy?
3 a What does the phrase 'neo-colonial umbilical cord' mean?
  b Does this phrase have a positive or a negative tone? Give reasons for your answer.

British colonial policy

In 1947 the British Colonial Office came out with a plan for the transfer of power to the colonies. According to the Colonial Office the empire had to be ended carefully and gradually. The plan anticipated reforms of the **Legislative and Executive Councils** and local government into representative institutions. Constitutional developments around these institutions would be flexible and take a long time.

The report of 1947 accepted that self-government was inevitable at some time in the distant future. The **preconditions** for self-government were seen as the existence of a nationalist movement, territorial unity, democratic representation and an efficient system of local government. The reforms also introduced two important changes from previous policy: the abandonment of indirect rule through chiefs in favour of local government through provincial councils; and a recognition of the educated African elites as the future leaders. The report suggested that the British were hoping to leave behind friendly nations which would continue to trade and have close relations with them.

The Colonial Office called a meeting of colonial governors to examine its policy on the transfer of power to the colonies in 1948. Not all the plans were disclosed, but the following steps were discussed with the governors.

- There were to be no attempts to cling to power in the colonies.
- Self-government was to be conceded at the earliest possible date.
- Maximum development needed to be secured before the end of colonial rule.
- Collaboration of the educated elites was to be achieved through constitutional development.
- African elites had to prove that they had the support of the rural and urban people. This suggestion was seen as a strategy to slow down the transfer of power as it would take time to get this support.

The Colonial Office reforms met with opposition from four sources: the colonial governors, the British government, the British people and African people.

New words

Legislative Council a consultative body of appointed colonial officials that discussed the affairs of a colony
Executive Council formed by the heads of government departments who advised the colonial governor on affairs of a colony
precondition a condition that must be fulfilled before any action can take place

▼ Source F
Sir Philip Mitchell, the colonial governor of Kenya, led the objectors

The government of Kenya considers itself morally bound to resist processes which might be called 'political progress' by the

misinformed or opinionated but would in fact, be no more than progress towards the abdication of its trust in favour of ... professional politicians. It may be difficult but will, for a long time, be necessary to dispose of the moral courage and political integrity to say no to proposals for the apparent progress of that kind.

▼ Source G
The Colonial Development and Welfare Act could not obtain all the funding it required because Britain herself needed lots of finances to off-set the fuel crisis. Restrictions on spending were placed on colonies which made the achievement of colonial development difficult.

(From: RD Pearce. *The Turning Point in Africa.*)

The colonial governors agreed that democracy was inappropriate for Africa. They accepted the recommendations on higher education and rejected the reform of the legislative and executive councils. The meeting ended supporting an evolutionary process to self-government.

The British public's strong sense of imperialism conflicted with the Colonial Office's plan to end empire.

▼ Source H
The *Daily Express* captured the public mood

*If dollars are scarce, Africa is ample
Immense the wealth of agricultural products
that her vast expanses will yield to those
who seek it with resolution in their hearts
out with bulldozers, the tractors, the trucks
forward with the railroads, the highways
let the scientists and the engineers go forth
upon their civilising mission.*

The African voice could also be heard in opposition, but on a different basis.

▼ Source I
New York Times, 30 November 1947
British Parley on Africa Scored

K Ozuomba Madiwe, president of the African Academy of Arts and Research, 55 West Forty-second Street, charged yesterday that the Conference of African Governors, recently held in London, was a 'conference for the execution of the exploitation of African peoples.' He criticised Great Britain for 'barring native legislators from the meeting.'

In the final analysis, the initiative for constitutional development lay with Africans as the tide of nationalism rose.

'Winds of Change' speech

In February 1960 the British Prime Minister Harold Macmillan on a visit to South Africa emphasised that the initiative lay with Africans in his address to the parliament in Cape Town.

▼ *Source J*

Extract from the 'Winds of Change' speech

> *The wind of change is blowing through [Africa], and whether we like it or not this growth of national consciousness is a political fact. We must accept it as a fact, and our national policies must take account of it.*

Activities ··

Do these activities on your own, and then compare your answers with the other learners in your group.

1 Can you identify any shifts in British policy as you read through Sources F, G, H and J?
2 Compile a list of the key elements of British decolonisation policy from Sources F, G, H, J and the text.
3 Did the 'Winds of Change' speech in Source J indicate any shift in policy?
4 Compare and contrast British and French decolonisation policies.
5 a Assess the role of Africans in the formulation of these policies.
   b What is the opinion of the role of Africans that is expressed in Source I?
6 To what extent were the British and French policies of decolonisation successful?
7 Were there any interests that the British and the French wished to protect in the colonies?

··

Unit 4

External factors and Africa's decolonisation

Unit outcomes

- Evaluate the impact of the Second World War in the process of decolonisation.
- Analyse the role of the United Nations and Pan-Africanism in Africa's decolonisation.
- Assess the effects of the anti-colonial attitude of the superpowers – the United States and the Soviet Union.
- Explore the relationship between the Cold War and African decolonisation.
- Understand concepts such as communist block, capitalist block, Cold War and Pan-Africanism.
- Evaluate primary sources and identify assumptions in sources.

Introduction

Changes in the international environment contributed to decolonisation. The Great Depression, the Second World War, the United Nations Organisation (UNO) and the rise of new super-powers provide a wider environment in which the process of Africa's decolonisation must be understood. Although the main responsibility lay with the Africans and the colonial powers these other factors shaped the world in which they operated. It is correct to say that the type of independence obtained by Africa was greatly influenced by the combination of these factors in different ways. The rivalry between the United States of America and the Soviet Union contributed to the British and French desire to leave behind friendly new states.

The Great Depression

The Wall Street Crash of October 1929 led to an economic crisis, called the Great Depression. It contributed to creating conditions that increased African suffering. In Africa the Great Depression led to a fall in the prices of minerals and agricultural products.

© Popperfoto. Photo: SAL

▲ Photograph of African soldiers fighting in the Second World War in the Burma campaign
(From: K Shillington. *History of Africa.*)

The colonial authorities, desperate for income, encouraged African peasants to grow more cash crops for export. As more products came on the market, the prices fell further, so the colonial powers resorted to raising taxes to meet budget requirements. The cost-cutting measures such as cutting back salaries and retrenching workers had a negative effect on Africans in the colonies.

African responses involved strikes, producer boycotts and the formation of youth political movements. It can be said that the Great Depression raised the political consciousness of the people.

The Second World War

In 1939 Britain and France dragged Africans into a war which had little to do with them. (See Chapter 3 for the causes and development of the war.) The Second World War, however, played an important role in leading Africa to independence.

To begin with, the restoration of Ethiopia's independence was a direct result of the Second World War. African soldiers participated in Ethiopia and went on to fight in North Africa, Europe and the Far East. The restoration of Ethiopia's independence inspired hope in Africans, 'if Ethiopia today, why not the rest of Africa tomorrow?' (Shillington, 371) was the general feeling.

The Second World War played a role in changing world opinion towards colonies. The Atlantic Charter of August 1941 between President Roosevelt of the United States and British Prime Minister Churchill promised the right of all people to self-government. This was a great source of inspiration for Africans still living under colonial rule.

▼ *Source A*
The Atlantic Charter
Clause Three:

... They [Britain and the USA government] respect the right of all peoples to choose the form of government under which they will live; and they wish to see sovereign rights and self-government restored to those who have been forcibly deprived of them.

(From: K Shillington. *History of Africa*.)

▼ Black South African soldiers in North Africa learn to identify mines during the Second World War
(From: T Cameron. *An Illustrated History of South Africa*.)

African experience of the war included high consumer prices resulting from war-time **inflation**, **forced cropping** and an increased African urban population. Nationalist leaders used these circumstances to organise protests against colonial rule. The huge urban populations were a new source of strength in public rallies and demonstrations.

The ex-servicemen contributed to the dismantling of colonialism in several ways. The war had helped to diminish the European image. African soldiers had discovered that Europeans hurt, died, feared and sometimes lived in poverty just like many Africans. The war removed their fear of colonial authorities and white people in general. Nationalist leaders such as Nkrumah in 1947 used the soldiers' protest marches to campaign against colonial rule and, importantly, the soldiers themselves became supporters of national movements for independence.

Activities ....

1 In what ways did the Great Depression contribute to the independence movement?
2 Was the Second World War a significant factor in the process of attaining African independence? Give reasons to support your answer.
3 Why do you think the Atlantic Charter, particularly the clause shown in Source A, was a serious challenge to colonialism?

....

Extension activity ....
Imagine that you were a nationalist leader in 1945. How would you have used the Atlantic Charter to help your cause?

....

The United Nations Organisation

One of the most significant consequences of the Second World War was the formation of the United Nations (UN) in 1945. The UN became a very influential venue for the discussion of the decolonisation process around the world. African nationalists used the UN to mobilise world opinion against colonialism and apartheid in South Africa. With the inauguration of the new democratic government in South Africa in 1994 the UN concluded its anti-colonial work, almost 49 years after it began. The principles used to guide this process could be found in two chapters of the UN Charter. Part of Chapter 11 can be found in Source B below, while Chapter 7 dealt with the trusteeship system (see Source I in Unit 1).

▼ *Source B*
Charter of the United Nations
Chapter 11 Declaration Regarding Non-Self-Governing Territories
Article 73
Members of the United Nations which have or assume responsibilities for the administration of territories whose peoples have not yet attained a full measure of self-government recognize the principle that the interests of the inhabitants of these territories are **paramount**, *and accept as a* **sacred trust** *the obligation to promote to the utmost, within the system of international peace and security established by the present Charter, the well-being of the inhabitants of these territories, and, to this end:*

a) to ensure, with due respect for the culture of the peoples concerned, their political, economic, social, and educational advancement, their just treatment, and their protection against abuses;

b) to develop self-government, to take due account of the political **aspirations** *of the peoples, and to assist them in the progressive development of their free political institutions, according to the particular circumstances of each territory and its peoples and their varying stages of advancement.*

The process leading to the drafting of the UN Charter faced serious obstacles. Britain, France and Belgium had problems with the Atlantic Charter that promised self-determination (independence) to the colonised. Neither De Gaulle nor Churchill was ready to grant self-determination. They were also not prepared to place the former German colonies, which they administered, under international supervision.

The Soviet Union and United States wished to obtain specific independence dates for the trustee territories. They also wanted to see a transparent system of administering them. Although the wishes of the Soviet Union and the United States were not granted, the UN gained the right to send groups to inspect the process to self-determination. Source C reflects the opinion of such a group.

▼ *Source C*
UN Mission Urges More Self-Government In Report on British Tanganyika Territory
Special to the New York Times
LAKE SUCCESS, 7 Dec. – The British administering authorities of the African territory of Tanganyika have been urged by an on-the-spot United Nations mission to

encourage the 6,000,000 African inhabitants in the area to seek increased participation in government affairs.

UN contributions to anti-colonialism

Although the colonial powers were often an obstacle to the process of decolonisation, the UN was still important in many ways.

- The **public diplomacy** of the UN opened up space to question colonial powers on their running of the colonies.
- The UN framework made the exchange of political ideas easier.
- The UN machinery was used for publishing and distributing anti-colonial material.
- The UN provided leadership in forming world opinion on issues. World opinion favoured decolonisation and this pressure was felt by the colonial powers.
- Independent Asian countries, and later on African countries, used the UN to work for the independence of the remaining African colonies. Notable was the work of the UN in the independence of Namibia and in the anti-apartheid campaigns.
- The UN created special agencies (organisations) to deal with decolonisation and trustee territories.

Activities . . . .

1 a Summarise the role of the colonial powers according to Source B.

b What was the UN's role?

2 How did the Charter try to please the colonial powers?

3 If you were a British official how would you interpret Source B?

4 Write down how you would use Chapter 11 (Source B) as a leader of:

a a nationalist movement

b an independent state.

5 Do you think the practice of submitting reports on trustee territories as shown in Source C is a good thing? Give reasons for your answer.

Extension activity . . . .

Do you think the UN is a useful organisation in today's world? Give reasons for your answer.

Pan-Africanism

Pan-Africanism was an important ideological basis of nationalism. Pan-Africanism is a contribution made by Africans in the diaspora (outside Africa) towards awakening African political consciousness. Pan-Africanism has a number of varieties. The movement directed by

New words

inflation a general increase in the prices of goods and services causing a fall in the buying power of money
forced cropping forced cultivation of cash crops such as cotton
paramount distinguished as being first among others
sacred trust safeguarded or reserved trust
aspirations earnest desires or hopes
public diplomacy diplomatic activities done in the open

Du Bois appealed to and organised the educated. Garvey's movement aimed at awakening the majority of people to their African origins. In Africa Pan-Africanism came to mean the movement towards African unity against colonialism. But all of these variations stress unity on the basis of a common African ancestry.

Origins of Pan-Africanism

Pan-Africanism started in North America and in the Caribbean. The first Pan-Africanists claimed for all blacks the same equality of human values with other peoples. Pan-Africanism, as a positive declaration of Africanness, was a reaction to the racist world. In the Americas and Africa black people were considered less than human by the Europeans. They faced segregation in every aspect of life. Pan-Africanism therefore started as a political response to the injustices against Africans.

The first Pan-Africanist movement started as an organisation of educated people of African descent. The movement was organised around a series of conferences between 1900 and 1945. The first of these conferences was held in 1900 in London. The leading figure at the time was William Edward Burghardt du Bois, an African American historian. In 1919 Du Bois organised a second Pan-Africanist conference in Paris. It was meant to coincide with the occasion of the First World War Peace Conference.

▼ William Edward Burghardt du Bois
(From: WE Burghardt du Bois. *The Souls of Black Folk.*)

The Pan-Africanist conference called for the protection and advancement of the natives of Africa and of African descent. But the great powers gathered in Paris did not listen to this call. The third conference was held in London and Brussels in 1921 and was followed by a fourth in Lisbon in 1923. The fourth conference called for 'black men to be treated as men, we can see no other road to peace and progress'.

The last Pan-African congress of this kind was held in London in 1945. It had a big impact on the African movement for independence. For the first time an impressive number of Africans from the mother continent attended the conference. Amongst these were Kwame Nkrumah, Jomo Kenyatta, ITA Wallace-Johnson from Sierra Leone and several Nigerians. This group of Africans returned to Africa inspired and determined to gain their independence. The closing press statement said: 'We are determined to be free. If the Western world is still determined to rule mankind by force, then Africans as a last resort, may have to appeal to force in the effort to achieve freedom.'

The African national struggle was transformed into radical politics that speeded up the arrival of independence.

Garveyism

Marcus Garvey's Pan-Africanism aimed at reaching the black man in the street. Garvey's methods and speeches impressed many, and his message reached black people everywhere, in the Caribbean, the plantations of the deep south of America and even in the heart of Africa.

Garvey organised 'the back to Africa movement'. He promoted a growing recognition of African kinship (family connections) among African Americans. Garvey did not only dream of an African homeland free from the oppression of biased society, he began to organise people to get back to Africa.

He organised black people in America to fight for self-improvement. 'Up you might race, you can accomplish what you will', he would urge his listeners. Through slogans such as 'Africa for the Africans', 'Renaissance of the negro race', and 'Back to Africa', Garvey moved the minds of African Americans and stirred many people to a strong sense of racial consciousness.

In Africa, it was Marcus Garvey's call of 'Africa for the Africans' which inspired young nationalists in the 1920s and 1930s.

▼ Marcus Garvey, president of the Universal Negro Improvement Association
(From: *The Horizon History of Africa.*)

Photo: South African Library

Negritude

In French West Africa Negritude provided Africans with a sense of black self-respect. It is interesting that this movement had its roots in the Caribbean Islands with people like Aime Cesaire. In Africa it was taken up by Leopold Senghor, who later became Senegal's leader.

Activities ....
1 What do you understand by Pan-Africanism?
2 What conditions made Pan-Africanism attractive for Africans in Africa and African Americans in the diaspora?
3 Do you think Africa needs Pan-Africanism? Give reasons to support your answer.
4 What are the different methods used to organise Pan-Africanism?
5 Why was Garveyism popular in Africa?
....

Superpower anti-colonialism

America's anti-colonial stand was clear in the Atlantic Charter which got adopted as Chapter 11 of the UN Charter. Between 1941 and 1945 the USA criticised Britain for going against the undertaking in the Atlantic Charter. The British were unhappy with taking self-government to mean independence, and because of this they fought to ensure that the UN Charter did not include the word 'independence'. The Soviet Union and China had pressed for the word 'independence' to be included in the Charter. However, America, France, the Netherlands and

South Africa objected to inserting 'independence', insisting that the future lay in interdependence.

From May 1945 when China had made the proposal that split the San Francisco Conference finalising the UN Charter, the issue of African independence would be fought along new lines, between the West and East. The end of the Second World War had brought about the redivision of the world. Britain and France experienced a decline in their status as international powers. This led to the related decline of Western Europe and saw the rise of the USA as the leader of the West. The Soviet Union emerged out of the Second World War as the only other superpower besides the USA. The West was rather suspicious of Stalin, the leader of the post-war Soviet Union.

The emergence of two main blocks, the communist block centred on the Soviet Union and the capitalist block led by the USA, had serious consequences on the process of decolonisation. The superpowers wanted to dominate international relations, which led to the development of global political strategies for decolonisation. The USA encouraged a process of decolonisation that would leave African states within the Western influence. To achieve this they began a process of diplomatically encouraging Britain to decolonise. Although they were critical of continued colonialism they were careful not to offend their partners in the Western alliance.

The Soviet Union was seen by many Africans as a source of hope. The Soviet Union, Cuba and China pressed for African independence. In the era of the Cold War (see Chapter 4), the Soviet Union block developed global strategies which would benefit from friendly African independent states. In this context it is only fair to state that the superpowers used the cause of African independence for their own selfish reasons. Had the ideological concepts of 'liberty and freedom' for all citizens of the world been important, the USA would not have been so patient with the colonial powers. It was patient with them because of its interest in getting the new states under Western influence.

The benefit of the rivalry between the Soviet Union and the West was that Africa gained great importance. It is this new significance that led some, not all, colonial powers to reassess their decolonisation policies. Continued foreign domination could not be defended in the post-war world. The colonial racial policies, forms of social and economic relations, were challenged as they contradicted the principles of self-determination in the UN Charter. African countries used this international climate to press for their independence and a place in the world.

Activities

1 a What is the British stand on independence?
 b What are the American pronouncements on independence?
2 To what extent was the USA's anti-colonial policy in her own best interests?
3 In what ways would America benefit from the independence of Africa?
4 What choice of partners did new African states have in the post-war world?
5 In the same way, examine the Soviet motives for the decolonisation of Africa.
 a What interests did they want to serve in the decolonisation of Africa?
 b How would that help them to grow as a superpower?

◄ Congolese demonstrators in Leopoldville in 1959
(From: D Wilson. *A History of South and Central Africa.*)

The Cold War in Africa

In Africa the Cold War had a direct impact on the independence of the Congo, formerly Zaire. The sudden departure of the Belgians from the Congo created a crisis. After riots in Leopoldville (now Kinshasa) on 5 January 1959 the Belgian government announced that the Congo would be given independence. Elections were to be held in December of the same year. Until this time, the Belgians had insisted that the Congo was an integral part of Belgium. The time for organising a transition to independence was so short that in December of that year chaos broke out, leading to a civil war between different parties. The struggle soon separated into the pro-West Shombe breaking away with the mineral rich Katanga, and Patrice Lumumba and Joseph Kasavubu holding on to the rest of the country. By June 1960 when independence celebrations were meant to be held the country had sunk into crisis.

The mineral wealth such as uranium and its location in the centre of the continent attracted the interest of superpowers. The Congo crisis provided an opportunity for the Cold War, which was taken up as the sources show.

▼ Source D
Document 3:
On 4 November 1965, Che Guevara, who was in the Congo, received a cable from Oscar Fernández Padilla, head of the Cuban intelligence station in Dar-es-Salaam. The cable said:

I am sending you, via courier, a letter from Fidel. Its key points are:

1 *We must do everything except that which is foolhardy.*

2 *If Tatu [Guevara] believes that our presence has become either unjustifiable or pointless, we have to consider withdrawing.*

3 *If he thinks we should remain we will try to send as many men and as much material as he considers necessary.*

4 *We are worried that you may wrongly fear that your decision might be considered defeatist or pessimistic.*

5 *If Tatu decides to leave [the Congo], he can return here or go somewhere else [while waiting for a new internationalist mission].*

6 *We will support whatever decision [Tatu makes].*

7 *Avoid [being destroyed].*

(From: Rafael [Fernández Padilla] to Tatu, 4 November 1965, Archives of the Cuban Communist Party CC, Havana.)

▼ Source E
New York Times, 16 July 1960
Khrushchev tells the West to hands off Congo
Replies to New Republic's Appeal For Intervention by Soviet if Needed
By Seymour Topping
Special to the New York Times

Moscow, 15 July – Premier Khrushchev acceded quickly today to an appeal by the Government of the Congo for Soviet intervention if the West does not end its 'aggression' against the new African republic.

'If the states which are directly carrying out imperialist aggression against the Congo and those who are pushing them on continue their criminal actions, the USSR will not shrink from resolute measures to curb aggression.'

The Congolese appeal to Mr Khrushchev dismayed Western diplomats here, who saw it as a propaganda coup that would enhance the Soviet leader's efforts to pose as the guardian angel of the African peoples. It was believed here that unless the Congo can be pacified quickly the situation could provide an opening wedge for Soviet penetration into the heart of Africa.

▼ Source F
New York Times, 26 April 1966
How CIA put instant air force into Congo
Intervention or Spying All in a Day's Work
Special to the New York Times

Washington, 25 April – The CIA operation in the Congo was at all times responsible to and welcomed by the policy makers of the United States.

It was these policy makers who chose to make the agency the instrument of the political and military intervention in another nation's affair, for in five years of strenuous effort it was only in Langley that the White House, the State Department and the Pentagon found the peculiar combination of talents necessary to block the creation of the pro-Communist regime, recruit the leaders for a pro-American government and supply the advice and support to enable that government to survive ...

When the Communist and Western worlds began to wrestle for control of the vast, undeveloped Congo in 1960 after it had gained independence from Belgium, a mod-

est CIA office in Leopoldville mushroomed overnight into a virtual embassy and miniature war department.

Activities ....

1 How would you classify Sources D, E and F above?
2 Why is it necessary to have intelligence reports on a situation?
3 What can we learn from intelligence reports?
4 Are intelligence reports reliable historical sources?
5 What can historians do about the bias and hidden signifiers or system of signals used in intelligence reports?
6 Is the posting by the diplomatic correspondent in Moscow, Source E, biased?

7 a Which side do you think the Moscow correspondent is supporting?
  b How do you know?
8 Why does Source F sound like it is celebrating CIA involvement in Africa?
9 Is it justifiable for countries to intervene in other countries? Give reasons to support your answer.

....

Extension activity ....
Is there a role for government intelligence agencies today? What do you think their role could be?

....

Patterns of decolonisation

Unit outcomes

- Understand the different patterns of decolonisation.
- Use historical sources to reconstruct the process of the transfer of power.
- Discuss how and why various liberation struggles developed.
- Learn about new concepts such as constitutional transfer of power, liberation movements and settler colonialism.

Introduction

African countries gained their independence in many different ways. The majority of the countries obtained their independence through constitutional means. This type of independence depended on the colonised and the colonisers agreeing on the timing of the process and the form of the new state. It was the constitution which specified the organisation of the new state. Both the British and the French employed this method in some colonies. For the French in Algeria, the Portuguese, the Belgians and the settler colonies of Zimbabwe and South Africa it took liberation wars to get them to the negotiating table. Two other ways of gaining independence were less problematic: the trusteeship territories and the former Italian colonies.

The constitutional arrangements of the British and the French differed in content and the way the process was handled. The British constitutional framework depended on the concept of **devolution** while the French was based on **integration**. The British process involved the colonisers dealing with each separate colony, while the French method aimed at creating a closely knit community. The only common ground was that they both attempted to work on a constitution that would specify how the state would be organised.

New words

devolution delegation of power by colonial power to the colony or new independent state
integration combination of colonies into one community

The Second World War gave rise to independence

The defeat of the Italians in Africa during the Second World War led to the restoration of Ethiopia's independence by 1941. In North Africa the war against the Italians carried on until 1943. Libya, a former colony of the defeated Italians, obtained its independence in 1951 with the help of the United Nations. In the Sudan the British used the opportunity granted by the Second World War to seize it from Egyptian control, and in 1944 the British granted independence to the Sudan, but the Egyptians rejected the idea. In 1952 Nasser overthrew the old regime and immediately assured Sudan of its independence. In 1956 the Sudan obtained its independence. By 1956 France had conceded independence to Morocco and Tunisia.

The British pattern of decolonisation

The British had governed each territory as a self-governing colony. Their plans for the transfer of power followed the same pattern of treating each colony separately. The process of transforming the legislative councils into bodies with an elected majority was carried out within each colony. The model used was the British Parliamentary system, but how each colony finalised that in their constitutions was done separately. Beginning with Ghana in 1957, Britain negotiated with each colony to set up the institutions that would have to be in place at independence. The British hoped that by giving Africa new democratic constitutions it would follow British Parliamentary democracy. Source A is a newspaper report giving an example of the constitutional negotiations.

▼ *Source A*
New York Times, 29 April 1954
British Give More Self-Rule to Gold Coast; Natives to Get Ministries Whites Now Hold

London, 28 April – The Gold Coast is to take another big step toward self-rule. The British government has accepted proposals from Prime Minister Kwame Nkrumah and his Government under which the last three

British Cabinet Ministers will be replaced by natives ...

The new constitutional proposals for the former colony in West Africa will be laid before Britain's **Privy Council** shortly, Mr Hopkinson declared. They include the extension of the **direct ballot** to areas that now vote by tribal groups and a definite reduction in the initiative the Governor normally will exercise ...

The Gold Coast has proposed to insert a constitutional guarantee that any business enterprise that is **nationalized** will be given fair **compensation**, Mr Hopkinson revealed. This clearly was made necessary by the past **radicalism** of Dr. Nkrumah and his Convention People's Party.

New words

Privy Council body of advisers chosen by the prime minister
direct ballot one man one vote
nationalized made into national/public property
compensation money or goods given to make up for a loss
radicalism extreme political solutions
ratified accepted or confirmed by signing a document

The French pattern of decolonisation

As discussed earlier, the 1958 referendum called for all the colonies to decide the form of government they preferred. All, except Guinea, chose to become autonomous (self-governing) states within the community whose external affairs would be controlled by France. Once the decision had been made the French Parliament **ratified** it and actual independence was a mere formality. When Mali requested its independence in 1960, it started a rush by the other colonies.

▼ Source B
New York Times, 13 July 1960
Three More Nations Gain Freedom Through Pact Signed by France
By W Granger Blaire
Special to the New York Times

Paris, 12 July – The rush to freedom in the French Community continued today as three more autonomous African republics signed independence accords with the French Government.

The designation of the Congo, Chad and Central African Republics as independent states brought to seven the number of African members of the Community to be granted full sovereignty in the last twenty-four hours ... Yesterday independence was pledged to the Council of the Entente which is composed of the Ivory Coast, Niger, Dahomey and Voltaic Republics in West Africa.

When the independence accords are ratified by the French Parliament and the legislation Assemblies of the Union republics, the three new states will proclaim their independence.

UN trusteeship territories

The sources below provide evidence on the independence of the United Nations trusteeship territories. The timing and form of independence depended on the territorial choices, the reaction of the colonial power responsible and the United Nations. The last of these territories only obtained independence in 1990.

▼ Source C
New York Times, 20 October 1958
Cameroon Gets Freedom Pledge
Paris Backs Independence For African Trust Territory After Interim Self-Rule
By TF Brady
Special to the New York Times

Paris, 19 Oct. – France has recognized the right of her United Nations trust territory of the Cameroons to choose independence ...

Like Togoland, the Cameroons was a German colony until the Treaty of Versailles, both territories were split into British and French mandates under League of Nations authority. The mandates were converted into trusteeships by the United Nations after World War II.

▼ Source D
Tanganyika in 4 Day Celebration as Nation Gains Independence
By L Ingalls
Special to the New York Times

Dar-es-Salaam, Tanganyika, Saturday, 9 Dec. – Tanganyika became an instant sovereign state today. An instant after midnight the green, gold and black Tanganyika flag was raised in a ceremony here that brought to an end the territory's years as a German colony and then as a British-administered United Nations trust territory.

▼ *Source E*

Togo Change Approved By UN
Assembly Vote to Conclude Trusteeship Under Britain, Backs Gold Coast Merger
By K McLaughlin
Special to the New York Times

> United Nations, NY 13 Dec. – The General Assembly approved today termination of trusteeship for British Togoland and merger of the territory with the Gold Coast in an independent state.

▼ *Source F*

New York Times, 28 October 1966
League Mandate in Africa Ended by 114 to 2 UN
By R Daniell
Special to the New York Times

> United Nations, NY 27 Oct. – The General Assembly adopted a resolution tonight to terminate South Africa's mandate from the League of Nations to administer the neighbouring territory of South West Africa [Namibia]. The vote was 114 to 2 with 3 abstentions.
>
> The resolution declared that 'South West Africa comes under the direct responsibility of the United Nations'.
>
> South Africa, which contests the right of the United Nations to rescind the mandate unilaterally, has promised to resist with all resources at her disposal any attempt to carry out the terms of the resolution.

Activities ·

1 What are the differences in the pattern of independence between the British and the French?
2 Use the maps on pages 192 and 193 in Unit 1 to write down the names and dates when British colonies and French colonies attained their independence through constitutional means.
3 Why were the French colonies all independent within a period of three years?
4 From the sources on French territories construct the process they followed to attain independence.
5 Use Sources C to F on the trusteeships to write a paragraph explaining the problems faced by Africans in attaining independence.

· ·

Liberation struggles

Some colonial powers and settler regimes were determined to maintain colonialism or racial oppression. The Portuguese, the French in Algeria, the white rebels in Zimbabwe and the minority government in South Africa objected to granting independence to the majority made up of African people. Portugal created the myth that the colonies were provinces of Portugal and there could be no independence for them. The French held on to Algeria despite the people's desire to be independent, and white Rhodesians, fearing that Britain might move to negotiate independence with the African population, declared themselves independent without permission (which is called a unilateral declaration of independence).

In contrast to the post-war thinking that emphasised self-determination, the southern African white settler territories pursued policies based on the belief of white superiority. Their position on independence revolved around a number of issues from opposition to decolonisation and communism to a suspicion of the UN to a wish to strengthen white privileges against blacks.

The settler states of South Africa and Rhodesia and the Portuguese in Angola and Mozambique were opposed to decolonisation. White South Africa in particular was fearful of political rights being granted to Africans north of the Zambezi River. They feared that these political rights might encourage African nationalism within their own borders. They also feared the hostility of the independent states which they thought would take on communism and spread it to South Africa.

In choosing to present themselves as anticommunist the settler states placed themselves on the side of the West. In fact, despite its anticolonial feelings, the USA established close relations with South Africa and the Portuguese colonies. They saw themselves as united against the communist danger. In this way southern Africa became part of the Cold War.

The United Nations, a body that could organise the international community for action on any issue, was regarded by the settler regimes with strong suspicion. South Africa felt threatened on the question of its authority in South West Africa. In 1950 the International Court of Justice ruled that the territory should be placed under the United Nations Trusteeship, but South Africa rejected the ruling and made it into its fifth province.

The settler states rejected self-determination. Instead, they retained and intensified colonial forms of domination. Despite all this, South Africa and Portugal enjoyed good relations with the West. It was only in the 1980s that ordinary people in Western countries pressed their governments to impose sanctions against South Africa.

Africans in these territories tried all legal means to negotiate with the settler states for some accommodation of their political rights. The peaceful strategies included writing petitions, boycotts, peaceful marches, stayaways, defiance campaigns, days of prayer and, in some cases, strikes. The settler governments of southern Africa responded with violence. Beginning in Mozambique at Mueda in 1960, in Luanda in February 1960, and Sharpeville in March 1960, the settler regimes opened fire, killing peaceful demonstrators in numbers.

The shootings in these territories emphasised that the settler states would not negotiate. These shootings were followed by the banning of African political activities. The road to peaceful negotiations and protests came to an abrupt end. The African nationalist movements took a strategic decision to answer force with force and fight for their independence.

Through its liberation committee the Organisation of African Unity (OAU) soon provided moral and material support for the liberation movements, and by early 1964 the neighbouring countries that were independent could provide military bases to the liberation movements. Through diplomatic work the African liberation movements managed to obtain support from the Soviet Union, China, Eastern Europe and ordinary citizens in the West. Soon the Western governments and the media called African liberation movements 'terrorist organisations'. In doing this they gave their support to the white settler states.

The rising tide of resistance in Portuguese Africa led to a military coup in Portugal by young officers. These officers pledged independence to Angola, Mozambique, Sâo Tomé e Príncipe, Cape Verde Islands and Guinea Bissau. The independence of Angola and Mozambique provided new fronts from which the liberation movements launched their war. The cost of maintaining the Rhodesian war became too high to continue and so, in 1979, Zimbabwe negotiated its independence with Britain and celebrated its independence in 1980. Namibia followed in 1990 after South Africa's military failures in Angola.

By 1990 there remained one obstacle to Africa's total political freedom: South Africa. With no **buffer zones** remaining, the international sanctions biting, and the internal struggle intensifying, the National Party government faced a serious crisis. The solution lay in negotiating a new order, a democratic society for South Africa. The process leading to the negotiations saw the release of political prisoners, most prominently, Nelson Mandela. On 10 May 1994 Nelson Mandela was inaugurated as the first president of a new South Africa, thereby erasing the last trace of settler colonialism.

New words

buffer zone neutral state located between two hostile states

Activities

1 What factors led to the establishment of the liberation movements?
2 To what extent was the taking up of the liberation war inevitable?
3 Do you think that the use of military force to bring about political change is justified?
4 What are some alternatives to the use of military force to bring about political change?

Extension activity

Do some research to help you write an essay on the following topic:
Describe the events leading to the independence of Zimbabwe from the break-up of the Central African Federation in 1964 to the independence of Zimbabwe in 1980.

Unit 6
Independence and political challenges

Unit outcomes

- Analyse different positions on democracy.
- Appreciate the political changes following independence.
- Recognise the political factors and actors in post-independence Africa.
- Understand more about the origins and role of the Organisation of African Unity (OAU).
- Learn about new concepts such as constitutional democracy, dictatorships, one-party states and military rule.
- Practise skills such as judging information, empathising and solving problems.

Introduction

This unit looks at the challenges facing Africans after obtaining independence. African attempts to deal with the challenges have resulted in diverse systems of government. The renewed presence of democratic governments in the 1990s ends the discussion of political developments in Africa.

Political systems: democracy debated

Sources A and B are a sample of the debates that took place in and outside Africa.

▼ Source A

New York Times, 27 March 1960
Africa Needs Time
By Julius Nyerere

Within ten years, Africa will have won its fight against foreign domination. Then the continent will be free to concentrate on its battle for the consolidation of its freedom, the achievements of economic, political and moral equality before the world.

The slogan 'Africa must be Free' must not be confined to the idea of freedom from foreign rule. It must, if it means anything at all, mean freedom for the individual man and woman – freedom from every form of oppression, indignity, intimidation or exploitation. It must include the right of the individual citizen to re-elect or to

replace the Government of his own country. It must also, of course, include freedom of the Government to govern, without fear of any attempt to replace it by means other than that of the ballot box.

It is important to emphasize the difference between democracy itself and the various forms it can take. To my mind, there are two essentials for democracy. The first of these is the freedom and well being of the individual; the second is that the method by which the Government of a country is chosen must ensure that the Government is freely chosen.

New words

consolidation strengthening
checks and balances of power fair distribution of power between institutions of government
accountability responsibility; obligation to explain why you have done something
universal adult suffrage right to vote extended to all adults

▼ Source B

New York Times, 18 March 1959
Africans Favor One-Party Rule
By Thomas F Brady
Special to the New York Times

Ibadan, Nigeria, 17 March – Abdoulaye Diallo, Guinea's Minister to Ghana, said at a conference of African intellectuals and political leaders that his country's method was democratic because the ruling party had its roots in the people and reflected their will through constant consultation. But the Minister continued, there is no opposition for opposition's sake and no struggle by individuals to take over power from other individuals in Guinea. Such struggles are a waste of time and energy and therefore inefficient in new countries, he said, where social programs are the first consideration.

Mr Diallo's proclamation of a one-party philosophy which appears to be that of

Prime Minister Kwame Nkrumah of Ghana as well as Premier Sekou Toure of Guinea followed a discourse on the role of opposition in new countries by S. N. Einsenstadt, Professor of Sociology at Hebrew University, Jerusalem.

David Apter, a Professor of Political Science at the University of Chicago replied to Mr Diallo, stressing the value of an opposition as the representative of minority interests, as a critic of government and as a source of information for the people.

Most African countries started out with constitutions that provided for multi-party systems, the separation of powers, **checks and balances of power**, representative structures and regular elections. The politics under this system involved compromise, bargaining and **accountability**. However, the stability of these governments was limited. Countries such as Botswana managed to retain a democratic system of government, but many more failed to face the tough challenges and found solutions which limited their citizens' freedom.

Activities

Work in groups for these activities.
1 What is your definition of democracy?
2 Compare your definition with Nyerere's thoughts on democracy in Source A.
3 In what ways are Nyerere's views (Source A) different from Mr Abdoulaye Diallo's position on democracy outlined in Source B?
4 Do you think African leaders understood the functioning of a democratic government?

Extension activity

Look at the views on democracy expressed in Sources A and B. What do you think the politics coming out of these positions would be?

Reasons for the failure of constitutional democracy

Colonial legacy

The political institutions inherited by newly independent states were imposed on them by the departing colonial powers. Colonialism did not provide Africans with democratic institutions of government. But at independence colonial powers prescribed a parliamentary system of government to a people who had not experienced it. Ghana provides an early example of the limitations of this situation as Source C discusses.

▼ Source C

1 **Universal adult suffrage** as a general basis for election to the legislature was not introduced till 1954, practically at the end of the colonisation period.
2 The first political party formed with the aim of forming a government, the United Gold Coast Convention People's Party was only launched on 4 August 1947.
3 The first party which ... operated as a modern mass-based party, the Convention People's Party was not launched until 12 June 1949.
4 The first constitution under which a cabinet, selected from the majority party after elections, functioned was the 1954 constitution.
5 At independence the judiciary they inherited had known no independence. It had been an active machinery of the colonial government, its members were active in the formulation of colonial policy and legislation, there was no independence of the judiciary.

(From: Kwame Arhin. *The Life and Work of Kwame Nkrumah.*)

At the time of independence parliamentary democracy was very new to most Africans. They had had no or little experience of the separation of powers between the executive (cabinet), the legislature (parliament), and the judiciary (the law courts).

Africa's history as a problem (**tribalism**)

Although nationalism brought many people together against colonialism, the new political groupings were still very weak. African countries are made up of many ethnic groups. The new leaders faced the challenge of finding a form of government that would bring all these ethnic groups together under one government. Even before independence had been won, trends towards ethnic groups demanding their own independence threatened to break up the new states. African internal divisions and especially a strong sense of regionalism gave rise to violent conflicts, resulting in Katanga breaking away from the Congo (1960–63), Biafra breaking away from Nigeria (1967–70), the civil wars in Sudan (1955, 1962–72), Ethiopia, Chad, and recently in Somali, Rwanda and Burundi.

New words

tribalism discrimination based on ethnic identity
federal structure organisational system that brings together independent states into a union as one state

Rewriting of constitutions

African nations had many good reasons for rewriting the independence constitutions. In several countries, as in Kenya, political leaders undertook to rewrite the independence constitutions in order to deal with the **federal structure** imposed on them. In Uganda the conflict between the Kabaka, the traditional ruler of the Buganda Kingdom, and the government resulted in the rewriting of the constitution. The aim was to reduce the influence and power of the traditional ruler in internal politics. Lesotho under Leaboa Jonathan rewrote the constitution to limit the role of King Moshoeshoe II, the traditional ruler, in government.

Division of leaders from the masses

Another problem that emerged in post-colonial Africa was that the leaders lost contact with the lives and interests of their people. This led to a struggle for power between the elite politicians. The new independent leaders used these conflicts to obtain unquestioning loyalty from party members. Disloyal party members were no longer rewarded with appointments to office. This led to power being concentrated in the hands of the president. Those opposed to the rulers had no choice but to leave the party. This led to the rapid growth of political parties.

Ideological conflicts

Africans' experience with capitalism had been rough. After independence some African rulers were opposed to the West. They denounced their unfair and unequal relationship with their former colonial masters and began to adopt socialism as an ideology to help them reorganise their societies. In this situation the socialist parties tended to look at other political parties as traitors who should not be allowed to participate in shaping the future of the country. Based on the new ideology the leaders rewrote independence constitutions, ending up with single-party systems of government.

Foreign military involvement

Foreign military involvement in some African countries contributed to political instability in post-colonial Africa. Foreign political and military intervention took place in countries which failed to find their way to national unity and agreement. The Democratic Republic of the Congo (formerly Zaire) witnessed foreign intervention following the disorganised manner in which the Belgians transferred political power. France's intervention in the Central African Republic helped the local dictators to rise to power. Military interventions sometimes inflamed existing conflicts into open civil war, as in the case in Chad. The French support of

Profile: Foreign military intervention – a case study of Angola

Angola has experienced war since 1961. The war has gone through three phases: the national liberation war 1961–74, the first civil war 1975–91, and the ongoing civil war since 1993. During the war for independence Portugal, the colonial power in Angola, was supported by countries belonging to the North Atlantic Treaty Organisation (NATO). The national liberation movements also obtained foreign support from countries in the Eastern Block, the Soviet Union, China and Eastern European countries. When Portuguese control crumbled in 1974, the rivalry between liberation movements (MPLA, FNLA and UNITA) led to war between them.

The United States of America and South Africa intervened on behalf of UNITA and FNLA. This intervention by Western countries on behalf of UNITA and FNLA was countered by Cuban forces and Soviet Union supplies in support of the MPLA. The Angolan conflict was thus turned into an international conflict which was a part of the Cold War (see Chapter 4 for more on the Cold War). It could be argued that the international involvement fuelled the conflict further.

The end of the Cold War contributed to the Angolan peace agreement of 1991. Since then the United States, the former Soviet Union, and Portugal have worked together to monitor the peace process in Angola. However, it is the United Nations Organisation that has played a significant role in the peace process. The UN intervention in Angola has taken the form of three verification missions. All three United Nations Verification Missions (UNAVEM) have failed to bring peace to Angola and the country continues to be at war even by January 1999.

the Christian South against the Muslim North in Chad was disastrous. White mercenaries attempted to overthrow the governments of Benin (formerly Dahomey) in 1977 and the government of the Seychelles in 1981. All these foreign military activities worked against stability and the success of democracy in Africa.

The military aggression of apartheid South Africa against its neighbours created instability, especially in Mozambique and Angola. The South Africans aimed to undermine the new republics so that they would be unable to support the liberation movement's fight against apartheid. The regime's support of pro-South African puppets of the National Resistance Movement of Mozambique (RENAMO) and the National Union for the Total Liberation of Angola (UNITA) totally destabilised these countries.

◀Clearing landmines in Angola, 1993

Activities

1 What do you think of South Africa's involvement in regional conflicts? For more information look at the role of South Africa in the OAU on pages 227 to 228.
2 Do you think the superpowers used Angolan territory and people to continue their own conflict?
3 What role do you think other powerful countries should play in the civil wars in Africa?
4 As a class discuss the ethics of the use of landmines in southern African civil wars.

Corruption

In much of Africa holding a government post was seen as a sure road to wealth. The competition for public office led to widespread practices of favouritism, which is known as nepotism. This involved being appointed to a position on the basis of a relationship with those in power. The buying of favours from those in office and other corruption contributed to people losing faith in the leaders. When government contracts were awarded to friends, relatives or those paying bribes, any legitimacy of the government was further eroded. Economic mismanagement, corruption and nepotism became widespread because of a failure to create checks and balances in government. The judiciary, parliament, the executive and bureaucracy came to be under the control of political leaders. These conditions bred instability and unconstitutional solutions.

Harassment of opponents

Ghana, the first country to obtain independence, pioneered the path to harassment of the opposition.

▼ Source D

New York Times, 1 November 1959
Jailings in Ghana Arouse Protests
By John B Oakes
Special to the New York Times

ACCRA, Ghana, This country's tough Preventive Detention Act passed last fall, has resulted in the imprisonment for up to five years of about forty-five persons, without hearings, trials or appeals.

The Act is one of several security measures that have aroused bitter criticism from such opposition as still exists. For all practical purposes this is a one-party state. In fact, it is virtually a one man state.

Activities

1 To what extent were African leaders responsible for the failure of democracy?
2 Were the troubles facing African countries unavoidable?
3 How would you have tried to solve these problems if you were one of the independence political leaders?
4 Imagine that you are an opposition leader in Ghana in 1959. How difficult would it have been for you to operate as an opposition leader?
5 Should governments pass laws such as the Preventive Detention Act in Source D? Give reasons for your answer.

In search of solutions

African leaders looked for solutions to their problems at two levels. Solutions to problems affecting the entire continent were sought through organisations like the Organisation of African

Unity (OAU) and the UN. However, most problems arose from within the boundaries of the new states, so the solutions looked for were national. This section considers the OAU, the rise of dictatorships (single-party and military governments), and the re-emergence of democracy.

Pan-Africanism and the OAU

Since independence in 1957, the government of Ghana had pursued an active policy of Pan-Africanism. Ghana had committed itself to supporting Africa's total independence. In 1958 Ghana convened two conferences in Accra: the Conference of Independent African States (CIAS) followed by the All-African People's Conference (AAP). The latter brought together political parties and trade unions from independent and non-independent states. The CIAS and the AAP succeeded in:

- bridging the division between two Africas: Arab Africa north of the Sahara and Black Africa south of the Sahara;
- focusing Africa's energies on the liberation of the entire continent;
- supporting the creation of the Commonwealth of African States.

Activities ....
The banner at the top in Source E reads: 'Hands off Africa! Africa must be free!'
1 How does this slogan sum up the ideology of Pan-Africanism?
2 What is the mood of this slogan?
....

The two conferences inspired many leaders to carry on with their liberation struggles. Also in 1958 African nationalists in East Central Africa formed a regional Pan-Africanist Freedom Movement for East Central Africa. This movement aimed at coordinating nationalist efforts to secure the rapid transfer of power.

However, the unity and high hopes of the Pan-Africanist movement did not last. The Algerian war of independence against France and the crisis in the Congo divided the movement. The French refusal to grant Algeria independence led some African states to recognise the provisional government set up by the National Liberation Front (FLN), while other former French colonies under the leadership of Houphonet-Boigny of Ivory Coast supported France. This group of countries formed an association called Union Africaine et Malgache (UAM), otherwise called the Brazzaville Group.

▲ *Source E* The All-African People's Conference in Accra, Ghana in 1958. The banner reads: 'Hands off Africa! Africa must be free!' (From: K Shillington. *History of Africa*.)

In the Congo the Brazzaville Group supported Kasavubu. Radical African states, including Ghana, Guinea, Mali, Morocco and the United Arab Republic (Egypt), formed the Casablanca Group and supported the FLN and Lumumba in the Congo crisis.

Efforts to resolve the differences between the two groups were ongoing, and by 1962 the two problems that had divided the Pan-Africanist unity were resolved. Algeria won its independence from France, and the Congolese leaders, Lumumba and Kasavubu, agreed to form a united government.

On 25 May 1963 thirty-two independent countries met in Addis Ababa, Ethiopia, and formed the Organisation of African Unity (OAU). It was less than what Nkrumah had hoped for, a closely integrated United States of Africa, but was rather a consultative body offering a mechanism to settle disputes between African states. Two significant principles were laid down from the beginning: boundaries inherited at independence were to be kept intact at all costs, and a commitment was made to the total liberation of Africa from colonialism. In this regard the OAU set up a Liberation Committee based in Tanzania. Non-interference in the internal affairs of member states was made an important part of the charter. Tribalism was condemned as a backward element in African politics.

Despite the many weaknesses of the OAU, it has remained a symbol of the determination of Africans to free themselves from foreign domination. Through the OAU Africans express their desire to assume control over their own destiny. Its greatest weakness is that there is nothing in the charter to force member states to follow its rules.

In June 1991 the OAU leaders signed a treaty to work towards forming an Economic Community of Africa by the year 2000. The strategy involves strengthening existing regional economic organisations such as the Economic Community for West African States (ECOWAS was founded in 1975) and Southern African Development Conference (SADC was established in 1980). Both organisations have expanded their agendas to include political and security matters in their work. On the political front these organisations are promoting democratic forms of government. West African states with strong military governments such as Nigeria have more serious obstacles in achieving their goals. In southern Africa almost every country is a democracy, with the exception of Swaziland and the new member, the Democratic Republic of the Congo.

Activities

1 In what ways is the OAU a Pan-Africanist body? Look at the extract from the OAU Charter in Source F for clues.
2 What do you think are the weaknesses and strengths of the OAU?

▼ *Source F*

Extract from the OAU Charter

The purposes of the OAU as stated in Article II(1) of its Charter are:

a) to promote the unity and solidarity of the African states;

b) to coordinate and intensify their cooperation and efforts to achieve a better life for the peoples of Africa;

c) to defend their sovereignty, their territorial integrity and independence;

d) to eradicate all forms of colonialism from Africa; and

e) to promote international cooperation, having due regard to the Charter of the United Nations and the Universal Declaration of Human Rights.

(From: D Mazzeo. *African Regional Organisations.*)

The role of the OAU in conflict resolution

Two examples of the work of the OAU can help us to assess its successes and failures. From the beginning the OAU pledged to work for unity and solidarity among African nations. This pledge to work for unity was often tested over the issue of boundaries. Since the early 1960s Africa has experienced several disputes over boundaries. Among the serious problems inherited by new independent states were frontier disputes. The OAU undertook to preserve the colonial boundaries as a basis for new nation-states. It has been successful in settling most of the frontier disputes through diplomacy and following the principles agreed upon by member states. A look at Morocco's frontier disputes illustrates the failures and successes of the OAU.

▼ *Source G*

A small war broke out in October 1963 between Morocco and Algeria. It concerned a frontier area of Algeria that was claimed by Morocco. Acting as mediator, the OAU was able to bring about a cease-fire, and, in February 1964, an agreement for peace.

Each side gained something and agreed to the economic development of mineral deposits at Tindouf in Algeria. But this failed to satisfy Morocco. OAU peace efforts had to continue. They were crowned with success by a new agreement of May 1970. Other disputes of this kind were settled; and the OAU proved a valuable instrument of peace.

(From: Basil Davidson. *Modern Africa.*)

However, the OAU failed to solve the large dispute involving Morocco and POLISARIO, a liberation movement of the Western Sahara. In 1976 Morocco wanted to share out the ex-Spanish colony, initially with Mauritania. This move would have prevented the formation of the Republic of Western Sahara. OAU efforts to end the war and settle the conflict diplomatically resulted in the recognition of POLISARIO's government and the proclamation of the state of Western Sahara in 1984. Morocco left the OAU in protest and stands out as the only country out of 55 outside the OAU.

The OAU has also played a manager role in conflict resolution and management in civil war situations. Civil wars have scourged Africa since independence, affecting huge states such as the Sudan, Ethiopia, Nigeria, Angola and Chad. The small states of Rwanda and Burundi have also experienced recurring bouts of civil war. The last led to a gruesome genocide in April 1994, which received worldwide media coverage.

▼ Source H

In April [1994] there were eight million people living in Rwanda. By today, more than three million have fled the country, and almost one million have been killed.

Today, Rwanda is like an open grave. There are corpses everywhere. Of men and women, children and babies. They have been slaughtered by their own countrymen; beaten to death, stabbed to death.

They are lying in pools of blood on the floor of their homes, on the grass outside their houses, in the fields that they have farmed. They are lying in the roads, they are floating down the rivers, they are rotting inside churches, they are being eaten by their own dogs. They are one million dead.

(From: http://www.idt.unit.no/~isfit/speeches/mollan.html)

The OAU has played an active role in ending civil wars in much of Africa. Through the ministerial councils and annual presidential summits, the OAU has mediated between the conflicting parties. In recent years the OAU has come up with new ways of tackling civil wars. Source I below portrays the work of the OAU.

▼ Source I

Prevention, Management and Resolution of Conflict

The establishment of the Mechanism for Conflict Prevention, Management and Resolution followed the realisation by the OAU that greater responsibility should be taken for peace efforts on the African Continent in order to promote peace and enhance development after the Cold War.

During 1995, South Africa actively participated in the activities of the OAU's Mechanism for Conflict Prevention, Management and Resolution (the Central Organ). South Africa attended several meetings pertaining to the Organisation's endeavours to assist Burundi in solving its internal political problems. This included two visits to Burundi where the South African component of the Central Organ team was led by the South African Minister of Foreign Affairs.

In regional security matters, South Africa, Botswana and Zimbabwe constitute the Southern Africa Troika which is involved in preventive diplomacy pertaining to the Lesotho constitutional crisis. Visits to Lesotho were undertaken at Ministers' level as well as Foreign Affairs officials' level during which consultations and discussions were held with the Government, the Lesotho Defence Force, Police and the extra-parliamentary political leadership.

(From: http://www.southafrica.net/government/foreign/prevent.html)

Activities ·······························

Discuss these questions as a class.

1 What is the role of the OAU in conflict resolution in Africa?

2 How valid is a military solution to political conflicts?

3 What are the advantages and disadvantages of diplomatic solutions?

4 What recommendations would you suggest for solving Africa's boundary disputes and civil wars?

5 Where do Sources H and I come from? What is the significance of their origin?

Take a case study of a boundary conflict or civil war and carry out research looking for:
- the causes of the conflict;
- the course of the conflict;
- OAU efforts to resolve the conflict;
- any international involvement in resolving the conflict.

···

Rise of dictatorships

Africa has experienced different types of dictatorial systems of government (hereafter referred to as dictatorships). The systems of government are called dictatorships because they did not allow political competition in the form of other political parties. In this chapter we explore two kinds of dictatorships: single-party systems and military rule.

Single-party systems

Africa has experienced many forms of single-party dictatorship. Although each one of them was a response to different challenges, they were all attempts at finding an appropriate form of government. Three types of single-party systems of government are discussed below.

The debate about single-party forms of government dates to the pre-independence period. African leaders such as Kwame Nkrumah, Sekou Toure and Julius Nyerere maintained that multi-party systems of government were not suitable for Africa. They argued that having opposition parties for their own sake was a luxury Africa could not afford. They also insisted that the task of nation building required all the energies of a nation which opposition parties would only undermine. Intellectual explanations of the suitability of single parties also drew on African traditions of governance.

The first type of single-party system developed in African countries where the struggle for independence was waged by single parties. These countries inherited independence without opposition parties. In Tanzania, the Tanganyika African National Union (TANU) had sole control over the new state. In French West Africa, an inter-territorial political party, the RDA, with branches in the separate colonies, led many of these territories to independence. In places such as the Ivory Coast and Guinea the RDA obtained independence without any challenges. Hence in Tanzania, the Ivory Coast and Guinea (Conakry) the single mass movements for independence came to rule the new states.

The second type of single-party system involved negotiations between the ruling party and the opposition to form a single party. In Zambia Kaunda's UNIP (United National Independence Party) experimented with a multi-party political system for nine years before adopting a single-party system. Through negotiation UNIP leadership persuaded the opposition to join them in a single-party rule. After a referendum that asked citizens to decide for a single-party state, Zambia became a single party state constitutionally from 1973.

The third type of single-party system was imposed forcefully on society. In Ghana Nkrumah slowly eliminated the opposition parties. He used the legislative system which made laws that eliminated opposition politics. Below are a few examples of the use of the law in removing the opposition.

▼ Source J
New York Times, 18 October 1960
Ghana Defeats Critics
Special to the New York Times

ACCRA, 17 Oct. – ... Before the House was a bill providing for £350 or £980 fine or three years in prison or both as punishment on summary conviction for an act calculated to bring the person of President Nkrumah into ridicule, contempt, or hatred. ... Government spokesmen denied that the bill would result in denial of the right to criticise the government.

▼ Source K
New York Times, 5 November 1963
Ghana Enacts Law to Detain Prisoners

ACCRA, 4 Nov. (Reuters) – An amendment allowing the Government to detain in prison for five years after he has served a five year sentence was passed by parliament today.

Enacted under a certificate of urgency, the amendment would permit such detentions if they were considered in the interest of defence and security ... Some members had compared the act to measures adopted in South Africa.

▼ Source L
New York Times, 3 February 1964
Intimidation Widespread in Vote for One-Party State
By Lloyd Garrison
Special to the New York Times

ACCRA, Ghana, 2 Feb. – Ghana has become an official one-party socialist state following a nationwide referendum marked by widespread fraud and intimidation.

In many areas thousands of voters had no choice. In all but a few wards in the Northern Region, voters found that the 'no' boxes were sealed ... There was no campaigning against the referendum. In Accra several cars were seen with homemade 'Vote No' signs on their bumpers. The drivers were arrested.

Activities ....
1 Summarise the contents of Sources J, K and L.
2 What do these sources lead you to conclude about the rule of Nkrumah?

....

Such single-party systems degenerated into dictatorships that ruled all who opposed or dared to challenge the leaders through terror and prosecution. These dictatorships were accompanied by practices such as press censorship, arrests of opponents without trial, banning political activities, corruption and intimidation of the society at large.

The military in politics
By the mid-1970s about half of Africa's independent states were governed by military rulers. Some of the factors that contributed to the rise of the military dictatorships are:

- the failure of parliamentary democracy and its administrative institutions;
- widespread popular discontent;
- the collapse of law and order;
- intervention by foreign powers;
- personal ambition for power and privilege;
- politicians' dependence on security forces to maintain themselves in office;
- the lack of mechanisms for changing governments;
- the rigging of elections.

Many of the military rulers came to power through military *coup d'états*, whereby a group of soldiers took over the running of the country. Most early military coups were greeted by popular outbursts of street celebrations and parties. The soldiers always promised to deliver the people from the tyranny of the civilian rulers by cleaning up the corruption and restoring the rule of law. Although they promised to return the government to civilian rulers after the clean-up operations, in most cases they held on to power until they were removed through another *coup d'état*.

Some of the military rulers became widely known for their tyranny. The best example has been Idi Dada Amin of Uganda and Bokassa who declared himself emperor of the Central African Republic. In some countries such as Ghana and Nigeria there has been more than one military coup.

Below are some examples of dramatic press reports about the coups.

▼ Source M
New York Times, 24 February 1966
Nkrumah Is Reported Out After Ghana Army Coup
By Reuters

LONDON: Thursday 24 Feb. – The Army has taken over in Ghana and dismissed President Kwame Nkrumah who is at present on a trip to Peking and Hanoi, according to an Accra radio broadcast heard here this morning. Reports reaching London said there was sporadic firing in the centre of Accra.

▼ Source N
New York Times, 26 January 1971
Obote Ousted By Ugandan Army
By Reuters

KAMPALA, Uganda, Tuesday, 26 Jan. – Uganda's Army ousted President Milton Obote yesterday and set up a military government.

Thousands of cheering Ugandans thronged the streets of this East African capital celebrating the Army take-over, while the President himself was still heading home after attending the conference of Commonwealth leaders in Singapore.

The new leader in Uganda is Major General Idi Amin, who rose from private to become commander of the Army and the air force and who will now head the military government.

Activities ....
1 What do Sources M and N illustrate about the different ways single-party states emerged in Africa?
2 Was there any truth in the arguments put forward in favour of the single-party systems?
3 Consider the map in Source O on page 232.
   a What are the countries that have experienced military rule?
   b Provide the dates of the various coups.
   c Indicate whether they were former British or French colonies.
4 a Compile a list of all the reasons which led to military coups and rule.
   b Do you think the solution to the reasons in (a) above was a military rule?
5 Should the military be involved in politics?
6 Look at Source P on page 233. What reasons are given for the large number of military coups in Africa?

....

◀ Idi Amin at the time of his military take-over, January 1971
(From: P Mutibwa. *Uganda since Independence: A Story of Unfulfilled Hopes.*)

Profile: Idi Amin

Idi Amin was born around 1925 in northern Uganda. As a boy he tended the family goats and he managed to acquire a primary school education. In 1944 he enlisted in the King's African Rifles and fought in the Second World War in Burma. In 1953 he fought against the Mau Mau in Kenya under the British.

President Obote trusted Idi Amin with secret missions inside and outside Uganda. In 1971 Amin seized power. His regime was harsh and brutal and he murdered thousands of his opponents. He also expelled Asians from Uganda. Amin was deposed by rebels led by Yoweri Museveni and backed by the Tanzanian army in 1979. He fled into exile and settled in Saudi Arabia.

Re-emergence of democracy in Africa

From the late 1980s into the 1990s Africa has witnessed a dramatic shift from single-party states to multi-party political systems. This has been described as a resurgence of democracy in Africa. The dominant system of government in Africa is no longer that of military rule and single-party state systems. Democratically elected governments are now the dominant feature of the African political landscape.

Explanations for this rapid political change involve both internal and external factors to Africa. Although opposition politics had been outlawed in many parts of Africa, the people's spirit to resist oppression had not been broken. Trade unions, churches, women's organisations, non-governmental organisations and student bodies continued to be sites of opposition to single-party and military dictatorships. These organisations have been given the label of civil society. It is important to note here that societies across the continent fell back on the type of organisation used against colonialism. Just as the earlier organisations of civil society succeeded in bringing down colonialism, the single-party and military dictatorships also fell. Another important comparison to make is the drama that accompanied the movements for re-democratisation in Africa. The demonstrations for democracy brought thousands of people into the streets. In many countries it was the labour movements, the college and university students and the urban youth who filled the streets. Methods of protest included strikes, public demonstrations, and food riots culminating in the looting of stores.

This civil disobedience found external support as the struggle for democratic change in the 1980s became a worldwide trend. From the Marcos in the Philippines to the collapse of East European communist dictators at the hands of civil society, these changes provided Africa with a model for change. The collapse of the communist block marked the end of the Cold War and the rise of the West as the dominant force in the world.

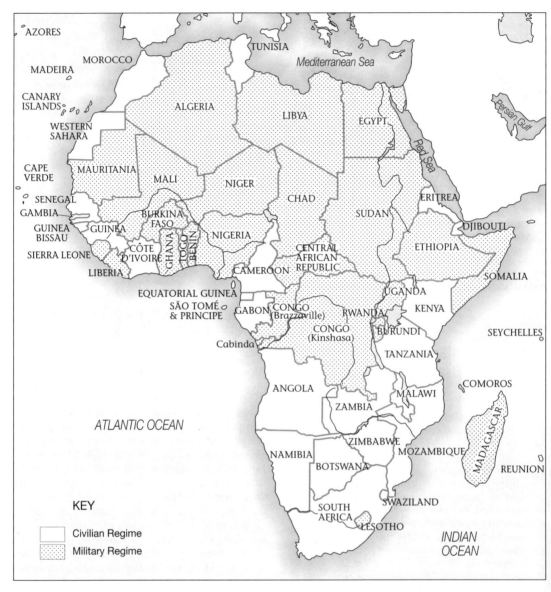

▲ **Source O** Military and civilian regimes of Africa

Civil societies in Africa found open and hidden support for democratic change in the West. Pressure from the West for political change in Africa thus played an important role. Soon the International Monetary Fund (IMF), the World Bank and other foreign donors demanded political changes before they would provide loans. The political crisis facing Africa had in part been fuelled by the economic hardships in the countries. The foreign donors, IMF and World Bank all believed that political freedom would stimulate economic growth in Africa.

In Angola, Mozambique, Liberia and Ethiopia where civil wars raged in the 1980s, the changing international political arena and war fatigue in the population led to negotiations for a peaceful end to the conflicts. In 1992 multiparty parliamentary elections were held in Angola, Mozambique had elections in 1994, and in 1997 Liberia became a multi-party democracy. Charles Taylor was instantly transformed from a terrorist into a president of the democratic nation of Liberia. When General Sanni Abacha of Nigeria died in June 1998 his successor, President Abubaka, promised to return Nigeria to civilian rule by May 1999. We will await that day!

History has come back to where it all started at independence with parliamentary democracy. The greatest threats to democracy in Africa remain poverty, illiteracy, and the closure of political negotiation by the governments.

Activities

1 What do you understand by democracy?
2 Is democracy suitable for Africa?
3 What do you consider to be the role of civil society in a democracy?

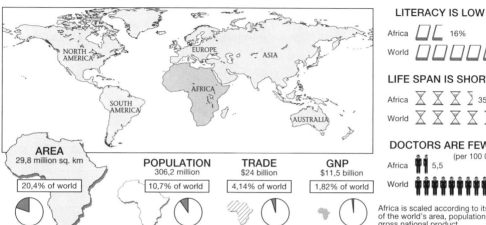

LITERACY IS LOW

Africa ⌇⌇ 16%

World ⌇⌇⌇⌇⌇⌇ 52,3%

LIFE SPAN IS SHORT

Africa ✗✗✗⟩ 35 years

World ✗✗✗✗✗ 48 years

DOCTORS ARE FEW
(per 100 000 persons)

Africa 5,5

World 54,3

Africa is scaled according to its percentage of the world's area, population, trade and gross national product.

AREA
29,8 million sq. km
20,4% of world

POPULATION
306,2 million
10,7% of world

TRADE
$24 billion
4,14% of world

GNP
$11,5 billion
1,82% of world

▲ Source P

One of the key problems confronting Africa, and a major reason for the large number of military coups, is the slow economic progress being made in many of the newly independent countries. The maps and charts here illustrate some of the problems.

(From: 'Black Africa'. *The New York Times*. New York Arno Press, 1973.)

Extension activity

Botswana, Namibia, Zimbabwe, Mauritius, Eritrea and Djibouti are all countries that have maintained multi-party democratic governments since independence. Do some research to write a short history on their transition to independence.

Unit 7 — Economic challenges at independence

Unit outcomes

- Examine the roots of African poverty.
- Understand the requirements of national development.
- Contrast private enterprise and nationalisation.
- Learn new concepts such as colonial legacy, balance of payments, debt crisis and private enterprise/liberalisation.
- Evaluate various development strategies.
- Interpret statistics.

The colonial legacy

African countries were not wealthy at the time of their independence. The colonial powers did not pass on large amounts of money to the new rulers. In some cases African states inherited debts that had been contracted during colonial rule. Another **myth** is that African countries inherited strong economies at independence. There were hardly any secondary industries in Africa at independence, and those that did exist mostly specialised in the export of raw materials. The economies inherited at independence were structured to benefit foreign companies.

The terms of trade of the export economies were unfavourable to Africa. Terms of trade refer to the relationship between a country's export and import prices. Without industries that manufactured goods, Africa depended on expensive imports to meet people's needs. The terms of trade were negative because the raw materials' prices were low whereas the imports were very expensive.

The other important **legacy** was that the new states joined a world of business that was organised by the rich Western countries. The markets for foreign trade were controlled by the rich countries of Europe and America.

The colonial economies forced Africans to grow cash crops for export instead of concentrating on food production for the people. With independence many rural people came to the towns. This rural to urban migration and an increase in Africa's population required more food.

The **infrastructure** left in Africa at independence was organised to meet the requirements of export economies. Roads and railways moved produce from the interior of Africa to the coastal towns.

At independence few Africans had the money to buy and own big companies such as mining companies, so most of the economies continued to be controlled by foreign investors. This continued control of the economies and others areas of African life after independence was called neo-colonialism by Nkrumah.

New words

myth fictitious idea
legacy something passed down by a former holder of office or position
infrastructure structures in a country such as roads, railways, factories, buildings, port facilities, etc.

Activities

1 Does neo-colonialism still exist in Africa today? Do some research on this question and hold a class discussion to talk about your findings.

Years of economic optimism

African independence coincided with economic optimism in the world. Experts, economists, politicians, businessmen, managers, academics and civil servants all shared the view that economic development – properly directed – would close the gap between the rich and poor countries within a short time. The development of industries was the aim and almost all the experts were convinced that it could be achieved by state action. African leaders did not question this opinion, rather, they welcomed it.

The feeling of optimism got a boost from the booming commodity prices. Throughout the 1960s when **commodity prices** were high, African exports grew by 6 per cent per year. Agricultural production also increased by 2,7 per cent per annum in the same period.

But as early as 1965 African leaders knew that political independence was not adequate. President Kaunda of Zambia explained as follows: 'Political independence only serves as a key to the door of economic and social progress ... We must open the door for all the people. The question now is – how do we do it?' (July, 469).

African leaders found two answers to this question. Some saw the hope of economic progress in socialism and adopted marxist centralised planning. Others found the capitalist system the answer to development. However, both groups did not question the leading role of the state in directing the economies.

The key to **industrialisation** in Africa was cheap power. **Hydroelectric schemes** became the favourite development projects. Western experts were quick to point out the advantages of such projects, for example, they would supply electricity to industry and households, fishing industries would provide much needed proteins, and great irrigation projects could be developed. From Nasser's Aswan Dam in Egypt to Nkrumah's Akasambo Dam, African leaders borrowed a lot of money to make the dream come true. But, the hydroelectric projects did not generate the predicted industrialisation of Africa for reasons ranging from poor planning to ecological factors that restricted fishing and agricultural industries, and mismanagement due to lack of expertise.

The 'import substitution industries' in the processing of food, drinks, clothing, car assemblies, tanneries, breweries and many other low level industries emerged under state direction. The African **private sector** was very small. The construction industry boomed as the new governments built new offices, schools, hospitals and houses for the government officials. In socialist states the nationalisation (taking over of control by the state) of insurance, shipping, mining, banking, import and export companies created a sense of control and ownership in the 1960s and 1970s.

In the first decade of independence African countries experienced modest growth in economic terms, but this honeymoon soon came to an end by the middle of the 1970s.

Lack of development and decline

The sources of stagnation (lack of activity and development) and decline in Africa continue to generate heated debates. Foreign observers often suggest that African economic problems are self-inflicted, that is, generated within Africa. However, most African leaders understand the problems as arising from the world economic order that places Africa in a dependent situation. The external factors mentioned by Africans include:

- the 1973–82 tenfold rise in oil prices leading to a 600 per cent rise in energy expenses;
- worldwide disruption and inflation caused by the rise in oil prices;
- the collapse in the prices of raw materials exported from Africa;
- sharp price rises for imported manufactured goods;
- a worldwide growing protection of the industries of a particular country against foreign competition;
- reduced amounts of foreign aid.

Those who put the blame on African governments raise issues such as:

- political instability as a result of military coups;
- financial and economic mismanagement;
- overspending leading to **budget deficits** and therefore external borrowing;
- corruption and inefficiency causing governments to collapse;
- failure to diversify and develop economies;
- nationalisation of foreign companies;
- commitment to socialist policies;
- huge civil services and social expenditures on education and health.

It is, however, certain that both external and internal factors played an important part. The consequence of all these factors was an overwhelming economic crisis.

New words

commodity prices prices of goods
industrialisation process of the development of industries
hydroelectric schemes schemes to generate electricity using water power
private sector businesses not under state control
budget deficit amount of money by which the annual expenditure is greater than the annual income

Activities

1 Hold a class debate on the causes of the economic crisis in Africa. One group should argue that external factors caused the economic crisis and the other group that internal factors were to blame.
2 Which of the colonial legacies could Africa change?
3 Which of the internal causes of the crisis could not be avoided?
4 Use Source A to calculate the decline of the commodities in percentage by dollar and oil value.

Falling value of African exports
What commodities could you buy in 1975 and
1980?
(From: B Davidson. *Modern Africa.*)

One tonne could buy	Barrels of oil	Capital US$
Copper		
1975	115	17,800
1980	58	9,500
Cocoa		
1975	148	23,400
1980	63	10,200
Coffee		
1975	148	22,800
1980	82	13,300
Cotton		
1975	119	18,400
1980	60	9,600

Extension activity ·····················
Take each commodity in Source A and draw a simple line
graph to show its decline in value.
··

The debt crisis

Budget deficits, **negative balance of payments**,
and the **financing of development projects**
throughout the 1960s and 70s resulted in heavy
borrowing by African states. When African
countries found it difficult to meet loan payments, the IMF and World Bank lent additional
funds that aimed at stabilising the economies.

The situation had grown worse despite the strict
measures imposed by the IMF and World Bank. By
1988 sub-Saharan Africa owed approximately
$135 billion. The national figures were disturbing:
Zambia and the Democratic Republic of the Congo
(Zaire) owed over $5 billion, Zimbabwe owed $2,5
billion, Ghana $2 billion, the Ivory Coast $10 billion, and Nigeria's $21 billion in 1984 had shot to
$33 billion by 1991. Between 1982 and 1991
Africa paid out $217 billion servicing debts
against a net resource flow of $214 billion. By the
end of the 1980s the debt crisis had had disastrous
consequences on governments' ability to provide
basic services to their people.

New words

negative balance of payments when payments
out of a country are greater in value than earnings
received by that country
financing of development projects raising funds
for development projects

The painful road ahead

We discussed that African leaders saw the economic crisis as generated by external factors
while the World Bank and IMF emphasised internal factors. The OAU promoted self-reliance
through regional cooperation in industrialisation
and food production. They hoped that through
regional bodies such as SADC (Southern African
Development Community) and ECOWAS (Economic Community of West African States) the situation could be stabilised. The return of peace in
Southern Africa will enable SADC to pursue
regional development as a way of reducing
dependence on the Western countries.

The other alternative development strategy
preferred by the IMF and World Bank involved
reducing government interference in the
economies. It promoted free markets (liberalisa-
tion), reducing the size of state bureaucracies,
and spending less on the social services and the
army. However, the economic reforms empha-
sizing reducing state participation from the
economies in favour of free market, private
investment and encouraging foreign investment
have led to retrenchment and massive unemployment. It remains to be seen if these reforms
can survive the political unrest being caused by
widespread poverty.

Countries owing money and religious leaders
have increased their pressure on the World
Bank, IMF and Western countries to write off
(cancel) the debts. In January 1998 the World
Bank President Mr Wolfensohn responded to
the pressure with new measures as discussed in
Source B.

▼ *Source B*

*The issue of debt is a quite different and
difficult issue. It was so difficult that
together with the International Monetary
Fund, we were able to get going 15 months
ago an initiative called HIPC (Heavily
Indebted Poor Countries) which was
designed to do something that had never
been done before which was to relieve the
debt of **multilaterals**, and of **bilateral** and
private creditors from countries that were
highly indebted.*

*This was on the very simple basis that the
Archbishop of Canterbury and the Pope
have both pointed out: that if someone is so
much in debt that the repayments and the
interest that they have to give back is more
than they get, there is no way they can move
forward. I couldn't agree more with the economics. The question is how to deal with it.*
Addis Ababa, 27 January 1998.

1 Who does the artist show as bearing the burden of the African crisis?
2 Who does the artist show as benefiting from the African crisis?
3 What do the people benefiting from the African crisis use to continue to enjoy the benefits?
4 Does the artist show any biases in this piece of work?

Up to nineteen African countries may benefit from debt deals under the HIPC. Uganda was the first to sign an agreement that took effect in 1998. Although Africa will enter the next century with a burden of debt, economic growth in the 1990s has shown a positive trend. One of the continent's assets has been the determination and spirit of its people.

▼ Source C

(From: *Journal of African Marxists*, 1986.)

Activities

1 What is the debt crisis?
2 Discuss ways in which the debt crisis affects the African economies.
3 How did African governments run the debt so high?
4 List all the possible solutions mentioned in Source B above.
5 What are the advantages and disadvantages of each one of these solutions to Africa's problems?
6 What do you think of the view that the solutions to Africa's economic problems should be African rather than foreign?
7 Summarise the main challenges facing African states after independence in the fields of economics, politics, administration and social developments?
8 Evaluate the policies and practices undertaken by African independent states to counter the challenges in the political, economic, administrative and social sectors of their nations?
9 In your own words, what do you think of the developments in Africa since independence?

Extension activity

Look closely at Source C and then answer the questions which follow.

Unit 8 Africa's social and cultural revolution

Unit outcomes

- Evaluate changes in education and public health services after independence.
- Appreciate the cultural regeneration which has occurred since independence.
- Learn about new concepts such as cultural productions, male supremacists and Acquired Immune Deficiency Syndrome (AIDS).
- Practise the skills of comprehension, historical explanation and investigation.

Cultural revolution

Independence marked the beginning of a social and cultural regeneration (renewal and growth) for Africa. With independence literacy, creative writing, African theatre, art, sculpture, music and dancing became a channel of African cultural expression. The colonial rulers viewed African cultures and history as irrelevant and backward, but nationalism and independence inspired a pride in African culture and history.

Independent Africa recorded significant changes in creative writing and drama, new dances and rhythms. The publication of the African Writers Series by Heinemann publishers made the African novel very popular across Africa. Novelists such as Chinua Achebe, Camara Laye and Ngugi wa Thiongo became household names and their writing was studied in literature classes in universities and schools. Chinua Achebe even went on to win the Commonwealth Prize for his book *Beware, Soul Brother*. His novel *Things Fall Apart* is probably the most widely read novel in Africa.

Wole Soyinka's biography illustrates African achievements in literature.

African drumming, dancing and singing could not be stopped by the missionaries or colonial officials. With independence and freedom, African musicians lifted African music to international fame. Performers such as Fella from Nigeria, Hugh Masekela and Miriam Mabeka of South Africa, Franco and Kanda Bongo Man from the Democratic Republic of the Congo, Salif Keita of Mali and Thomas Mapfumo of Zimbabwe are world famous musicians. African musicians have been very successful in mixing traditional rhythms and instruments with modern ones, with the products remaining truly African.

Profile: Wole Soyinka

© INPRA

Wole Soyinka was born in Nigeria in 1934. In 1986 he became the first Black African to win a Nobel Prize in literature. Wole Soyinka is an outstanding playwright, novelist, critic, editor and poet. His first play, *Invention* (1955), and a subsequent play were staged in London. His first novel, *The Interpreters*, was published in 1965 and has been called the first truly African novel. Soyinka has also directed films. Most of his work deals with the interplay of African and Western cultures in society.

He has been critical of both the colonial and independent regimes in Africa, which has earned him periods of house arrest, imprisonment and exile. Soyinka has been a leading figure in the campaign for democracy in Nigeria.

CHINUA ACHEBE
Things Fall Apart

Profile: Thomas Mapfumo of Zimbabwe

Thomas Mapfumo, born in 1945, became a pioneer of popular African music in Zimbabwe. He is the originator of the chimurenga music style which combines the rhythms of the thumb piano (*mbira*) with more modern instruments. His first recording in 1977 in Shona, *Hoyaka* ('watch out'), was banned by the white minority government.

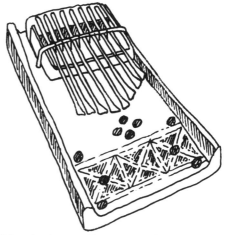

▲ A thumb paino or *mbira*

Extension activity

Discuss the types of media found in South Africa. What role should the media be playing in South Africa?

Cultural regeneration was helped by the rapid growth of the mass media in independent Africa. National news agencies, newspapers, television, cinemas, and, above all, radio broadcasting, made it possible for Africans to speak for themselves. National broadcasting corporations in independent Africa served as the channels for promoting African culture.

The African film industry has also played an important role in challenging the fantasies on Africa produced by Hollywood, such as Tarzan. Indeed, the African presence on the world's cultural stage has shown the strength and depth of Africa's diverse cultures.

Activities

1 In what ways did independence inspire a cultural revolution?
2 Do you think the cultural revolution contributed anything positive to Africa?
3 Wole Soyinka, a writer, and Thomas Mapfumo, a musician, have both been persecuted by the state. Do you think that writers, scholars, musicians and artists should participate in politics?
4 As a project, pick a South African writer, dramatist, musician or any artist to do some research on.
  a Comment on the nature of his or her work.
  b Apply the historical skills of interpretation (found on page 197) to discuss his or her work.
  c Do historians work differently from writers, poets, dramatists or musicians?
5 How did the mass media contribute to national development in independent Africa?

Education

The expansion of education after independence was Africa's greatest achievement. Basil Davidson summarises the achievements in Source A below.

▼ Source A

In 1960, when the tides of independence began to flow in most parts of the continent, the proportion of young Africans enrolled for study in primary schools south of the Sahara Desert stood at around 36 per cent of all young Africans of school-age ... in 1981, some twenty years later, the same proportion stood at 78 per cent. The content of primary education had meanwhile improved. Young Africans no longer had to learn of their former colonial masters; now they could learn the history of their own peoples. There was a comparative enlargement in secondary and higher education. Colonial Africa had almost no universities; independent Africa has many, as well as vocational colleges.

Women in Africa have always suffered under male supremacist attitudes and customs, and they have continued to suffer under them since independence. But they have begun to suffer less. In 1960, for example, the same set of education figures for sub-Sahara Africa showed that only 24 per cent of school-age girls could go to school, but in 1981 this proportion stood at 64 per cent.

(From: B Davidson. *Modern Africa: A Social and Political History.*)

Health services

Considerable improvement was achieved in the health services in the years following independence. With the help of overseas donors African governments invested a great deal of effort into providing primary health care clinics in the villages. These efforts led to significant improvements in health, diet and hygiene at local level. Some governments, such as that of Zambia, also constructed general hospitals in each province. The post-independence period saw the construction of large hospitals in the capital cities. In some countries teaching hospitals became important parts of the local universities.

The new health institutions were accompanied by inoculation campaigns against diseases such as polio, smallpox, cholera and others. Although the struggle against malaria still has to be won, the improvements in health provision have reduced mortality (death) rates. However, the subsequent rise in population is now checked by the outbreak of AIDS (Acquired Immune Deficiency Syndrome), and declining living standards arising from Africa's economic stagnation.

Activities

1 In what areas of education does Davidson (Source A) see changes after independence?
2 Why was change necessary in the areas given in your answer to question 1?
3 What role should education play in developing a nation socially, politically and culturally?
4 Do some research to find out more about the possible impact of the AIDS virus on Africa's population, economy and social structure. Hold a class discussion to report on your findings.
5 How can the spread of AIDS be prevented?

CHAPTER ASSESSMENT

For the following essay questions you should do at least three essay plans and then write one of the essays. For help in planning and writing essays refer to the section on essay writing on pages 41 to 42.

1 In 1960 Harold Macmillan said, 'The wind of change is blowing through [Africa] ...'.
  Describe the factors which led to African states gaining independence.
2 'African states remained unstable after independence because of the legacy of problems which they inherited from the period of colonial rule.'
  Critically discuss this assertion by considering the period 1945 to 1970.
3 'The drive towards unity in Africa and the wish to have greater influence on world politics led to the formation of the OAU.'
  Explain the formation, aims, principles and problems of this body.
4 Africa became a fruitful ground for intervention by rival power blocks in the Cold War years. Discuss the Russian and American involvement in Africa during the period of the Cold War.

Further reading

David Birmingham. *The Decolonisation of Africa*. Athens: Ohio University Press, 1995.

P Curtin, J Vansina, S Fierman, and L Thompson. *African History*. New York: Longman, 1995.

Basil Davidson. *Modern Africa: A Social and Political History*. London: Longman, 1989.

The Diagram Group. *Nations of Africa*. New York: Facts on File Books, 1997.

John Iliffe. *Africans: The History of a Continent*. Cambridge: Cambridge University Press, 1996.

Robert July. *A History of the African People*. Prospect Heights: Waceland Press, 1997.

RD Pearce. *The Turning Point in Africa*. London: Frank Cass, 1982.

Kevin Shillington. *History of Africa*. New York: St Martin's Press, 1995.

HS Wilson. *African Decolonisation*. New York: Edward Arnold, 1994.

South Africa (1924–48)

contents

chapter outcomes

knowledge outcomes

As you work through this chapter you will learn about:

- the development of a system of economic, social and political segregation in South Africa;
- the changing nature of a rural and urban society;
- the development of the South African economy;
- the changing pattern of parliamentary politics;
- key forms and episodes in resistance to white domination;
- the interrelationship between South Africa and a changing international political and economic order

skills outcomes

As you work through this chapter you will apply skills such as how to:

- explain continuity and change, cause and consequence, similarity and difference;
- discuss the nature of historical evidence;
- expand on specific concepts relevant to this period of South African history such as segregation, civilised labour, migrant labour and urbanisation;
- analyse and organise material and sources;
- develop empathy for people;
- develop arguments and take positions in key historical debates.

value outcomes

As you work through this chapter you will get the chance to think about:

- the nature and causes of racism;
- the position of women and youth in South African society;
- the position of workers in an industrial economy.

Timeline

1902	Treaty of Vereeniging
1905	SANAC Report
1907	Transvaal and Orange River Colonies granted self-government
1910	
1910	Union of South Africa
1912	Formation of the South African Native National Congress (later renamed the African National Congress)
1913	Native's Land Act
1919	Formation of the Industrial and Commercial Workers Union (ICU)
1920	
1920	NRC recognised as the only local labour recruiter
1921	Founding of the Communist Party
1922	Rand Revolt; Formation of Inkatha kaZulu
1924	General election – South African Party defeated and new government formed by the National Party and Labour Party
1929	'Swart Gevaar' general election won outright by the National Party; Collapse of share prices on Wall Street Stock Exchange marks the beginning of the Great Depression
1930	
1932	Gold standard abandoned; Report of Native Economic Commission
1933	Coalition formed between National Party and South African Party – merged and formed United Party
1934	Formation of the Gesuiwerde (Purified) National Party
1935	All-African convention formed
1936	Parliament passes Native Representatives Act and the Native Trust and Land Act
1938	Great Trek centenary celebrations
1939	Outbreak of the Second World War; Smuts becomes prime minister
1940	
1944	Establishment of squatter camps
1945	End of the Second World War
1946	Mine workers strike; Passive resistance campaign
1948	General election won by National Party

This chapter covers Specific Outcomes 1, 2, 3, and 9 of the Human and Social Sciences learning area.

Unit 1 Segregation

Unit outcomes

- Discuss the origins of segregation.
- Identify the Acts that were the building blocks of the system of segregation.
- Debate and explain the impact of segregation.

Introduction

South Africa stands out in the twentieth century world because of the central and lasting role played racism has played in the history of the society. The system of apartheid which was developed after 1948 became justifiably notorious, but in many ways it was far from new. Many of the key elements of apartheid had evolved much earlier in the century as part of the system of **segregation** which took shape in the first decades of the century and which was further refined in the 1920s and 1930s.

New words

segregation a political and social system designed to keep groups of people separate

reconstruction economic and political rebuilding

imperial values beliefs which stressed the importance of the British Empire

compensation goods or money given to make up for losses suffered in the war

---

Reconstruction

In May 1902, after three years of warfare, the British army finally defeated the Boer Republics. Lord Milner, British High Commissioner and governor of the newly conquered republics was faced with the difficult task of rebuilding shattered economies and societies. The form of **reconstruction** favoured by the British administration had important consequences for the modern history of South Africa.

Britain had been critical of the Boer treatment of Africans before and during the war, but hopes that British victory would improve the situation of black South Africans were quickly disappointed. At the Peace of Vereeniging signed on 31 May 1902 which concluded the Boer War it was agreed that 'The question of granting the franchise to natives will not be decided until after the introduction of self-government'.

On first reading, this clause does not seem terribly important, but it ensured that Africans would be denied the vote in most of South Africa.

- Self-government would allow colonists to control their own internal affairs. The Transvaal and the Orange River Colony were granted self-government in 1907. In both colonies parties with strong support amongst Afrikaners won the first elections.
- In the Boer Republics Africans had been denied the vote. The majority of colonists in Natal were against Africans having the vote. It was only in the Cape Colony that a minority of Africans had the vote.

There was little prospect that a majority of white colonists would extend the vote to Africans without strong pressure from Britain.

The Peace of Vereeniging was not the only example of Britain giving in to colonists' demands. British policy was, in fact, broadly shaped by the view that South Africa should be ruled by whites.

▼ Source A

Milner, for example, voiced this belief

A political equality between black and white is impossible. The white man must rule, because he is elevated by many, many steps above the black man: steps which it will take the latter centuries to climb, and which it is possible the vast majority of the black population may never be able to climb at all.

◀ Alfred Milner

© Cape Town Archieves

Discuss the following questions as a class.
1 Why do you think Britain did not insist that Africans be
  granted the franchise (vote)?
2 If Britain had forced colonists to accept an African
  franchise should it have been given to all adult
  Africans or only to those with a Western education?
3 a Who was Alfred Milner?
  b Summarise the opinion he gives in Source A.

British policy in South Africa

While Britain supported the idea that South Africa should be a white man's country it also believed that some whites were more desirable than others. British policy was to spread **imperial** values and to ensure that people of British descent became the majority of whites. Milner hoped to increase the British element in the population until it reached 60 per cent, but this goal was never achieved and the Afrikaners remained the majority of the white population.

The Milner administration nonetheless moved quickly to help the defeated Boers. They were aided in re-establishing their farms and herds and government assistance was provided to increase white production on the land. Africans who had taken control of land and cattle from Boers during the war – often with the encouragement of the British – now found that their claims were rejected and they were forced to hand back land and cattle to the Boers with minimal or no **compensation** for their losses.

British officials were keen to modernise white farming but their main concern was to rebuild the gold mining industry. Gold had been a particular focus of British interest in the years before the Boer War. Milner and his officials saw gold mining as vital to the future of both South Africa and the wider British Empire.

The new administration in the Transvaal set about creating the conditions for the mining industry to expand. The most important concern of mine owners was labour supply. South Africa had large deposits of ore but much of it was of a low grade and located deep under the ground. The costs of mining this ore and extracting gold from it were high. The mine owners believed that it was only with large amounts of cheap labour that gold mining could expand and profit. They saw a solution in a large supply of low wage African migrant workers who left their families in the rural areas and came for limited periods of time to the industrial centres.

In the years immediately after the Boer War, mine owners reduced wages in order to cut costs but then found that the supply of migrant workers dwindled. Africans living in South Africa complained of low wages, dangerous working conditions, high death rates, and harsh treatment by mine police. Many were reluctant to work on the mines under these conditions. The mines were forced to rely on labour from Mozambique instead, but they still could not meet their needs. They remained reluctant to increase wages. Instead, with the support of the British administration between 1904 and 1906, over 60 000 Chinese workers were brought to South Africa on a temporary basis. This measure solved the labour shortage.

After 1906 an increase in mine wages and the effects of droughts, cattle diseases, taxation and land shortage on rural Africans resulted in a steady increase in the flow of African labour to the mines. Finally in 1920, after years of costly competition over local labour supplies, all the major mining houses recognised the Native Recruiting Corporation (NRC) as the only local labour recruiter. In the years that followed the blue and white buildings of the NRC – better known as Teba after its first head – became an increasingly common sight in the countryside. Cheap migrant labour was the foundation of the South African economy.

In these decades gold was South Africa's biggest export and earner of foreign revenue. It employed 60 per cent of all workers in industrial employment, and by 1920 over 200 000 workers were employed in the gold industry. While South Africans now made up over 30 per cent of migrant workers, the majority of workers came from Mozambique and other African countries.

The South African Native Affairs Commission (SANAC) and segregation

Another major problem facing the British after the Boer War was to create a set of policies particularly in relation to the administration of the African population which would be acceptable to mine owners, farmers and to elected representatives in the four colonies. In 1903 Milner established the South African Native Affairs Commission (SANAC) led by Sir Godfrey Lagden with instructions to draw up a native policy which would be supported by all four colonies.

SANAC reported in 1905. Its main argument was that separate areas and systems of government should exist for blacks and whites. It recommended that separate areas of land (reserves) should be set aside for Africans in rural areas. But it also recommended that the reserves should be small so that Africans would be forced to work in white dominated towns, farms and mines. SANAC supported the system of migrant labour arguing that the labour supply should consist of men without their wives and families who would be temporarily employed and would return to the reserves when they were no longer needed. It suggested that separate locations (townships) should be set up for Africans in urban areas. It also argued that Africans should have separate political institutions and that tribal structures should be strengthened in order to provide authentic African leadership.

▼ Source B

Lagden made this comment when arguing that 'surplus' or idle Africans should be returned to the reserves

> A man cannot go with his wife and children and his goods ... on to the labour market. He must have a dumping ground. Every rabbit must have a warren where he can live and burrow and breed, and every native must have a warren too.

(From: Reader's Digest. *Illustrated History of South Africa*.)

Activities ·····························

1 What is Lagden saying and implying in Source B?
2 What does this tell us about Lagden's attitudes to Africans?

···

The Commission drew on many existing ideas and practices within colonial society and presented them in a systematic form. Its recommendations provided a vision of the future which formed the basis of the doctrine of segregation. Over the following five years this approach won broad support in colonial society and the term segregation was in common use by 1910. Although criticism of political segregation was voiced by the Cape Colony, where some Africans had the vote, the doctrine of segregation nonetheless provided sufficient common ground to allow the four colonies to join together in the Union of South Africa in 1910. Black South Africans were not represented in the negotiations that resulted in the Union, and their views were almost completely ignored.

New words

reconciliation create good relations after a period of conflict
entrenched made stronger and longer lasting

Laying the foundations for segregation

While important ideas were developed before the Union it was in the years 1910–24 that key elements of a segregationist legal framework were put in place.

The first national elections held in 1911 were won by the South African Party (SAP) which had English-speaking support but was dominated by Afrikaners. The SAP was led by two former Boer generals: Louis Botha was appointed prime minister, and the deputy leader of the party was Jan Smuts. Both men believed in

◄ Lagden and SANAC
(From: Cory Library, Rhodes University, Grahamstown.)

© Cory Library/Pic A 1319

reconciliation between English and Afrikaans-speaking South Africans and were sensitive to the needs of the mainly Afrikaner farmers, but they also believed that segregationist policies were the best framework for race relations. Between 1911 and 1924 a number of laws were passed which established the basic principles of segregation and set the scene for future years.

The 1911 Mines and Mine Works Act **entrenched** a system of job reservation which effectively barred blacks from doing skilled jobs on the mines. The act was welcomed by many white workers who feared that they might be replaced by lower paid black workers.

The 1913 Native's Land Act established the basis for territorial separation by setting aside reserves for exclusive African occupation and preventing Africans from buying land outside these areas. Africans were allocated just over 7 per cent of the land area of South Africa. The Act also discouraged the practice of sharecropping – Africans using white farmers' land in order to grow crops and handing over a share of their harvest in return. Africans living on white farms were allowed to remain as labour tenants. In exchange for providing the farmer with labour they would be allowed to keep some livestock and use some land to grow their own crops.

Most mine owners welcomed the Act because it formalised the inadequate reserves which provided the basis of the migrant labour system which was central to the mining industry. While many white farmers were opposed to reserves being set aside for Africans, they welcomed the fact that only a limited amount of land was available to Africans and that steps had been taken against sharecropping.

The 1920 Native Affairs Act paved the way for a separate system of tribally based, but government-appointed district councils in reserve areas.

A crucial issue for segregationist policies was what to do about Africans living in urban areas outside of mine hostels. In 1923 the Natives (Urban Areas) Act gave local authorities powers to establish separate locations for Africans and restricted the purchase of land by Africans outside these locations.

Debating segregation

Segregation was not accepted by everyone. The fact that the Union had been achieved on the basis of the political and economic subordination of black South Africans contributed to the formation of the South African Native National Congress (SANNC) – later renamed the ANC – in 1912. The men who formed the SANNC were mainly the products of missionary education and members of a small African middle class. They had hoped that their education and achievements would lead them to be accepted into a common colonial world, but after 1910 it had become clear that this would not happen without a struggle.

Just after the SANNC was formed it faced a major new threat to the position of Africans – the 1913 Native's Land Act. The leadership of the SANNC was horrified by the Act. They organised protests against it in South Africa and sent a delegation to appeal directly to the king and British parliament not to ratify (approve) the Act but they had no success. Within, SANNC there was also a wide range of opinion, about the Act. While one group objected to any dis-

▼ SANNC leaders Pixley Seme and Sol Plaatjie
(From: Reader's Digest. *Illustrated History of South Africa*.)

crimination amongst British subjects, others were willing to accept the system of reserves so long as Africans were granted more direct political representation.

Africans who were not part of the educated elite also objected to the small area set aside for reserves. But there were many people who welcomed the fact that they had some space in which to maintain important elements of their own way of life.

There were also critics of segregation in white society. While some liberals supported segregation, others argued from the 1920s that segregation could not be the basis for the future because economic development was drawing black and white closer together in a single economic system and a common society.

Explaining segregation

For many years historians have debated why segregation, with its emphasis on racial separation, became such a central feature of white politics in South Africa in the first decades of the twentieth century.

Some historians have suggested that attitudes formed on colonial frontiers in the seventeenth, eighteenth and nineteenth centuries continued to shape the thinking of many whites well into the twentieth century. In this view, white settlers living isolated lives on the edges of colonial society and in constant conflict with Africans developed strong racial attitudes which stressed both white supremacy and the need for racial separation. The Great Trek of the 1830s, when Boer farmers moved out of the colony, resulted in these attitudes being carried deeper into the interior. The clashes between Boers and Africans that took place in the interior deepened this racism. It was also reflected in the constitution of the Boer Republics which laid down that there could be no equality between blacks and whites in either church or state.

In the late nineteenth and early twentieth century, with the rise of new cities and diamond and gold mining, this frontier tradition played a decisive role in setting the political agenda. In the words of CW de Kiewiet, a leading scholar in this **school of thought**:

> *What had hitherto been a rural and even a frontier problem now was fast becoming an urban problem as well. It was a new social disease that was destined to become chronic. Into the new urban and industrial communities the native policy of the frontier farmers intruded itself.*

(From: *The Imperial Factor in South Africa*.)

White workers, many of whom moved to the towns from rural communities in the late eighteenth and early nineteenth century, were seen as playing a crucial role in spreading this disease of racism.

New words

school of thought a particular set of ideas or way of thinking

frontier mentality a way of thinking about and explaining the world which develops among people living on a frontier

Many of the historians who saw this racism as rooted in a frontier tradition saw an alternative political tradition in British values, which emphasised the ideal 'equal rights for all civilised men' which it was argued was reflected in the existence of the Cape franchise. In the Cape Colony by the 1890s all adult males, regardless of race, who occupied property of at least 75 pounds and could write, had the right to vote. Historians like Macmillan and De Kiewiet argued that in twentieth century South Africa a **frontier mentality** and the values of the Boer Republics triumphed over the more liberal traditions of Britain and the Cape Colony.

◄ Early unskilled road workers
(From: *The Star*. Barnett Collection.)

© City Council of Pretoria

Other historians took a different view. They suggested that British policy makers – like Lord Milner – played an important part in promoting the idea of segregation. They also argued that segregation was not left over from an earlier historical period, but was the result of the desire of mine owners and farmers for cheap labour. They pointed out that segregationist policies, by denying Africans the vote and establishing the reserve system, ensured a flow of cheap and controllable migrant labour to the mines. The argument was that this labour was cheap because migrants' families stayed in the countryside and provided for many of their own needs by farming the land. Migrant workers' wages did not therefore have to support the whole family. Segregationist policies were also seen as being of benefit to farmers, in denying Africans rights to the land defined as white, and by forcing sharecroppers and tenants to become labour tenants and labourers.

Marion Lacey, for example, argued that segregation policies allowed miners and farmers to combine to 'super exploit' African workers while Martin Legassick wrote: 'the policy of segregation was a specific and self-conscious attempt to formulate a 'native' policy appropriate to the conditions of capitalist economic growth' (Dubow. *Racial Segregation and the Origins of Apartheid in South Africa*, 2).

While most historians would now agree that segregation should be understood in the context of the emergence of an industrial society there is still considerable disagreement about how best to explain segregation. Some historians would still argue that racial attitudes, with roots in earlier periods, played an important, if not the only, role in shaping popular support for segregation. Other historians suggest that it is important to remember that mine owners and farmers disagreed about more than they agreed on, and segregation cannot therefore be seen as the result of an easy compromise between them. Other historians have argued that it is not possible to explain segregation in terms of narrow economic interests. Rather the influence of segregationist ideas was the result of the fact that they appealed to many different elements within white society – sometimes for different reasons – and even won some support within African society. Shula Marks has pointed out that segregation

> was a many faceted policy made up of varying components which could be, and were, subtly shifted in response to circumstances and the needs of different interests of the dominant white group in South Africa. Indeed its great strength ... was its very elasticity, its ability to serve the needs of very different interests (Dubow, 3).

As we have seen, in the years 1900–24 segregationist ideas and policies played an increasingly important role. In the years 1924–48 a segregationist social order was further entrenched and debated. From the account so far, and from the material to come, you must decide how you would explain the rise of segregation and the shift to apartheid after 1948.

Activities ....

1 Based on the text in this section on segregation, do you think that a frontier tradition played a part in the development of segregation in the period 1900–24?
2 Were white workers the main supporters of segregationist policy? If not, what other groups were in favour of it?
3 a Did mine owners and farmers agree on the exact form segregation should take?
  b Describe and explain any areas of disagreement you think may have existed.
4 Were all Africans opposed to all aspects of segregation?

Unit 2

Rural South Africa

Unit outcomes

- Discuss the reserves and their role in the development of migrant labour.
- Understand the forces that drove many whites to the cities.

Reserves

By the 1920s, communities living in areas set aside for Africans under the 1913 Land Act were dominated by a system of migrant labour which affected almost all aspects of their lives.

This does not mean that keeping livestock and growing crops were no longer significant, but their relative importance to a rural economy had diminished. In the late nineteenth and early twentieth century many Africans had been able to produce enough food to feed themselves and to sell some to meet their needs for cash to pay taxes and to buy goods. But from the turn of the century, African families in these areas came under increasing pressure. Two devastating cattle diseases, rinderpest in 1896–7 and East Coast Fever from 1904–13 killed as much as 80 per cent of the herds in some districts.

At the same time, the collection of taxes became even more efficient. In the reserves all men aged eighteen and over had to pay a poll tax of one pound and there was a tax of ten shillings for each dwelling. As the population grew in the increasingly overcrowded reserves, land which was farmed every year became exhausted and provided less crops. Households also had access to less land, and some did not have any rights to land for cultivation. This fragile rural economy

became more vulnerable to drought. In many districts larger quantities of grain had to be imported to feed the local population.

Rural production did not collapse completely but fewer families were able to produce enough from the land to feed themselves, and even fewer were able to produce enough to be able to sell crops on the market to get cash to pay for taxes or to buy goods. In this situation migrant labour became increasingly important. By the 1920s between 30 and 40 per cent of the adult male population were away working in industrial centres. Migrancy, which previously had been most common amongst young, single men, now involved increasing numbers of married men who had to leave home for longer and longer periods of time in order to help meet the basic needs of their families. The number of men who stayed in the towns, and stopped supporting their families in the reserves, also grew. Women whose husbands were temporarily or permanently absent took on larger responsibilities for maintaining the households, fields and herds.

The government attempted to limit the number of Africans settling permanently in the cities through pass laws. These tried to ensure that Africans only stayed in town as long as they were in white employment. But passes had a limited effect and other forces persuaded migrant workers from the reserves to return home. Despite the declining rural economy and increasingly long periods away from home, many migrants continued to see working in the mines or the cities as a means to maintain a rural way of life. Towns were seen as alien places where people had lost touch with their

▲ Government officials collecting taxes in the reserves

NATIVE LABOUR PASSPORT. (To be held by Employer.)

LABOUR DISTRICT OF JOHANNESBURG.

Form 1 L.

▲ *Source A*   A photograph of a pass

own traditions and way of life. Towns were viewed as places controlled by whites where blacks had no rights and everything had to be paid for.

Activities

Study Source A, the photograph of a pass, carefully.
1 What kinds of information had to be filled in on a pass?
2 Why do you think all this information was required?
3 Try to speak to someone who had to carry a pass and find out what life was like for them.

In the reserves, chiefs still had some power and authority. Many migrants criticised aspects of chiefly rule, but administration by chiefs was still seen as preferable to being directly controlled by white officials. In the cities, if individuals did not have money to pay rent they could find themselves with nowhere to live, but families living in the reserves knew that even if they had no money they would not be evicted from their homes. Many migrants invested in cattle and in building up other resources of their rural households in the hope that they would eventually be able to retire to the countryside and live as elders in their own communities. From the perspective of the people living in rural areas, migrant labour, despite all its problems, was seen as better than individuals moving permanently to the towns.

▼ Source B
The historian, William Beinart, commented on migrant labour

One of the greatest ironies of the early twentieth century was that both the country's major industry (mining) and many rural communities favoured a system of labour mobilisation in which male migrants worked for only a limited period and returned with their wages to their homes ... In some senses, there was agreement on this aspect of what became segregation policy.

(From: *The Political Economy of Pondoland to 1930*.)

But this did not mean that rural communities were content with the division of land established by the 1913 Land Act, with having to carry passes, or with their exclusion from other rights in society.

Activities
1 Why did African production for the market in rural areas grow less and less in the first decades of the twentieth century?
2 Why do you think that many rural communities preferred migrant labour to people leaving rural areas to live in cities (as mentioned in Source B)?

White farmlands

While black farmers in the reserves faced increasing difficulties, white farmers found that more assistance was made available to them by governments committed to food self-sufficiency based on white farming. An expanding network of railways and roads connected white farmers to towns and markets. The state and private institutions made increasing amounts of credit available to farmers. By the 1920s a **state-subsidised** system of grain storage was established, and the state provided funds for research to assist white farmers and to establish agricultural schools. After 1922 many **cooperative associations** were established to provide better marketing facilities and to reduce the prices paid by white farmers for agricultural implements, fertiliser and other necessities. From the end of the 1920s price subsidies were also provided for white farmers. Between 1911 and 1936 the government spent 112 million pounds supporting – mainly white – agriculture.

Despite all this assistance, by the 1920s, not all white farmers in South Africa were prosperous. Many farms were unprofitable. **Yields** were low and the cost of land was high in comparison to the amount of money that could be made from farming. In many areas rainfall was low and unreliable and there was a constant threat of drought. By the end of the 1920s many farmers were deeply in debt and, partly because of Boer inheritance practices, which led to farms being subdivided between all the sons on the death of the father, farms were shrinking in size. Some of the most successful farmers were known as cheque-book farmers – men with other interests and sources of income – for example, lawyers, who could survive the bad years and prosper in good years. Many farmers, who did not have resources outside agriculture, were forced to sell their farms or have them **repossessed** by their creditors.

Labour relations on white farms were an ongoing source of conflict and struggle. Sharecropping was one source of disagreement. **Absentee landlords** and poor Boers found sharecropping an effective way of getting a return from the land.

New words

state-subsidised government provides money to lower the costs involved
cooperative associations organisations formed by groups of farmers to assist each other
yields the amount of crops harvested
repossessed taken back
absentee landlords landowners who did not live on the land they owned, but rented it out to others

▼ Source C

A sharecropper's daughter recalled of her father

> *Napthali was a hard worker. Indeed, he worked very hard in his fields. He produced a lot from the soil. Hundreds of bags, half of which he gave to Theuns (the farmer), who in turn would proceed to sell*

> *them and get a lot of money from the labour to which he had never contributed anything.*

(From: T Matsitela. 'The life story of Mma-Pooe, In S Marks and R Rathbone (eds.) *Industrialisation and Social Change in South Africa.*)

▼ *Source D* Sharecroppers at work

In return for their labour and skill, sharecroppers got access to better quality and larger areas of land closer to markets than was available in the reserves.

As some white farmers grew wealthier and the number of absentee landlords decreased, farmers increasingly wanted to farm the land themselves and sharecropping was seen as an obstacle. This fact, in part, explains why the 1913 Native's Land Act set out to end sharecropping, although in fact it continued in some areas of the highveld for many years. Farmers who wanted to work the land themselves wanted labour rather than crops from tenants on their land. Some Africans were prepared to work for wages, but most Africans living in white farming areas, like Africans living in the reserves, were determined to continue working the land and keeping livestock for themselves. As a result, an arrangement known as 'labour tenancy' became increasingly common.

Activities . . . .

Source C describes the life of a sharecropper and Source D shows black sharecroppers at work. Study these sources closely and then answer the questions below.

1 What motivated black workers to enter into sharecropping agreements?

2 Why did white landowners enter into sharecropping agreements?

3 What reasons did some white farmers give for wanting to end sharecropping agreements?

· ·

Labour tenants worked or sent family members to work for part of the year for the farmer in exchange for the right to stay on a farm, keep animals and grow crops. In many cases some of the tenants' children would work for the white farmers, while the tenants' wife or wives would work their own plot of land. One point of conflict was when tenants resisted white landlords' demands that their wives should work in white households or even on white farmers' land. 'I must work for the baas' argued a Transvaal tenant, 'but not my wife ... I buy a woman to work for me!' The children of tenants also got tired of working for their fathers and the farmers. As a result, many ran away from the farms to towns, in spite of the strict pass laws that were meant to keep them in the countryside.

Most white farmers were opposed to any extra land for the reserves because they feared that tenants would leave the farms if there was extra land available in the reserves. Most Africans living in the reserves preferred to work on the mines to working on the farms because the mines paid much better wages.

Whites move to the cities

While large numbers of African tenants remained on the farms in the 1920s, the early decades of the twentieth century saw a mass departure of white tenants and farmers from the land. As we have seen, many white farmers were not able to survive the difficult conditions and were forced to sell their farms. Some went to the towns while others joined the ranks of the landless bywoners which had long been a feature of Boer society. By the 1920s bywoners were a vanishing feature in the countryside.

White farmers could get much more labour from African families because both women and children were expected to undertake hard work, unlike bywoner families who did not easily accept that women and children should work on the land. Another ironic feature of South African history is the large-scale movement of Boers to the towns in the early twentieth century. This was partly the result of the fact that Boer farmers preferred black tenants to white tenants on their land. Displaced bywoners and bankrupt farmers also found it difficult to rent land because landlords often preferred renting lands to African communities who could afford higher rents than individual Boer families. Some bywoners continued to scrape out an existence in the countryside through transport riding, putting up fences or selling wood, but there was less demand for their services in the 1910s and 1920s. Many had little option but to head for the cities.

With few skills suitable for urban living, many Afrikaans-speaking whites from the countryside struggled to establish themselves in South Africa's growing towns. In Johannesburg, after the Boer War, Afrikaners ran small brick making works and transport businesses, but could not compete with new industries and forms of transport – trams and railways. Unskilled and supervisory jobs on the railways and mines provided an alternative source of employment. Whites in these positions feared that their employers might

◀ A bywoner dwelling (From: *Carnegie Commission Report 1936*. South African Library.)

replace them with African migrant workers who did not have their families with them in the cities and could, and did, work for lower wages. Faced by this threat to their jobs, but with the advantage of having the vote, white workers stressed that they deserved protection by the state because they were whites. They succeeded in persuading the government to pass laws, such as the 1911 Mines and Mine Works Act, to reserve certain categories of more skilled work on the mines for whites.

The mine owners did not oppose job reservation along racial lines, partly because they found advantages in these racial divisions in controlling the work force. But the mine owners did object to the proportion of relatively highly paid whites in the work force. It was attempts by employers to reduce the numbers of white workers, in order to reduce costs, that led to a major strike on the Rand by white workers in 1922. The strikers rallied round the famous slogan 'workers of the world unite and fight for a white South Africa', but the strike was put down with great force by the Smuts-led government.

In these difficult decades the numbers of whites who could not make a living within rapidly changing rural and urban societies, and who were described as 'poor white', grew considerably. By 1927 the number of **destitute** whites had grown so much that the Carnegie Corporation of New York decided to fund a Commission of Inquiry into the problem of poor whites in South Africa. The Commission reported in 1932 that of a white population of 1,8 million more than 300 000 were extremely poor and 'unfit, without help from others to find a proper means of livelihood for himself or ... his children' (*Illustrated History of South Africa*. 332).

New words

destitute very poor

Activities

1 Why was there an exodus of white tenants and farmers from the land in the 1920s?
2 What kinds of employment were open to the whites?
3 What factors caused the major strike on the Rand in 1922?

Africans in the city

Unit outcomes

- Describe how the government dealt with the increasing numbers of black people settling in the cities.
- Evaluate the impact of the 1923 Natives (Urban Areas) Act.

Introduction

While the rapid growth of the white population in the cities created a range of social and political problems, it did not threaten a segregationist framework. However, the growing black population, settled permanently in the towns, was seen as a major threat to the evolving system of segregation. In the early decades of the twentieth century, while most black workers were migrant workers living in mine compounds, increasing numbers found work in the towns as washer men, store men and labourers.

By 1906 there were 30 000 male domestic workers in Johannesburg alone. Most of these workers remained committed to returning home, but some chose to settle permanently in the towns. The problem on the Rand was to find a place for permanent residents to live. In 1893 the Kruger government had laid out an African location but as the African population grew the location soon became too small and the African residents moved into neighbouring coloured and white areas creating multi-racial settlements. Between 1905 and 1912 areas of **freehold** African **tenure** were also established in Sophiatown, Newclare and Alexandra. Many of these inner city areas became overcrowded slums which local authorities feared were breeding grounds for diseases, posing a health hazard to neighbouring white suburbs. These fears were increased by outbreaks of bubonic plague, smallpox and tuberculosis. The authorities also feared that the multi-racial, unregulated nature of these slum areas would encourage popular revolt. Growing militancy in black urban areas after 1912 with strikes, anti-pass campaigns and boycotts increased this anxiety.

By 1924 the black urban population of the Rand had risen to 103 000 including 13 000 women and 25 000 children. Growing numbers of women and children were an indication of an increasingly settled African urban population.

In 1922 a report of a commission on urban Africans led by Frederick Stallard, made influential policy proposals for dealing with urban Africans.

New words

freehold tenure a right of ownership forever

▼ Source A

One of the Stallard Commission's recommendations was that

... natives – men, women and children – should only be permitted within municipal areas so long as their presence is demanded by the wants of the white population ... The master less native in the urban areas is a source of danger and a cause of degradation of both black and white ... If the native is to be regarded as a permanent element in municipal areas ... there can be no justification for basing his exclusion from the franchise on the simple ground of colour.

Activities

1 Summarise the main points of Source A.
2 What was a 'master less native' and why were they seen as a source of danger?

The twisted logic of Source A is worth noting. If Africans were permanent residents in urban areas and could therefore be regarded as in some sense members of a common society they could not be denied the vote. Therefore it must be ensured that they did not become permanent and that they remained separate.

Removals and locations

The 1923 Natives (Urban Areas) Act gave local authorities the power to establish African locations on the outskirts of urban and industrial areas.

Africans who were living in 'white' areas could be forced to move to these locations, and restrictions were placed on blacks purchasing land outside the location.

The Act also tightened the pass laws. Africans who were considered not to be needed by white employers or who were believed to be leading 'an idle or disorderly life' could be **deported** to the reserves.

Johannesburg was one of the first councils to try to use the laws. In December 1924 the council proclaimed the city slums to be 'white' areas and tried to force black workers out of these areas. Lawyers working with the communities challenged this. They argued that people could not be thrown out of their homes unless alternative accommodation was provided for them. The Supreme Court agreed and the council found itself caught in a trap. It could not clear the black inhabitants out of the slums until it built houses for them, but it was not prepared to spend the money on housing.

Other councils, which did not have as large a black population, and did not face the same legal challenges, found it easier to segregate their towns. Between 1924 and 1926, sixty-four local authorities established separate locations for their black populations. By 1937 one thousand seven hundred segregated locations had been set up. Local authorities still found it difficult to remove people from slum areas and to establish control over locations. They also achieved little success in expelling 'surplus' populations from the urban areas. This failure was partly because of popular resistance, but it was also because local industries were keen to have a large pool of labour to choose from and local authorities were reluctant to deport large numbers of workers. There was also a steady flow of people to the towns. As we have seen in the 1920s and 30s, large numbers of tenants were fleeing from the oppressive conditions on white farms. Johannesburg had one of the fastest growing black populations: between 1924 and 1936 it rose from 103 000 to 320 000.

New words

deport send home

Activities

Look closely at the two maps of Johannesburg that make up Source B.

1 Use the key to describe what you see in each map.
2 What has happened to the number of registered black occupied stands between 1915 and 1938?
3 Has the size of the black location changed at all between 1915 and 1938?
4 What changes do you think the differences shown in these maps brought to the lives of black people in Johannesburg between 1915 and 1938?
5 How did the situation develop and change for black people after 1938?

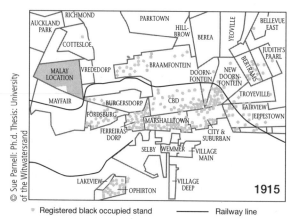
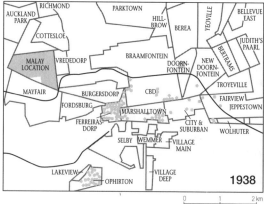

• Registered black occupied stand ——— Railway line

▲ Source B

Industrialisation and segregation in Johannesburg in 1915 and 1938

Unit 4

The 1924 Pact government

Unit outcomes

- Understand how the Pact government was formed.
- Describe the effect of the Balfour Declaration and the Statute of Westminister on South Africa's status in the British Empire.
- Analyse the racial policies of the Pact government.
- Explore the relationship between the Pact government, labour and the economy.
- Work through a suggested answer to an essay question.

Introduction

In 1924 the ruling South African Party (SAP) under General Smuts was defeated in a general election. In 1923 the National Party led by General Barry Hertzog and the Labour Party led by Colonel FHP Cresswell formed an electoral alliance or pact on the basis of a programme to put 'White South Africa first'. In 1924 the National Party won 63 seats and the Labour Party won 18 which gave them 81 seats, a majority of 29 over the 58 seats won by the SAP.

The Labour and National parties

The Labour Party had been formed in 1910 with the aim of representing white workers. Its main concern was to protect white workers from being replaced by cheaper black workers – a crucial issue in the period 1910–24. Its main support came from English-speaking workers and it attracted limited support amongst Afrikaner workers, but it could not match the support amongst Afrikaners achieved by the National Party formed in 1914. The National Party's main support was in rural areas but it also had supporters amongst urban Afrikaners.

The National Party protected and advanced the interests of Afrikaners. One of its key campaigns was for language equality and greater recognition for Afrikaans. It also supported looser ties with the British Empire and among its members were strong supporters of **republicanism**. Although it initially gained little support amongst the established Afrikaner middle

class, in the unstable years after its birth it gained a strong following amongst the unemployed and unskilled members of the community. It also established a support base amongst ministers of religion, civil servants, teachers, lawyers and small businessmen, many of whom were struggling to establish themselves in an English-dominated world.

When the Pact government took office, Afrikaans was given the status of an official language. DF Malan, Minister of the Interior, insisted on bilingualism throughout the civil service. As a result, many more jobs were available in the civil service for Afrikaners.

New words

republicanism rejection of having a king or queen as the formal head of state

Background to the constitutional position of the Union of South Africa in the British Empire

With the creation of Union in 1910, South Africa joined Canada, Australia and New Zealand as one of the self-governing dominions of the British Empire.

These overseas British dominions occupied in many ways, a subordinate status to that of Britain. In internal affairs Britain reserved the right to veto legislation and, by the Colonial Laws Validity Act (1865), any act of a self-governing colony that was inconsistent with British Law was invalid. In practice, the British parliament never interfered in the domestic affairs of a dominion. In external affairs, dominions had no authority at all: they did not have their own ambassadors, they could not make foreign treaties, and they could not declare war.

When Great Britain declared war on Germany on 4 August 1914, the whole of the British Empire was automatically at war. There was no question of a dominion electing to be neutral.

During the First World War, General Smuts spoke of the concept of a 'British Commonwealth of Nations'. This term gradually replaced the term 'British Empire', when referring to

Britain's self-governing overseas dominions. At the Peace Conference in 1919, the dominions were individually represented and their representatives signed the Treaty of Versailles – Generals Louis Botha and JC Smuts signing on behalf of the Union of South Africa.

South Africa joined the League of Nations in 1920 and was given the Mandate of South West Africa, which she administered on behalf of the League.

By 1920 Smuts considered that a South African republic was unnecessary, because the Union had been shown to have independent status within the British Empire. Nevertheless, in 1917 and again at the Imperial Conference in 1921, he pressed for a precise interpretation of dominion status.

The Pact government and the Balfour Declaration

In 1926 JBM Hertzog, as prime minister in the Pact government, attended the Imperial Conference in London. Hertzog took the lead in pressing that South Africa and the other dominions should be more independent of British control. A committee under the chairmanship of Lord Balfour and including the prime ministers of South Africa, Canada, Australia and New Zealand was established to define the relationship between Britain and her dominions.

After careful deliberation, the Balfour Declaration was issued:

> They (Britain and the dominions) are autonomous communities within the British Empire, equal in status, in no way subordinate one to another in any aspect of their domestic or external affairs, though united by a common **allegiance** to the Crown, and freely associated as members of the British Common Wealth of Nations.

Hertzog was pleased with the outcome of the conference and felt sure that his goal of a sovereign, independent South Africa was not far away. On his return to South Africa he was hailed as the 'father of his country's new found independence'.

The Statute of Westminster (1931)

The Balfour Declaration had to be carried into law. This was done by the British House of Commons in 1931 by legislation known as the Statute of Westminster. Dominion status was firmly established:

- the legislative independence of the dominions was formally recognised
- the governor-general could now no longer act as the representative of British government
- the offices of the governor-general and the high commissioner were separated, thereby emphasising the difference of policy.

The impact of the Statute of Westminster on South Africa

Hertzog now came to believe that being a dominion within the Commonwealth was not a threat to the Afrikaner cause and that republicanism was no longer an important issue. He acted according to this new-found independence:

- in 1927 he created a Department of Foreign Affairs
- in 1929 he sent South Africa's first ambassadors abroad.

The passing of the Statute of Westminster necessitated amendments to the Union's new constitutional position. Therefore, in 1934 the Union Parliament passed the Status of the Union Act which proclaimed the Statute of Westminster as law in South Africa and confirmed the supremacy of the South African parliament and its complete independence from Britain.

The Seals Act (1934) extended the Status Act by ensuring that South African laws would be signed by the British Monarch and a minister of the South African government.

In the following years, South Africa continued to assert her independence by, for example:

- passing her own act of abdication when Edward VIII abdicated in 1936
- declaring war against Germany in 1939
- proclaiming Elizabeth II Queen of South Africa in 1952
- becoming a republic and withdrawing from the British Commonwealth of Nations in 1961.

New words

allegiance loyalty

The Pact government and segregation

The Pact government set about entrenching and extending the segregationist framework which had been established by the South African Party.

Hertzog declared at an election meeting in May 1926

Next to the European the native stands as an 8 year old child to a man of great experience ... Another point of difference of the greatest importance is that of national character and customs ... How much of this difference is something which will eventually disappear when the native becomes civilised cannot be determined with any certainty. The time has come for a fixed native policy; a policy that will do away with all uncertainty on the part of the native as to what his place will be in the political society during the time of his cultural immaturity. To take away the uncertainty, it is not only necessary that he realises clearly that equality with the European as regards political rights is impossible, but in the clearest words the native must understand that the European is determined that South Africa will be ruled by the white man ... We must not give him rights calculated to arouse false hopes in him; and as far as he already has such rights we must make sure that he renounces them in favour of what will be, for him, more conducive to progress and happiness.

▲ Barry Hertzog

Activities ·

Carefully read through Source A and then answer the following questions.

1 What are the most important differences which Hertzog sees between what he describes as natives and whites?

2 Does Hertzog believe that these differences will disappear over time?

3 Hertzog says the time has come for a 'fixed native policy'. What message does he wish this policy to convey to Africans?

4 Hertzog is determined that Africans must renounce any rights which might give them false hopes. What rights and hopes do you think he has in mind?

5 Hertzog is speaking to an audience of white voters. Do you think that this affects what he has to say and how he says it?

· ·

The 1926 'Natives' Bills

Hertzog was determined to do away with the Cape franchise, which he saw as an obstacle to the 'fixed' and segregationist native policy he wanted to achieve. In 1925 he offered to increase the size of the African reserves in exchange for the loss of the vote. In 1926 he placed the 'Native' Bills before parliament.

The Representation of Natives in Parliament Bill aimed to remove African voters from the common voters role in the Cape and to provide Africans throughout the Union with seven white representatives in parliament.

The Natives Land Act (Amendment) Bill made additional land available for inclusion in their reserves.

The Union Native Council Bill provided for a 50 man advisory African Council.

While National Party policy at this time was committed to full segregation of Africans, its policy in relation to the coloured community was that they should be allowed to develop economically and politically alongside white society. In the run-up to the 1924 election the National Party sought the support of coloured political leaders, promising to extend the vote to coloureds throughout the Union and to release coloureds from the economic colour bar. Partly as a result, the National Party benefited from the support of coloured voters in the Cape in the 1924 election. In 1926 Hertzog introduced a Coloured Persons Rights Bill which proposed to extend political rights to coloureds outside the Cape.

This set of Bills was not passed by parliament. They involved amendments to the constitution and therefore required a two-thirds majority of both houses (at a joint sitting) in parliament.

The South African Party, led by Smuts, strongly criticised the Bills. He argued that the Land Bill was insufficient and likely to increase rather than to diminish territorial, racial intermingling. He criticised the proposals to give Africans separate representation in parliament as an attempt to weaken the political influence of whites. As a result of the SAP's opposition, Hertzog could not achieve the two-thirds majority required to pass the Bill.

Activities

Did Smuts' criticisms of Hertzog's Bills suggest a fundamental difference in policy between the NP and the SAP?

Pact and the Indian community

The Pact government also introduced new legislation in relation to the Indian community. After 1910 the SAP government had made a series of attempts to encourage the repatriation – the return to India – of members of the Indian community. In 1914, for example, the Smuts-Gandhi agreement was signed which made provision for the voluntary repatriation of Indians with a free passage, but the majority of Indians chose to remain in South Africa, and the continued presence of Indians in 'white' residential and business areas became an important issue in the 1924 election. In 1925 Dr Malan, the minister of internal affairs, introduced a Bill into parliament which provided for the compulsory segregation of Indians in business and residential areas and attempted to reduce the Indian population to an '**irreducible minimum**' by encouraging repatriation.

The Indian community responded by attempting to gain support from overseas, particularly in India. In 1925 a **deputation** was sent to India to meet the British Viceroy and to address a series of public and private meetings. The Indian government sent a fact finding mission to South Africa. A Round Table Conference between the South African and Indian governments was arranged in 1926. This resulted in an agreement to undertake combined action to assist repatriation including the appointment of an agent of the Indian government. The South African government agreed in return to drop its attempts to extend and enforce the residential and commercial segregation of Indians, but very few Indians were interested in being repatriated.

Activities

Study Source B and then answer the questions that follow.

1 From which two countries were the delegates at the Round Table Conference?
2 What was the reason for the conference?
3 a Discuss the arrangements the delegates arrived at with regard to the main reason for their conference.
  b How successful were these arrangements?

New words

irreducible minimum the smallest number possible
deputation a group of people given the right to speak or act for others

▼ *Source B* Delegates who attended the Round Table Conference in 1926

Pact and white labour

When the Pact government was formed, Cresswell was appointed minister of labour and several measures were taken to improve the position of white workers. These measures were not revolutionary. Labour, though in power as part of the Pact government, remained a minority party with only eighteen seats in parliament. Cresswell failed to persuade the cabinet to pursue his dream of the replacement of African mine labour with white workers, but the industrial labour policy of the Pact government was to support the employment of 'civilised labour' at a 'civilised' rate. This basically meant giving preference to the employment of whites at higher wages than those paid to blacks.

In many ways the Pact's programme extended earlier forms of protection for white workers and attempted to involve them more fully in structures designed by the government.

The Industrial Conciliation Act of 1924 incorporated trade unions and employers in industrial councils, restricted union capacity to initiate industrial action, and laid down tight legal control over disputes.

The Wages Act of 1925 and the establishment of wages boards allowed minimum wages to be established for 'civilised' labour.

The Colour Bar Act of 1926 excluded black mine workers from many skilled jobs on the mines and reserved them for white and coloured workers.

The responsibility for providing jobs for the growing white population in the towns was placed on the mines and on the public service. White employment was encouraged and expanded in all government departments and state enterprises. Railways and harbours became major points of white employment. In 1924, for example, 9,5 per cent of railway employees were white; by 1928 this figure had risen to 28,7 per cent. Tariff protection for industry was also made conditional on the employment of a 'fair' amount of white labour.

Activities

1 What kind of work does Source C show the white labourers doing?
2 What impact did the 'civilised labour' policy of the Pact government have on patterns of employment on the railways?

White labour essentially traded its use of strikes for the promise of government protection, while businessmen accepted increased government regulation of industrial relations in return for

▲ *Source C* Afrikaner labourers on the railways

greater stability. There was a steady expansion of white employment. Even in the mining industry where the proportion of whites in the labour force had dropped from about 11 per cent prior to the 1922 strike to 8 per cent after it, white workers formed 10 per cent of the work force by 1926. There was also a dramatic reduction in industrial conflict. In the years 1919–22, 2,8 million working hours were lost as a result of strikes, but only 114 000 hours were lost in the years 1924–32.

Activities

Did the election of the Pact government in 1924 allow white workers to reverse their defeat in the Rand Revolt of 1922?

Pact and the economy

Part of the reason why the Pact government was able to deal with white workers so effectively was that the period it was in power coincided almost exactly with a time of sustained economic growth which continued until the end of the 1920s.

The fact that Pact supported white workers in some ways and that it was strongly rooted amongst white farmers has led some historians to suggest that it was hostile to business interests, but there is little evidence that Pact policies were intended to be damaging to either mining or industry.

The Pact government recognised that the gold mining industry provided the foundation for the South African economy and was a vital source of state revenue. Consequently, it was very cautious in its treatment of it. There was also a general belief that gold supplies would be exhausted in the not too distant future and that it was necessary to develop other forms of industry to sustain the society and make it more self-sufficient. It was hoped that wider industrialisation would provide for more jobs and a larger internal market – especially for farmers.

The Pact government was the first to introduce a **systematic** programme for the development of secondary industry in South Africa. It took the form of **tariff protection** for South African industries from foreign competition. Under the Customs Tariff Act of 1925, goods from outside South Africa were subjected to import duties which made them more expensive than local products.

Pact also regarded it as essential that South Africa should have its own substantial iron and steel industry. Therefore, the government established Iscor (The Iron and Steel Corporation) in 1927 which was largely state-run and state-directed.

In the short term these efforts had limited impact and it was not until the 1930s that secondary industry started to expand rapidly in South Africa.

The Pact government was also sensitive to the needs of white farmers who formed a large part of its support base. The National Party was overwhelmingly a rural party. It took steps to promote the external marketing of fruit, dairy and other products through subsidies. It reduced the taxes on imported fertilisers and farm implements. It paid particular attention to the needs of white farmers who were struggling to remain on the land. For example, it provided them with easier access to credit through the Land Bank.

New words

systematic thoroughly planned
tariff protection placing heavy taxes on imported goods to protect local products from competition

The 1929 general election

The government's failure to carry the Natives Representation Bill set the stage for the 1929 election. Although Smuts emphasised his commitment to comprehensive segregation, the National Party, using 'swart gevaar – black peril' electoral tactics portrayed the SAP as being in favour of black rule and succeeded in playing on the racial fears of the white electorate. By this time the Labour Party was deeply divided between moderate and radical members and made little impact on the election. The National Party won 78 seats, the SAP won 61, and the Labour Party only won 8 seats. The National Party could therefore comfortably govern the country alone.

Activities

1 Did the Pact government in the period 1924–29 introduce fundamental changes in segregationist policy or did it do little more than to continue the existing direction of segregationist policy?

2 Were there any significant differences between the NP and the SAP in relation to 'native' policy in the period 1924–29?

Understanding historical skills and concepts

Answering an essay question

One of the essay questions that is often asked on this unit of work, particularly in the final exam, is: 'Analyse the extent to which the Pact government was successful in the period 1924–29.'

The sections on 'Essay writing' (pages 41 to 42) and 'Preparing for the Grade 12 final exams' (pages 357 to 358) will help you to analyse what this essay question is asking and help you to plan your answer.

The material which follows covers the content that should be included when you answer this essay question. Carefully work through each section of the suggested answer. You will notice that in some sections you have been given new information on topics that are not in the main text, and in other sections you could add more details from the main text.

Background

In 1923 the National Party under JBM Hertzog and Cresswell's Labour Party formed an election pact. They wanted to defeat the government of the South African Party (SAP) led by Jan Smuts. Once elected, the Pact government had three main aims:

- to make South Africa safe for the white man – both politically and economically
- to promote economic development
- to secure the constitutional independence of the Union.

Political measures (main text, page 259)

To protect white labour from the threat of cheap black labour, a 'civilised labour' policy was introduced. All state departments gave preference to white (civilised) labour, paying them higher wages than blacks. Other measures in favour of the white worker were:

- Department of Labour created (1924)
- Industrial Conciliation Act (1924)
- Wages Act (1925) which laid down minimum wages
- Mines and Mine Works Act or Colour Bar Act (1926) which provided protection for skilled white workers
- Old Age Pension Act (1926).

Economic measures (main text, page 260)

The economy was encouraged in various ways and, at the same time, there were good rains:

- agriculture: Export Boards, import tariffs, the Land Bank
- mining and secondary industry protected by import tariffs
- diamond and gold production increased and there were new diamond discoveries
- Iscor was established (1928).

Recognition of South Africa's sovereign independence (main text, page 256)

a **The Balfour Declaration**
- Imperial Conference of 1926
- recognised in British law by the Statute of Westminster in 1931, and incorporated into South African law by the Status Act of 1934
- the Seals Act of 1934.

b **Department of External Affairs**
This was established in 1927. The first ambassadors were sent to The Hague, Washington and Rome.

c **The flag question**
'For a long time various members of all three political parties, had felt that SA ought to have her own flag. In 1925 Dr DF Malan, the minister of the interior, introduced a Bill which provided for a national flag, but at Smuts' insistence it was agreed to hold the Bill back. It was re-introduced during the 1926 parliamentary session. A bitter dispute arose over the flag's appearance. One extreme wanted nothing but the Union Jack, at the other extreme were people like Dr DF Malan who wanted a flag with no British symbols on it.' (From: CFJ Muller. *500 years.*)

A compromise was the obvious solution, but Malan was most unwilling to agree. The dispute caused increasing concern among the various population groups, and a split threatened to develop in the Labour Party when the leader, Cresswell, supported the Nationalists on this issue. The prime minister was urged to delay the passing of the Bill for another year. He agreed to do so in spite of strong opposition from Malan.

Finally Malan agreed to accept the compromise. The resulting Bill gave South Africa two official flags: one was the national flag consisting of three horizontal stripes of orange, white and blue with miniature versions of the Union Jack and the two republican flags on the middle stripe; the other was the Union Jack, which could not be flown alone, but only together with the national flag in certain specified places such as the Houses of Parliament and the more important government buildings. The SA national flag was flown for the first time in South Africa on 31 May 1928.

d The recognition of Afrikaans

As a champion of Afrikaans, Hertzog worked hard to obtain full recognition for his mother tongue. He was strongly supported by his minister of interior, Dr DF Malan.

Bilingualism was enforced in most branches of the government service despite severe opposition. Most English officials were unilingual and were gradually replaced. Gradually the policy of bilingualism came to be accepted as being in the best interests of the country.

On 8 May 1925, Afrikaans became an official language in place of Dutch, and this was entrenched in the constitution. In a stirring speech, Dr Malan argued that Afrikaans was sufficiently developed to serve as an administrative, legislative and educational instrument. His motion was accepted unanimously. The government issued a grant for a Verklarende Woordeboek (explanatory dictionary), and the translation of the Bible was completed in 1933.

Hertzog's four 'Race Bills', 1926 (main text, page 257)

In 1925 Hertzog outlined his policy of political and territorial segregation, and in 1926 he introduced four Bills:
- to remove the African franchise in the Cape Province
- to set up an advisory Native Council

- to make additional land available in the reserves he introduced The Native's Land Act (Amendment) Bill and a Coloured Persons Rights Bill.

Smuts opposed the Bills and Hertzog could not get the two-thirds majority of both Houses sitting together, which he needed to have the Bills passed. The Bills were withdrawn – to be resubmitted to parliament in modified form in 1936.

The 1929 ('Swart Gevaar') election (main text, page 260)

Hertzog and his government could face the electorate with confidence; apart from the so-called 'Race-Bills', his policies had been successful: 'the Union prospered economically, there was industrial peace, the budget was balanced and the finances restored. He had kept his promise to obtain formal recognition of the Union's independent status. He had satisfied the Afrikaner by his language policy' (From: DW Kruger. *The Making of a Nation*).

Hertzog's election platform was that of the preservation of 'white South Africa'. The Nationalists claimed that Smuts was aiming to make South Africa a 'black state'; he was threatening the country with the 'Black Peril'.

These tactics worked and the National Party won 78 of the 148 seats, thus obtaining an absolute majority for the first time. The Pact had indeed had a successful first term of office.

Unit 5

Patterns of resistance (1924–30)

Unit outcomes

- Evaluate the different forms of resistance to government rule.
- Discuss the reasons for the rise and decline of the Industrial and Commercial Workers Union (ICU).

Introduction

The years of the Pact government witnessed white politicians debating the precise form of segregation within parliament, but much more dramatic political struggles were occurring outside parliament in the cities and countryside.

The ANC

The leadership of the ANC in this period was drawn from the small, educated African middle class and the membership was at best a few thousand. In the years after it was founded in 1912 it had concentrated on the politics of 'petition and polite protest' and many of the leaders still hoped that British intervention would improve the position of westernised, educated Africans. John Dube from Natal, the first president of the ANC, for example, placed 'hopeful reliance on the sense of common justice and love of freedom so innate in the British character' (Lodge, 23). But, two delegations who went to Britain in 1914 and 1919 to plead for help came away without success.

◀ John Dube

In the years after the First World War, the ANC was influenced by the experiences and demands of less secure and wealthy lower middle class members suffering from low wages and lack of housing. Partly as a result, it was drawn into an upsurge of protest and strike action on the Rand in 1918, but much of the leadership was uncomfortable with radical protest and from 1920 onwards the movement mainly restricted itself to more moderate forms of politics. In the early 1920s it participated in the Joint Council Movement with white liberals and took part in government advisory conferences. The ANC also found its leading position in resistance politics being challenged by a number of newcomers.

The Communist Party of South Africa (CPSA)

The Communist Party, which was founded in 1921, was strongly influenced by the Russian revolution of 1917, the Communist International and the experiences of Eastern European immigrants. The party initially focused on white workers, and communists were active in the 1922 Rand Revolt and supported the Nationalist/Labour Pact in the 1924 election. The party also argued that working class unity should overcome racial divisions. The emphasis on white supremacy which brought the Pact to power led the party to rethink its tactics. At its annual conference in 1924 it decided that 'our main revolutionary task is among the natives'. The membership of the CPSA was even smaller than that of the ANC but it was well organised with a centralised structure.

The Industrial and Commercial Workers Union (ICU)

The organisation that dominated resistance politics in this decade and gained a mass following was the ICU. The rise and fall of this movement has provided historians with a number of puzzles to solve. The ICU started out as a trade union organising workers in urban areas, but it gained its greatest following in rural areas. At the heights of its power in 1927 the ICU claimed a membership of 100 000 but within three years it had collapsed. As you read the account of the history of the ICU which follows, see if you can work out why this happened.

The ICU developed out of attempts to organise dock workers in Cape Town. It was founded in 1919 and led a successful strike in the same year. Its secretary was Clements Kadalie – a mission educated migrant worker from Malawi (then called Nyasaland) with a powerful personality. In 1920 Kadalie linked up with other emerging worker organisations, including those led by Selby Msimang in Bloemfontein and Samuel Masabal in the Eastern Cape.

▼ Source A
The ICU's declared aim

Bring together all classes of labour, skilled and unskilled, in every sphere of life ... To obtain and maintain equitable rates of wages and reasonable conditions of labour, to regulate the relations between employer and employed and to endeavour to settle differences between them ... and to promote co-operation, insurance, sick and out-of-work benefits and old-age-pensions.

Activities
1 a What kind of organisation is being described in Source A?
   b Is it a political party?
   c Is it a trade union?
2 What does the letterhead of the ICU (Source B) show?
3 What do you think could be the significance of the telegraphic address for the ICU shown on Source B?

The growth and decline of the ICU
The ICU grew steadily in the years immediately after its formation, becoming a general rather than a craft or industrial union. Its formation was strongly influenced by local leaders and circumstances in the different industrial centres. The ICU branch in Durban led by AWG Champion, who had been a mine clerk, concentrated on fighting issues in the law courts and won many workers' cases against employers. Some employers were fined under the Masters and Servants Acts for beating workers. The courts also ruled that Africans entering Durban no longer had to be dipped with their belongings in disinfectant tanks like animals. In Bloemfontein the ICU used the Wage Board to get minimum wages established for the city's black workers. Some time after the ICU was established in Johannesburg it was involved in a strike which the newspaper *The Star* called the 'native unions first strike on white lines'. The strike was at a metal factory in Mayfair where 52 members of the union demanded an hour's break for breakfast. The workers got their demand (Callinicos. *Working Life*, 162).

By the mid-1920s serious conflicts had developed within the organisation. There were tensions within the leadership and it was accused both of taking decisions without proper consultation and of misappropriating (stealing) funds. With its organisation in urban areas faltering, ICU organisers increasingly turned their attention to rural areas. Between October 1926 and July 1927, forty-three branches were opened in three provinces. By the end of 1927 there were more than one hundred ICU branches. As the ICU shifted in focus from the town to the country its emphasis shifted from the trade union demands to broader political demands for African freedom and the return of the land.

▲ *Source B* Letterhead of the ICU (From: Luli Callinicos. *Working Life*.)

© UNISA Photographic Library

▲ Kadalie and Champion

Kadalie', an old man recalled years later (Callinicos. *Working Life*, 163). In the Eastern Transvaal, members were told that the ICU would restore freedom by Christmas of 1927. Inspired by these hopes many rural Africans bought ICU membership cards and stopped carrying passes, paying taxes and fees. An ICU provincial leader, Thomas Mbeki, toured Eastern Transvaal towns telling Africans to walk, not in the streets as the whites demanded, but on the pavements with the whites. A number of strikes started on the farms.

The ICU also gained considerable support in Natal. Tenants who had been stripped of much of their land and livestock believed that the ICU would give them farms and cattle and the union initially played along with this view. Kadalie even remarked at a meeting in Escourt that it would not be long before 'the natives would take over the farms of the white man'. As time passed by and neither farms nor cattle were provided in either Natal or the Transvaal, support for the ICU started to fade away. Farmers also hit back. They evicted supporters from their farms, burnt their huts and confiscated their cattle. Farmers also threatened organisers, smashed local ICU offices and persuaded local magistrates to ban meetings and to prosecute union leaders.

Activities

1 Explain the reasons for the large following of the ICU.
2 Why did the ICU increasingly turn its attention to the rural areas?

Africans living on white farms were under mounting pressure. Farmers in many districts demanded more and more of the land for their own crops and cattle, leaving little room for tenants. It became harder for sharecroppers to survive and harsher terms were imposed on labour tenants. Many farmers demanded six or more months of labour a year from tenants and expected more of tenants' family members to work for them. In the mid-1920s, partly as a result of the assistance provided to white farmers by the Pact government, farmers expanded their production and intensified their demands on tenant and other farm workers. This led to growing conflict on many farms and encouraged the expansion of the ICU in the countryside.

By 1926, ICU organisers were operating in the rural Transvaal. It was not long before Sunday meetings were attracting thousands of people. Many of these people had high hopes that the ICU would help them get rid of the white farmers and return their land to them. 'Man, we thought we were getting our country back from

Conflicts within the ICU leadership also flared up and accusations of corruption continued. After 1924 communists joined the ICU aiming to help build it as an organisation of the working class. They were frustrated by high levels of internal disorganisation and the lack of a clear focus on industrial workers. Communist Party criticism was resented by the leadership and some of the organisers. In 1926 members of the Communist Party were expelled. As a result, many of the ICU's most dedicated and experienced organisers were removed.

When faced with growing difficulties in the organisation – including a breakaway by the Natal section, under the leadership of Champion – Kadalie attempted to restructure the ICU as a trade union run along British lines. The National Council of the ICU sought help from the British Trade Union Council, who sent out a Scottish trade unionist William Ballinger. Ballinger, however, found the ICU accounts in chaos and criticised Kadalie's leadership. Eventually Kadalie resigned and established a breakaway section with headquarters in East London. With leaders and organisers locked in conflict and accusing each other of mismanagement, members had little hope that their needs and interests would be given attention. By 1928 thousands of members were leaving. People complained that the ICU 'promised the worlds things and none of its promises have ever been fulfilled, so they are no more following' (Callinicos. *Working Life*, 166).

ICU aftermath

By 1930 the ICU had crumbled but it left a significant political legacy. Jason Jingoes later wrote about the impact of the movement:

> Although the initials stood for a fancy title, to us Bantu it meant basically: when you ill-treat the African people, I See You; if you kick them off the pavements and say they must go together with the cars and the ox-carts, I See You; I See You when you do not protect the Bantu ... I See You when you kick my brother, I See You (Callinicos. *Working Life*, 168).

And in the words of an old woman recalling the ICU many years later: 'for a short while at least we too tasted freedom' (Callinicos. *Working Life*, 168).

The ICU also had an important impact on other resistance movements. The Communist Party, after its rejection by the ICU, began to establish its own industrial unions and placed more emphasis on recruiting African members. By 1928 three of the central committee members were black, as were a majority of the party's 1 750 members. The party also took a renewed interest in the ANC, which it had previously dismissed as a reactionary movement. In 1928, partly under the influence of the Communist International, the party adopted a slogan defining its aim as being to establish 'an independent native Republic as a stage towards a workers and peasants republic'. The idea of stages of change which this slogan reflected made it easier for the Communist Party to come to terms with cooperating with the more conservative ANC, in order to achieve the first stage of transformation and establish a 'Native Republic' under African leadership.

By 1927 many ANC leaders, aware of the successes of the ICU and threatened by the Pact government's plans to do away with voting rights for Africans, were losing faith in the politics of diplomatic persuasion. In 1927 Josiah Gumede was elected as president of the ANC and the movement announced plans to embark on a path of mass organisation. Gumede, like a number of leaders of the ICU, had been influenced in the early 1920s by the teachings of Marcus Garvey.

Garvey was a West Indian who had moved to the United States during the First World War. Preaching the unity of all blacks, he claimed that liberty would only come about through the return of all African Americans to their ancestral homes. Gumede was responsive to other influences as well. He accepted an invitation to tour the Soviet Union, and he returned to South Africa considerably impressed with what he had seen of a communist country.

Inkatha

It was not only the ANC and the Communist Party that were affected by the rise and fall of the ICU. The Zulu National Council, or Inkatha kaZulu was also partly shaped by these events.

The first Inkatha kaZulu was founded in 1922 by a group of African Christians (amakholwa).

▼ *Source C*

A white missionary present at an early meeting of the organisation commented on the role of the Zulu king

> They consider that the native is victimised in many ways and receives unfair and unjust treatment from the white man; that this will continue as long as the natives are divided; that the native people will never be strong until there is unity amongst them ... They are casting around for a rallying point – a central figure and that figure would seem to be Solomon.

▲ King Solomon

1 According to Source C, what role did the founders of Inkatha want Solomon, the Zulu king, to play?

2 Do you think that using the Zulu king as a symbol of national unity was a good idea? Divide the class into two groups; one to argue in favour of the proposition, the other to argue against it.

....

The word Inkatha means 'a grass coil placed on the head for carrying a load'. The Inkatha yeSiswe or grass coil of the nation was a ritual object inherited by Shaka's successors and kept at the royal headquarters.

The Inkatha organisation was formed at a time when Zulu society was facing many challenges. For example, as pressure on the land mounted there was a growing number of landless families. Some chiefs, landowners, shopkeepers and teachers feared that they might find themselves attacked by poor people. These fears were increased by the threat that militant organisations, like the ICU, might win significant support amongst Zulus who had lost, or were in danger of losing, their land and livestock.

Not only the wealthy and the powerful supported the king. In pre-colonial Zululand the king had represented the unity of the people and had provided a key link with the ancestors who were believed to be responsible for the well-being of the community. At a time of growing hardship, when many less important chiefs increasingly seemed only to serve the interests of the government and not their subjects, Solomon, who was not recognised by the government, was seen by many Zulu commoners as a figure who could unite and protect Zulu society.

Other people also looked to the king. Some whites placed their hopes on Solomon. George Heaton Nicholls, and a number of leading sugar planters, believed that the influence of the king could prevent growth in support for organisations like the ICU and the Communist Party, which were attempting to build a working class following. Some mine owners also supported Solomon because they found members of the royal family helpful in recruiting migrant workers in Zululand and in smoothing over difficulties in the workplace.

But in the 1920s the Pact government refused to recognise the Zulu king, and by the early 1930s the first Inkatha had lost its importance.

Extension activity ....
Write an essay in which you evaluate the impact of the ICU on resistance politics from 1924–30.

....

Unit 6

The Great Depression

Unit outcomes

- Evaluate the effects of the Great Depression on South Africa.
- Explore the reasons for economic growth after the Depression.

Introduction

In October 1929 the Wall Street Stock Exchange in New York crashed with people scrambling to sell shares. By the end of the month nearly 15 000 000 000 (fifteen billion) dollars had been wiped off the value of shares. As we have seen in previous chapters, from Wall Street the crisis spread to the rest of the American economy and from there to the rest of the world. At first, South Africa was not significantly affected, as few South Africans had investments in the United States of America. In December, Prime Minister Barry Hertzog announced that 'there was no reason to expect a slump' in South Africa. This comment proved to be a mistaken prediction.

The effects of the Great Depression on South Africa

The world price for major South African exports such as wool, sugar and maize fell dramatically. The diamond industry suffered particularly severely and a number of major mines were forced to close. Wages dropped and unemploy-ment increased as many companies went bank-rupt. To make matters worse, during 1932–33 the country experienced one of the worst droughts of the century. Many farmers who had borrowed heavily in the boom years of the late 1920s, went bankrupt when the banks called in their loans. Many of these broken farmers had little choice but to move to the cities where they increased the numbers of unemployed. Whites joined the queues at soup kitchens and begged on the streets. Migrant workers, retrenched by the mines, farms and factories, returned to the drought-stricken reserves either to find that their families were starving, or that they had gone to farms and towns to find food and work.

▼ *Source A*

Verse from 'In the Gold Mines', a poem by BW Vilikazi written on returning to his homestead in the 1930s

I carried my bundle to seek my home,
But was hit in the face by cropless stalks,
By empty huts and abandoned homes;
I paused and scratched my head, puzzled;
Where was my wife? My mothers-in-law?
I was told they had gone to the white man,
To the white man for whom I work.
I shut my mouth and spoke not a word.

(From: Emilia Potenza. *All That Glitters.*)

◀ *Source B*
A soup kitchen

© City Council of Pretoria

Activities

1 Carefully read through Source A and then answer these questions.
   a What does the poet find when he returns to his homestead from the mines?
   b Why have the poet's wife and mother-in-law 'gone to the white man'?
   c How did events in far-away New York contribute to this situation?

2 Source B shows the queue at a soup kitchen.
   a Describe whom the photograph shows standing in the queue.
   b What kinds of containers have the people brought to be filled?
   c Who would organise and sponsor soup kitchens like the one in Source B?

South Africa recovered more quickly from the Great Depression than many other countries. This was because gold production continued and prospered. Financial insecurity and instability led people to buy gold and while the prices of many other goods and services fell, the price of gold was fixed by international agreements so that gold could be used as an international currency for settling debts. With growing demand, a fixed price and falling costs, the profits from gold mining increased.

In September 1931 South Africa was shocked to hear the news that Britain had decided to abandon the gold standard. This was the system under which a government was obliged to exchange its paper money for gold, if it was required to. The value of paper money was therefore **underwritten** by gold stored in national vaults. Britain went off the gold standard and **devalued** the pound in an attempt to encourage its economy to grow more rapidly, and recover from the effects of the Depression. A number of other countries followed this example.

In South Africa, Jan Smuts, the leader of the opposition, urged Hertzog to follow Britain's example, but the Nationalist government believed that the country's currency should remain linked to gold. This decision was based on these arguments.

- The belief that support for the gold standard was good for the mining industry.
- The view that a strong currency would help the economy by allowing goods to be imported more cheaply.
- The idea that not following Britain's lead would show South Africa's economic and political independence.

New words

underwritten guaranteed
devalue reduce the value or price

◀ **Source C**
Suffering under the gold standard
The sufferer: I'm sure this is very good for me – but I wish I knew why!
(From: *The Cape Times*, 14 November 1931.)

	1924–25	1925–26	1926–27	1927–28	1928–29	1929–30	1930–31	1931–32	1932–33
Number of establishments	6 009	5 957	6 012	6 162	6 238	6 472	Industrial census not taken	Industrial census not taken	6 543
Number of workers									
Total (x 1 000)	115	121	127	132	141	142			133
Whites (x 1 000)	41	44	47	50	54	55			57
Blacks (x 1 000)	74	77	80	82	87	88			76
Salaries and wages									
Total (x R1 000)	22 120	23 924	25 662	27 774	29 730	31 206			26 712
Whites (x R1 000)	14 808	16 032	19 336	18 952	20 260	21 484			19 292
Blacks (x R1 000)	7 300	7 890	8 326	8 882	9 470	9 722			7 420
Value of output									
Gross value (x R1 000)	114 608	127 532	134 438	151 284	161 296	156 850			134 664
Net value (x R1 000)	49 492	53 582	59 352	62 584	67 552	68 388			61 400

▲ *Source D* Development of secondary industry in South Africa (1924/5 to 1932/3)

Activities ....
1 What does Source C show?
2 Who are the people riding on bicycles?
3 What do you think is the opinion of the cartoonist regarding the gold standard? Give reasons for your answer.

....

Hertzog's way of thinking about the gold standard proved to be seriously misguided. The highly valued South African pound, which made South Africa's exports relatively expensive, made it very hard for South African exporters to compete in world markets. Wool producers were particularly hard hit. Uncertainty about whether or not South Africa would finally be forced to abandon the gold standard also resulted in investors moving large amounts of money out of the country. It has been estimated that between 1931 and the end of 1932, thirty-six million rand was sent out of the country. Mounting economic and financial crisis resulted in the gold standard being abandoned in December 1932.

Activities ....
Study the figures given in Source D for the development of secondary industry in South Africa.
1 Explain the general increase in all the figures between 1924/5 and 1929/30.
2 Why do you think no industrial census was taken in the years 1930/31 and 1931/32?
3 Explain the drop in most of the figures between 1929/30 and 1932/33.

....

In January 1933 Tielman Roos and Smuts discussed the formation of a national government. Roos wanted to be prime minister, but Smuts refused.

However, the idea had been planted, and Smuts approached Hertzog about a coalition between the National Party and the SAP. Hertzog's cabinet was divided on the issue, but Hertzog went ahead with the negotiations for a few reasons.
• He felt that the National Party on its own had very little chance of winning the next general elections.
• A coalition was needed to solve South Africa's economic problems, especially those of the farmers.
• He also felt that with the passing of the Statute of Westminster and the 'achievements' of the Pact Government, the time had come to bring the 'two streams' together. The future of the Afrikaner seemed assured, as did South Africa's independence. He no longer felt that it was essential to turn South Africa into a republic.

In February 1933 Smuts and Hertzog agreed on coalition. In March Hertzog, as prime minister, formed the Coalition Government. Smuts became deputy prime minister and minister of justice. Six nationalists and six members of the SAP made up the new government.

DF Malan did not agree with the coalition and he refused to be part of the government.

However, he remained in the National Party, because he wanted to make sure of winning his parliamentary seat in the next general election.

Despite fears that going off the gold standard would damage the mining industry, South Africa's economic recovery in the 1930s continued to be fuelled by gold. Over the next ten years the world price of gold doubled and lower grade ores, which were more expensive to mine, were now also mined on a scale which had previously been impossible. As a result, employment increased. The number of African workers on the mines increased from about 200 000 in 1929 to 383 000 in 1941, while the number of white miners rose from 22 000 to 41 000.

Government policy on taxing the mines also shifted. Before the Great Depression the mining industry had not been a major source of taxation, but economic thinking was changing in the post-depression world. One important influence, which you dealt with in Chapter 2, was Franklin Roosevelt's 'New Deal' policy in the USA. In 1933 an excess profits tax was imposed on the gold mining industry. Annual state income from the industry rose from about £1 to 6 million between 1925 and 1930 to over £13 million in 1933 and to £22 million in 1940. With these enlarged tax revenues the state could start ambitious new projects and policies.

White farmers who, as we have seen, suffered heavily in the Depression, received greatly expanded support through loans from the Land Bank and from state grants. They also benefited from state intervention to support agricultural prices. Control Boards were established to manage markets and in 1937 the system as a whole was regulated by a Marketing Act.

The manufacturing industry, which had also been deeply affected by the Depression, got less state support than agriculture but grew more rapidly. A growing market, created by the expansion of both urban areas and the mining industry, provided an important **stimulus** for the establishment of new factories. Employment in metal and engineering trebled to over 50 000 between 1932 and 1940. Industries such as clothing, textiles and food processing also expanded rapidly, so that their work forces grew even more rapidly than those of the mining industry. In 1930, a total of 6 472 factories employed 141 616 workers. By 1939, the number of factories had grown to 8 614, employing 236 123 workers.

New words

stimulus encouragement

Activities

1 With a partner discuss and make a list of the economic, social and political effects of the Great Depression on South Africa.
2 What factors caused the economy to make such a remarkable recovery in the years following the Great Depression?
3 Who are the people that benefited from this improvement in the economy, and how did they benefit?

The reserves and the 1932 Native Economic Commission

Unit 7

Unit outcomes

- Assess the condition of the reserves in the 1920s and 30s.
- Analyse the validity of the reasons given by the Native Economic Commission for the condition of the reserves.

Introduction

As we have seen previously, the reserve areas of South Africa were home to a growing population which depended heavily on migrant labour and which, by the 1930s, no longer had sufficient land and other agricultural resources to provide for its most basic food requirements.

▼ *Source A*

In 1930 a Native Commissioner in Sekhukhuneland, in the Northern Transvaal, Major DR Hunt, commented

> [the] district produces very little itself and is very nearly dependent on what is sent from beyond its own borders. It produces very little indeed for its own living. If we in Sekhukhuneland had to depend on local revenue, I am quite certain that it would be necessary to reduce taxes, or else to provide additional prison accommodation for the adult, male population.

Activities . . . .

1 When Hunt refers to 'what is sent from beyond its own borders' in Source A what do you think he is referring to?
2 What was the main form of local revenue to the state and why was it so low?
3 Why do you think Hunt refers to 'additional prison accommodation'?

. . . .

The situation in the reserves

By the 1920s there was increasing concern about the deterioration of the reserves. Mine owners feared that if the reserves collapsed the migrant labour system, upon which they depended for a supply of cheap labour, would not be able to survive.

Many white politicians and government officials feared that if the reserves deteriorated rapidly, poverty would force people to abandon rural areas and move to the towns in large numbers. They believed that this rapid urbanisation would undermine attempts to maintain a segregated social order. They were also frightened that a rapidly growing, poor urban population would be very expensive to administer and might become rebellious.

There was also great concern about the destruction of natural resources. It was argued that overcrowding and poor farming methods were leading to the loss of fertile soil. This concern about soil erosion was heightened in the early 1930s by news of the American 'Dust Bowl', which was created when farmers used land too intensively, causing massive soil erosion and the collapse of farming in large areas.

The growing concern about conditions in the reserves, rapid urbanisation and a context of heated debate sparked by Hertzog's Native Bills, led to the appointment of an official commission of inquiry in 1930 known as the Native Economic Commission. The commissioners toured the whole country taking evidence before presenting their report in 1932. The report also drew together much of the segregationist thought of the 1920s and like the SANAC report of 1905 set out a far-reaching and influential programme for the future.

The report argued

> that when Europeans first came to South Africa the Native population was living under a primitive subsistence economy.
> The white man came in with a money economy. The conflict of the two systems lies at the root of much of the native problem in its economic aspect.

The impact of colonial rule had been to allow for rapid growth of human and animal population in African areas. 'Tribal war was succeeded by peace, enforced by the white man, better transportation relieved famine, measures against human and animal diseases increased numbers.'

While the increase in the human population was a problem, 'at the root of the whole evil was overstocking [too many livestock – especially cattle] which was the result of the religious, rather than economic way in which Africans regarded their cattle'.

Overstocking in combination with backward farming methods had led to soil erosion and famine and threatened to produce an ecological catastrophe. The commission argued that the collapse of the reserves would lead to 'the rapid increase in the drift to the towns which has already assumed such a magnitude as seriously to disturb the European mind and to create grave problems of urban housing, administration and Native morality'.

Activities

Imagine that you live in a reserve like the one shown in Source B. Write a few paragraphs describing the conditions, the people you live with, and what your life is like.

For the commission the main question was 'how best the native population can be led onward, step by step in an orderly march to civilisation'.

The main problem in their view was not 'a small, vocal, satisfied, semi-civilised group of urban Africans; but millions of uneducated, tribal Natives held in the grip of superstition and of an anti-progressive tribal system'.

The commissioners did not believe that chiefs and the tribal system should be done away with but that the system should be modernised. This process would also allow educated Africans 'to find a fruitful field for using their energies and their knowledge to uplift their own people' rather than becoming 'exiles' amongst the whites.

The commission's key conclusion was that:

The most promising factor is the availability for development of such a large potential

source of wealth as the reserves undoubtedly possess. In the economic development of the Reserves must undoubtedly be sought the main solution to the Native economic problem.

The commissioners recommended a range of measures to develop reserve areas.

- That there should be a major reduction in the amount of livestock that Africans were allowed to keep in the reserves.
- That grazing land and agricultural land should be divided and fenced.
- That agricultural demonstrators should be appointed to help teach farmers in the reserves to employ more modern and 'scientific' methods of farming.

Activities

1 a Read through the text in this unit and summarise the Native Economic Commission's explanation for the problems in the reserves.
  b Do you think this explanation is convincing? Give reasons for your answer.
  c Was the problem too many people and cattle or too little land?
  d Why do you think that the commission placed so little emphasis on land shortages?
2 Why do you think that the commissioners were so keen that the solution to the problems of educated Africans should also be found in the reserves?
3 If you had been living in a reserve area at this time and were told the solution to rural poverty was to reduce the amount of cattle, how would you have felt?
4 What was the commission's solution to the economic problems facing Africans?
5 Outline what you see as strengths and/or weaknesses of the commission's recommendations.

◀ **Source B**
In the reserves

Unit 8 Urban life

Unit outcomes

- Understand why people left the land and moved to the cities.
- Explain why increasing numbers of women came to the city.
- Create an empathetic picture of life in the city for a young woman.

Leaving the land

In the 1930s changes taking place in the countryside along with the expansion of employment in mining and manufacturing led many people to move temporarily or permanently to South African cities – especially Johannesburg, Cape Town, Durban, Pretoria and Port Elizabeth. Increasing poverty in the reserves forced many people to look for employment in the cities. Some of those who found work in urban areas saw little reason to return home.

There was also a steady stream of both blacks and whites to the cities from white farming areas. Partly as a result of increased assistance from the government, white farming expanded and became more commercialised. Farmers demanded more labour from their black tenants and allowed them less land and livestock. Many youths were under pressure from both their fathers and farmers to work long and hard on the land. With tenants allowed ever decreasing access to land and cattle the only thing some youths could see in the future was more hard work for no reward. Faced with this prospect many youths left the farms against the wishes of both their fathers and the farmers and headed for the cities. Many white farmers and bywoner families also found that they were no longer wanted or could no longer survive on the land in more competitive times which encouraged more intensive forms of farming.

In 1936, according to the official population census of that year, the urban population numbered more than 3 million and comprised 31 per cent of the total population. Johannesburg, the largest city, had 519 000 inhabitants: 258 000 whites, 229 000 Africans, 22 000 coloureds and 10 000 Asians.

The government tried to limit the flow of Africans to the cities by implementing pass laws. African males were not supposed to leave farms or reserves without a pass signed by a white official or farmer, and when they reached urban areas they had to report to an official within 24 hours and obtain a permit to seek work which was valid for six days. If this permit could not be produced on demand from an official or policeman these Africans would be jailed or expelled from the town. Part of the reason for these regulations was to prevent Africans living in town except as labourers for whites. The pass laws resulted in many otherwise law-abiding individuals ending up in court and in prison. In 1930 some 42 000 Africans were convicted for pass law offences in the Transvaal alone. Between 1921 and 1936 the number of urban Africans trebled, rising from about half a million to just over one and a half million. In 1937 the pass laws were made even stricter, but despite these harsh measures the African population in the towns continued to increase.

Life in the city

The 1923 Native (Urban Areas) Act set out a framework for urban segregation but the process of turning this model into reality was slow and uneven. Nonetheless, separate black locations were developed and extended. By 1930, for example, the Johannesburg Council had bought a portion of the Klipspruit farm and began to build houses. The new township was named Orlando after one of the councillors. It was the start of what eventually became the sprawling and famous township of Soweto.

▼ Source A
An official commented in 1932

We are building the township for the better class of Native, who has a sense of beauty and proportion. This will undoubtedly be somewhat of a paradise which will enhance the status of the Bantu.

(From: *Umteteli wa Bantu.* 30 January 1932.)

▼ *Source B* Modern Orlando

▼ *Source C*

A different view of Orlando is provided by the commentary from a film about the history of Soweto

The houses were built cheaply and had neither floor nor ceiling, no water tap, no electric lights, no parks, no sports grounds, no banks. All shopping had to be done in Johannesburg. Public transport was especially inadequate and very expensive. People would now have to spend a quarter of their salary getting to work. Not surprisingly most people did not want to move from the city centre. Orlando represented loneliness and exile.

(From: *Soweto: A History.*)

Activities

1 a What are the different attitudes expressed in Source A and Source C?
  b Why do you think there is this difference?
2 a Describe what Source B shows you of modern Orlando.
  b Do you think it is more like the description in Source A or Source C?

The attitudes in Source C, combined with a rapid growth in the urban population and slow delivery of houses in the new location, ensured that thousands preferred to move into the freehold areas such as Alexandria and Sophiatown, and the inner city slum yards like Doornfontein remained densely inhabited.

◄ *Source D*
Doornfontein in the 1930s
(From: E Hellman.
Rooiyard.)

Doornfontein had originally been a middle class white suburb, but most of the whites living there moved north to Parktown. The large stands were divided up and sold. The people who bought these smaller stands wanted to make as much money as possible. So they packed the stands with cheap tin shacks and rented them out to the poor.

▼ *Source E*

Historian Luli Callinicos describes conditions in the yards which gives us some idea of what life must have been like for the people

> *The yards were crowded with boxes, bins and pails that did not fit into the small rooms. All the cooking was done outside and there were always large packing cases piled up next to the braziers for use as fire wood. Two garbage tins served all the people [which] were constantly overflowing attracting many flies. The unhealthy surroundings were made worse by the fact that there were only six lavatories ... to serve the whole yard. These were so neglected and overused that the children avoided them and used the alley-way instead ...*
>
> *The interiors of the greater numbers of the rooms created a striking contrast ... The walls were well scrubbed and the belongings of the family tidily arranged. This cleanliness was achieved by the constant preoccupation of the women with washing, polishing and dusting.*

(From: *Working Life*.)

Activities

1 What do Sources D and E tell you about life in Doornfontein in the 1930s?
2 Why do you think people chose to live there?

In 1933 the Johannesburg Town Council declared the city to be a white area. All blacks without special permission had to move out of town, either into municipal hostels that provided for single migrant workers, or to locations. In 1934 the Slums Act was passed which gave the Council the power to demolish slums and one by one the slum yards were cleared and the buildings demolished. As more and more people were forced out of the yards the freehold townships like Sophiatown became full to bursting and Orlando started to fill up. By 1937 the manager of the Native Affairs Department was pleased to report: 'The resistance of the natives to slum clearance has almost disappeared. Four years ago not more than 12 per cent of those removed from the slum areas actually took up residence in the locations and the hostels. The figure is now over 90 per cent.'

As the housing shortage intensified, getting a house in a location became increasingly difficult.

Women in the city

One of the most important features of the movement to the cities was that it included increasing numbers of women. For example, in Johannesburg in 1927 there had only been one African woman to every six African men. By 1939 the proportion was one to three. In twelve years the number of urban women had doubled. This made for a more settled population – more men found partners in town and did not return to rural areas and more families were formed in the cities. These developments increased the number of people who saw themselves as permanently based in town and not just temporary residents there.

However, in the 1930s most African women in the towns were newcomers who had grown up in the countryside but had to leave because of poverty. Women went to town to try to find work, to escape harsh conditions on white farms or to find their husbands who had stopped supporting them. Some of these women found work in factories or in white households as domestics. Many survived outside of formal employment. They took in washing, made or repaired clothes, sold fruit or vetkoek, but probably the most single profitable activity was beer brewing. Large numbers of single men in town meant that there was a large market for beer. While some men wanted traditional beer which had little alcohol in it, others wanted more powerful potions and brewers added a range of substances including methylated spirits to give their brew a 'kick'. In a good week in the 1930s, a woman could earn R2, which in those days was the same as the wage earned by a male worker. However, they also ran considerable risks. Brewing and selling liquor was against the law and there were regular police raids during which women were arrested and stocks of beer destroyed.

Not only African women came to town in large numbers. In the 1930s many of the factory workers were white women and the majority of these women were young Afrikaners who, like their African counterparts, had grown up in the countryside. By the 1920s around 12 000 Afrikaners were leaving the land every year. Often daughters went first. African communities were very reluctant to allow women to go to town because their labour provided the backbone of the rural economy. Afrikaner women, however, did not work on the land and could be more easily spared.

▼ *Source F*

Hester Cornelius, a union organiser, wrote

What sometimes breaks my heart is to see little girls of scarcely 16 years old and sometimes 15 coming from the farms, in possession of a letter from the parents to please look after Aletta: that they had to allow her to be uprooted because there is no other future for their little girls: also a testimonial from the school principal who reports that Aletta cannot continue her education because her parents are in great need, they are only bywoners and have another six or seven children to care for.

(From: Luli Callinicos. *Working Life*.)

Because women were paid relatively low wages, white women were often able to find jobs more easily than their menfolk. They – like African migrant workers – sent money home to support their struggling families in the countryside. The income of young Afrikaner women also often played a vital role in supporting their parents and siblings after they had moved to the city.

▼ *Source G*

Hester Cornelius again provides a description of their lives

We were four garment workers, who had to live together in Vrededorp. All four of us earning very little because the wages were R1.75 a week ... Our little room was in a backyard and was so small that we could not move. All the furnishing that we had was a single bed, a small table and a few soap boxes for chairs ... We had two blankets which we had brought with us from the farm. Our sheets were made from mielie bags which we joined together and which we washed every Saturday ... The hardest time was in winter. Each of us had to have a coat, so we had to cut down on our food. For months we ate only bread and jam ... So it continued until one of us became seriously ill. The doctor diagnosed malnutrition ...

(From: Luli Callinicos. *Working Life*.)

Activities

1 In small groups discuss what life must have been like for these Afrikaner women. Use the evidence in Sources F and G to help you.
2 Write a few paragraphs in which you imagine that you are a young woman who has just moved to the city. Explain why you moved to the city and describe your life and the work that you do. Also think about what you would do for pleasure.

By the early 1930s there were also hundreds of white families living in the slums. From the late 1930s the Johannesburg municipality started to build sub-economic housing on the sites of the demolished inner city slums and two hostels for white women workers were established in the early 1940s. The hostels and houses provided for whites were of a slightly higher standard than those provided for blacks, but perhaps the most important difference was that white housing was close to the shops, services and employment, while black locations were usually situated far away from such facilities.

Whites living in a shack

Fusion and segregation

Unit outcomes

- Discuss the effects that the United Party had on segregation.
- Explain the reasons for the emergence of the Purified National Party.
- Evaluate the significance of the Afrikaner Broederbond in South Africa in the 1930s.

The formation of the United Party

As we have seen, the Great Depression and National Party's attempt to remain on the gold standard caused a political crisis which was only resolved when the National Party and the South African Party formed a coalition government in 1933. At the end of the year the two parties merged and formed the United Party of South Africa, which had a big majority of seats in parliament.

The more extreme nationalists in the SAP, especially those from Natal, held the view that fusion would undermine South Africa's relationship with Britain and the Commonwealth. This group, led by Colonel Stallard, formed the Dominion Party in 1934.

There were two main issues which were difficult to resolve in the discussion around the formation of the United Party. The first was South Africa's role and rights in the British Commonwealth. Smuts placed a higher value than Hertzog on continuing ties with the British Empire, and believed that in the event of war South Africa had to fight alongside Britain. The second was Hertzog's determination to do away with the franchise for Africans in the Cape. Both issues were left largely unresolved for future negotiations.

The question of the vote for Africans was, however, rapidly placed on the agenda by Hertzog. With the new United Party controlling a vast majority of seats in parliament he reintroduced legislation to further reduce the significance of the Cape franchise and was able to get the two-thirds majority he needed to change the constitution. A joint sitting of both Houses in 1936 produced a vote of 168 to 11 in favour of the Native Representatives Bill. This legislation removed Africans from a common voters roll in the Cape. Cape Africans would continue to vote as individuals for the House of Assembly, but in future they would do so on a separate voters roll for three white members to represent their interests. Africans elsewhere in South Africa would be able to vote for three white members of senate to represent them and an effectively powerless native representative council was set up as a forum for debate and consultation. While there was considerable opposition to this Bill outside of parliament – which we will discuss later – the overwhelming majority within the House of Assembly demonstrates the extent of support within white society for political segregation.

The Hertzog government had already done much to destroy the effectiveness of the African vote. In 1930 it gave white women the vote thereby reducing the African electorate from 3,1 to 1,4 per cent of the total. It liberated white adult males in the Cape and Natal from the property and income test in 1931 and thereby added another 10 000 to the voters' roll. The African vote was therefore numerically insignificant.

Placing of Africans on a separate voters roll provided a powerful symbol of the fact that Africans should not think of themselves as participating in a common political system.

Activities ·······························

Write a paragraph giving your view of the significance of the Native Representatives Bill.
···

Native Trust and Land Bill

Together with the 1936 Native Representatives Bill, the Native Trust and Land Bill set out to entrench territorial segregation. It allocated a further 702 million morgen to be added to the 1 004 million morgen already reserved for Africans under the 1913 Land Act. The total area allocated to Africans now reached 13 per cent of the land within South Africa. The additional land was to be purchased by the state on behalf of Africans. The state did not plan simply to hand land over to the African communities. In line with the recommendations of the Native Economic Commission it intended to exercise close control over the land to make sure that it was used 'scientifically' and that measures were taken to prevent overstocking and soil erosion. From 1939 'Betterment' policies were pursued on trust land which involved separating agricultural and **arable land**, **culling** livestock and enforcing concentrated 'village' patterns of settlement. These schemes changed over the years and affected different communities in different ways but they set out a programme of massive state intervention in rural society and sparked off bitter resistance in many areas.

The passage of these two Bills represented a key moment in the history of segregation in South Africa, but the broad agreement within white society on the outlines of 'native' policy did not last for very long.

New words

arable land land that can be used for growing crops
culling reducing numbers by shooting or forced sale

Activities

1 In what ways did the content and implementation of the Native Trust and Land Act reflect the thinking of the Native Economic Commission?
2 Hertzog and some other politicians argued that the additional land that was provided more than compensated Africans for the loss of franchise.
   a Do you think that Sources A and B below agree with this view? Give reasons for your answer.
   b Do you think that it is true that many Africans were more concerned with land than the vote?
   c Do you think that land was adequate or appropriate compensation for the loss of the franchise?

▼ Source A
Chief Maitse Moloi sent a telegram to General Hertzog

Message from the Transvaal and Free State Chiefs. Away with the Franchise. Give us land.

▼ Source B
Another leading chief from the Transvaal, Chief Sekhukhune, commented

It is considered in the interests of the natives that the bills should go through and thus additional land made available but the Cape vote should not be taken away and the Transvaal natives should be allowed to send representatives to parliament.

The emergence of the Purified National Party

Fusion saw an increase in agreement within white politics, but it also brought about the deepening of divisions amongst Afrikaner nationalists and led to the emergence of a new party – The Gesuiwerde (Purified) National Party. Although this started as a small movement, within fifteen years the Purified Nationalists became the government of South Africa, and started building the apartheid system.

A group within the National Party, mainly based in the Cape and led by Dr DF Malan, could not accept a coalition government with Smuts and broke away. In 1935 this group held only nineteen seats in the House of Assembly. This split was partly caused by differing interpretations of Afrikaner nationalism.

The focus of Hertzog's nationalism was gaining language equality for Afrikaners and the constitutional independence of South Africa from Britain. His definition of an Afrikaner was a broad one – including loyal English-speaking whites who accepted language equality. A strong sense of white South African interests affected his economic and political policies and his version of nationalism.

© South African Library

▲ DF Malan

DF Malan and his followers had a more narrow version of Afrikaner nationalism which emphasised the uniqueness of Afrikaner culture and of Afrikaners as a group. They saw, as a priority, legal equality for Afrikaners and also an improvement of the social and material circumstances of Afrikaners as a distinct nation within South Africa. The Purified Nationalists argued that entering the United Party would weaken the struggle for Afrikaner rights and advancement. They feared that coalition would prevent the establishment of an independent republic.

The Broederbond

These objectives were not only pursued by the Purified National Party but also by a wider grouping of political, cultural and economic organisations. The most important of these was the Afrikaner Broederbond. Originally formed as a cultural organisation with a membership of clerks, teachers and dominees it operated in strict secrecy. Potential members were carefully investigated before they were accepted. A member had to be a regular churchgoer and his children had to attend an Afrikaans medium school. In the 1930s the Broederbond managed to gain a firm foothold in almost all the country's cultural, political and economic activities. It sided with Malan and the Purified Nationalists in the dispute about fusion, and the two groupings became very closely linked. By 1933 Malan had joined the Broederbond.

One of the main goals of the Broederbond was to make sure that class divisions did not prevent Afrikaners from seeing themselves as part of one united nation or volk. As we have seen, Afrikaners were deeply divided along economic lines. While some had managed to stay on the land and a few had grown rich as farmers, many more had been forced to move to the cities and become workers, or had joined the ranks of poor whites. In the towns and cities some Afrikaners, who had received a better education, had managed to get better jobs as teachers, lawyers and civil servants and formed a growing middle class. Relatively few Afrikaners, however, had become successful businessmen. The business world remained dominated by English-speaking people. The Broederbond argued that divisions between Afrikaners were the result of imperialism and exploitation by foreigners and they aimed to restore the unity of the volk.

In order to work towards improving the economic position of Afrikaners and to challenge the dominance in business of English speakers the Broederbond played a central role in the 'economic movement'. This involved using Afrikaner resources and savings – particularly the funds accumulated by the more prosperous farmers – to build new enterprises. In 1934, for example, a 'people's bank', Volkskas – was started in Pretoria which grew to be one of the largest banking groups in the country. Possibly the greatest achievement of the economic movement was the collaboration between the life insurance company Sanlam and the Broederbond, which began in 1937. This brought considerable benefits to both organisations and helped Sanlam become a leading financial institution.

The Broederbond also kept a close watch on developments in the trade union movement. It saw the growth of class rather than national consciousness as a major threat to Afrikaner unity. Organisations like trade unions and the Labour Party, which were active amongst Afrikaners on the basis that they were workers whose main interests lay in joining together with other workers, whatever their language and culture, were seen as hostile groups whose power had to be broken to protect the 'volk'. The 'Nasionale Raad van Trustees' was formed to promote a new Afrikaner unionism which promoted Christian National principles, resisted socialist ideas and sought to keep blacks out of 'white' jobs. The Spoorbond Union of Railwaymen formed in 1934 by the first chairman of the Broederbond – Henning Klopper – was the most successful of these new unions and drove the National Union of Railway and Harbour Servants out of business in 1937. Beyond this, Afrikaner unions had very

▲ *Source C* The Great Trek centenary celebration

little success in these years and did not manage to draw many Afrikaner members away from the established unions.

Another event in which the Broederbond played a significant part were the Great Trek centenary celebrations in 1938 which centred on a symbolic ox-wagon trek from Cape Town to the newly completed Voortrekker Monument in Pretoria. At every town where they stayed the night, these trekkers received a warm reception organised by the town's dominees and members of the Broederbond, and the slow progress of the wagons played a part in a growing Afrikaner consciousness. Thousands of men grew bushy Voortrekker beards while women were seen in traditional Voortrekker dresses.

While the Purified National Party was closely connected to the celebrations, Hertzog and the United Party were marginalised. When the trekkers reached the Voortrekker Monument DF Malan, not Hertzog, made the keynote speech. He told a crowd of some 250 000 that just as 'the muzzleload had clashed with the assegai at Blood River to preserve the interests of the whites, now too it was the duty of Afrikaners to make South Africa a white man's land'.

In this atmosphere of heightened nationalism support for the Purified Nationalists grew although the political loyalties of Afrikaans-speaking people remained divided. Many stayed in the United Party and the Purified Nationalists were still far from securing a parliamentary majority when the Second World War broke out in 1939.

Activities

1 Write a paragraph describing the development of Afrikaner nationalism between 1934 and 1939.
2 How did the Purified Nationalists' version of Afrikaner nationalism differ from that of Hertzog and his supporters?
3 Imagine you are a young Afrikaner, man or woman, living in a town visited by the centenary trek in 1938 shown in Source C. What do you think and feel when the ox-wagons arrive?
4 Imagine that you are one of the people on the centenary trek.
  a Why have you joined this celebration?
  b Describe the reception that you receive at each new town.

Unit 10

Resistance in the 1930s

Unit outcomes

- Identify the reasons for the decline of the ANC and the Communist Party.
- Debate the effectiveness of the All-African Convention's resistance to the government's policies.

Introduction

The 1930s brought an increase in segregation and a further reduction in political rights for Africans. It would not therefore have been surprising if this had been a decade of bitter resistance to white rule. In fact, in comparison to the 1920s, the 1930s proved to be relatively tranquil. Part of the reason for this was that opposition outside parliament was in chaos.

The ANC and the Communist Party

As we have seen, the ICU had collapsed as a national movement by the end of the 1920s. After the election of Josiah Gumede the ANC appeared about to embark on more radical policies and tactics and started to work more closely with the Communist Party. But Gumede faced increasing opposition from more conservative elements within congress and in 1930 the ANC executive resigned in protest against his policies. Gumede was challenged for the leadership by Pixley Seme and the contest was played out at the ANC conference in April 1930. Gumede restated his support for working with the communists arguing that the ANC's demands were too mild and that its appeal for justice to Britain had brought no results. He argued: 'let us go back from this conference resolved to adopt a militant policy which will bring us liberation. This is the quickest, effective, most logical and least expensive road to emancipation.'

Seme, however, warned the delegates against the 'humbug of communism'. He and his supporters argued that only the ANC should be allowed to make political demands on behalf of Africans. They also insisted that what Africans wanted was not communism or socialism, but equal opportunities and a fair chance to participate within the current economic and political system. Seme and his followers also rejected mass action. Their chosen weapons remained persuasion, moral force and consultation.

Seme won by 39 votes to 14. Under his leadership, however, the ANC entered a long period of decline. Internal divisions continued, and the ANC's concern with winning the support of chiefs and protecting the interests of a small African elite, caused their popular support to decline.

The Communist Party also entered a period of decline in the 1930s. Policy shifts partly determined by changes in Moscow caused conflicts in the Communist Party. In 1928, as we have seen, the party adopted the 'Native Republic' slogan which ushered in a period of closer cooperation with the ANC. In 1930, convinced that the Great Depression was the start of the worldwide collapse of capitalism, the Communist International called for the withdrawal of all Communist Parties from any association with 'reformist' organisations and the launching of revolutionary campaigns. Despite some doubts about whether a revolutionary situation really existed in South Africa, the Communist Party obeyed these instructions and, in isolation, launched strikes and pass burning campaigns which proved to be damaging failures. Then from 1933, confronted by the rise of the Nazi Party in Germany, the Communist International urged alliances with reformist and anti-Fascist groups.

These twists and turns in policy and practice increased divisions in the party. Some people argued that if it emphasised black nationalism the party ran the risk of substituting race war for class war. They feared the party would lose support amongst white workers. Others argued that the party was too dependent on instructions from Moscow, and others wanted to restructure the party into small, highly disciplined revolutionary cells. These – often bitter – debates led to many leading members being expelled from the Communist Party and little attention being paid to organisational work. Membership dwindled and the party which had 1 750 members in 1928 had been reduced to only 280 members by 1940

Hertzog's 'Native' Bills and the All-African Convention

As a result of these developments, neither the ANC nor the Communist Party were in a position to lead effective resistance to Hertzog's 'Native' Bills. When Hertzog announced in 1935 that a special sitting of parliament would be held in 1936 to consider the Bills, there was widespread concern amongst middle class Africans. The newspaper *Bantu World* called for a national convention of Africans to consider how best to resist. On 16 December 1935 four hundred delegates from all over South Africa and representing a wide range of organisations, gathered in Bloemfontein for the founding conference of the All-African Convention (AAC). Professor Davidson Jabavu and Dr Alfred Xuma were elected as president and vice-president respectively. This new organisation echoed many of the positions and tactics of the ANC. Although the convention condemned the proposed Bills most delegates stressed their loyalty to the British crown and called on the British parliament to intervene on their behalf. They also accepted the idea of 'civilisation tests' and a qualified franchise for Africans. Calls by communists and other radical delegates for militant action to reinforce opposition to the Bills were firmly rejected by the leaders. Instead, apart from protest meetings throughout the country, the AAC's plan of action was based mainly on prayer meetings, appeals, petitions and meetings with government authorities.

Despite these efforts the Bills were passed with a massive majority in parliament in April 1936. The AAC met in June of that year to decide its next step. Two choices were debated by delegates. One strategy was to boycott the new Natives Representatives Council and the white MPs elected to represent Africans. The other approach was to use the new system to try and win more **concessions**. Jabavu argued that a boycott would probably fail, and urged delegates to accept a policy of participation under protest. This view won overwhelming support amongst the delegates.

New words

concession something given in response to arguments and/or demands

Activities

Divide the class into two groups. One group should argue in support of the position of the leaders of the AAC rejecting militant action. The other group should argue in favour of mass action – including strikes and demonstrations.

Unit 11 South Africa and the Second World War

Unit outcomes

- Discuss the debate surrounding South Africa's entry into the Second World War.
- Analyse the impact of the Second World War on South Africa's economy.
- Study the growth of the squatter communities as people continued to move to the cities.

The outbreak of war

On Sunday 3 September 1939 Britain declared war on Germany. This decision was to send shock waves through faraway South Africa and reshape the pattern of white politics.

The unity which Hertzog and Smuts had achieved through fusion and the formation of the United Party did not survive the outbreak of war. Hertzog summoned his cabinet to discuss how to respond. He argued that South Africa should remain neutral but he was unable to persuade a majority of the ministers to support him. The issue was then debated in parliament. Hertzog argued that to enter the war with the white population divided would undo the unity which had been achieved in the previous six years. He argued that it was in the country's best interests to remain neutral and pointed to the example of Ireland which had decided to remain neutral. He went still further in his argument – and offended a number of members of parliament – when he compared Hitler's efforts to achieve German liberty with his own struggles on behalf of Afrikaners.

Smuts agreed that South Africa could legally refuse to fight. He also argued that it would be in the country's best interests to enter the war, that South Africa could not survive alone and that it would be impossible to combine neutrality with maintaining South Africa's formal obligations to Britain and the Commonwealth. When the votes came, Hertzog's position was defeated by 80 votes to 67. Hertzog demanded that a general election should be called but the governor general refused and invited Smuts to form a government. Smuts became prime minister with the support of the sections of the United Party which supported entering the war and the Labour and Dominion Parties who had also agreed to support Britain.

At first it seemed that a common opposition to the war would lead to reconciliation between Hertzog and the Purified National Party led by Dr Malan. Encouraged by Hitler's early successes in the war, some of Malan's followers adopted anti-Semitic slogans and demanded that Afrikaans should be the only medium of instruction in educational institutions. Shaken by this turn of events Hertzog retired from public life and died in early 1942.

Activities

1 What were the main points of disagreement between Smuts and Hertzog in terms of their response to Britain's declaration of war against Germany?
2 Did they have any points of agreement?

New words

conscription force people by law to serve in the armed forces
enlist enter the armed forces
relegate reduce to a lower rank or task

Recruitment and combat

The deep divisions amongst white South Africans over the war ensured that there was no programme of compulsory **conscription** into the armed services. More than two million South Africans volunteered for service in the Second World War, including 120 000 blacks. Many black South Africans were hostile to the anti-democratic and racist elements within Nazism, and were also well aware that the strongest supporters of Germany in South Africa were also the most strident supporters of segregation. The African National Congress declared that the government was correct in going to war in support of Britain. There were also intensive recruitment drives amongst Africans – especially in the rural areas – and there is evidence which suggests that some officials and chiefs placed heavy pressure on their subjects to **enlist**. Many men were led to believe that they would get substantial rewards. As one man recalled: 'I believed that I would get something splendid because I was fighting for the government'. A common belief was that soldiers would be rewarded for their services with land grants.

◀ **Source A**
The Sixth South African
Armoured Transport
Division in Italy during the
war
(From: *Die Burger*.)

While African recruits were sought after by the defence force they were generally not armed and used as fighting troops. Instead they were used in a variety of non-combatant roles such as driving, digging trenches, cooking and carrying the wounded. Despite being **relegated** to these roles many black recruits performed outstanding feats of courage under enemy fire.

South African troops fought in East Africa, Madagascar, North Africa and Italy. The East African campaign was largely a South African effort. South African forces were also heavily involved in the North African campaign. Two divisions sent to Egypt as part of the British Eighth Army, saw action in the major battles of 1941 and 1942. There were 10 000 South Africans in the forces that were trapped by the German General Rommel at Tobruk. Many of them spent the rest of the war in German prisoner of war camps. Many South Africans also served – and died – under Field Marshall Montgomery at the Battle of Alamein where the Eighth Army stopped Rommels' drive to capture Egypt.

Activities

1 Carefully study Sources A and B and describe what you see in each of the photographs.
2 Who are the people in the foreground in Source A, and where do you think they are going?
3 a What are the soldiers in Source B doing?
  b What is the mood of Source B?

◀ **Source B**
Field Marshal Smuts
visiting troops in the
desert, North Africa
(From: United Party
Archives, Unisa.)

Army Service and a growing awareness of the atrocities committed by the Nazis had important influences on the thinking of servicemen. Some white soldiers returned to South Africa convinced that racism was wrong. Both the Springbok Legions and the Torch Commando which were formed after the war were partly inspired by this realisation. Many black servicemen were struck by the fact that South Africa claimed to be fighting for democracy and against racism while the majority of its own citizens were denied political rights and were discriminated against in numerous ways. Growing awareness of this contradiction also contributed to post-war political organisation. Many African servicemen were outraged at the very small rewards they received when they were discharged from the army. Instead of getting 'something wonderful' – particularly the hoped-for grants of land – Africans got two pounds sterling, some khaki clothes and/or a bicycle. Anger at these paltry payments fed into post-war protest.

War economy and society

The war helped bring about a boom in the South African economy which lasted until 1945. A war industry was established to produce a considerable proportion of the Defence Force's requirements for arms and this stimulated training, research and investment. The outbreak of war also led to the end of the flow of imported manufactured goods from Europe, particularly from Britain and this stimulated the local manufacturing industry as factories were set up to produce goods that had previously been imported.

These developments considerably expanded the demand for labour. One result was the opening of opportunities to new groups of workers. For example, many white women found jobs in the **munitions industry** while many black women entered factories for the first time, and the growth of manufacturing considerably increased the opportunities for male black workers to find employment in secondary industry. This rapidly expanding demand for workers resulted in the movement from the countryside to the towns gathering momentum. Growing landlessness in the reserve areas and further reductions in the amount of land and the number of cattle tenants were allowed to keep on white farms also contributed to this movement along with a series of crippling droughts which gripped the countryside.

Another factor which encouraged the large-scale movement of people to the towns was that, under pressure from the manufacturing and construction industry, which wanted more workers, the government relaxed influx controls and began debating the possibility of revising the pass laws. The higher demand for labour also resulted in higher wages for workers.

During the decade which ended in 1946 the black urban population of South Africa nearly doubled. Of vital importance were the relatively large number of women and even whole families that were part of this process. For them to move to the towns was not a temporary measure but a long-term strategy and they contributed to a rapidly growing, settled urban population.

However, despite the demand for labour and the relatively high wages, conditions in the cities were hard for many who lived there. Rents, along with the cost of food and transport, rose even faster than wages in the war years. The shortage of black housing became acute.

New words

munitions industry factories that make arms and ammunition

Squatter movements

From 1944 onwards vast squatter camps grew up on the outskirts of Johannesburg and, to a lesser extent, on the edges of other major cities. In Johannesburg, during the war years, very few houses had been built for blacks. Faced with a major housing crisis, the city council began to issue more and more permits to allow householders to take in subtenants. This was a short-term solution which led to more and more people crowding into the existing locations which did not have the facilities to cope with such a rapidly growing population. For example, Pimville – which is now part of Soweto – had only 63 water taps for 15 000 people. In March 1944 thousands of people, tired of waiting for houses began setting up homes on vacant land.

One of the main squatter leaders was James Mpanza, who founded the Sofasonke Party and established a settlement on open land near Orlando where the dwellings were made from hessian sacks and which became widely known as Masakeng – the place of sacks. By the end of April 1944, eight thousand people had streamed in and by the end of 1946 its population had risen to twenty thousand.

Mpanza had an eventful past. He had been a court interpreter in his younger days but then he had been sentenced to death for the murder of an Indian trader. He was reprieved at the last moment, converted to Christianity and late released. The way in which Mpanza presented himself as a squatter leader drew both on biblical imagery and forms of chieftainship. For example, he likened the position of the homeless to the 'children of Israel' and compared himself to Moses, leading his people across the River Jordan to the chosen site. 'The position of chieftainship is given to me, like Jesus,' he said.

Mpanza and his Sofasonke Party was only one of a number of movements which emerged in this period. The leadership of the camps, sometimes individuals, sometimes committees, established their own systems of administration and policing. They charged the inhabitants taxes and controlled trading in the camps.

The municipal authorities were horrified by this new development. Appeals were made to the central authorities to break up the camps but the government hesitated, which gave the squatters time to consolidate their positions. Even when the shacks of smaller settlements were demolished squatters simply moved to other pieces of ground. The Pimville squatter leader,

Oriel Monongoaha commented: 'The government was like a man who had a corn field which is invaded by birds. He chased the birds from one part of the field and they alighted in another part ... we squatters are the birds.'

The massive process of urbanisation that took place in the war years stretched government resources, challenged existing segregationist policies and aggravated the fears of white workers over competition for jobs and living space in increasingly crowded cities. It also provided the elements for a new style of militant mass-based black politics. These developments would have a crucial impact on the history of South Africa in the post-war years.

Activities

What do you think was the most important effect of the Second World War on South Africa? Write a paragraph giving your view. Consider both the political and economic effects of the war when preparing your answer.

◀ Squatters erect dwellings in Mpanza's squatter camp called 'Sackville'

Unit 12 Resistance during and after the Second World War

C NOTES

Unit outcomes

- Describe the various forms which resistance took during and after the Second World War.
- Understand the reasons for the cooperation between the ANC and the Communist Party.
- Discuss the role played by trade unions and the campaign of passive resistance.
- Give reasons for the formation of the ANC Youth League in 1943.
- Understand the causes of the 1946 mine workers' strike.

Introduction

In Unit 11 we looked at some of the political consequences of the war. In this unit we will consider more fully the changing nature of resistance during and immediately after the war.

Rural struggles

In the early 1940s there were a number of episodes of resistance in rural areas – especially in the Transvaal. These events were shaped both by the recommendations put forward by the 1932 Native Economic Commission and by the impact of the 1936 Native Land and Trust Act.

From the late 1930s large areas of land were bought by the newly established South African Native Trust (SANT) to be added to the land reserved for Africans. Much of this land was situated in the Northern Transvaal and it was in this region that the most bitter struggles took place. It seems a little strange that buying more land for Africans should have caused resistance. How can we explain this?

One important fact was that much of the land that was bought was owned by land companies who did not farm the land but simply extracted rent from African communities who lived on the land. Many of these communities had long lived on the land with little outside interference and some believed that the land was theirs as a result of this long history of occupation. When the SANT took over these farms, however, it began to interfere with the ways in which people lived and worked on the land. This was partly because of policies shaped by the report of the Native Economic Commission. The SANT attempted to divide up and fence grazing, arable and residential areas. In order to do this people were told to move to new settlements. In this reorganisation many people also received much smaller plots than they had had previously. The most hated aspect of SANT control was cattle culling. Officials believed that there were many more cattle than the land could carry, and they forced communities to sell off – often at very low prices – many of their animals. This cluster of policies was often described as 'Betterment'. In the Zoutpansberg an organisation called Zoutpansberg Balemi Association led by Alpheus Malivha, a Venda migrant worker and member of the Communist Party, led resistance to these measures in the early 1940s. In the area around Pietersburg resistance also developed from 1940. Officials reported that tenants living on SANT farms had asserted that the 'land belonged to them and that they could plough where they like as much as they liked. They stated that the land belonged to them and their grandfathers and they can do what they like'.

Fences were cut, land designated as grazing land was ploughed and many people refused to move to new settlements. Slowly, however, the SANT re-established control by deporting leaders, punishing rebels and by rewarding those who cooperated with the new system. A feeling of bitterness remained in many rural areas, which was intensified when the government pushed ahead with Betterment policies at the end of the war.

The Communist Party

At the beginning of the war the Communist Party was close to collapse. At first it opposed South Africa's involvement in the war, but after Germany attacked Russia in 1941 the party put considerable energy into supporting the war effort. With lower levels of internal conflict, heightened political consciousness amongst Africans and growing respectability amongst whites as a result of Russia's brave battle against the German army, the party started to gather new recruits. Its membership rose from a mere 280 in 1940 to well over a thousand by 1943 and the majority of the new members were black.

This membership, though still small, had a considerable impact. Party policy was to ensure that members were well trained and highly active in both political and trade union organisation. The party also took up a number of issues which were problems for ordinary people in the townships. It got involved in bus boycotts, rent struggles and anti-pass campaigns. It also recruited a number of migrant workers into its ranks – like Alpheus Malivha, who played a key part in linking urban and rural struggles.

Above all, the party in this period encouraged its members to join the ANC and to help build it as the main organisation of the African people. In the words of Elias Motsoaledi, 'the Party encouraged us to join the national liberation movement to give it a progressive outlook and lead it – to make it the mass movement it is supposed to be'.

This strategy was consistent with the decision taken in 1928 to work for a Native Republic of South Africa as the first of two stages towards socialism. Many years later Motsoaledi recalled that,

> as a result of education by the Party, I understood the long term programme of the Party and the short term programme of the ANC – then I came to understand the alliance – that when we achieve liberation the ANC struggle ceases and there is a continuation now with the class struggle.

Leading communists like JB Marks, Moses Kotane and Dan Tloome, put considerable energy into building the ANC as did many ordinary members. Rusty Bernstein, who was active in the party in the 1940s, later reflected: 'we made a really important organisational contribution to the ANC and gave them what they lacked, which was an organised, disciplined core'.

◀ JB Marks

◀ Moses Kotane

© E Weinberg

◀ Dan Tloome

© Inkululeku, 1947

Activities

1 Why was there an increase in rural resistance in the 1940s?
2 Do you agree that the Communist Party 'made a really important organisational contribution to the ANC'?

Trade unions

Trade unions for black workers also underwent a period of growth during the Second World War. After the Great Depression communists such as Gana Makabeni and socialists such as Max Gordon helped revive trade unions in the service and small industry sector. Attempts to organise Indian workers in Natal, from the late 1930s, were particularly successful. By the end of the war the Council for Non-European Trade Unions, which was formed in 1941, claimed 119 affiliates with 150 000 members and there was a marked increase in the number of strikes. While in 1940 there were 23 strikes, and these mainly involved white workers, in 1945 there were 63 strikes and these mainly involved black workers. The most dramatic example of trade union organisation and action in the years was the mine workers' strike of 1946.

New words

initiative take the lead in doing something

Mine workers, isolated in compounds and divided along ethnic lines, proved a difficult challenge for union organisers. In 1941 a new attempt was made to mobilise mine workers, largely at the **initiative** of the Communist Party. The African Mine Workers Union (AMWU) was formed under the leadership of JB Marks. In the war years, prices started to rise rapidly and many products – including foodstuffs – were in short supply. These food shortages affected the mines, where compound managers reduced the amount of meat miners received. To make matters worse, in 1942 it was announced that because mine workers were migrant workers, they would not get cost-of-living increases to help compensate for rising prices. The justification for this decision was that migrant families were able to support themselves through farming in the reserves. But in fact, as we have seen, the reserves' capacity to support migrant families effectively, had been undermined many years previously and it diminished even further in the 1940s. In 1944 the Lansdown Commission, established by the government to look into conditions on the mines, reported that the 'reserves are overpopulated and overstocked; they do not produce sufficient for the population to live on: their productive capacity is decreasing and the general health of the Reserve population is far from satisfactory'.

The declining value of their wages and the deteriorating conditions in the reserves angered many mine workers and encouraged them to join the new union. At the start of 1946 AMWU held a general meeting attended by about 2 000 members who drew up a list of demands which included a call for workers to receive payment of ten shillings a day. The Chamber of Mines failed to respond and on 12 August 1946, 50 000 workers stayed in their compounds. In all, 73 000 workers were involved and production stopped completely on ten mines and was seriously affected on many others.

Many factors were against the strikers. The mine owners and the government acted ruthlessly to crush the strike. The police opened fire on some strikers and beat others with batons, while compounds were sealed off under armed guard. The leadership of the union was arrested and tried under war regulations. The national executive of the Communist Party was charged with sedition (agitation against the state). Within a week the strike was over without any of the demands of the strikers having been met. AMWU was broken and it would be another 30 years before black mine workers were organised into a union once more.

Passive resistance

On 13 June 1946, Indian shops throughout South Africa were closed and Indian workers and hawkers stayed at home. In Durban, after a mass meeting of 15 000 people, a group marched to the corner of Umbilo Road and Gale Street. They pitched tents on the vacant pieces of municipal ground and proceeded to occupy it. Then they waited to be arrested. This episode was the start of a campaign of passive resistance, led by the Natal Indian Congress (NIC) and the Transvaal Indian Congress (TIC). This strategy drew some of its inspiration from the passive resistance campaign led by Mohandas Gandhi early in the century. Why did members of the Indian community feel that it was appropriate to embark on this kind of campaign in 1946?

▲ *Source A* A public meeting held in Durban in 1946

In 1943 the Smuts government passed a law which helped to both radicalise and unify Indian political activity. In order to win the support of whites at a time when a general election was due, the Trading and Occupation of Land Restriction Bill was introduced. This became known as the 'Pegging Act' because it was designed to 'peg' (stop) Indians from buying land from whites or settling in new areas in either the Transvaal or Natal for a period of three years. This Act affected both the middle classes and workers. Well-off members of the community were prevented from investing in property while workers faced being trapped in already desperately overcrowded slums. In 1946 parliament passed an Act which made the measure permanent and the passive resistance campaign was launched in response.

Dr TM Dadoo, Dr GM Naicker and The Rev Michael Scott were among the thousands who offered themselves for arrest as part of the campaign. The Indian community also sent a delegation to the United Nations organisation and the first of many resolutions condemning South African race policies was passed. The government of India broke off diplomatic relations with South Africa over this issue. The Smuts government simply ignored these diplomatic setbacks and as the resistance campaign dragged on without any clear results many people became discouraged and the campaign lost momentum. The resistors were not successful in getting the legislation repealed (withdrawn). Their actions impressed on the ANC leadership the need for militant strategy, and opened the way for cooperation between the ANC and the TIC and NIC. This relationship was formalised in the 'Doctors Pact' between Dr Xuma of the ANC, Dr Dadoo of the TIC and Dr Naicker of the NIC in 1947.

Activities ....

1 What specific grievance led to the public meeting shown in Source A?

2 What evidence does Source A provide that the general mood of those present was one of anger and defiance?

3 What actions does Source B call for from the Indian community?

....

The Ghetto Bill is now Law !

INDIANS!

THURSDAY, 13TH JUNE
IS
"RESISTANCE DAY"

....

The Joint Passive Resistance Council of the Natal and Transvaal Indian Congresses has declared THURSDAY, 13th JUNE, "Resistance Day," to mark the beginning of resistance against the Ghetto Act. The Indian community is expected to observe this day as a Day of Hartal.

All Indian businessmen are requested to close their shops, offices, factories and other businesses for the whole day on June 13th.

All Indian parents are requested NOT to send their children to school on this day.

All Indian workers, whose employers do not close their businesses, are asked to REMAIN AT WORK.

ATTEND
MASS MEETING
RED SQUARE - 5.30 P.M.
ON
"RESISTANCE DAY"

Square will be floodlit.   Seats provided for Ladies.

Issued by PASSIVE RESISTANCE COUNCIL of NATAL INDIAN CONGRESS

© SS Singh, Durban

ANC Youth League

The political and economic changes and the increase in popular struggles which took place in the war years persuaded many members of the ANC that new policy directions and leadership needed to be found. The election of Dr Alfred Xuma as president in 1940 had led to a restructuring of congress and greater levels of organisational drive. The pace of change was still too slow for a group of younger members including Peter Mda, Jordan Ngubane, Nelson Mandela, Walter Sisulu and Anton Lembede. Many of these men were relatively highly educated but they criticised the elitism of the ANC and insisted on the importance of building a mass-based membership and advocated a strategy of mass action: boycotts, strikes, civil disobedience and stayaways. In December of 1943 the annual conference of the ANC accepted the proposal to form a Congress Youth League. Membership was open to all Africans between the ages of 12 and 40. Anton Lembede – a 33-year-old lawyer was elected as its first president.

The Youth League spelled out an Africanist philosophy. Lembede, for example, wrote:

Africa is a black man's country ... Africans are the natives of Africa and they have inhabited Africa ... from time immemorial. Africa belongs to them ... Africans are one ... The basis of national unity is the nationalist feeling of the Africans ... irrespective of tribal connections, social status, educational attachment or social class.

The Youth League was hostile to cooperation with whites. Partly for this reason they were critical of the Communist Party. Walter Sisulu, later recalled: 'we tended to despise the blacks in the party. We felt that they were white led ... we felt that Africans should lead their own movement.' They also rejected the communists' emphasis on class divisions and struggles.

The 1948 Manifesto of the Youth League stated: 'here are certain groups which seek to impose on our struggle cut and dried formulae, which so far from clarifying the issues of our struggle, only serve to obscure the fundamental fact that we are oppressed, not as a class, but as a people, a nation'.

The division between the Communist Party and the Youth League was by no means absolute. Some Youth League members like David Bopape and Dan Tloome were also members of the Communist Party and some leading members of the League – such as Walter Sisulu – had by 1948 come to see value in an alliance with the party.

While the Congress Youth League did not itself develop a mass membership in this period, it did contribute to a growing emphasis within the ANC on mass politics and provided the training ground for a new generation of leaders. The 1949 Congress of the ANC saw the adoption of the League's Programme of Action and six of its members were elected to the national executive.

Activities . . . .
Use the text above to help you write a paragraph setting out what you consider the most important political ideas put forward by the Youth League.
. . . .

The National Party and the 1948 election ⌐ notes

Unit outcomes

- Analyse the factors which produced the defeat of the United Party in the 1948 general election.

Introduction

On 26 May 1948 South Africans went to the polls to vote in the first post-war general election. Smuts, who had consolidated his position as an international statesman during the war years anticipated he might lose some support but expected to retain power. Instead, a dramatic swing in support to the National Party saw the United Party lose its majority in parliament and Smuts lose his seat in the Standerton Constituency. What factors produced this remarkable and fateful result?

Build-up to the 1948 election

The victory of the National Party in 1948 was largely based on the additional support it gained in the farming districts of the Transvaal, the working class districts of the Witwatersrand and the lower middle class areas of Pretoria. By examining the difficulties confronting mainly Afrikaans-speaking white farmers and white workers during and after the war it is possible to gain some understanding of the swing in support from the United Party to the National Party.

Farmers had felt that they did not have sufficient workers as a result of the growing movement of Africans to the towns or at least into urban employment. In addition, farmers – and especially those who were less profitable – found they were getting lower prices for their products after the war. White workers' wages had remained static and in some cases declined during the war and the rapid expansion of African employment in secondary industry led many white workers to fear that they might lose their jobs to lower paid black workers. Afrikaans-speaking workers, in particular, were often clustered in the least skilled sections of the white workforce and felt especially vulnerable to being replaced. Their anxieties were increased by the **preferential treatment** given to the ex-servicemen – 106 000 of whom returned at the end of the war – in admission to apprenticeship and other forms of training for employment.

White workers also faced a housing crisis which had intensified in the war years and many white suburbs were flooded with African workers who sought places to stay in the back yards. There was also increasing concern about crime levels in many areas and this, along with higher levels of resistance – including strikes, marches and boycotts – led to the widespread belief amongst the white working and lower middle classes that law and order was breaking down and that white supremacy was under threat.

> **New words**
>
> **preferential treatment** special, better treatment

Fagan and Sauer reports

It was against this troubled backdrop that the National Party and the United Party developed policies which they believed could cope with the challenges posed in the wake of the Second World War. Two commissions helped spell out the competing visions of the future. One was set up by the UP and chaired by Justice Henry Fagan. The Fagan Commission Report rejected integration but also argued that complete segregation was totally impracticable. It argued that – partly because of the breakdown of economy and society in the reserves – the flow of Africans to the cities could not be reversed or halted and that measures should be taken which recognised the reality and contribution of a permanent urban African population. Fagan also maintained that a large pool of African labour in urban areas would help industry and commerce to ensure adequate supplies of workers and would therefore contribute to economic growth.

The National Party Commission chaired by politician Paul Sauer took a rather different view. The Sauer Commission Report argued that the country could either move towards equality between black and white communities or seek complete racial separation which would protect whites and ensure the development of Africans in 'their own areas'. The report refused to accept that the reserves were in a state of collapse or the extent of permanent settlement by Africans in the towns and cities. It declared that the process of 'detribalisation' of Africans had to be stopped, and recommended that Africans had to come to cities as temporary workers who would have to return to their homes in the reserves once their labour contracts had expired.

Activities

1 What were the main differences in the policies outlined by the Fagan and the Sauer Commissions?
2 What were the main similarities between the commissions?

The election campaign

DF Malan and the National Party fought a campaign based on elements of the Sauer report. They argued that the flood of Africans to the towns would be halted and even reversed and that in future they would have to develop 'along their own lines in their true fatherland, the reserves'. Furthermore, Malan promised that mixed marriages would be stopped, African parliamentary representation would be ended, black trade unions would be banned, job reservation tightened and Indian immigration stopped. Malan called this policy 'apartheid'. This programme appealed to both white workers who feared losing their jobs to African competition and white farmers who feared losing their workers to the cities. It also worked to broaden white fears that a segregated social order was under threat in the turbulent and changing post-war world.

The United Party's programme was based on acceptance of the main recommendations of the Fagan report. It argued that the reality of a black urban population should be accepted and proposed establishing African urban local authorities. The United Party also committed itself to maintaining white civilisation. It stressed its hostility to racial integration and proposed instead a modified form of segregation which took into account changing economic and political realities. Smuts approached the end of a long political career with a programme that did not easily translate into popular slogans or perfect solutions, was forced onto the defensive during the campaign and finally – as we have seen – suffered defeat at the polls.

The Nationalist victory was not a landslide. The Nationalist Party won 70 seats to the United

Activities

Study the text and then complete the summary of the factors which cost the United Party the 1948 elections.

UNITED PARTY: NEGATIVE FACTORS	NATIONAL PARTY: POSITIVE FACTORS
1 Over-confidence: comfortable victory in 1943 election; successful war policy; international status of Smuts – his interest and involvement with overseas affairs 2 Post war economic and social difficulties: • food rationing • white bread • shortage of housing • government administrative bungling • demobilised soldiers dissatisfied; plan for large scale immigration • fears of farmers and white workers (details from text) 3 Political weakening of UP Labour and Dominion Parties abandoned support for the UP over its Indian policy and moved towards the HNP 4 Election campaign badly organised: apathy of voters 5 Non-white policy was vague: based on the Fagan Report (give details from main text)	1 The Afrikaners were together politically – Havenga and the Afrikaner Party would work with the Nationalists 2 The Afrikaners were resentful and worried: • visit of British Royal Family in 1947 • UN criticism of SA policy on South West Africa • UP policy towards Indians was too liberal 3 Election campaign was vigorous and well-organised 4 Definite policy of apartheid as a counter to Asian and African nationalism – details from Sauer Report and main text

Party's 65 and it has been estimated that the Nationalists won less than 40 per cent of the votes cast. The fact that rural constituencies had fewer voters than the urban constituencies assisted the National Party which had strong support in rural areas. Many people believed that the Nationalist victory would be short-lived. They were wrong, but it was to be some years before the new rulers were confident of their continued hold on power.

CHAPTER ASSESSMENT

In small groups write essay plans for the following questions, and then choose one of the essays to complete. Each person in your group should write a different essay.

1 Examine Hertzog's racial policies, both political and economic, towards blacks (excluding Indians and coloureds) and evaluate the general reaction to these policies during the period 1924 to 1939.

2 What were the aims of the Pact government when it came to power in 1924, and to what extent had it achieved these aims by 1933?

3 'The desire to bring about a broader white unity, a South African rather than an exclusive Afrikaner nationalism, was the basis of coalition and fusion between 1933 and 1939.'
Discuss the validity of this statement.

4 Describe the divisions amongst Afrikaners in the period 1934–1943.

5 'The United Party under Smuts contributed much to its own downfall in 1948.'
Investigate the validity of this view, referring to the party's domestic and foreign policy during the years 1939 to 1948.

Further reading

L Callinicos. *Working Life.* Johannesburg: Ravan, 1987.

L Callinicos. *A Place in the City.* Johannesburg: Ravan, 1993.

TRH Davenport. *South Africa: A Modern History.* London: Macmillan, 1991.

Reader's Digest. *Illustrated History of South Africa.* Cape Town: Reader's Digest, 1994.

New Nation, New History. Johannesburg: New Nation and History Workshop, 1989.

South Africa (1948–98)

contents

chapter outcomes

knowledge outcomes

As you work through this chapter, you will be able to:
- discuss the main characteristics of the apartheid state;
- discuss the various forms of resistance to apartheid;
- analyse why apartheid collapsed;
- explain how it was that South Africa moved from apartheid to democracy.

concepts and skills outcomes

In this chapter you will apply the concepts and use the skills involved in:
- advancing a historical explanation for a complex set of events;
- interpreting a conflict situation;
- empathising with others;
- preparing for the final exams.

value outcomes

As you work through this chapter you will get the chance to think about:
- the morality or amorality of apartheid;
- whether those opposed to apartheid were justified in taking up arms against it;
- whether the policy of sanctions against apartheid was good or bad.

Timeline

The establishment of apartheid	1948	National Party government comes to power
	1949	Programme of Action adopted
	1950	Suppression of Communism Act
	1951	Legislation to remove coloured voters in Cape from common roll
	1952	Defiance Campaign
	1953	Public Safety Act
	1955	Freedom Charter adopted (26 June)
	1956	Women's protest in Pretoria (9 August)
	1959	Pan-Africanist Congress formed
Sharpeville and political repression	1960	Sharpeville massacre (21 March)
	1961	South Africa becomes a republic (31 May); MK formed and armed struggle begins (16 December)
	1964	Rivonia trial ends with sentences of life imprisonment
	1969	South African Students Organisation formed
	1972	Black People's Convention formed
	1973	Durban strikes
	1974	Coup in Portugal
	1975	Independence of Mozambique and Angola
Revolt and reform	1976	Soweto uprisings
	1977	Murder of Steve Biko
	1978	PW Botha becomes prime minister
	1979	African trade unions first registered
	1980	Independence of Zimbabwe
	1981	SADF raid on Maputo
	1982	National Party splits Conservative Party formed
	1983	Tricameral constitution adopted
	1984	Township Revolt begins
	1985	State of emergency; Meetings with ANC begin
	1986	End of Township Revolt
	1987	SADF aids Unita against Angolan
	1988	Cuito Cuanavale Namibia/Angola Accords signed
	1989	Botha replaced by De Klerk Harare Declaration
The years of negotiations	1990	De Klerk speech; Mandela released Increase in violence
	1991	Codesa
	1992	Threatened breakdown of negotiations; Negotiations resume
	1993	Interim constitution agreed to at Trade Centre
The new democracy	1994	First democratic election; Government of National Unity
	1995	First local government elections
	1996	The final constitution is approved

This chapter covers Specific Outcomes 1, 3, and 9 of the Human and Social Sciences learning area.

Apartheid in its early phase (1948–59)

Unit 1

Unit outcomes

- Understand what apartheid meant in this period, how it began to be applied, and the consequences of this.
- Discuss the main features of apartheid.
- Assess how apartheid developed and changed over time.

Unit timeline

1949: Prohibition of Mixed Marriages Act

1950: Population Registration Act; Immorality Act amended; Group Areas Act; HF Verwoerd appointed minister of native affairs

1952: Abolition of Passes Act

1953: Bantu Education Act; Separate Amenities Act

1954: Native Resettlement Act

1955: Removals from Sophiatown, Martindale and Newclare to Meadowlands, Soweto; Western Cape declared Coloured Labour Preference Area

1956: Industrial Conciliation Act provides for job reservation in any industry

1958: HF Verwoerd elected prime minister by the National Party caucus

1959: University apartheid legislation passed; Bantu Homelands Act

Introduction

One of the most important questions in recent South African history is the significance of 1948. On the one hand, the election of May that year saw the triumph of an Afrikaner nationalist party which then established itself in power for over four decades and successfully secured the transition to a republic outside the British Commonwealth in 1961. On the other hand, 1948 is usually taken to mark the beginning of the policy of apartheid.

In this unit we will focus on the start of apartheid. Now that apartheid has been dismantled – though its legacies (effects) continue – we can see the apartheid era as a distinct period in South Africa's history, one which can be divided into phases as it was implemented and then began to erode. In this unit we are concerned with the first of these phases, from 1948 to 1959.

Where does apartheid begin?

The term 'apartheid', first used in the early 1940s, occurred in the report by the National Party (NP) commission chaired by Paul Sauer which you read about in the previous chapter. The NP campaigned on the basis of that report in the 1948 election, and apartheid was a key slogan in that election. But what did it mean? How did apartheid differ from the racial segregation that had been in place before 1948? The idea of racial inequality was not new in 1948, nor was racially oppressive legislation: we noted examples in the previous chapter. Apartheid was, then, a continuation and extension of a previous policy which changed over time. It was not a master plan that was implemented overnight, but it took different forms at different times.

It is important to remember that the rest of the world, horrified by the Nazi holocaust (see Chapter 3), rejected racial discrimination after the Second World War. At that very time, the NP in South Africa took the opposite route, placing new and rigid emphasis on racial difference. To some extent this was to counter the less rigid approach adopted by the United Party during and immediately after the Second World War. We will consider some other reasons for apartheid below.

What was new about apartheid?

First, it involved extending racial segregation into new areas of life. Now whites were to be separate from all blacks, and each racial group was to live in its own area and be treated separately. Secondly, apartheid came to be defined in terms of 'separate development', which meant that Africans in particular should have separate political institutions.

The first important apartheid legislation included:

1 The 1949 **Prohibition of Mixed Marriages Act**, which made 'mixed' marriages between white and black illegal.

2 The 1950 **Immorality Act**, an amendment to a 1937 Act, which prohibited sexual intercourse between whites and blacks.

3 The **Population Registration Act**, which formed the basis of the new apartheid policies. Everyone was now classified into one or other racial group – white, coloured or 'native', or into an ethnic group, such as Malay, Griqua, Xhosa or Zulu. The classification was entered on an identity document. If there was doubt about a person's racial classification, a Racial Classification Board investigated the matter. One test used was the so-called pencil test, in which a pencil was pushed through the hair on a person's head to see if the texture was straight or not. If it was straight, the person was classified non-African, if it was not, African.

Many errors were made, and in some cases classifications were changed on review. Individuals who were wrongly classified were often rejected by other members of their families or by others in their community. In some cases members of the same family were classified differently; some were 'white', others 'coloured', some 'coloured', others 'Bantu'.

4 The **Group Areas Act** of 1950, another of the pillars of apartheid, extended residential segregation and set aside separate areas for each racial group to live. (See Source A for the 'ideal' apartheid model of how a city should be divided into racial compartments.) When an area was proclaimed for one race group, people belonging to other groups had to leave their homes and settle elsewhere. Entire communities were subjected to forced removals. The most publicised cases were those of District Six in Cape Town, which was declared 'white' in 1966, though most people living there were coloured, and Cato Manor in Durban.

▼ *Source B*

The impact of the Group Areas Act

Please don't talk about it to me. I will start to cry ... That's when the trouble started ...When they chucked us out of Cape Town. My whole life ... changed ... What they took away they can never give it back to us ... they destroyed us, they made our children ruffians.

(Statement by a woman living on the Cape Flats, outside Cape Town.)

▼ *Source C*

Group Areas removals to end of 1971

Group Areas Removals as of 31st December 1971	
	No. of Families resettled
Whites	1 433
Coloured people	41 199
Indians	26 294
Chinese	68

▼ *Source A* The model apartheid city (Adapted from: RJ Davies (1981). 'The spatial formation of the South African city', *GeoJournal* Supplementary Issue 2 pp. 59–72)

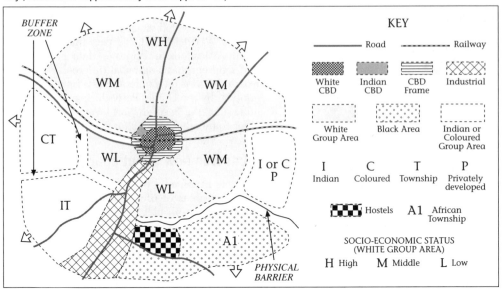

1 In 1997 the Land Court set up by the democratic government which took office in 1994 was to decide the future of District Six and Cato Manor.

   a Find out what has happened to these areas today.

   b Were those forced out given compensation, or able to return?

   c Who lived in these areas before forced removals took place, and who is living there now?

Extension activity

Some people say that the social impact of the Group Areas Act can be seen in the gang violence so widespread on the Cape Flats today. Discuss this statement in small groups to see if you agree with this or not.

◀ **Source D**

There's none so blind
(March 1949)
(From: J Leyden. *100 Not Out.*)

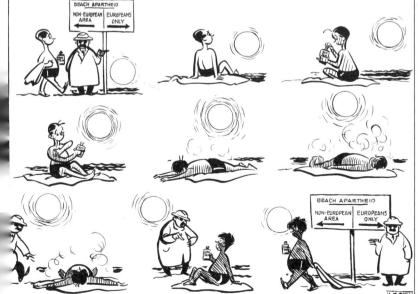

◀ **Source E**

The burning question (1950)
(From: J Leyden. *100 Not Out.*)

5 The **Abolition of Passes Act** of 1952 replaced the previous passes which Africans had had to carry. The new pass or reference book (often called the 'dompas') contained details of, for example, authorisation to be in a particular area. All Africans who were sixteen and over had to carry this book at all times and had to produce it to a policeman on demand. It took time to extend the pass system to African women (see Unit 2 on page 306).

The pass laws were often enforced in a very humiliating way. People were stopped in the street, and their pass was demanded. If they were not able to produce it, they were arrested and taken to jail. When the people came before one of the special pass courts, they were almost always unrepresented by any lawyer, and cases were dealt with very rapidly with sentences or fines imposed.

The pass system was essentially an influx control measure, linked to other legislation, which controlled the settlement of Africans in 'white' cities.

6 The **Separate Amenities Act** No. 49 of 1953 provided for what was sometimes called 'petty apartheid'. Public facilities were reserved for 'whites' or 'non-whites'. The Act specifically provided that separate facilities need not be equal to those enjoyed by another race group. In terms of this Act certain beaches were set aside for whites only, hotels excluded blacks, blacks had to use certain seats on trains and were unable to attend places of entertainment. Those who used the 'wrong' facility could be fined or imprisoned.

Activities

1 Discuss Sources D and E with a partner and then summarise the message of the cartoonist in each case.
2 Do you think the cartoonist is for or against apartheid? Give reasons for your answer

7 The **Bantu Education Act** No. 47 of 1953 provided for the government to take direct control of all education for Africans. Church schools were forced into the state sector or forced to close down.

▼ Source F

Speech by Hendrik Verwoerd, Minister of Native Affairs

The Bantu must be guided to serve his own community in all respects. There is no place for him in the European community above certain levels of labour.

(From: Parliamentary Debate, 1953.)

Activities

1 Why do you think Verwoerd believed what he said in Source F was true?
2 What 'levels of labour' did he mean?
3 What was the impact of this philosophy on the lives of individual Africans?

Profile: HF Verwoerd

Hendrik Frensch Verwoerd was born in the Netherlands in 1901 and came to South Africa as a child. A brilliant scholar, he became founding editor of the Nationalist newspaper *Die Transvaler*, then entered parliament in 1948, and was appointed minister of native affairs by Prime Minister Malan in 1950. He was often charming in public, but revealed himself to be a fanatic in the application of apartheid in its most extreme and logically consistent form. As South Africa became democratic and rejected apartheid, Verwoerd's name was removed from public places.

8 In 1959 the government applied apartheid to universities, setting up separate universities for different races, and preventing black students from studying at universities for whites. The minister of Bantu education said: 'our aim is to keep the Bantu child a Bantu child ... the Bantu must be so educated that they do not want to become imitators, that they will want to remain essentially Bantu.' (Giliomee and Schlemmer. *From Apartheid to Nation Building*.)

Extension activity

Find out more about the university apartheid legislation. Name some of the universities set aside for blacks and do some research to find out what kind of universities they were and how they developed.

9 The **Native Laws Amendment Act** of 1954 restricted the presence of Africans in urban areas by prescribing 72 hours as the longest any African could remain in an urban area without authorisation, and it also required African women to carry passes. The only rights that Africans were given to live in urban areas were set out in Section 10 of the Act: continuous employment for ten years with the same employer or continuous residence for fifteen years was required for the right to remain in an urban area. The government's policy was to promote migrant labour and reduce the number of Africans in the cities to the lowest number possible.

New words

precedent something that has happened previously, and often determines what follows

There were many other ways in which apartheid was applied. The **Separate Representation of Voters Act** of 1956 removed the vote from those coloured males in the Cape who had had the vote. This helped remove 50 000 voters likely to vote against the NP. When it came to power, the NP did not have a majority of votes and won with only an eight seat margin, so it had to do all it could to consolidate itself in power. It found it was not easy to remove the coloured voters, and it took over five years to achieve this. The coloureds were removed in part because the NP feared that if they continued to have the vote, there might be a **precedent** for Africans obtaining the vote in the future. Coloureds were given the right to elect four white representatives to parliament, but even that was removed in 1970. Africans, who had lost the right to vote in 1936, continued to elect seven white members of parliament and senators until that representation was removed in 1959, when Verwoerd adopted his bantustan policy, allowing eight states to move towards 'independence'. We will see what this meant in Unit 4 on page 317.

The impact of apartheid legislation

The apartheid legislation passed in the first decade of NP rule constituted a massive attempt at social engineering. Individual Acts had far-reaching effects. The Mixed Marriages and Immorality Acts broke up personal relationships, and forced some couples to leave the country. The

police spent time inquiring into very personal affairs, and people caught were harshly treated. Among those charged under these laws were ministers of the pro-apartheid Dutch Reformed Church. Much more importantly, the Group Areas Act broke up entire communities and led to large-scale forced removals. The anti-African legislation reviewed above further restricted the mobility of Africans and led to many cases of extreme hardship. Bantu Education impoverished generations of African children. The total impact was sufficient for the international community to call apartheid a crime against humanity.

How do we understand apartheid?

It was not clear at the time what apartheid meant. Malan said that total territorial segregation was not possible, but that it was possible for different groups to develop separately in their own areas. It was left for Verwoerd to take this further, as you will see in Unit 4.

Scholars have given different answers when asked to explain apartheid. Some see it as primarily a political phenomenon, to preserve racial identity and white supremacy; others see it as an extreme form of racial ideology, used to help consolidate white privilege and power. To some Marxists, whose approach is a materialist one, it was a way to secure the exploitation of cheap labour. As the economy grew under apartheid, it seemed that apartheid was important to the development of the capitalist economy. Liberal analysts pointed out ways in which apartheid was irrational and inefficient, and said that it violated free market principles. As the manufacturing industry grew, so apartheid seemed more and more contrary to economic rationality, and apartheid caused internal opposition and external condemnation, which both undermined economic growth.

To the extent that apartheid was a response to the way industrialisation and urbanisation were bringing people together, we may notice that its influx control aspects forced migrancy on people at a time when the subsistence economies in the reserves, on which migrancy depended, were collapsing. That was one of the many contradictions in the implementation of apartheid.

When elected in 1948 DF Malan said: 'In the past we felt like strangers in our own country, but today South Africa belongs to us once more. For the first time since Union, South Africa is our own. May God grant that it always remains our own.'

Activities

1 Who are the 'we' and 'us' Malan spoke of?
2 Was it right that one group should regard South Africa as 'its own'?
3 How could Malan reconcile his position with Christianity?
4 Imagine that you are forced out of your home under the Group Areas Act. Describe what impact this has on you and your family's life. (Try to find someone who was moved from their home under the Group Areas Act and interview him or her about how this changed his or her life.)
5 Imagine you are members of a Truth Commission such as that which sat in 1997 and 1998. You are interviewing DF Malan and HF Verwoerd about their policies of the 1950s. One group can formulate questions for them to answer; the other could work out how they might have responded to such questions.
6 You should now know the main features of apartheid.
   a What do you think was the main aim of apartheid?
   b Was it above all a means of protecting white rule?
   c Or a device to keep the National Party in power?
   d Or a way of keeping black labour as cheap as possible?

Extension activity

You should now have seen how apartheid evolved, and changed over time. Consider this in more detail. Try to research some case studies of how various individuals were affected by different apartheid policies.

Resistance in the 1950s (1949–59)

Unit 2

Unit outcomes

- Learn about the many different forms which resistance took in the 1950s, and something about how successful they were.
- Discuss the ideas of the Congress movement and why the Pan-Africanist Congress (PAC) was formed.
- Analyse resistance: from the Programme of Action to the Freedom Charter.
- Discuss the rise of Africanism.

Unit timeline

1949: ANC Programme of Action

1950: Suppression of Communism Act

1952: Defiance Campaign

1953: Public Safety Act; ANC call for a Congress of the People

1955: Congress of the People at Kliptown

1956: Congress leaders arrested and charged with treason

1959: Founding of PAC; Cato Manor women's protests

Introduction

Some of the members of the ANC Youth League, such as Oliver Tambo and Walter Sisulu, welcomed the coming to power of the apartheid government in 1948 because they believed that apartheid policies would so antagonise people that they would rise up and overthrow white supremacy. Though apartheid did provoke mass resistance, that resistance was unable to prevent the increasingly ruthless imposition of apartheid policies in the 1950s and beyond. As we shall see, resistance took different forms as apartheid was applied in new ways and as a result of ever-chang-

ing circumstances. In the 1950s most resistance was legal and above-ground. In this unit we will consider the major examples of that resistance.

Forms of resistance – the ANC Programme of Action

At its annual meeting in 1949 the ANC adopted the militant Programme of Action proposed by the Youth League. At that conference Alfred Xuma was replaced as president by Dr Moroka, and Walter Sisulu was elected the new secretary-general. The Programme of Action **envisaged** boycotts, strikes and other forms of civil disobedience (see Source A). Through such tactics, the Youth League hoped to mobilise a larger group of people to resist.

▼ *Source A*
Programme of Action, ANC Annual Conference, December 1949

> *The fundamental principles of the programme of action of the African National Congress are inspired by the desire to achieve national freedom. By national freedom we mean freedom from white domination and the attainment of political independence ... Like all other people the African people claim the right of self-determination ... [to achieve this] we ... undertake ... to employ the following weapons: immediate and active boycott, strike, civil disobedience, noncooperation, and such other means as may bring about the accomplishment and realisation of our aspirations ...*

(From: Johns and Davis. *Mandela, Tambo and the ANC.*)

Activities . . . .
Refer to Source A and answer these questions with a partner.
1 How did these new tactics differ from the old ones?
2 Why is there the emphasis in this document on 'political independence'?
. . . .

Government legislation

The first major piece of repressive legislation which the apartheid government passed was the Suppression of Communism Act of 1950. This outlawed the Communist Party of South Africa, which disbanded itself. White communists formed a new above-ground organisation, the Congress of Democrats, while a South African Communist Party was organised underground in 1953. It did not declare itself to the public until July 1960. White liberals, despondent after the National Party was returned to power in the general election of 1953, formed a non-racial Liberal Party, which in the beginning accepted the idea of a qualified franchise. It put up candidates in a number of elections but never with any success. The United Party, the official opposition in parliament, opposed the NP government on many issues, but its members themselves believed in white supremacy, so its opposition to apartheid was very selective. The most effective opposition to apartheid in this decade was mounted by the ANC and its allies, and by some rural communities, as we shall now see.

The Defiance Campaign

The Defiance Campaign was launched by the ANC and the South African Indian Congress as whites were celebrating the 300th anniversary of the arrival of the first settler, Jan van Riebeeck. A mass resistance campaign targeted six main apartheid laws: the Bantu Authorities Act, the Group Areas Act, the Separate Representation of Voters Act (which provided for coloureds to be removed from the common voters' roll), the Pass Laws, and Stock Limitation Laws. From 26 June, individuals began to present themselves for arrest by disregarding apartheid legislation and sitting in whites-only restaurants, entering areas reserved for whites, and burning passes in public.

▼ *Source B*

At the opening of the Defiance Campaign, the ANC wrote to the Prime Minister DF Malan

... as a defenceless and voteless people, we have explored other channels without success. The African people are left with no alternative but to embark upon the campaign ... it is our intention to conduct this campaign in a peaceful manner ...

Activities

1 What 'other channels' had been explored?
2 Do you agree that there was 'no alternative'?
3 Why was emphasis placed on the 'peaceful manner' of the Defiance Campaign?

By January 1953 over 8 000 volunteers had been arrested. The hope was that the prisons would become overcrowded and the police would not be able to cope, which would force the government to remove the legislation being protested against. But in October 1952 riots occurred in Port Elizabeth and East London, which the government linked with the Defiance Campaign. Nelson Mandela, one of the main organisers, had been arrested in July, and many other black leaders were banned from attending meetings or from travelling outside a limited area. New legislation was passed – the Public Safety and Criminal Laws Amendment Acts – to deal with transgressors and to provide for the declaration of a state of emergency if 'public order' was threatened. In the face of this, Albert Luthuli, who was elected in December 1952 to succeed Dr Moroka as president-general of the ANC, decided to call off the campaign. By then, membership of the ANC had risen from 20 000 to 100 000, and the world had been made aware of the oppression of the majority in South Africa as never before.

Profile: Albert Luthuli

© Paul Weinberg/South Photographs

Albert Luthuli, born around 1898 in what was then Southern Rhodesia, was trained as a teacher at Adam's College near Durban. He became a member of the Native Representative Council, and then in 1952 was given a choice of renouncing his membership of the ANC and support for the Defiance Campaign or being dismissed as a government-paid chief at Groutville. He refused to resign from the ANC and so was dismissed from his post. A tall, confident man, he held the office of president-general of the ANC from 1952 until his death. When awarded the Nobel Peace Prize in 1960, he returned to the statement he had made in 1952, in which he spoke of having spent thirty years of his life 'knocking in vain, patiently, moderately and modestly, at a closed and barred door'. Restricted to his home, he died when hit by a train under mysterious circumstances.

Source C

In *Long Walk to Freedom* Nelson Mandela wrote about the Defiance Campaign:

> [It] freed me from any lingering sense of doubt or inferiority I might still have felt; it liberated me from the feeling of being overwhelmed by the power and seeming invincibility of the white man and his institutions. Now the white man had felt the power of my punches and I could walk upright like a man ... I had come of age as a freedom fighter (130).

Activities

1 Why did the campaign have this psychological effect on Mandela and others?

2 a How successful was the Defiance Campaign?
  b What did it achieve?
  c Were the aims of the organisers realised? If not, why not?

3 Imagine you were one of the volunteers in the Defiance Campaign. Write a diary setting out what you did and how successful you were.

Extension activity

Read sections of *Long Walk to Freedom* and write an essay on Mandela's role in the Defiance Campaign.

The Congress of the People

With Luthuli restricted to a small area of Natal, it was ZK Matthews, the Cape president of the ANC, who in August 1953 called for an alliance of organisations to draw up a charter setting out the hopes of the people of the country. This led to the formation of the Congress Alliance, made up of the ANC, the South African Indian Congress, the Federation of South African Women, the Coloured People's Organisation, the white Congress of Democrats, and the South African Council of Trade Unions. Voluntary organisers spread over the country to get ideas from people for the charter. Exactly how those ideas were summarised into a single short document is not clear. The famous Freedom Charter

The Freedom Charter

We, the People of South Africa, declare for all our country and the world to know:

that South Africa belongs to all who live in it, black and white, and that no government can justly claim authority unless it is based on the will of all the people;

that our people have been robbed of their birthright to land, liberty and peace by a form of government founded on injustice and inequality;

that our country will never be prosperous or free until all our people live in brotherhood, enjoying equal rights and opportunities;

that only a democratic state, based on the will of all the people, can secure to all their birthright without distinction of colour, race, sex or belief;

And therefore, we, the people of South Africa, black and white together equals, countrymen and brothers adopt this Freedom Charter;
And we pledge ourselves to strive together, sparing neither strength nor courage, until the democratic changes here set out have been won.

THE PEOPLE SHALL GOVERN!
Every man and woman shall have the right to vote for and to stand as a candidate for all bodies which make laws;
All people shall be entitled to take part in the administration of the country;
The rights of the people shall be the same, regardless of race, colour or sex;
All bodies of minority rule, advisory boards, councils and authorities shall be replaced by democratic organs of self-government .

ALL NATIONAL GROUPS SHALL HAVE EQUAL RIGHTS!
There shall be equal status in the bodies of state, in the courts and in the schools for all national groups and races;
All people shall have equal right to use their own languages, and to develop their own folk culture and customs;
All national groups shall be protected by law against insults to their race and national pride;
The preaching and practice of national, race or colour discrimination and contempt shall be a punishable crime;
All apartheid laws and practices shall be set aside.

THE PEOPLE SHALL SHARE IN THE COUNTRY'S WEALTH!
The national wealth of our country, the heritage of South Africans, shall be restored to the people;
The mineral wealth beneath the soil, the Banks and monopoly industry shall be transferred to the ownership of the people as a whole;
All other industry and trade shall be controlled to assist the wellbeing of the people;
All people shall have equal rights to trade where they choose, to manufacture and to enter all trades, crafts and professions.

THE LAND SHALL BE SHARED AMONG THOSE WHO WORK IT!
Restrictions of land ownership on a racial basis shall be ended, and all the land re-divided amongst those who work it to banish famine and land hunger;
The state shall help the peasants with implements, seed, tractors and dams to save the soil and assist the tillers;
Freedom of movement shall be guaranteed to all who work on the land;
All shall have the right to occupy land wherever they choose;
People shall not be robbed of their cattle, and forced labour and farm prisons shall be abolished.

ALL SHALL BE EQUAL BEFORE THE LAW!
No-one shall be imprisoned, deported or restricted without a fair trial;
No-one shall be condemned by the order of any Government official;
The courts shall be representative of all the people;
Imprisonment shall be only for serious crimes against the people, and shall aim at re-education, not vengeance;
The police force and army shall be open to all on an equal basis and shall be the helpers and protectors of the people;
All laws which discriminate on grounds of race, colour or belief shall be repealed.

ALL SHALL ENJOY EQUAL HUMAN RIGHTS!
The law shall guarantee to all their right to speak, to organise, to meet together, to publish, to preach, to worship and to educate their children;
The privacy of the house from police raids shall be protected by law;
All shall be free to travel without restriction from countryside to town, from province to province, and from South Africa abroad;
Pass Laws, permits and all other laws restricting these freedoms shall be abolished.

THERE SHALL BE WORK AND SECURITY!
All who work shall be free to form trade unions, to elect their officers and to make wage agreements with their employers;
The state shall recognise the right and duty of all to work, and to draw full unemployment benefits;
Men and women of all races shall receive equal pay for equal work;
There shall be a forty-hour working week, a national minimum wage, paid annual leave, and sick leave for all workers, and maternity leave on full pay for all working mothers;
Miners, domestic workers, farm workers and civil servants shall have the same rights as all others who work;
Child labour, compound labour, the tot system and contract labour shall be abolished.

THE DOORS OF LEARNING AND CULTURE SHALL BE OPENED!
The government shall discover, develop and encourage national talent for the enhancement of our cultural life;
All the cultural treasures of mankind shall be open to all, by free exchange of books, ideas and contact with other lands;
The aim of education shall be to teach the youth to love their people and their culture, to honour human brotherhood, liberty and peace;
Education shall be free, compulsory, universal and equal for all children; Higher education and technical training shall be opened to all by means of state allowances and scholarships awarded on the basis of merit;
Adult illiteracy shall be ended by a mass state education plan;
Teachers shall have all the rights of other citizens;
The colour bar in cultural life, in sport and in education shall be abolished.

THERE SHALL BE HOUSES, SECURITY AND COMFORT!
All people shall have the right to live where they choose, be decently housed, and to bring up their families in comfort and security;
Unused housing space to be made available to the people;
Rent and prices shall be lowered, food plentiful and no-one shall go hungry;
A preventive health scheme shall be run by the state;
Free medical care and hospitalisation shall be provided for all, with special care for mothers and young children;
Slums shall be demolished, and new suburbs built where all have transport, roads, lighting, playing fields, creches and social centres;
The aged, the orphans, the disabled and the sick shall be cared for by the state;
Rest, leisure and recreation shall be the right of all;
Fenced locations and ghettos shall be abolished, and laws which break up families shall be repealed.

THERE SHALL BE PEACE AND FRIENDSHIP!
South Africa shall be a fully independent state which respects the rights and sovereignty of all nations;
South Africa shall strive to maintain world peace and the settlement of all international disputes by negotiation - not war;
Peace and friendship amongst all our people shall be secured by upholding the equal rights, opportunities and status of all;
The people of the protectorates Basutoland, Bechuanaland and Swaziland shall be free to decide for themselves their own future;
The right of all peoples of Africa to independence and self-government shall be recognised, and shall be the basis of close co-operation.

Let all people who love their people and their country now say, as we say here: THESE FREEDOMS WE WILL FIGHT FOR, SIDE BY SIDE, THROUGHOUT OUR LIVES, UNTIL WE HAVE WON OUR LIBERTY

© Mayibuye Centre

Source D

The Freedom Charter

was accepted at a meeting of 2 848 delegates held at Kliptown in Soweto, south of Johannesburg, on 25–26 June 1955. Police had prevented many more thousands attending. The Charter spelt out guidelines for a future non-racial country.

The ANC adopted the Freedom Charter at its annual conference in 1956. A group of 'Africanists' rejected it, for reasons we shall look at below. Some people opposed it as a socialist document. This is what Nelson Mandela had to say about the Charter in his statement to the court in the Rivonia Trial in 1964:

> 'The Charter' is by no means a blueprint for a socialist state. It calls for redistribution, but not nationalization, of land; it provides for nationalization of mines, banks and monopoly industry, because big monopolies are owned by one race only ... In this respect the ANC's policy corresponds with the old policy of the present Nationalist Party ... The ANC has never at any period of its history advocated a revolutionary change in the economic structure of the country, nor has it ... ever condemned capitalist society.

(From: *No Easy Walk to Freedom*.)

Mandela also wrote that the Charter 'is a revolutionary document precisely because the changes it envisages cannot be won without breaking up the economic and political set-up of present South Africa' (*Freedom in our Lifetime*, quoted Pampallis, *Foundations of the New South Africa*).

Activities

1 Carefully look at the terms of the Freedom Charter in Source D. Do you agree with Mandela's view that the Charter does not propose socialism, but is merely opposed to monopoly capitalism?

2 Assess the ways in which the Freedom Charter is, or is not, a 'revolutionary document'.

3 Hold a class discussion to decide to what extent the Charter has been put into practice in the new South Africa.

Women's protest in 1956

Many women members of the ANC Women's League participated in the Defiance Campaign. The campaign against the extension of the pass laws to women was taken up by the Federation of South African Women (FEDSAW), a non-racial national organisation founded in April 1954 and closely aligned to the Congress Alliance. FEDSAW drew up certain women's demands for the Freedom Charter. The demands 'for all mothers of all races', included:

- four months maternity leave on full pay for working mothers;
- day nurseries for the children of working mothers;
- birth control clinics.

(From: Suttner and Cronin. *Thirty Years of the Freedom Charter*.)

The highpoint in a series of protests against the extension of the pass laws to women took place on 9 August 1956, a day now celebrated as Women's Day, a public holiday. On that day in 1956, twenty thousand women walked peacefully to the Union Buildings in Pretoria to deliver petitions against the introduction of passes for African women. They failed to obtain an interview with Prime Minister Strijdom, but they sang this song, composed for the occasion: 'Strijdom, you have tampered with the women; you have struck a rock.'

Campaigns against passes for African women continued, and it was not until the late 1960s that all African women were forced to carry passes.

▼ Source E

Helen Joseph wrote about the occasion:

> When I reached the top [of the Union Building Stairs], I found [the women] there sitting quietly in the amphitheatre, resting peacefully. It had been a long and tiring morning for them. Babies were unstrapped from their mothers' backs and fed, umbrellas went up against the hot sun. Two thousand women were sitting where no black women had sat before. It was a triumph. Their signed protests had been handed to their leaders and now they could rest. 'We have not come here to beg or plead but to ask for what is our right as mothers, as women and as citizens of our country ...'
>
> Four women had been chosen as leaders for the day, Lilian Ngoyi, the African, Rahima Moosa, the Indian, Sophie Williams, the coloured and I, the white. We reflected the multiracial membership of the Federation of South African Women. We took those piles of protests and left them outside the doors of the ministers' offices, when our knocking brought no response. I suppose we had really expected no less, in view of our four unacknowledged letters announcing the forthcoming visit. It made no difference to us. We had recorded our protest for all time.

(From: Helen Joseph. *Side by Side*.)

◀ The march on the Union Buildings, 9 August 1956

Profile: Lilian Ngoyi

© Mayibuye Centre

Lilian Ngoyi (1912–80) grew up in poverty and became a garment worker. She began her political career as a trade union organiser, and joined the ANC at the time of the Defiance Campaign in l952. She became president of the ANC Women's League, then of the Federation of South African Women. With Helen Joseph, she was one of the leaders of the protest of 9 August 1956. Later that year she was arrested and she was one of those charged in the Treason Trial. She was subsequently banned for many years.

Activities

Another women's organisation which played an important role in resisting apartheid, a role acknowledged by Mandela in his speech of 11 February 1990, was the Black Sash.

a Find out what this organisation stood for, and why it had that name.

b How did it differ from, for example, the Federation of South African Women, in membership, objectives and actions?

2 By protesting, as in Source E, women challenged the sexist idea that their role should be a passive, subordinate and politically inactive one. Why had such an idea emerged, and why did it come under attack at this time, not only in South Africa but in other countries as well?

3 a What did the women hope to gain by their protest on 9 August 1956 as discussed in the text and Source E?

b What did they achieve?

4 Imagine you were one of the women who travelled a long way to march in Pretoria on 9 August 1956. Write a diary of that memorable day.

Extension activity

Women played a key role in protest in the squatter settlement of Cato Manor, Durban, in 1959, when the police tried to enforce the pass laws and a regulation preventing the brewing of beer. At the municipality's beer halls, sorghum beer was sold to African men and the officials did not want women to sell beer at their shacks. When women attacked a beer hall, the police retaliated by breaking up a crowd of women with great brutality. The women's struggles continued and merged with resistance against the forced removal from Cato Manor to KwaMashu.

Find out more about the role of the women in this particular protest.

© Mayibuye Centre

◀Source F
The treason trialists

Activities

1 Who is the tall man standing in the centre of the third row from the bottom in Source F?
2 Can you identify any of the other people in Source F?

On 5 December 1956 one hundred and fifty-six leading members of the Congress Alliance were arrested and charged with plotting to overthrow the state. The prosecution claimed that the Freedom Charter was a communist document, and that the ANC and its allies wished to use violence to bring about a transfer of power. The trial began in 1957. A number of those charged were acquitted early on in the process, and in March 1961 the last 30 were also acquitted. Though the state failed to prove its case, it had used the trial to weaken the liberation move-

ment. The trial prevented many leaders from doing anything else for many years, but it also brought them together in one place and helped to unite them.

Other resistance

There is no space here to provide a comprehensive survey of resistance in the 1950s. Some of this was organised by the ANC, such as the bus boycott in Alexandra township north of Johannesburg in 1957. This was called when the bus company increased bus fares by a penny. For three months the residents of Alexandra walked the sixteen kilometres to work, and eventually the fares were lowered. While the ANC was active in some urban resistance, it was not until the earl-

1960s that it accepted that rural-based struggles were equally important.

Much of the resistance of the 1950s was not organised from the urban areas by political organisations. Instead, much of it took place in rural areas, was related directly to local issues, and was not organised from outside. Sometimes there were connections: resistance among the Pedi in Sekhukhuneland was influenced by ideas brought back by migrants from the Rand, who formed a rural migrant-based organisation, Sebatakgomo. Much rural resistance focused on issues such as the imposition of the Bantu Authorities Act, which enabled the government to remove 'troublesome' chiefs and install those who would work within the new system.

▼ *Source G*

Map of reserve-based resistance (Adapted from: Tom Lodge. *Black Politics in South Africa since 1945*.)

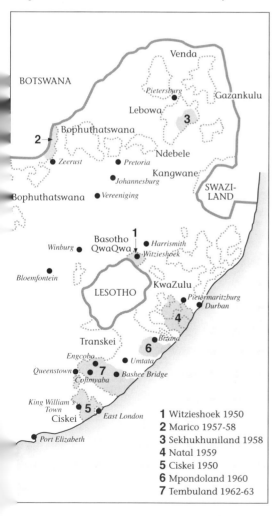

1 Witzieshoek 1950
2 Marico 1957-58
3 Sekhukhuniland 1958
4 Natal 1959
5 Ciskei 1950
6 Mpondoland 1960
7 Tembuland 1962-63

Activities

Find out more about other examples of resistance in this decade. Some examples as shown in Source G include:

- the resistance in Witzieshoek, close to the Lesotho border, in 1950–51;
- in 1957–58 women in Zeerust protested against the carrying of passes;
- in 1958 in Sekhukhuneland there was protest against the enforcement of cattle culling;
- in 1960 in eastern Pondoland in the Transkei, in what is now the Eastern Cape, there was massive resistance against the state's interference in local affairs and apartheid laws. The 'peasants' revolt' was ended after a state of emergency was proclaimed in November 1960.

The formation of the Pan-Africanist Congress (PAC)

In the mid-1940s a group of men within the ANC began calling themselves Africanists. This group included Robert Mangaliso Sobukwe, Potlako Leballo, and Ashley Peter Mda, and was increasingly unhappy with ANC policy in the 1950s. They opposed the multi-racialism of the Congress Alliance, believing that leadership of the struggle for liberation was being taken over by white and Indian communists. They rejected the Freedom Charter, particularly those sections which guaranteed minority interests, and the statement that South Africa belonged to all who lived in it, black and white. They believed in the slogan 'Africa for the Africans', and saw most whites as settlers without valid claim to the land they owned.

The Africanists broke away from the ANC in 1958, and in April the following year formally established the PAC. Sobukwe, the leading theoretician among them and a lecturer in African languages at the University of the Witwatersrand, was elected president, with Leballo as national secretary. Most of the other members of the executive of the party were former ANC Youth League members.

The Africanists felt that South Africa belonged to the African people; white colonisers had seized much of the land unlawfully. They identified the struggle for freedom in South Africa with that of Africans in other parts of Africa, and wanted to work together with Pan-Africanists elsewhere to establish a United States of Africa. They were inspired by the anti-imperialist leadership of Kwame Nkrumah of Ghana and Tom Mboya of Kenya, whose most famous saying was that whites should 'scram' out of Africa.

◀ Sobukwe and the PAC executive in 1959 (From: South African Library)

PAC leaders defined 'African' as a person who owes loyalty to Africa and accepts the democratic rule of the African majority. One of the important early leaders in the organisation was Patrick Duncan, a white ex-liberal. But 'African' was also used by the Africanists in racial terms, for they realised that the masses could be mobilised through a racially assertive nationalism. They advocated a militant strategy of mass action, involving boycotts, strikes, civil disobedience and non-cooperation, and wished to take advantage of opportunities presented by popular protests. The PAC quickly attracted members because of its apparent militancy. It appealed especially to migrant workers with links to the rural areas, where access to land was the main issue.

▼ Source H

At the founding of the PAC on 6 April 1959 Sobukwe said:

> The Africanists take the view that there is only one race to which we all belong, and that is the human race ... Against multi-racialism we have this objection; that the history of South Africa has fostered group prejudices and antagonisms, and if we have to maintain the same group exclusiveness ... we shall be transporting to the new Afrika [sic] these very antagonisms and conflicts. Further, multi-racialism is in fact a pandering to European bigotry and arrogance. It is

> a method of safeguarding white interests ...
> (From: Fredrickse. *Unbroken Thread.*)

Sobukwe also said that on that day Van Riebeeck had planted white supremacy, and on that day it would be buried. One of the PAC's first acts was to organise the anti-pass law campaign of March 1960. Within hours of the launch of that campaign, the Sharpeville massacre, which we will look at in Unit 3, occurred.

Activities

1 Write an essay showing in what way the philosophy of the Africanists differed from that of the ANC.
2 Critically assess Sobukwe's notion of 'Africanism' in Source H.
3 Do you agree with the reasons the PAC gave for breaking with the ANC?
4 What do you know of the later history of the PAC? Why was its early success not sustained? Do some research and also look at page 349 of this book.

Extension activity

Tom Lodge, the author of *Black Politics in South Africa since 1945*, calls the 1950s 'a decade of defiance'. Decide whether this is an adequate phrase to describe this period, bearing in mind the following.

• How successful was resistance in the 1950s?
• Why did resistance take the forms it did in this decade?

The Sharpeville massacre and the birth of the republic (1960–63)

Unit outcomes

- Understand what happened at Sharpeville, and what the significance of the massacre was.
- Learn about the establishment of the republic, and see that development in context.

Unit timeline

21 March 1960:	Shooting at Sharpeville
30 March 1960:	Declaration of a state of emergency
April 1960:	ANC and PAC declared un-lawful organisations; attempted assassination of Verwoerd
October 1960:	Referendum on the republic among white voters
31 May 1961:	Establishment of a republic
mid-1961:	Discussions in the ANC about adopting the armed struggle; formation of Umkhonto we Sizwe
1961:	Albert Luthuli accepts Nobel Prize for peace
16 December 1961:	MK sabotage campaign laun-ched; MK manifesto issued

Background to the Sharpeville massacre

The newly formed PAC decided to act before the ANC by holding a pass campaign in March 1960. Like the ANC, the PAC planned a campaign involving the burning of passes in public. Members of the PAC were then to march to police stations and demand to be arrested. It was hoped that so many people would be arrested that the jails would not be able to cope with the influx, and the government would have to abolish the pass system.

On 21 March in the township of Sharpeville, near Vereeniging, a large unarmed and peaceful crowd gathered around the police station. The police were nervous, and when it seemed that the fence around the station was about to collapse, they started shooting. People tried to run away, and many were shot in the back. Within a few minutes, 69 lay dead and 180 were wounded.

By the end of March a state of emergency had been declared, giving the police vast powers to crush protests. Though the pass laws were suspended for a brief period, they were soon implemented as harshly as before. Verwoerd, who survived an assassination attempt in April, made it clear that the government would make no concessions.

▼ *Source A* Wonder if I could have taken a wrong turning somewhere? (From: *Cape Times*, 23 March 1960.)

Activities

1 Why did the events of 21 March 1960 have such far-reaching results?
2 Why did the police act as they did?
3 Was the Sharpeville massacre itself a 'turning-point' in our history?
4 a What is the significance of the date of Source A?
  b Who does the torchbearer represent?
  c How would you answer the question that the cartoonist is making the torchbearer ask?

The banning of the ANC and PAC

The banning of the ANC and PAC in early April 1960, in terms of the Unlawful Organisations Act, legislation passed specifically to achieve this, was indeed a turning-point in South African history. The Communist Party had been banned in 1950 in terms of the Suppression of Communism Act, but that Act required a lengthy process of enquiry and report, and the government wished to act quickly. It was warned at the time that banning the organisations would drive them underground and into exile, and virtually force them to adopt the armed struggle as the only viable strategy of resistance. And yet, as was also predictable, despite enormous efforts by the state to suppress these organisations, that proved impossible. Even if the ANC and PAC had not been banned, they might, like SWAPO in Namibia, have adopted the armed struggle anyway in the face of fierce repression.

The banning was an immediate response to the violence that occurred at Sharpeville. After the shootings, the organisations called on their followers to observe a day of mourning. Passes were burnt and a general strike called. On the day of the strike, before a state of emergency was proclaimed, the Minister of Justice Erasmus, moved the **first reading** of the Unlawful Organisations Bill, which empowered the government to ban the two organisations. The government told parliament that banning the organisations would restore 'stability' and promote 'law and order'. The United Party supported the measure as an emergency one, but one member of parliament, pointing out that the ANC was the mouthpiece of the great majority of Africans, predicted that 'banning would create a vacuum which would leave unruly and terrorist groups in control', and the **Natives' Representative** Lee-Warden warned that the organisations themselves would resort to guerrilla warfare and sabotage.

Both organisations set up headquarters in exile. The following year the armed struggle began, as the ANC formed Umkhonto we Sizwe and the PAC Poqo.

New words

first reading the first time legislation is brought before parliament (there is no debate on the legislation at this stage, but there is at the second reading)
Native Representative member of parliament supposed to represent the interests of Africans

▼ Source B

In October 1960 Albert Luthuli went to Oslo to accept the Nobel Peace Prize. Here are extracts from his speech accepting the prize.

I, as a Christian, have always felt that there is one thing about 'apartheid' or 'separate development' that is unforgivable. It seems utterly indifferent to the suffering of individual persons who lose their land, their homes, their jobs in the pursuit of what is surely the most terrible dream in the world. This terrible dream is not held on to by a crack-pot group on the fringe of society ... It is the deliberate policy of a government, supported actively by a large part of the white population ... the golden age of African independence is also the dark age of South Africa's decline and retrogression ... there is nothing new in South Africa's apartheid ideas, but South Africa is unique in this: the ideas not only survive in our modern age, but are stubbornly defended, extended and bolstered up by legislation at the time when in the major part of the world they are now largely historical ...
(From: *New Age*, 14.12.61)

Activities

1 Write an essay on 'the parting of the ways' between South Africa and the rest of the world in relation to racial policies.
2 Summarise the message of Luthuli's speech in Source B.
3 Look closely at Source C.
  a Why was the rest of the world so critical of South Africa's racial polices by this time?
  b How did that criticism develop in the years that followed?

The adoption of armed struggle as a strategy

It was, ironically, shortly after Luthuli's speech praising the non-violent nature of the struggle in South Africa, that the armed struggle began. The ANC as such did not adopt the armed struggle, for it was a mass political organisation, the members of which had joined to fight a non-violent struggle. Mandela and other leaders in the

'South Africa is the polecat [skunk] of the world,' wrote an Afrikaans intellectual in an article assessing the country's ostracism by the world community (1960)
(From: A Berry. *Act by Act.*)

ANC formed Umkhonto we Sizwe (MK) in 1961 to perform sabotage. A number of whites served on its National High Command, under which served regional commands. On 16 December 1961 government buildings were attacked, and within eighteen months 200 acts of sabotage had been carried out.

The reasons for the adoption of the armed struggle were set out in the founding manifesto of Umkhonto we Sizwe, issued on 16 December 1961, the day on which Afrikaners remembered the covenant made at Blood River in December 1938 (also known as Dingane's Day).

▼ *Source D*

Extracts from the manifesto of MK

[MK] will carry on the struggle for freedom and democracy by new methods, which are necessary to complement the actions of the established national liberation organisa-tions ... The people's patience is not end-less. The time comes in the life of any nation when there remain only two choices: submit or fight. That time has now come to South Africa. We shall not submit and we have no choice but to hit back by all means within our power in defence of our people, our future and our freedom ...

We of Umkhonto we Sizwe have always sought to achieve liberation without blood-shed and civil clash. We hope, even at this late hour, that our first actions will awaken everyone to a realisation of the disastrous

situation to which the Nationalist policy is leading. We hope that we will bring the Government and its supporters to their senses before it is too late, so that both the Government and its policies can be changed before matters reach the desperate stage of civil war.
(From: Barrell. *MK.*)

Activities . . . .

1 What is the aim of MK according to Source D?
2 Divide into two groups. Assume you are all members of the ANC in 1961.
   a Some argue the case for adopting the armed strug-gle, others the case against.
   b Then each group consider, from today's perspectives, whether the decision to launch the armed struggle was indeed the right one.

Extension activity . . . .

Find out about Poqo, the armed wing of the PAC. How successful was it?

The making of the republic

Afrikaner nationalists had long wanted to see South Africa become a republic, cutting its ties with Britain. Under Prime Minister DF Malan the goal of a republic had been soft-pedalled, but the movement for a republic gained momen-tum under his successor, Strijdom, and was realised under Strijdom's successor as prime minister, Hendrik Verwoerd.

Background

Smuts had accepted South Africa's position as a dominion in the British Empire, then the Commonwealth, and realised that many English-speaking South Africans had deep ties to Britain and other parts of the Empire/Commonwealth. During the Second World War, some Afrikaners, Verwoerd among them, advocated the establishment of a Boer republic which would be Christian-National in character and in which English would only be a second language. After the war, realising that achieving such a republic was impractical, republicans argued for a 'democratic' republic in which English-speakers would have full rights. After coming to power in 1948, DF Malan's priority was to consolidate the NP in power. He said that a republic would only come about after a referendum of whites, and through-out the 1950s the NP had too precarious a hold on power for them to risk a referendum defeat.

In January 1960 Verwoerd announced in parliament that the time to establish a republic had arrived. The republic would be democratic and Christian, and the equality of the two official languages would remain. There would be no drastic constitutional change: the governor-general would be replaced by a state president, chosen by parliament, who would be the constitutional head of state and above politics. Verwoerd deliberately played down the changes that a republic would bring in order to gain votes in the referendum on the issue. He accepted the idea that the new republic would be in the Commonwealth, though he preferred one outside that body.

Verwoerd gained support from his forthright reply to Macmillan's wind of change speech (see Unit 4). He also gained white support from the way the Sharpeville crisis was handled, and by the fact that he survived an assassination attempt at the Rand Easter Show in April: a deranged farmer, David Pratt, shot him twice in the face, but he made a remarkable recovery, which some attributed to Divine Providence. When the Belgian Congo obtained its independence at the end of June, chaos erupted there, which encouraged whites to support the strong South African prime minister. In the referendum campaign held in October, Verwoerd appealed to English-speakers to support a republic as a way to bring about white unity, and the NP warned that the chaos of the Congo would come to South Africa if it did not become a republic.

A brilliant example of propaganda is the letter in Verwoerd's handwriting, shown in Source E, sent to voters and dated 21 September 1961. It began: 'Dear Friend ...' and warned that unless a republic was introduced, South Africa would follow the Congo into chaos and the white man would be forced out. Over a million copies of this letter were distributed.

Activities

1 What was wrong with Verwoerd's argument in the letter in Source E?
2 Are such tactics legitimate in an election or referendum campaign?

> Libertas
> Bryntirion
> Pretoria
> 21/9/60.
>
> Dear Friend,
> The time is approaching when all of us must help to decide at the referendum what the immediate future of our country and people must be.
> Only in a republic will we be able to unite in giving our full attention to what is of vital importance. This includes the development of a safe future for our white population, coupled with justice towards the non-whites. It is also necessary to ensure prosperity for everybody.
> Above all, however, we must create a republic in which we can all co-operate in truly building one South African nation. Self-preservation and the interests

3 What is the difference between propaganda and factual information?

In October 1960 a referendum was held among white voters, and a majority of 74 580 votes or 52 per cent voted for a republic. Verwoerd had all-along said that a simple majority would be sufficient for that goal to be realised. Few English-speakers voted for the republic, fearing that it might mean leaving the Commonwealth and leave South Africa isolated in the world. Some in Natal spoke of secession but, as in 1909, that was not realistic.

Extension activity

1 Under what circumstances are referenda held?
2 Are they more democratic than general elections?
3 An important referendum was held in March 1992 to secure the support of white voters for continuing negotiations for a democratic country (see Unit 8 below). Why was it held?

Black opposition to the republic

On 20 April 1961 Nelson Mandela wrote to Dr Verwoerd, informing him that a conference held at Pietermaritzburg in March had decided that the white minority government was not entitled to introduce a republic 'without first seeking the views and obtaining the express consent of the African people'. He went on to call for a national convention representative of all South Africans to meet and draw up a new non-racial and democratic constitution. If no convention was called by 31 May, country-wide demonstrations would be held.

On 23 May 1961 Mandela wrote to Sir De Villiers Graaff, leader of the Opposition, asking him to support the call for a national convention, but again got nowhere. On 26 June he again wrote to Dr Verwoerd, after the strike on 31 May had been suppressed, saying that 'no power on earth can stop an oppressed people, determined to win their freedom. History punishes those who resort to force and fraud to suppress the claims and legitimate aspirations of the majority of the country's citizens.' (Ebrahim. *Soul of a Nation*.)

The republic came into being on Union Day, 31 May 1961. Few constitutional changes were made, as Verwoerd had promised. He had also said that he would do everything he could to retain South Africa's membership of the Commonwealth. In March he went to the meeting of Commonwealth prime ministers in London and when he came under pressure from others over his government's apartheid policies, and it seemed that South Africa's application to remain in the Commonwealth as a republic might be rejected, he withdrew it. He said: 'No self-respecting member of any voluntary organisation could, in view of ... the degree of interference shown in what are South Africa's domestic affairs, be expected to wish to retain membership in what is now becoming a pressure group.' He predicted the break-up of the Commonwealth. On his return to South Africa, his supporters welcomed him back and proclaimed that his journey had ended in triumph, and that Providence had produced a 'miracle'. On 31 May CR Swart, a former minister of justice, became the first president of the new republic.

Activities ···

1 Why was the republic born when it was?
2 What was the black response to the new republic, and why was black opposition rejected? (Source F)
3 Speculate on whether, without Verwoerd, the republic would have been achieved. (Asking such questions is to engage in counter-factual or 'virtual' history. It may help one's understanding of the event to speculate in this way.)

···

▼ *Source F*

Say 'No' to Verwoerd's Republic
Editorial in *New Age*, 15 September 1960

The Minister of Bantu Administration, Mr De Wet Nel, told an audience last week that a good reason for having the republic was that the Bantu would then know who was baas – the Queen or the Prime Minister. To make this clear would be to the benefit of the country and in particular of the Bantu.

As far as we are concerned, Mr. Nel has given us a very good reason for not having the republic. Not that we prefer the Queen to the Prime Minister as baas, but we don't want any baas at all.

We are republicans. We don't believe in kings and queens and their divine right to rule over us especially when they live 6,000 miles away from us and know nothing about our problems.

But we believe in a people's democratic, republic, not in Verwoerd's fascist republic, where the Prime Minister will be baas and the majority of people will have no rights at all. The very fact that Verwoerd wants a republic is good enough reason for us to oppose a republic, for history has shown that whatever Verwoerd wants is in the interests only of a tiny section of the Whites, and can be achieved only at the expense of the interests of the majority of the population, Black as well as White.

A Verwoerd republic will:
- *entrench White supremacy;*
- *perpetuate the·rule of the Nationalist Party;*
- *end up as a Christian National authoritarian police state.*

Moreover, a victory for Verwoerd in the coming referendum will consolidate his shaky regime at a time when his prestige has never been lower as a result of the disasters of Sharpeville and Langa and the whole period of the emergency. On the other hand, a defeat for Verwoerd would shatter the myth of his infallibility and might very well be the beginning of the end of his hated rule.

We therefore issue a call to all democratic-minded Europeans to cast their vote against the republic in the coming referendum. There can be no question of boycott or indifference in this matter. A chance exists for delivering a shattering blow to the

Verwoerd Government; that chance must not be thrown away through neglect.

At the same time, it is as well to point out that the curse of apartheid will remain with us irrespective of the outcome of the referendum on October 5. Therefore the struggle for a genuine people's democratic republic, in which all peoples, of all races, creeds and colours, will enjoy equal rights and apartheid will be made a crime, must be intensified. Freedom will not come as a result of a referendum or election restricted to European voters only. It will only come as the result of mass struggle in which all sections of our people join hands to rid the country of the curse of the colour bar and White supremacy.

Extension activity

How significant was it for South Africa that it was no longer a member of the Commonwealth from 1961? (It resumed its membership in 1994, once a democratic government was installed.)

To answer this question, you will need to do some research on South Africa's position in the world before and after 1961. Were ties with trading countries cut? Did isolation increase? What role was the Commonwealth to play in bringing about negotiations in South Africa?

Apartheid and resistance in the 1960s and early 1970s (1960–76)

Unit outcomes

- Understand in greater depth the meaning of apartheid and how it changed over time.
- Learn more about different forms of resistance to apartheid and how they changed over time.

Unit timeline

Apartheid

1966: Declaration of District Six a white area; assassination of Verwoerd; Vorster becomes prime minister

1970: Bantu Homelands Citizenship Act

1976: 'Independence' of Transkei

Resistance

1963: Arrest of Rivonia trialists

1964: End of Rivonia trial: life-sentences imposed and leaders sent to Robben Island

1968: Formation of SASO, first major black consciousness organisation

1973: Durban strikes

1975: Independence of Mozambique and Angola

Introduction

In this unit we shall look at how apartheid changed after the Sharpeville massacre, and then what forms resistance took from the early 1960s to the year of the Soweto uprising.

Verwoerd redefines apartheid

When he visited South Africa in early 1960, the British Prime Minister Harold Macmillan addressed a joint sitting of both Houses of Parliament. He warned the white South African legislators that a wind of change was blowing through Africa, the wind of African nationalism. A growing number of countries were becoming independent in tropical Africa, and he urged the South African government to move away from apartheid. Verwoerd responded that South Africa was a different case, and that South Africa would not bow to outside pressures for change.

▼ **Source A**

Extract from Verwoerd's speech

We settled in a country which was bare. The Bantu, too, came to this country and settled certain portions for themselves. It is in line with thinking on Africa to grant them there, those fullest rights which we, with you, admit all people should have. We believe in providing those rights for those people in the fullest degree in that part of southern Africa which their forefathers found for themselves and settled in. But we also believe in balance. We believe in allowing exactly those same full opportunities to remain within the grasp of the white man in the areas he settled, the white man who has made all this possible.

(From: Liebenberg and Spies. *South Africa in the Twentieth Century.*)

Activities

1 Critically evaluate the history in Source A. Was the country 'bare' when whites settled it?
2 What did Verwoerd mean by speaking of providing rights 'in the fullest degree'?
3 What did he mean by 'balance'? Was it a true balance?

New words

ideologue one who holds a certain ideology, that is, a system of thought or a set of beliefs

Verwoerd had become prime minister in 1958. The leading **ideologue** in the formation of apartheid, he decided in 1959, in the face of international pressure against apartheid, that the bantustan policy should be taken to its logical end, and bantustans be granted their 'independence'.

PW Botha, one of his ministers, speaking in the Senate on 11 May 1964, said:

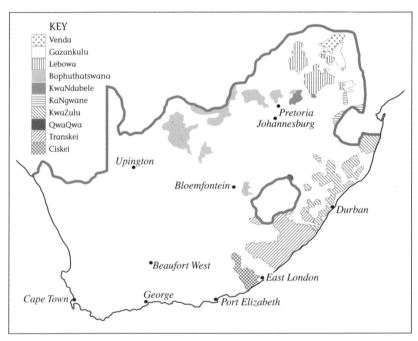

◀Source B
Forced removals

KEY

→ Removal

◻ Homelands 1970

■ Major Resettlement Camps

Mohodi

*Restaurant
Kwaggafontein*

Rooigrond

*Pretoria
Johannesburg*

Upington

*Mzimhlope
Sahlumbe
Pietermaritzburg*

Bloemfontein

Onverwacht *Compensation*

Durban

Thornhill *Elakhanyeni*

Beaufort West *Sada*

Glenmore *East London*

Kamaskraal

Cape Town

George

Port Elizabeth

◀Source C
Map of bantustans or
'homelands'

KEY

Venda

Gazankulu

Lebowa

Bophuthatswana

KwaNdabele

KaNgwane

KwaZulu

QwaQwa

Transkei

Ciskei

*Pretoria
Johannesburg*

Upington

Bloemfontein

Durban

Beaufort West

East London

Cape Town

George

Port Elizabeth

*there is no permanent home for even a sec-
tion of the Bantu in the White area of
South Africa ... the destiny of South Africa
depends on this essential point. If the principle of permanent residence of the Black
man in the area of the White is accepted
then it is the beginning of the end of civilisation as we know it in this country.*

Once they had removed all blacks from the
common voters' role, the government decided to
turn the African reserves into separate countries. Ten separate 'homelands' were established
and Africans given political rights there (see
Source C above). Those rights were used to
justify denying Africans in the rest of South
Africa all rights. Many Africans were forced

Profile: Mangosutho Buthelezi

© Eric Miller/i-Afrika

Mangosutho Gatsha Buthelezi, born in 1928 and descended from Cetshwayo, had been expelled from the University of Fort Hare in 1952 for African National Congress activities and become an adviser to the Zulu king. Having attempted unsuccessfully to resist the imposition of the bantustan system on his people, Buthelezi decided to work through it, and became chief minister of KwaZulu in 1972. He emerged as the most outspoken bantustan leader, rejecting independence for his fragmented and impoverished territory. Though he was accused of lending credibility to the bantustan policy, he argued that use should be made of any platform to fight apartheid, even a platform created by apartheid. He supported **federalism** as a device which would allow for redistribution to Africans, while **allaying** white fears, and he encouraged foreign investment in South Africa on the grounds that it provided jobs for Africans.

In the mid-1970s he revived Inkatha as a mass organisation with the **tacit support** of the ANC. In the Soweto Uprising (see Unit 5), he backed the Zulu hostel-dwellers against the youth, and Black Consciousness supporters condemned him as a sell-out, and threatened his life at the funeral of Robert Sobukwe in March 1978. He fell out with the ANC at a meeting with the exile leadership in London in 1979. He refused to adopt a different strategy, and continued to reject the armed struggle, though he worked for the release of Nelson Mandela who was in jail. He remained the single most important figure in KwaZulu-Natal until the 1994 election, in which he agreed to participate at the very last minute. The IFP won 10 per cent of the vote in that election, and control of KwaZulu-Natal. After the election, Buthelezi became minister of home affairs in the Government of National Unity.

from urban and rural areas to the bantustans, where there was no work and few resources. Eventually more than three and a half million people were moved (see Source B). The Transkei, the largest block of African territory, was the first bantustan to be given self-government. Elections were held there in 1963, a step in a process that was to lead to the 'independence' of the territory in October 1976. The Transkei was followed by Bophuthatswana, Venda, and the Ciskei, but in KwaZulu, Mangosutho Buthelezi who was the chief minister of KwaZulu, refused to accept 'independence' for his bantustan.

No other country, besides South Africa itself, recognised any of the bantustans as legitimately independent countries. Instead, they were denounced as creations of apartheid. In them new leaders emerged, people who saw an opportunity to gain power and throw off apartheid.

Government policy was that all Africans should be linked to one or other bantustans. By legislation passed in 1970, all Africans were to be citizens of different bantustans. That meant that no Africans would be citizens of, or have permanent homes in, white-ruled South Africa.

Activities

1 What does the pattern of forced removals in Source B show?
2 Look closely at Source C.
   a Why were the bantustans shaped like they were, with such small patches of land?
   b Why did they come into existence in those places?
   c What were the aims of the bantustan policy?

New words

federalism system of government in which power is divided between the centre and the regions or provinces
allaying putting to rest
tacit support not open support

You must remember that this new policy accompanied great repression. We have explored the bannings of the liberation movements (see Unit 3), and now legislation was passed to give the police a freer hand: 90-day detention without legal process was introduced, then extended to 180 days, and beyond. Reports of the torture of prisoners began to be heard, and political prisoners began to die under suspicious circumstances.

This repression and intensification of apartheid accompanied a period of economic growth, for South Africa recovered rapidly from the crisis of 1960 (see Unit 3). As 'stability' was restored, so foreign investment increased. Anglo American became an international giant and expanded from gold mining into many different areas of the industrial economy.

While the policy of apartheid was greatly refined by Verwoerd, it did not depend on one individual. On 6 September 1966, Verwoerd was assassinated in the House of Assembly as he was preparing to make a speech. Under his successor, John Vorster, who was elected by the NP caucus to succeed him, apartheid was continued, though it took on new forms.

Apartheid under Vorster

Under Vorster South Africa's remarkable economic growth continued. But Afrikaner nationalists were now divided into the far-right, determined that there should be no concessions, and those who were open to change. Professor Willem de Klerk, speaking in October 1966, described the two schools of thought as the 'verkramptes' (conservatives) and the 'verligtes' (enlightened). The new prime minister supported the verligtes, and set out to improve South Africa's position abroad. His 'outward policy' meant allowing Malawi to send a black diplomat to South Africa, and adaptations in sport policy, allowing a New Zealand Maori to tour

South Africa. In 1968 Albert Hertzog, son of the former prime minister, was dismissed because of his hard-line refusal to accept the new approach, but other verkramptes, including Dr AP Treurnicht, remained within the National Party. The new party which Hertzog formed, the Herstigte Nasionale Party, was crushed in the election of 1970.

Vorster's 'outward policy' did not get far. After the military coup in Portugal in April 1974, which signalled the independence of Mozambique and Angola, Vorster realised that he had to change his policies. He began to campaign for peace in Rhodesia and urged the parties to a settlement. His pressure on Ian Smith helped lead to Smith's acceptance of black majority rule in 1976. But the credit which Vorster's new policies won him in Africa was lost when South African troops invaded Angola in late 1975, to try to prevent the MPLA coming to power there. After the Soweto uprising (see Unit 5), Vorster made major concessions on South West Africa/Namibia, accepting a Western-brokered plan for a transition to independence in which a United Nations Transitional Assistance Group would 'supervise and control' an election. But implementation of that plan had got nowhere by the time Vorster had to leave office, disgraced as a result of the Information Scandal, in September 1978 (see Unit 6). We shall see how the Namibian issue was finally resolved in Unit 7.

▶ *Source D*
"Vote for him? Next thing we'd have blacks living right next door to us! Not likely!" (1974)
(From: J Leyden. *100 Not Out.*)

© The Star

Balthazar Johannes (John) Vorster was born in 1915. Interned during the Second World War for his anti-Nazi sympathies, the usually grim-faced Vorster became Verwoerd's minister of justice in 1962, and introduced detention without trial to deal with political opposition. As prime minister from 1966, he was more flexible than Verwoerd, welcomed diplomats from Malawi and pursued an 'outward' policy which involved talking to black African heads of state, provided that apartheid was not discussed.

Activities

1 To what extent, and why, did Vorster adapt apartheid in his years as prime minister?
2 In your view, was Vorster an effective ruler of South Africa?
3 Look closely at Source D. What message is the cartoonist conveying?

Resistance in the period

The nature of resistance in this period was shaped by the new climate in which it took place. The liberation movements had now gone into exile, and resistance internally was crushed in the early 1960s, but arose in new forms from the late 1960s.

As it was soon clear that sabotage would not topple the regime, the leadership of MK began to plan to undertake guerrilla war. But in 1963 the police raided the headquarters of the organisation at Lilliesleaf farm, Rivonia, north of Johannesburg. At the Rivonia trial which followed, the MK leaders were charged with planning a violent revolution to overthrow the government. Sentenced to life imprisonment, the African prisoners were sent to Robben Island.

© Mayibuye Centre

Bram Fischer (1908–75) was born into a leading Afrikaner Orange Free State family. He became an advocate and joined the Communist Party in the 1930s. He was the main defence lawyer for the ANC members charged with sabotage in the Rivonia trial of 1963, but was later arrested himself and charged under the Suppression of Communism Act. He then jumped bail and went underground, until he was caught and sentenced to life imprisonment. He became ill in jail and was allowed to leave only when on the point of death.

For more information on Fischer see Stephen Clingman's *Bram Fischer, Afrikaner Revolutionary*.

The ANC and MK from Rivonia to Soweto

In the decade after the Rivonia trial, the ANC was extremely weak. Its underground structures were largely destroyed at the time of the Rivonia arrests. Some of its top leadership fled the country and others, including Chris Hani, left to undergo military training abroad. It took years to mount any campaign, and then it was a disaster. South Africa was at that time surrounded by countries hostile to the ANC. In 1967 MK cadres (soldiers) and forces of the Zimbabwe African People's Union crossed the Zambezi River into Zimbabwe. But the MK cadres did not reach the Limpopo River before they were killed or forced to scatter, and other attempts to reach the country failed in these years.

At its conference in 1969, held at Morogoro, Tanzania, the ANC for the first time formally opened membership of the ANC to non-Africans, though they were still barred from membership of its National Executive

Committee. (Informally, Jack and Ray Simons had been admitted to membership before Morogoro.) The conference confirmed that the ANC should intensify armed struggle, but should also campaign internationally for support and try to build underground structures within the country to aid the guerrillas and to support a possible insurrection. But all this remained a dream for a long time to come. Throughout this period, MK did not fire a shot in South Africa. Oliver Tambo proved an able leader, holding together the bulk of a very diverse organisation in exile (some who pushed an Africanist line were expelled).

The PAC, on the other hand, won some new recruits (some from the Coloured Alliance organisation joined the PAC in London), but suffered greatly from fighting in its exile wing; its internal structures had been broken by the police in the early 1960s. For a decade there was relatively little activity within the country while harsh repression prevented political protest. From 1968, however, new and forceful African voices began to be heard.

Black Consciousness

Bantu Education and the creation of new black universities created a larger body of black students, which, in the late 1960s, began to challenge the university authorities and then the state itself. In 1969 black university students broke with the white-dominated, liberal National Union of South African Students, and came together under the leadership of a medical student, Steve Biko, to form the South African Student's Organisation. They called for unity of blacks (Africans, coloureds and Indians) against apartheid, and argued that blacks should lead the fight. Biko rejected the use of 'Non-white' as negative, and promoted 'Black' as a positive term. The Black Consciousness (BC) movement, in which he was the leading figure, stressed the need for the psychological liberation of blacks, and tried through a variety of programmes – clinics, crèches, and literacy training, among others – to reach out to the masses. At first the emphasis on race meant that the government tolerated BC as fitting its 'separate development' philosophy. From 1973, however, after the formation of a Black People's Convention (BPC) with an overtly political agenda, BC leaders began to suffer harsh state repression. Biko suffered various forms of harassment before his murder (see Unit 5).

Although the ANC acknowledged that the BC movement had helped to activate the people into struggle it also spoke out about BC limita-tions: '[BC] saw our struggle as racial, describing the entire white population of our country as "part of the problem"' (Pampallis).

Activities
1 What is your assessment of BC?
2 Did its positive role outweigh its limitations?

Another form of resistance occurred in Durban from January 1973, when factory workers in their tens of thousands went on strike, for the first time since 1960. As one worker put it: 'I make blankets for Mr Philip Frame, [but] I can't afford to buy blankets for my children' (Pampallis, 247). The long growth phase was over and the South African economy now began to falter. From the Durban strikes over the next decade and a half a large new labour movement would emerge which would eventually form an important component in the anti-apartheid movement. By the late 1970s it was clear that existing labour legislation, which prohibited Africans from belonging to registered trade unions, was ineffective, and in 1979 that legislation was amended.

▲ Miriam Makeba

Sport and culture in the age of apartheid

History is not just about politics. If space permitted we could include much about other areas of life. Consider the following snippets.

- Basil D'Oliviera left South Africa to play cricket for England, and in 1968 the government refused to allow the English cricket team to play in this country because D'Oliviera was included. After that, South Africa was gradually excluded from most international sport.
- New forms of music developed: musicians such as Dollar Brand (later Abdullah Ibrahim), Hugh Masekela, Miriam Makeba and others became successful jazz musicians, but most had left the country by the early 1960s because they saw no future for themselves under apartheid. From 1951 a lively magazine aimed at African readers, *Drum*, published the work of new writers, such as Es'kia Mphahlele, Can Themba and Todd Matshikizi.

Activities

1 Interview someone who was an adult in the 1950s or 1960s about their life at that time. What music did they listen to, what sport did they play, etc. Write up a report on this person and present it to the rest of your class.
2 Account for the changing strategy of the resistance forces in the years under discussion in this unit.
3 Explain why and how resistance was crushed in the early 1960s.
4 Why did resistance revive from the late 1960s?
5 How significant is resistance in this period?

Unit 5

The Soweto uprisings and the aftermath (1976–77)

Unit outcomes

- Learn about the different perspectives which people can have about events.
- Understand what caused the Soweto uprisings, and appreciate the consequences.

Unit timeline

May 1976:	Desmond Tutu warns John Vorster of the danger of violent protest
16 June 1976:	Outbreak of the uprising in Soweto
August 1976:	The uprising spreads from Soweto to the Western Cape
September 1977:	The murder of Biko in detention
November 1977:	The United Nations imposes a mandatory arms-embargo on South Africa
1977:	The NP Cabinet approves a new constitutional plan
1978:	The first of the Soweto generation to return with arms as MK cadres are arrested.

Introduction

In this unit we will learn about one of the most important events in the history of the anti-apartheid struggle. The Soweto uprisings feature prominently in the accounts of the liberation struggle as the first major step on the way to the ending of apartheid. We need to understand what happened and why, and how the Soweto uprisings contributed to the destruction of apartheid.

As with all such events, we shall see some of the ways in which it remains controversial both in its causes and its significance. Remember that history is often contested and debated, and people approach the past from different perspec-

tives depending on their points of view. Interpretations of important past events can never be final. For relatively recent events, such as the Soweto uprisings, we may not have a full picture, and interpretations may change as more evidence becomes available.

The order of events

After the initial event, it is important to notice how the uprisings escalated and spread to new parts of the country. As with most such events, it is difficult to know exactly when it ended. Think of other violent protest movements in South African or other history. Although the Soweto uprisings petered out in the course of 1977, their consequences were felt long after that.

The uprising began when the police opened fire on a protest march by schoolchildren in Orlando, Soweto, on 16 June 1976. The marchers, who were unarmed, were heading for the Orlando football stadium, where a mass rally was planned, to show opposition to learning through the medium of Afrikaans. The police were determined to prevent the students from holding their rally. They therefore blocked the march. Stones were thrown at them, and they began firing on the marchers. Soon after the first shots were fired, killing Hector Petersen among others, street battles were fought between the schoolchildren and other young people and the police in many parts of the sprawling Soweto township. The protesters set up barricades to try to prevent the police gaining access, and they attacked state property, especially beerhalls and other buildings belonging to the West Rand Administration Board, which ran the township.

Two white employees of the Board were killed and many schools and beerhalls were set alight. Large numbers of suspected activists were detained by the police. Some were shot and killed by police, who often fired from the safety of their vehicles. John Vorster appeared on television and announced that instructions had been given to the security forces to maintain order 'at all costs'.

Within weeks, battles with the police had spread from Soweto to many other African townships in the Transvaal and elsewhere. On 11 August fierce clashes with the police occurred in the Cape Town African townships of Langa, Guguletu and Nyanga, and in early September the protests were joined by coloureds in their suburbs of Cape Town. Soon the coloured townships were also the scene of violent clashes with the police. What had begun with a protest against the use of Afrikaans in schools had become a general revolt against apartheid.

Activities
1 Why did Source A become so well-known?
2 What does it tell us about the way the uprising began?

Discuss these questions in small groups before you answer them.

3 This was clearly a different kind of anti-apartheid struggle from the Defiance Campaign of 1952, or from the anti-pass campaign of 1960. What are the differences that you can think of?

4 Why did the police open fire in Soweto with live ammunition to stop a march by unarmed young people?

5 a Was the march, or the proposed rally, a threat to the police, or to anyone else?
  b If the police wanted to stop the march, why did they not use other methods?
  c If you had been police commissioner in Soweto on that day, how would you have handled the situation?
  d Do you think that the methods that the police used were effective or counter-productive? Give reasons to support your answer.

◄ **Source A**
Photo taken by Sam Nzima of the body of 13-year-old Hector Petersen being carried away after being shot in Orlando West, Soweto, on 16 June 1976. If there is one image that sums up the Soweto uprisings in most people's minds, it is this one.

► **Source B**
Students demonstrate against Afrikaans (Soweto, 16 June 1976)

▼ **Source C**
Police beating students attending a political meeting

© TRACE

These questions are not easy to answer. We still do not know exactly what instructions had been given to the police before 16 June 1976. Were they told to be 'tough', and given orders to shoot to kill? On 18 June the prime minister made his 'maintain order at all costs' speech. Remember that any mass organisation by blacks was seen as a potential threat to 'law and order' as defined by the apartheid state.

Activities

1 Study Sources B and C and imagine that you were a student on one of these occasions. Write a diary of what happened to you on the day.
2 a What sources of information could there be on why the state acted as it did to crush the revolt?
  b Why could that information no longer be available?

Extension activity

In 1997 the Truth Commission enquired into some aspects of the Soweto uprisings. Do some research to find out what it said about the revolt and those involved in it in its final report.

▼ **Source D**
A pamphlet issued by the schoolchildren of Soweto appealed to parents

... you should rejoice for having given birth to ... a child who prefers to die from a bullet rather than to swallow a poisonous education which relegates him and his parents to a position of perpetual subordination.

Activities

1 Why do you think the schoolchildren had to convince their parents of the justice of their struggle as is shown in Source D?
2 Imagine you were a parent at the time. How would you have reacted?

There was soon a cycle of funerals of those shot by the police, more attacks on the police at the funerals, and more funerals. To explain why people were so angry, and were prepared to put their lives at risk in showing resistance to the apartheid system, we must look at the causes of the uprisings.

Causes of the uprisings

As with most such events, we cannot just isolate one cause because there were many causes. The immediate cause of the protest march which was met with police bullets on 16 June 1976 was the regulation issued by the Bant

Education Department that Afrikaans was to be used on an equal basis with English as a language of instruction in secondary schools. So we can ask: why was there resistance to this? What did Afrikaans symbolise to the schoolchildren? Clearly this was not the only cause of a revolt that became widespread and involved many who were not directly affected by this regulation.

▼ Source E

Soweto Students Representative Council statement, August 1976

Twenty years ago, when Bantu Education was introduced, our fathers said: Half a loaf is better than no bread. We say: Half a gram of poison is just as killing as the whole gram.

▼ Source F

Desmond Tutu, then Bishop in Johannesburg, wrote an open letter to Prime Minister Vorster three weeks before the uprisings began. In this he said:

I have a nightmarish fear that unless something drastic is done very soon, then bloodshed and violence are going to happen in South Africa, almost inevitably. A people can take only so much, and no more ... A people made desperate by despair and injustice and oppression will use desperate means.

Activities ....

1 a What do you know about Bantu Education (see Source E)?
  b Why was it so bitterly resented?
2 Carefully read through Source F.
  a How was Bishop Tutu able to anticipate the revolt?
  b How do you explain that Vorster did not react to this warning?

....

Was the uprising planned?

In exploring any such event, one of the main questions to ask is: was it organised, and if so, by whom? Historians agree that although the initial march of 16 June 1976 was planned, there is no evidence that any group, such as the ANC, organised the Soweto uprisings as such. They began and spread spontaneously in response to a particular event, the shooting of marchers, and the consequences that followed from that event. To understand why they occurred, however, we have to remember the context in which they occurred.

In the previous unit we considered the rise of Black Consciousness. The ideas of Black Consciousness were widespread and gave black people a new self-confidence and assertiveness.

There are other relevant factors that are part of the background to the Soweto uprisings.

- The uprisings began at a time of a serious economic downturn. This had begun in 1974 and was in part related to a worldwide recession which followed the imposition of much higher oil prices by the oil producing nations. In South Africa, prices had increased a lot, but wages had not increased at the same rate. Many black people were without jobs and so found it very difficult, if not impossible, to pay their rent.

- As we saw in Unit 4, in 1975 first Mozambique and then Angola gained their independence from Portugal, and black-led governments took over – Frelimo in Mozambique and the MPLA in Angola. This inspired many blacks in South Africa to think that it was intolerable that they should still live under a white-minority government. In the case of Angola, South African troops had entered the country to try to prevent the MPLA coming to power, and had moved north to the outskirts of Luanda, the capital. This invasion had been covered up for a time, but by early 1976 news of it had leaked out, and it became widely known that the South African Defence Force had been forced to withdraw early that year, in the face of the support which Cuban forces had given the new MPLA government. To many black people in South Africa this seemed to show that the forces of the apartheid state were not, after all, unbeatable.

Activities ....

1 What else in the background to the Soweto uprisings do you think could be relevant to an explanation of why they occurred? (Check back to the timeline at the beginning of this chapter for clues on this.)
2 Not all black people participated in the revolt.
  a Why do you think some townships exploded, while others did not?
  b Why did hostel-workers in Soweto and elsewhere take the side of the state against the protesters?

....

The revolt was not successful in that it did not achieve its aim which was to remove the apartheid government. Unarmed people could not possibly defeat those who had guns and were prepared to use them. In the end, according to the official record, over 700 people died, but the real figure was probably higher. If the revolt was crushed relatively easily, why is it considered a major blow against apartheid and the point from which the decline and fall of apartheid can be traced? We shall consider this question in the section on consequences below.

The death of Steve Biko

The world was shocked when the police opened fire on children in Soweto in June 1976. It was further shocked when the single most prominent new black leader in South Africa was murdered by the police in September 1977. We have considered Steve Biko's early career as a Black Consciousness activist in Unit 4. On 18 August 1977 he and his companion Peter Jones were detained at a police roadblock set up outside Grahamstown. On 12 September he died from massive head injuries sustained when he was assaulted by the security police in their headquarters in Port Elizabeth. After the assault, he was treated appallingly, and taken to Pretoria in the back of a Landrover. As the leading advocate for the Biko family said at the **inquest**, he 'died a miserable and lonely death on a mat on a stone floor of a police cell'.

Biko had been harassed by the police for years. They suspected that he was trying to coordinate resistance, and had travelled to Cape Town, breaking his banning-order, to carry this further. The Minister of Justice, Jimmy Kruger, reacted to his death by claiming that he had died of a hunger-strike. He also said that Biko's death 'left him cold'.

September 77

In Port Elizabeth weather fine

It was business as usual

In Police Room 619

(From: 'Biko' by Peter Gabriel. In: B Pitjana et al. *Bounds of Possibility*.)

New words

inquest official inquiry into a death

Extension activity ....

The first book on Biko was Donald Woods's *Biko*, that was made into the film *Cry Freedom*. Try to see the video of this film. (Refer to Source D in Unit 6.) Can you find anything to be critical about?

....

What happened to Biko in the hands of the police in Room 619 took years to emerge. The inquest which opened in Pretoria in November 1977 revealed that he had suffered brain damage and other injuries, then been kept naked and chained while transported overland from Port Elizabeth to Pretoria. The magistrate who presided at the inquest failed to find any person responsible for his death. Biko's family sued the state for damages and in 1979 settled for an out-of-court

Profile: Steve Biko

Steve Biko was born in King William's Town in the Eastern Cape in 1946. He attended a Roman Catholic school in Natal, then the University of Natal Medical School. It was under his inspiration that African students broke with the National Union of South African Students and established their separate South African Students Organization in 1969 (see page 322 of Unit 4). Dropping his medical studies, the charismatic Biko emerged as an outstanding organiser and theoretician, promoting Black Consciousness through his writing, speeches and actions. From 1973 he endured banning and other forms of state harassment.

payment. Years after the inquest, the police who had assaulted him gave new evidence when applying for amnesty to the Truth and Reconciliation Commission. The Biko family, opposed to the amnesty process, continues to believe that the police were not telling the whole truth.

▼ Source G

Extract from editorial in *Isaziso*, September 1977

Vorster's belief that Biko was not known is nonsense. His police will tell him that 25 000 people attended Steve's funeral and twelve buses were turned back by police in the Transvaal. Vorster's and Kruger's funeral combined would be so cold and insignificant that they will never match up to Biko's in the number of mourners and sympathisers, let alone telegrams and messages from all over the world. For that matter, no Black faces would be seen at their funerals ... Black people in South Africa have lost one of their greatest leaders, but Biko's death has not been in vain. His spirit is very much alive ...

(Karis and Gerhart. *Protest to Challenge, vol. 5*.)

▲ Supporters at Biko's funeral

Activities

1 Why did the writer of the editorial in Source G say the things he did?
2 Do you think he was right or wrong? Give reasons for your answer.
3 Write an essay on the life and death of Steve Biko, explaining his historical importance.
4 If you look at Nelson Mandela's autobiography, *Long Walk to Freedom,* you will find that he devotes little attention to Biko.
  a Why is that, do you think?
  b Try to find information on relations between the ANC and the Black Consciousness movement in the 1970s.
5 What is the cartoonist implying in Source H?

Consequences of the Soweto uprisings

Many of those involved in the protests realised that they would not be able to win the struggle for freedom by peaceful means, and decided that they now wanted to fight back with weapons. Many young men, in particular, left the country to join the liberation movements. Many of them were followers of Black Consciousness when they left, but there was no external Black Consciousness organisation engaged in armed resistance for them to join.

◀ **Source H**

'Follow me' (22 September 1977)

(From: J Leyden, *100 Not Out.*)

The most organised liberation movement was the ANC, and most therefore joined it, greatly strengthening that organisation. Within a year of the outbreak of the revolt, the first members of 'the class of 76' were returning to the country with landmines, hand grenades and AK-47s.

▼ Source I

Statement by 'Tokyo' Sexwale to the Pretoria Supreme Court, 1978, after he was convicted and before he was imprisoned on Robben Island, explaining why he took up arms. He was one of those who left Soweto to take up arms.

> It was during my primary school years that the bare facts concerning the realities of South African society and its discrepancies began to unfold before me. I remember a period in the early 1960s, when there was a great deal of political tension, and we often used to encounter armed police in Soweto ... I remember the humiliation to which my parents were subjected by whites in shops and in other places where we encountered them, and the poverty. All these things had their influence on my young mind ... and by the time I went to Orlando West High School, I was already beginning to question the injustice of the society ... and to ask why nothing was being done to change it.

Sexwale then explained how after the revolt he went abroad and joined the ANC, and returned to undertake sabotage.

Activities

1 What factors does Sexwale describe as having an influence on him in Source I?
2 Imagine that you are someone similar to Sexwale. Write an account of your childhood in Soweto and the reasons why you went into exile and then returned to South Africa.
3 What do you know of Sexwale's later career?

Though the Soweto uprisings were suppressed, they were a major disaster for the state. Around the world people were appalled when they read or heard that in apartheid South Africa police had opened fire on unarmed schoolchildren, and then that Steve Biko had died while in police custody. The government came under much stronger international pressure to change its apartheid policies. The most important step taken against it by the international community was the imposition, in November 1977, of a mandatory arms embargo by the United Nations.

There was also new pressure coming from internal events. As happened at the time of the Sharpeville massacre (see Unit 3), the economy suffered severely, as people no longer wished to invest in South Africa. Businessmen and others urged the government to take action to prevent another such revolt occurring.

In the face of this new pressure, the government began to think of ways to respond. Its officials began to say that (old-style) apartheid was dead, and the government began to formulate a new scheme in which coloureds and Indians would be brought into central government as inferior partners with whites. In 1977 the NP **caucus** approved in principle a plan for a new constitution which would bring coloureds and Indians into central government and provide for an executive state president with greatly extended powers. The process of drawing up this new constitution was a very long drawn-out one: a President's Council was established in 1980 which produced final proposals in late 1982, and the new constitution did not take effect until 1984 (see Unit 6 for more information), but the origins lie in the aftermath of the Soweto uprisings.

At that time the government also decided that Africans in the urban areas should be treated differently from those in the rural areas and the bantustans. The government's own commission of inquiry into the uprisings, the Cillié Report, recommended changes in policy to urban Africans. Looking back, we can now see that from the time of the Soweto uprisings apartheid was never the same again: the state was now more defensive, and desperate, in its efforts to keep a system going which had been challenged so dramatically.

The Soweto uprisings also helped to inspire later resistance, including the school boycotts of 1980, and above all the Township Revolt of 1984–86 (see Unit 6).

New words

caucus meeting of officials (often members of a party in parliament)

Activities

PJ Koornhof, Minister for Cooperation and Development, told the National Press Club in Washington DC in June 1979 that 'apartheid is dead'.
1 Why did he say that?
2 What did he mean by these words?

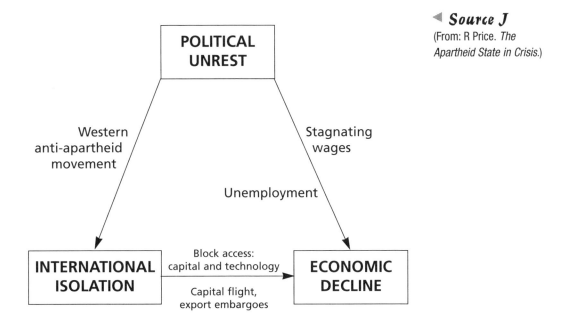

◀ *Source J*
(From: R Price. *The Apartheid State in Crisis.*)

3 Do you agree with what he said? Give reasons for your answer.

4 Source J shows how a political scientist tried to set out the changed environment before and after the Soweto uprisings.

a What is he is trying to say?

b Do you find this diagram helpful?

c Can you think of how you could improve on this diagram?

Extension activity ....

There was space here only to tell the history of the revolt in brief outline. Can you tell more of the story with information from your own community or from a library accessible to you?

a What happened in your local community at this time?

b Do you know anyone who was involved in the Soweto uprisings whom you can interview about what happened to them?

c Can you think of any other source of information about the uprisings which you could consult?

Unit 6 — Total strategy, tricameralism and the Township Revolt (1977–86)

Unit outcomes

- Understand how and why the apartheid system changed from the late 1970s.
- Discuss how and why the major resistance of the mid-1980s occurred.
- Formulate the relationship between these two phenomena.

Unit timeline

State policy

1975:	Independence of Angola and Mozambique
1976:	Soweto uprisings
1977:	Defence Force White Paper
1978:	Operation Reindeer (Cassinga massacre); PW Botha becomes prime minister; National Security Management System set up
1980:	Independence of Zimbabwe; MK attack on Sasol plant
1981:	SADF attacks houses in Maputo; Operation Protea
1982:	SADF attack on Maseru, Lesotho
1983:	Operation Askari (December)
1984:	Lusaka Accord; Nkomati Accord

Tricameralism and resistance

1983:	New tricameral constitution approved; Labour Party agrees to work within the new system; birth of the United Democratic Front (UDF) at a meeting in Mitchell's Plain, Cape Town (August)
1984:	(September) new constitution brought into effect; Township Revolt begins in Vaal Triangle; Army sent into Vaal Triangle (October); Township Revolt spreads
1985:	From its exile headquarters in Lusaka the ANC calls on the people of South Africa to 'make the townships ungovernable' (January)
1985:	Uprising spreads to most of the country; ANC holds conference at Kabwe, Zambia; imposition of the first state of emergency; Botha's 'Rubicon' speech; financial sanctions imposed
1986:	General state of emergency; press censorship; harsh repression
1986–87:	Township Revolt peters out
1988:	UDF and other bodies restricted

Introduction

In the aftermath of the Soweto uprisings, the state adopted a 'total strategy' policy. PW Botha, who succeeded John Vorster as prime minister in September 1978, sought to reform the apartheid system to meet the new circumstances. This helped produce new forms of resistance, the most important of which was the Township Revolt which began in September 1984. State policy and resistance, as we will see, were closely linked.

New words

mastermind the person or organisation behind something

Total strategy and destabilisation

In response to the Soweto uprisings, and to the changed regional situation, with the independence of Mozambique and Angola, the state adopted a 'total strategy' policy. This was first advanced in the Defence Force White Paper of 1977. South Africa, it was said, was facing a 'total onslaught', **masterminded** by the Soviet Union. In response, it was necessary to meet it with a 'total strategy', in which all sectors of the state would be mobilised to face the enemy.

PW Botha became prime minister in September 1978 as a direct result of the Information (or Muldergate) scandal. This involved the use of large secret funds, in a special Defence Force account, for various purposes, including the establishment of a pro-government English-speaking newspaper in Johannesburg, *The Citizen*. Vorster had supported these ideas, put to him by Connie Mulder, the Minister of Information, and his chief official, Dr Eschel Rhoodie. One result of the scandal was that it divided the Transvaal members of the NP caucus, the parliamentary members meeting together. When Vorster was forced to resign, as news of the scandal leaked out, it was the caucus which met to elect a new leader. Botha, the Cape leader of his party, gained the support of the Free State group, which was sufficient to win him enough votes to secure election as new *Hoofleier*.

Botha was keen to reform apartheid but had to wait for the *verkramptes* in his party to do something for which they could be said to be *volkskeurders* (schismatics or defectors). In 1982 Treurnicht forgot that he had been a member of the cabinet when it had approved power-sharing in principle and challenged Botha on the idea of power-sharing. Botha was able to accuse him of directly challenging the leader of the NP, and he was told to submit or leave. Treurnicht left and formed the Conservative Party, which grew to become the official opposition to the NP government in parliament, but which was to be sidelined once the transition to democracy began (see Unit 8).

Profile: PW Botha

© i-Afrika

PW Botha, born in 1916, became a full-time NP organizer in 1936, and a member of parliament in 1948. From 1966 he was minister of defence, and he persuaded Vorster that it was necessary to invade Angola in late 1975 to try to ensure that the Marxist MPLA party did not come to power there. A forceful man, he was able to persuade his colleagues to grant huge increases in the defence vote in parliament. After he became prime minister, the army was given increasing powers, and there was much talk of the 'total onslaught' and of a total strategy to combat such an onslaught. Vast destabilisation of neighbouring countries occurred. Though he told his electorate soon after becoming prime minister that they must 'adapt or die', his reformist vision did not extend very far.

Under Botha an elaborate, secret National Security Management System was created, with numerous Joint Management Centres bringing together security and other officials to plan counter-revolutionary strategy. One of the major aspects of this was destabilisation policy. As ANC attacks on targets inside the country mounted, it was deemed necessary to strike at the bases from which they came. And so numerous raids were carried out on neighbouring countries. Some were in direct retaliation for MK attacks, others were more random, giving rise to the idea that the South African government wanted to destabilise its neighbours to make the point that black governments, especially socialist ones, did not work.

In the case of Mozambique, the destabilisation policy led to the Nkomati Accord (see Source A below), by which that government agreed no longer to allow MK to operate from its soil. A similar, secret agreement with Swaziland had been made two years before. Forces within the South African state continued to supply Renamo, which was fighting the Frelimo government of Mozambique, but these agreements were major setbacks for the ANC, which had to withdraw its cadres from those territories. Its main training camps in the region were in Angola and from the early 1980s the South African government tried to make a deal with Angola to close them down. This was finally achieved in the New York Accords of December 1988 (see page 344 of Unit 7).

▼ *Source A*
The Nkomati Accord (March 1984)

> *'Agreement on non-aggression and good neighbourliness between the Government of the People's Republic of Mozambique and the Government of the Republic of South Africa.' Each party undertook 'to respect each other's sovereignty and independence and ... to refrain from interfering in the internal affairs of the other'*
> (From: Legum. *The Battlefronts of Southern Africa.*)

Both Machel and Botha said they signed the accord as a way of obtaining peace in the region. But the ANC was not consulted and its National Executive Committee said that the Accord:

> *cannot but help to perpetuate the illegitimate rule of the white settler minority ... a just and lasting peace in our region is not possible while the fountain-head of war and instability in this area – the apartheid regime and the oppressive system it maintains in South Africa and Namibia – continues to exist. (Legum.)*

1 a What is the significance of Source A?
  b Did the Nkomati Accord achieve anything?
2 Should Machel have signed it?
3 Why was the South African government so keen on the Accord?
....

Much state policy was initiated in the 'bush war' in South West Africa/Namibia. The first major cross-border raid by the South African Defence Force (SADF) took place in early May 1978, to attack what the SADF said was the military headquarters of the South West African People's Organisation (SWAPO), then waging an armed struggle against South African occupation of Namibia. At Cassinga there were large numbers of women and children refugees from Namibia, and over 600 of them were killed in the raid. For years SWAPO was able to use this massacre to their political advantage. There is evidence that the Cassinga raid was launched as a deliberate move to sabotage the agreement being negotiated on Namibia by the Western countries (see Unit 4).

More cross-border raids followed and from 1981 the SADF was in permanent occupation of a portion of southern Angola. Increasingly it found itself engaged in conflict with the forces of the Angolan army itself, not only those of SWAPO. After one particularly large operation in late 1983 (Operation Askari), the South African and Angolan governments agreed to an arrangement by which a joint monitoring committee was set up to secure the withdrawal of the South African troops from southern Angola. SWAPO's forces were not to take their place. But the agreement did not work well, and in May 1985 an SADF commando was discovered in the Cabinda enclave in the north of Angola, bringing further negotiations with Angola to a halt.

Tricameralism

In 1977 the NP caucus had approved in principle constitutional proposals providing for bringing coloureds and Indians into central government, and for an executive state president with increased powers. An advisory President's Council was appointed in 1980 and it produced the final constitutional proposals in late 1982, providing for new houses of parliament for coloureds and Indians. There was then a referendum among white voters to approve these proposals. They contained no provision for a fourth chamber for Africans,

who were therefore clearly excluded from the new constitutional order. The Coloured Labour Party reversed its previous position in early 1983 and decided to participate in the tricameral system, to try to work against apartheid from within. This helped to give some legitimacy to the new system, which was clearly designed to provide more support for the government, from within the country and from abroad. Most Indians and coloureds rejected the idea of participating in such a racially based system, in which the white House had more power than the other two combined, and so could stop them from passing laws which the white House of Assembly rejected.

Botha also removed some apartheid laws, most notably the pass laws (1986), which had broken down, and in 1979 he brought African trade unions within the industrial framework, by allowing them to register. This was to prevent uncontrolled strikes, and to facilitate negotiations with employers. Some jobs previously reserved for whites were now opened to all, and private schools and universities were allowed to admit students of all races, while theatres and luxury hotels were opened to all. The attempt to provide elected community councils in townships, financed through local rates and rents, only increased opposition to the entire system of apartheid rule. And critics said that Botha's reforms were merely cosmetic, and were designed to entrench the pillars of the apartheid system.

Under the tricameral constitution, which took effect in September 1984, Botha became the country's first executive state president, with greatly increased powers. Always authoritarian in manner, he became more short-tempered as resistance grew. His 'Rubicon' speech of August 1985, which failed to deliver on expectations for change, was a disaster for the country, and in May 1986 he ended the attempt by the Eminent Persons Group to bring about negotiations between the government and the ANC (see Unit 7).

In late 1997 Botha was subpoenaed by the Truth and Reconciliation Commission to give evidence in public before it, but he refused to attend and was then served a summons to appear in court. He was later fined, and then appealed against the fine.

New words

affiliates people connected to an organisation
decentralised not organised around a central group
government collaborators those who worked for or aided the government

The founding of the UDF

In January 1983 the Reverend Allan Boesak called for all opposed to the tricameral system to join hands in solidarity, and in August that year the United Democratic Front (UDF) was formed at a meeting held at Mitchell's Plain, Cape Town. On that occasion Boesak brought the crowd to its feet with 'three little words, words that express so eloquently our seriousness in this struggle: *all*, *here*, and *now*. We want all our rights, we want them here, and we want them now'. Delegates from 565 organisations, with 1,5 million supporters, attended the launch, and 400 immediately became UDF **affiliates,** many of them youth, student and civic organisations, two-thirds of them from the Western Cape. The UDF was a very democratic organisation: all affiliates had equal voting powers on committees. It was a federation, deliberately **decentralised** so that the state would not easily be able to destroy it. At its peak the UDF claimed the support of about 700 affiliates, representing people in every part of the country.

◀ *Source B* Photograph of Goniwe speaking at a funeral

Some were critical of the UDF. The National Forum, a Black Consciousness grouping, said: 'Any black person genuinely committed to liberation from white oppression will reject participation by members of the white oppressor class in the liberation struggle. The UDF is the old white-dominated SACP/ANC alliance dressed up in a new disguise' (Fredrikse, 209).

Activities

1 What is your view of the UDF? Explain why you hold that view.
2 Why did the UDF take the form it did?

The Township Revolt

There are three key questions to be asked about the Township Revolt.
• What led to this event and how did it begin?
• What was its nature – was it a kind of civil war?
• What were the consequences of the Township Revolt?

How did the Township Revolt begin?

A UDF-affiliated civic association in the Vaal Triangle decided to support a refusal to pay rents, to force a reduction of rental charges, and to try to secure the resignation of the local council, which was seen to be made up of **government collaborators**. The rent strike was accompanied by a boycott of the local schools and a work stayaway. A clash with the police followed, which inflamed the situation, the boycott and strike spread, and further violent clashes with the police occurred. In October 1984 the army was sent into the Vaal Triangle townships, and the troops searched house to house for guns. This inflamed the situation and intensified the revolt, which then spread to other townships in the East Rand and elsewhere.

What the government and the media called 'unrest' quickly became a mass uprising, which spread rapidly from the industrial centre of the Reef to the Eastern Cape – where even small towns in the Karoo were now for the first time caught up in the struggle – to the coloured townships of Cape Town, and the shantytowns of the Bophuthatswana and Ciskei bantustans.

In January 1985 the ANC called on South Africans to make the townships 'ungovernable'.

Within months, the police had to acknowledge that some of the Eastern Cape townships were 'no-go' areas, where teenage comrades manned barricades and engaged in street battles with the police, in which they threw home-made petrol bombs or stones. In response, some police decided to 'take out' activists. The most notorious case was the brutal killing of the 'Goniwe 4', named after Matthew Goniwe, a charismatic schoolteacher at Cradock (see Source B).

Resistance was more widespread than in the Soweto revolt of 1976 (see Unit 5) and it drew wider support from almost all sections of a black population now much more politicised and organised in a network of community and local associations, many of them linked to the UDF. And now various forms of resistance came together:

- work stoppages for political reasons (stayaways);
- boycotts of schools and white-owned businesses;
- rent and service boycotts – by September 1986 over 300 000 African households were refusing to pay rents and for services;
- rallies were soon forbidden, but funerals took their place. They were often highly charged and emotional, with speeches made, liberation songs sung and ANC and SACP banners unfurled. The police often tried to intervene, using teargas and sometimes shooting, but the deaths of mourners often required further funerals.
- attacks by MK guerrillas increased, often against police stations and increasingly using AK-47s. There was also a shift from attacks on property to attacks on soft targets, involving loss of life and injury.

The ANC slogan of ungovernability shifted to that of 'people's power', and in some townships the comrades began to act as if they had local power. Street committees were formed, streets and parks were renamed and people's courts established to hand out 'people's justice'. Abuses of power worked to the advantage of the state. In particular, those deemed to be collaborators or agents of state control were turned on, and many were killed by the notorious necklace method, in which a tyre soaked in petrol was placed around the person's neck and set alight. Many councillors were killed, while hundreds lost their homes or businesses.

Consequences of the Township Revolt

One of the main consequences of the revolt was that support for the armed struggle grew, and the ANC became recognised as the dominant anti-apartheid organisation. Support for Inkatha dropped outside KwaZulu-Natal. The UDF, the new trade union federation Cosatu (see Source C),

▲ *Source C* Workers launch Cosatu in the Western Cape

and the National Union of Mineworkers, the single most powerful trade union, increasingly identified themselves with the leadership of the ANC and saw themselves as participating in a common struggle. In 1985, for example, the UDF associated itself with the Freedom Charter. Meanwhile, a National Education Crisis committee was set up. One of its activities was the writing of a new syllabus for history in schools.

The state met what it saw as a 'revolutionary struggle' with very harsh repression. The state of emergency first imposed in mid-1985 was extended to the whole country the following year, and from June 1986 emergency regulations made it difficult or impossible to cover what was happening in the townships. The press was censored, and television coverage, which had played an important role in alerting the outside world to what was happening, dried up. Even a film about Steve Biko was banned, as Source D shows.

The state did not only use repression. Its counter-revolutionary strategy was carried out through the elaborate system of Joint Management Centres set up by the security forces. Power passed to some extent to a group of 'securocrats', concerned above all with the re-establishment of 'order'. The police and army worked closely together, and used vigilantes – organised mobs of conservative people, sometimes called witdoeke after the white scarfs they wore – against the comrades. The Special Branch of the Police and the army's Special Forces engaged in acts of assassination to 'eliminate' activists. The state president himself authorised the bombing of Cosatu House, a centre for anti-apartheid groups, in Johannesburg in May 1987. Far more people were detained than ever before. In the last eight months of 1986 over 29 000 people were held. Patrick Lekota and other leading figures in the UDF were arrested and put on trial for 'treason'. Eventually the UDF and many of its affiliates and associated organisations, including the National Education Crisis Committee (NECC) and the End Conscription Campaign (ECC), were themselves restricted in February 1988, when the Minister of Police, Adriaan Vlok, declared them to be a threat to security.

The 'securocrats' were not only concerned with repression. They planned a multifaceted strategy to try to bring the 'unrest' under control. Money was allocated for the upgrading of African townships where there had been strong resistance, such as Alexandra outside Johannesburg. But such acts won no support for the regime. Resistance continued, as we shall see in the next unit.

▼ **Source D** The screening of *Cry Freedom* banned (From: I Berry. *Living Apartheid.*)

Activities

1 Speak to someone who was involved in the Township Revolt. Find out about their experiences and report back on them to other members of your class.
2 Consider the impact of these events on your local environment. Write a brief history of how they affected your town, village or area.
3 What do you know about Cosatu, the trade union federation being launched in Source C. Do some research to find out more about this organisation and its role in South Africa today.
4 What effect does an event like that shown in Source D – the banning of *Cry Freedom* – have on society?

From the Township Revolt to the advent of De Klerk (1985–89)

Unit 7

Unit outcomes

- Explore the difference between public and secret acts.
- Gain insight into some of the problems historians face when trying to reconstruct relatively recent history.
- Explain why dialogue between the government and the ANC began.
- Account for the independence of Namibia, South Africa's colony.

Unit timeline

1985: PW Botha offers Mandela freedom on condition; Mandela refuses the offer

1986: Eminent Persons' Group visit to South Africa; the Township Revolt subsides

1987: Dakar conference

1988: Battle of Cuito Cuanavale; Calueque incident; negotiations between Angola, Cuba and South Africa; beginning of formal meetings between Mandela and government officials; New York Accords

1989: PW Botha suffers stroke and decides to resign as head of the NP; FW de Klerk elected the new leader of the NP; Botha meets Mandela at Tuynhuys; De Klerk takes over as state president; Namibian election

1990: Namibia's independence

Introduction

In the mid-1980s few South Africans or international commentators thought that South Africa could avoid a civil war. As we saw in Unit 6, 1984 to 1986 were years of fierce resistance in the townships, and many thousands died. Yet it was at that time of great conflict that the first steps were taken towards the negotiations which took place in the early 1990s. In the first part of this unit we shall ask two main questions: How did the process of dialogue begin?, and Why did it begin when it did?

Then, in the second part of the unit, we shall consider the question: How and why did South Africa withdraw from its colony, Namibia?

Activities

Before you read further, consider the above questions. Write down your preliminary answers, so that you can compare what you know now with what you know after working through this unit.

Background

By early 1987 the Township Revolt had petered out and a kind of quiet returned to the townships. Rent boycotts continued, as did boycotts of elections for local councils. Those elected were never accepted as legitimate and trustworthy leaders. Cosatu, which was to some extent protected by the importance of its members to the economy, continued to call strikes; a general strike of June 1988 brought out over a million workers. The UDF, restricted from February 1988, transformed itself into a loose Mass Democratic Movement, which in early 1989 launched a successful hunger strike of political prisoners, which forced the state to release a number for fear of the consequences were they to starve to death. Attacks by MK continued and peaked in 1988. An increasing number of the attacks were on civilian targets, giving whites, who had not previously been directly affected by the protests, a new fear of what might happen to them in public places.

This increased the general loss of confidence in the regime, which the downturn in the economy since 1985 greatly intensified. Financial sanctions imposed in August that year brought about a major collapse of the Rand, and from 1986 economic and other sanctions imposed by the United States Congress and the European Union began to bite.

It was against this background that a process of dialogue began which was to lead eventually to the fundamental change we will consider in Unit 8.

The beginning of dialogue

Some of this dialogue was known to only a few people at the time, and only gradually has information about it emerged. If you can get hold of a copy, read the book by Allister Sparks, *Tomorrow is Another Country*. This was the first book to tell a previously hidden story. Pay special attention to the sources he uses. Are they mainly written or oral sources?

Many of the meetings held in the late 1980s were secret. Oral testimony is clearly an important source for secret meetings.

Activities ....

1 How can we judge whether such oral testimony is reliable?
2 What other sources could there be?
3 A number of those involved have subsequently written memoirs (their personal memories) of this time, most notably Nelson Mandela himself.
   a What assessment can you make of these memoirs?
   b Are there reasons why they may not be completely authoritative on the matters they discuss?

Dialogue with Mandela

One of the many kinds of dialogue which began to take place in the late 1980s involved talks between Nelson Mandela and government officials. By the early 1980s Mandela was internationally known as the most famous apartheid prisoner, and the campaign for his release put mounting pressure on the government. In January 1985 President Botha offered him freedom if he would renounce violence. Mandela's response, read on his behalf to a Soweto meeting in February, was as follows: 'I cherish my own freedom dearly but I care even more for your freedom ... I cannot sell my birthright ... Only free men can negotiate. Prisoners cannot enter into contracts ...'

Still pursuing the idea of releasing him conditionally, the Minister of Justice, Kobie Coetsee, met him in the Volks Hospital in Cape Town in November 1985, and that meeting eventually led to a series of discussions between Mandela and government officials, including the head of the National Intelligence Service, first when Mandela was in Pollsmoor prison close to Cape Town, and then when he was living in a house within the grounds of Victor Verster prison near Paarl. Eventually, PW Botha himself met Mandela at Tuynhuys in July 1989 and a joint statement was issued which was vague about the issue of violence: Mandela did not renounce it, but agreed to work for a peaceful solution to the conflict.

▼ *Source A*

The Botha-Mandela meeting
(From: A Sparks. *Tomorrow is Another Country*.)

© T Ehlers

Activities....................

1 What does Source A tell you about the relations between the people in this photograph?
2 What do you think they are thinking about each other?

Extension activity ....

If you have access to the book by Sparks mentioned above, or to Mandela's *Long Walk to Freedom*, make a list of the steps in the process leading to discussions, between 1985 and 1990, putting down the dates (if they are given) at which each took place. If you have access to both books, do you notice any differences between the two accounts?

The ANC and Broederbond meet

A second set of talks took place between members of the ANC in exile, including Thabo Mbeki, and members of the Broederbond and other Afrikaners. These talks were held in England. The Afrikaners included the brother of FW de Klerk. These talks were reported to the government. Eventually, in September 1989, officials of the National Intelligence Service met secretly with ANC leaders Thabo Mbeki and Jacob Zuma at a hotel in Switzerland.

These were all exploratory talks, in which the state tried to find out what the ANC stood for, especially on the question of the continuation of the armed struggle, and its links with the communist party, and whether a compromise settlement was possible involving a deal with the ANC.

The ANC and business leaders

Alongside the secret meetings, public meetings took place between the ANC and a number of different groups of South Africans from September 1985 onwards. These included business leaders, and a large group of Afrikaners who met the ANC at Dakar in 1987 (see Source B below). These talks were denounced by PW Botha, but they helped give the ANC legitimacy as an important player in the future of South Africa. The ANC was becoming increasingly accepted in the international community as the main organisation speaking for the oppressed in South Africa.

▼ *Source B*

The Dakar conference (1987)

A conference organised by the Institute for a Democratic Alternative for South Africa (Idasa) took place in Dakar, Senegal, from 9 to 12 July 1987. Sixty-one people from South Africa, the majority Afrikaans-speaking, met a 17-person delegation from the African National Congress. PW Botha harshly criticised those who attended, seeing it as an act of betrayal. The meeting discussed strategies for bringing about fundamental change in South Africa; the building of national unity; the structures of the government of a free South Africa; and the economy of a liberated South Africa. A statement issued after the meeting spoke of it being: 'part of the process of the South African people making history', and of a shared commitment towards the removal of the apartheid system and the building of a united, democratic and non-racial South Africa. The statement continued:

> The main area of concern arose over the ANC's resolve to maintain and intensify the armed struggle. The group accepted the historical reality of the armed struggle and, although not all could support it, everyone was deeply concerned over the proliferation of uncontrolled violence. However, all participants recognised that the source of violence in South Africa derives from the fact that the use of force is fundamental to the existence and practice of racial domination ... [The] Conference unanimously expressed preference for a negotiated resolution of the South African question. Participants recognised that the attitude of those in power is the principal obstacle to progress in this regard. It was further accepted that the unconditional release of all political leaders in prison or detention and the unban-

ning of all organisations are fundamental prerequisites for such negotiations to take place.

▲ Delegates at the Dakar conference

Activities

1 Do you have any criticisms or praise of anything said in Source B?
2 Did events turn out as the statement hoped they would?

International pressure increases

A Commonwealth summit meeting held in Nassau, Bahamas, in 1985 could not reach agreement on whether sanctions should be imposed on South Africa. Most Commonwealth leaders wanted to impose economic sanctions to show their rejection of apartheid and believed that sanctions would help bring the apartheid regime to its knees. South Africa's main trading partner was Great Britain, however, and Mrs Thatcher, the Conservative British prime minister, was strongly opposed to sanctions. She argued that they would not be effective, and would in fact be counter-productive, because they would cost Africans jobs, both in South Africa and in neighbouring countries. She believed that imposing sanctions would merely solidify the opposition of the South African government to change.

The Eminent Persons' Group

A compromise was worked out at the Nassau meeting: an 'Eminent Persons' Group' (EPG) would travel to South Africa to study the prospects for change and report to the next Commonwealth summit. A seven-member group arrived in South Africa in early 1986, met Nelson Mandela in Pollsmoor prison, and proposed almost exactly what De Klerk was to announce in February 1990 (see page 347 of Unit 8). But then, in May 1986, the South African Defence Force launched commando and air attacks on supposed ANC bases in Zambia, Zimbabwe and Botswana, aborting the EPG mission. Shortly afterwards, the Botha government imposed a nation-wide state of emergency, which gave the police enormous powers to try to end the Township Revolt.

Activities

1 Was Source C accurate?
2 a Do we now know that Botha was pushed towards such talks?
  b If not by the EPG, then by what other considerations?

Operation Vula and the Harare Declaration

As the ANC came under pressure to work for a negotiated settlement, Oliver Tambo, its leader, approved a secret plan, known as Operation Vula, which involved sending into South Africa senior members to organise underground support and promote mobilisation within the country. At the same time, the ANC publicly issued a set of liberal-democratic constitutional guidelines, and in August 1989 was to propose a detailed programme for moving to negotiations with the apartheid government.

The Harare Declaration stated the ANC belief that 'a **conjuncture** of circumstances exists which, if there is a demonstrable readiness on the part of the Pretoria regime to engage in negotiations genuinely and seriously, could create the possibility to end apartheid through negotiations'. The Declaration laid down five preconditions for negotiations:

- lifting the state of emergency
- ending restrictions on political activity
- legalising all political organisations
- releasing all political prisoners
- stopping all political executions.

Why did dialogue take place between the ANC and the government? Let us look at the different answers that have been suggested to this question. Was it because the government's attempt to crush the resistance movement had failed? Govan Mbeki of the ANC has claimed that 'Mass mobilisation of the people had clearly knocked the Nationalists off balance ...' (*Sunset at Midday*, 101). On the other hand, the ANC had come under increasing pressure from Western governments to seek a negotiated solution. For the ANC there was clearly the danger that making a compromise would be seen by some of its supporters as a sell-out.

New words

conjuncture where things (such as circumstances, time, etc.) join together
coercion force

◄ *Source C*

Cartoon by Abe Berry showing the EPG pushing Botha towards 'Talks with Mandela'
(From: I Berry. *Living Apartheid*.)

From the Township Revolt to the advent of De Klerk (1985–89) **341**

Activities

1 Why was the ANC prepared to agree to a compromise?
2 Was this a result of its weaknesses or its strength?
3 What were these weaknesses or strengths?

Reasons for dialogue

The ANC

Support for the ANC and its ally, the UDF, had increased massively in the mid-1980s, but by late 1986 it was clear that the state had the power to crush the uprising. The ANC knew that its position would be weakened if Namibia became independent as a result of an agreement which required the ANC to leave Angola, as subsequently happened (see below). While its military wing, MK, had scored dramatic propaganda successes, it had come nowhere near overthrowing the state. Any success from Operation Vula, which was discussed above, would take time. As the international campaign for negotiations increased, the ANC was under strong pressure to follow that route to change.

The government

There are a number of factors to consider in explaining why the government began to explore the possibility of a compromise settlement with the ANC. Here are some of the most important ones:

- the internal situation, with the economy in decline, and the likelihood of more resistance, of greater intensity, in the future;
- the growing international pressures against South Africa, which now for the first time involved trade and financial sanctions against the country (remember from Unit 5 that a mandatory arms embargo had been approved by the United Nations in 1977);
- the escalating war in Angola which is discussed below.

Remember that dialogue began when the country was under the state of emergency imposed to crush the Township Revolt. Censorship imposed under the state of emergency kept much of the news of what was happening from both a local and an international audience, but sufficient leaked out to give South Africa a very bad press, and a reputation for using brutality to maintain apartheid policies. Business could not develop in such a climate. If there was no economic growth – and South Africa had entered a period of negative economic growth – all the social and economic problems facing the country would get worse. The government came to realise that **coercion** was no long-term solution, and that the only peaceful way out was by negotiations.

The decision to withdraw from Namibia

Many whites in South Africa and in Namibia itself assumed in the mid-1980s that independence for Namibia was a long way off. Back in 1978 the South African government had approved a plan for a United Nations-supervised election to be held in Namibia, an election for a Constituent Assembly which would write a constitution for an independent Namibia. But the South African government made clear that it did not like the idea of the United Nations, which it regarded as being pro-SWAPO, entering the territory, and many members of the South African government had made it clear that they regarded SWAPO as a pro-communist and terrorist organisation. They did not want to see 'the red flag' flying in Windhoek.

South Africa's strategy, therefore, was to refuse to allow the implementation of the United Nations Resolution 435 of 1978, which provided for a UN Transitional Assistance Group (UNTAG) to enter the country to supervise the holding of the election which would precede independence. Instead, the South African government gradually transferred power to internal groups in South West Africa (as Namibia was often still called) which were sympathetic to South Africa.

A major step in that process occurred in June 1985, when a new transitional government of national unity was installed in Windhoek. The new internal government was not elected, and remained dependent on South Africa. A South African-appointed administrator-general was the key official in the territory. Implementation of UN Security Council Resolution 435 seemed very unlikely because from the early 1980s the South African government was adamant that it would not withdraw from Namibia unless there was a parallel and total withdrawal of Cuban forces from Angola.

We learned of the arrival of the Cubans in Angola in 1975 in Unit 5. Refer back to this section if you have forgotten why they were there.

In December 1988 a deal was struck, and South Africa signed agreements with Angola and Cuba which provided for the implementation of UN Resolution 435 and the withdrawal of Cuban forces. Implementation of Resolution 435 meant the withdrawal of South African troops and administration from Namibia according to the timetable laid down in the Western Plan of 1978. And this led to Namibia's independence, achieved on 21 March 1990.

When trying to understand how this withdrawal and independence happened we need to consider the following:

- Chester Crocker, the Assistant American Secretary of State for Africa, was the mediator in the negotiations which took place in 1988. For years he had tried to negotiate a deal between Cuba, Angola and South Africa. The Americans wanted a 'triumph' before President Ronald Reagan left office, and they secured one in large part because by 1988 the Cold War was winding down (see Chapter 4), and the Americans won the support of the Soviet Union, which helped persuade Angola and Cuba to settle.
- South Africa was persuaded to risk implementing UN Resolution 435 in part because it would, in doing so, win rewards: diplomatic support and no further sanctions so long as the Namibia process was on track. One of those rewards was the removal of MK bases from Angola.
- By 1988 the war in southern Angola was deadlocked, and there was the serious risk of it escalating into a major war, which neither the Cubans nor the South African government wanted. For the situation on the battlefield see the map and text below.

Cuito Cuanavale (November 1987 to March 1988)

This 'battle' (or siege) remains controversial, and there are very different interpretations of what happened. Some of those who have written about the 'battle' agree with the Minister of Defence, Magnus Malan, that it was a South African victory, which paved the way for the negotiations on Angola and Namibia which followed. Another school of thought accepts the view expressed by Fidel Castro of Cuba in July 1988, that it was a major defeat for the apartheid regime, a disastrous military humiliation which forced South Africa to enter negotiations which it had been resisting for years. In *Sunset at Midday*, for example, Govan Mbeki refers to Cuito Cuanavale as 'a disastrous military humiliation for South Africa' (106).

Why are there such different interpretations, and is it possible to **reconcile** them?

Some commentators think that neither side won or was defeated. Rather, it was a military **stalemate**. But it is also important to be clear what one is referring to. The South African officials who referred to a victory were thinking of the larger picture: in August 1987 the South African forces did defeat a major advance by the forces of the Angolan government against the rebel movement Unita, backed by the SADF, in south-east Angola. Castro and others who speak of a victory think that the South Africans were aiming to capture the town of Cuito Cuanavale and that they did not succeed in that goal. Certainly, the town was not captured, but General Jannie Geldenhuys, chief of the SADF, claims it was never the SADF's objective to capture it.

It is not possible to say definitely what South African intentions were, for the military records, which might supply the answer, are not open to researchers. Another way in which the South Africans were 'defeated' was that the Cuban forces in April/May 1988 moved down close to the Namibian border for the first time, changing the military balance of power in the region. They now posed a major military threat to the South African forces, which had lost the air superiority they had previously enjoyed. An incident at Calueque close to the Angola/Namibia border in late June 1988, in which twelve South African soldiers died, served to show how dangerous the situation was, and helped persuade the negotiators to move towards a settlement.

▲ Map showing the location of Cuito Cuanavale

New words

reconcile bring together
stalemate situation of deadlock in which no one party or group can win

Negotiations and agreement

A series of meetings was held between May and December 1988, in places as far apart as London, Cairo, Brazzaville and New York, between the Angolans, the Cubans and the South Africans, with the Americans as mediators. These led ultimately to the December Accords.

Implementation of Resolution 435 began on 1 April 1989, and in November of that year the Namibians went to the polls in the election supervised by the UN. The Constituent Assembly met between November and February, and on 21 March 1990 Sam Nujoma was sworn in as the first president of independent Namibia by the UN secretary-general, minutes after the South African flag was lowered for the last time.

Activities ....

1 What do you think South African occupation of (a) Angola, and (b) Namibia, achieved?
2 Analyse why the South Africans withdrew from Namibia.
3 Relate the movement towards Namibia's independence to events in South Africa itself. Show in as much detail as possible, by referring to specific events, how they were related.

Extension activity ....

If you know or can find anyone who was involved in the war in Namibia/Angola, interview them about their experiences. Alternatively, ask members of your family what they remember of the battle of Cuito Cuanavale, or other aspects of the war in southern Angola.

◀ ***Source D***

South African troops withdrawing from Angola, August 1988

© South African Government Communication Information Service

Unit 8

The transition to democracy (1989–98)

Unit outcomes

- Understand how South Africa moved from apartheid to democracy, and what that new democracy meant.
- Learn more about the problems of writing contemporary history, and especially about the different sources available.

Unit timeline

1989: (January) PW Botha suffers stroke; De Klerk elected leader of the NP; (July) PW Botha meets Mandela at Tuynhuys, Cape Town; (August) PW Botha resigns as state president; FW de Klerk becomes acting state president; (September) Election: NP suffers setback; De Klerk sworn in as state president; (October) release of eight leading political prisoners from Robben Island

1990: (2 February) De Klerk's 'Rubicon' speech before parliament
(11 February) Nelson Mandela released
(May) Groote Schuur meeting between government and ANC
(August) ANC agrees to suspend the armed struggle; violence spreads from KwaZulu-Natal to the Rand

1991: (July) Inkathagate scandal;
(December) first meeting of Codesa

1992: Break-down of Codesa; mass action; Boiphatong massacre; Bisho massacre; Record of Understanding

1993: Assassination of Chris Hani;
(November) interim constitution agreed to

1994: (April) First democratic election
(May) Mandela sworn in as first democratic president

1995: Beginning of work of Truth and Reconciliation Commission (TRC)

1996: Final constitution approved by Constitutional Assembly and Constitutional Court

1997: Final constitution comes into effect

1998: TRC finishes its work

Introduction

At the beginning of 1990 apartheid was still firmly in place, the liberation movements were still banned, and Nelson Mandela remained a prisoner. By the end of April 1994 the political situation had been transformed: South Africa had a new, democratic constitution and most apartheid legislation had been repealed. These years are not only of world historical importance, marking a turning-point in our history, they are also difficult ones to study, for many complex and different processes were taking place simultaneously. It is not possible here to do more than mention some of them.

Activities

Before proceeding further, consider what possible sources there are for these years. An obvious one is the people who have lived through these years. You will know such people – ask them what their experiences were.
Secondly, ask yourself what you would want to know about the years from 1989–98.

Background

In this unit we are concerned with a very recent period in our history. We cannot yet see these years in perspective. On the one hand, to write contemporary history we have a lot of evidence not available to historians of earlier periods. On the other hand, some of the key evidence is not yet available to historians. Historians have not yet had the opportunity to draw upon official and other archives for material. More was being learnt about these years as this chapter was written, thanks to the Truth and Reconciliation Commission. Despite this, we must try to make sense of what happened in these years. Interpretations differ greatly. We must try to present as objective a picture as possible. As always, as historians we need to define the main questions to ask.

The main questions to ask about these years

In the following pages you will find a selection of some of the sources available for this period. What are some of the questions that need to be asked about this period? The political changes, those involving the move from apartheid to democracy, are perhaps the most obvious.

- Why did the process of repealing apartheid laws and moving to a new **dispensation** take the form it did, with many stops and starts?
- What did the repeal of these laws mean on the ground?
- What was the role of political violence, and of the 'third force' in this process?
- What was the nature of the compromise reached and written into the new constitution?

Other questions could include:

- What was the role of the international community in this process?
- Why did the African National Congress abandon its nationalisation strategy and accept the idea of economic growth based on free enterprise?
- What was the legacy of apartheid, and how did that affect the consolidation of our democracy?
- What did democracy mean to ordinary people, and how much content did it have?

New words

dispensation order of things
imperious commanding, bossy

Developments within the National Party in 1989

After he suffered a minor stroke on 18 January 1989, PW Botha decided that, to lessen his responsibilities, he would resign as leader of the National Party, but remain head of state. This was the first time there had been such a division of power, and it was unclear what relationship would exist between the party leader and head of state. The National Party caucus (the members of parliament) immediately voted for a successor as leader, and FW de Klerk was elected by 69 votes to 61. Relations were not good between De Klerk and Botha, and many in the National Party thought that his failure to set an election date was harming the party. After Botha

did call an election for 6 September, he was forced to resign as president in August by his ministers, all of whom he had antagonised by his **imperious** style.

▼ Source A

In his television address to the nation in which he announced his resignation, PW Botha said

> It is evident that after all these years of my best efforts for the National Party, and for the government of this country, I am being ignored by Ministers serving in my Cabinet. I consequently have no choice but to announce my resignation.

Activities

1 What do you think Botha was referring to by his 'best efforts for the National Party and for the government ...' in Source A?
2 Explain why relations between Botha and his ministers broke down.

FW de Klerk

Botha's resignation was important for various reasons. Even after his meeting with Mandela in July, he remained unwilling to release him before he had renounced violence, and there is no evidence that suggests he might have taken the other bold steps De Klerk was to take in February 1990. With his resignation, power passed to De Klerk, who had the reputation for being a conservative, and so was able to count on the support of the right-wing of the party. At the same time, however, he was a member of the small Dopper church (Reformed Church) and a man of strong moral principles. On taking office, he felt a 'calling' to serve the nation, and soon became more aware than he had been as a minister of the pressures mounting on the government. He therefore decided to make a bold move, and seize the moral high ground. This happened on 2 February 1990.

Background to 2 February 1990

In the September 1989 election, the NP did badly, and its majority in parliament was cut from 80 to 20 seats. De Klerk had asked for a mandate to bring about what he had called, in very vague terms, 'a drastically different South Africa', and could argue that he had received such a mandate. He realised that unless he acted, the NP might become a minority party, in a political system providing vast power to the majority party, at the next election in five years' time. If he unbanned the ANC, he hoped it might split, and that the transition from liberation movement to political party would be very difficult. He hoped therefore that it could be prevented from getting two-thirds of the votes in an open election. And before the ANC could come to power, he intended to help shape a new constitution in which any majority party would have drastically reduced power, and in which minority group rights were protected.

Activities

1 Some historians emphasise the role of great men in history, others rather the importance of social processes. In this particular case, some argue that De Klerk played a vital role and that without him there would have been no transition to democracy, but civil war instead. Others argue that the pressures building for negotiations did not depend on a single individual and that such a transition was more or less 'inevitable'. What is your assessment?
2 Consider why apartheid collapsed. Was this because it had proved impractical and impossible to implement? (Clearly, it had not prevented more and more blacks from settling in the cities.) Or do we need to look to external reasons why apartheid collapsed, in particular the opposition it aroused?

De Klerk and violence

One of the criticisms against De Klerk is that he did not do enough to stop the violence. In late 1989 Dirk Coetzee, the former head of the special police unit based at Vlakplaas west of Pretoria disclosed that he had been part of death-squad activities. After he left there in 1984, the unit was renamed C10 and placed under the command of Eugene de Kock. De Klerk reduced the importance of the security forces in November 1989, but he allowed many of the operatives to continue, gave De Kock and others extravagant payments, and took no decisive action to end the activities of what some called a 'third force'. De Kock was later found guilty of many murders and other crimes and sentenced to over 200 years in jail.

Activities

1 What is your assessment of De Klerk with regard to his role in continued violence?
2 Look at Source B.
  a Do you accept the proposition in the first sentence?
  b Why did De Klerk highlight the election of September as such an important event?

▼ Source B

De Klerk's speech to parliament, 2 February 1990

He began as follows: 'The general election of September 6, 1989, placed our country irrevocably on the road of drastic change'. He then promised that a process of negotiation would be given the highest priority, and that a constitutional dispensation would be created in which every inhabitant of the country would enjoy equal rights.

[About three-quarters through his address, he reminded the audience of the promise he had made in his inauguration to give attention to the obstacles in the way of negotiation. He then announced the lifting of the ban on the African National Congress, the Pan-Africanist Congress and the South African Communist Party. After mentioning changes to the security regulations, he added: 'the government has taken a firm decision to release Mr Mandela unconditionally. I am serious about bringing this matter to finality without delay.' Nelson Mandela's release followed nine days later.]

Extension activity

Most people saw De Klerk's speech as a dramatic breakthrough, the kind of Rubicon speech which PW Botha had promised in 1985 and not delivered.

The leader of the right-wing Conservative Party, Andries Treurnicht, called it 'a most revolutionary speech', and he and his colleagues walked out of the Assembly.

What is your assessment of the significance of the speech?

Nelson Mandela's release from jail

Mandela delivered a speech from the balcony of the Cape Town City Hall on 11 February 1990 after his release that afternoon after 27 years in prison. He was then 71. He began as follows: 'Friends, Comrades and fellow South Africans. I greet you all in the name of peace, democracy and freedom for all ...' He praised those who had supported the ANC and others who had worked against apartheid.

▼ Source C

Mandela also defended the continuance of the armed struggle

Our resort to the armed struggle in 1960 with the formation of the military wing of

the ANC, Umkhonto we Sizwe, was a purely defensive action against the violence of
apartheid. The factors which necessitated
the armed struggle still exist today. We
have no option but to continue.

[But he immediately added] We express the
hope that a climate conducive to a negotiated settlement would be created soon so
that there may no longer be the need for
the armed struggle ... I myself have at no
time entered into negotiations about the
future of our country, except to insist on a
meeting between the ANC and the
Government. Mr de Klerk has gone further
than any other Nationalist president in taking real steps to normalise the situation.
However there are further steps as outlined
in the Harare Declaration that have to be
met before negotiations on the basic
demands of our people can begin. I reiter-
ate our call for, inter alia, the immediate
ending of the state of emergency and the
freeing of all and not only some political
prisoners ...

[Towards the end of his speech, he said] the
future of our country can only be determined
by a body which is democratically elected on
a non-racial basis ... Universal suffrage on a
common voters' roll in a united, democratic
and non-racial South Africa is the only way
to peace and racial harmony ....

Activities

1 Why did Mandela say what he did about the armed
struggle in Source C?
2 Did his call for a negotiated settlement contradict
what he said about the continuation of the armed
struggle?
3 Why did Mandela say that he had not entered into
negotiations himself?
4 Was the country's future in fact decided by a body
'democratically elected on a non-racial basis'? (If you
do not know the answer to this question, you will find
it below.)

The release of political prisoners

This was one of the key preconditions for negotiations. De Klerk announced in his speech of
2 February that those in jail because they were
members of previously banned organisations
would be released, but not those convicted of terrorism, murder and arson. In his speech on his
release Mandela called for 'all' political prisoners to
be freed. This issue caused much disagreement
between the parties in the following years. The government was reluctant to release people who had
committed major crimes, and whose motivation
was not always obvious. In the end, a man convicted of planting a bomb in a Durban bar which had
killed civilians (Robert McBride) was released, as
was a mass murderer (Strijdom). Others remained
in jail, in particular, members of the PAC.

▲ Mandela was welcomed by a crowd of 100 000 ANC supporters at the Soccer City Stadium in Soweto two days
after his release from prison in 1990.

Activities

What criteria do you think should have been used to decide who should, or should not, have been released in this process?

The PAC in exile and after

Harsh repression and a lack of leadership brought the PAC to the brink of disintegration by the end of the 1960s. Rivalries continued among the exiled leadership, based at Dar es Salaam in Tanzania. In the mid-1960s the PAC absorbed members of the Coloured People's Congress who rejected the ANC's approach as reformist. For a time the controversial Patrick Leballo hoped to wage an armed struggle from Lesotho, and he worked closely with the Lesotho Liberation Army, but he was effectively sidelined at a conference at Arusha in 1978. After David Sibeko, his rival, was shot by members of the PAC's armed wing, the Azanian People's Liberation Army (APLA) in Dar es Salaam, John Pokela became leader there but proved weak and ineffective. The PAC in exile failed to win the international support given to the ANC, and APLA achieved little before the 1990s.

After being unbanned in February 1990, the PAC continued to refuse to suspend its armed struggle. In 1993 its armed wing APLA conducted a number of terrorist attacks aimed at white civilians. Members of a church congregation were fired upon at Kenilworth in Cape Town, and shots were fired into a pub in the Cape Town suburb of Observatory. Though the party did then decide to suspend the armed struggle and participate in the democratic election of April 1994, many of its members did not support that decision and in the election the PAC received only 1,5 per cent of the total vote.

From Mandela's release to the April 1994 election

You will find the timeline at the beginning of this unit useful as you work through the events of this section.

The bumpy road to Codesa

In May 1990 the government and the ANC met formally for the first time, at Groote Schuur, the president's residence, in Cape Town, to discuss how the obstacles in the way of negotiations might be removed. At another meeting between

◀*Source D*
The dismantling of apartheid

the two parties in Pretoria in August that year, the ANC agreed to suspend the armed struggle. This was a necessary precondition for formal negotiations to take place. As violence spread from KwaZulu-Natal to the Rand, the ANC accused the government of not acting to stop it, and relations between Mandela and De Klerk soured.

Another reason why the start of formal negotiations was delayed was uncertainty over the form they would take. The ANC wanted an elected body to write the constitution, but the government knew that the ANC would dominate such an elected body, and wanted to build in safeguards to protect minority rights. In the end, agreement was reached on a two-stage process: an unrepresentative body, to be known as the Convention for a Democratic South Africa (Codesa), would draft an interim constitution, which would embody a set of constitutional principles. Then a democratically elected constitutional assembly would draft the final constitution, which would have to be based on those constitutional principles.

In the meantime, in early 1991, De Klerk announced that parliament would repeal the remaining pillars of apartheid, and in that parliamentary session the Population Registration Act, the Group Areas Act and others were repealed. Remarkably, De Klerk was able to take his party with him in this great shift in policy. In time the NP itself was transformed into a non-racial party, though it remained largely under white leadership.

Activities ....
Imagine you were De Klerk in 1991 as shown in Source D. How difficult was it for you to go ahead and repeal apartheid laws?

From Inkathagate to the break-down of Codesa
Before Codesa met in December 1991, the government was weakened by the revelation in July 1991 that state funds had been going to Inkatha, allegedly for anti-sanctions activities. Codesa was made up of nineteen parties: besides the government, the ANC and the other major parties, a number of small parties, some of them from the bantustans, attended. The right-wing Conservative Party, and the Pan-Africanist Congress refused to participate at this stage, the CP because it rejected the idea of negotiating with 'the enemy' and the PAC because it wanted an elected constituent assembly. Codesa adopted a Declaration of Intent in which the parties committed themselves to an undivided South Africa 'free from apartheid or any other form of discrimination or domination'.

Activities ....
1 Imagine that in 1991 you were asked to attend Codesa. Write an imaginative account of the experiences of:
 a an ANC delegate; and
 b an NP delegate at Codesa.

In March 1992 De Klerk won a referendum among whites over whether he should continue with the negotiations. A further meeting of Codesa in 1992 broke down in disagreement over the percentage required for breaking a deadlock over the final constitution. The ANC, already angered by what it said was De Klerk's failure to stop the violence, broke off further negotiations when a particularly brutal and large massacre occurred at Boiphatong. Inkatha supporters from a nearby hostel **ran amuck** among residents of a squatter settlement. The ANC then embarked on a campaign of 'rolling mass action' to put pressure on the government to act to stamp out the violence. De Klerk continued to argue that he could do no more, and that there was no 'third force' behind the violence. In KwaZulu-Natal, meanwhile, the struggle between the ANC and Inkatha continued to lead to many deaths. In all, perhaps 15 000 people were to die during the transition period from 1990 to 1994 in acts of political violence.

New words
ran amuck went wild

Extension activity ....
The transition to democracy is often referred to as a 'peaceful' one, yet large-scale loss of life occurred. Others write of a low-intensity civil war in these years.
Try to find out more about the causes of the violence, and its different types, write an essay setting out your findings on this question: 'What were the causes of the political violence which plagued the transition to democracy, and do you think the government of the day could have done more to stamp it out?'

From Bisho to the interim constitution
Another massacre took place at Bisho in September, when the forces of the Ciskei government fired on ANC marchers. This served to highlight for the ANC and the government the dangers of the situation. To prevent the country from descending into civil war and anarchy, the two sides agreed to a Record of Understanding in late September. This excluded the Inkatha Freedom Party and alienated Buthelezi. Thereafter the negotiations were mainly

★ ★
CAPE EDITION ★ ★ ★ ★ ★

Sunday Times

THE PAPER FOR THE PEOPLE   APRIL 11 1993   PRICE R3 incl VAT   A TIMES MEDIA PUBLICATION

Four shots kill SACP chief after lone drive

Tragedy strikes two days after peace call

HOW HANI DIED

By CHARMAIN NAIDOO,
CHARLES LEONARD and
CHARLENE SMITH

AS CHRIS HANI drove into his driveway just after 10am yesterday, a red Ford Laser pulled in close behind. The driver, a white man, followed Hani to his front door.

Four shots rang out. Hani was hit at point-blank range in the chin, behind the ear and in his chest.

Mr Hani, 50-year-old revolutionary turned peacemaker, lay dead, clutching a newspaper to his chest.

The assassin sauntered back to his car, reversed out of the driveway and drove around the corner.

Alerted by the sound of the gunshots, Mr Hani's daughter, Nomakhwezi, 15 — only member of his family at home at the time — opened the front door to be confronted by the sight of her father's bloodied body in his blue track suit and running shoes.

Her screams alerted a neighbour, who ran to the Hani house from next door and found the hysterical girl bent over her father's body.

"It was pitiful. The child was wailing. I quickly took her away from the sight of her dead father, bleeding all over the patio," said the neighbour, who did not want to be named for fear of reprisals.

Cordon

She took Nomakhwezi to the nearby home of the ANC's PWV chairman Tokyo Sexwale.

As the killer drove away, a woman who lives nearby took down the registration number of his car and reported the killing to the police.

By 10.30am, police, SADF personnel and traffic police had cordoned off the entire block bordering Hakea Street.

Mr Hani's body was removed in a police mortuary van at 12.50pm.

ANC members formed a column on either side of the van and broke into an emotional rendition of the farewell song for fallen comrades. *Hamba Kahle M'Komto.*

As the van slowly drove through the large crowd, ANC national chairman Oliver Tambo, his wife Adelaide and son Dali arrived. With them was the Mandela lawyer Ismail Ayob.

Mr Tambo, in obvious pain and leaning heavily on his walking stick, insisted on saying a personal farewell to his friend.

Alone

Soon afterwards, white-haired Walter Sisulu arrived alone, with a driver.

Mrs Winnie Mandela, who arrived with a three-car entourage, also paid her last respects.

This was to have been a rare weekend off for Mr Hani, who broke his usual security routine to drive alone to the shops. His driver, who doubles as his bodyguard, was not at the house when the assassination took place.

He arrived after the cordon had been erected and broke down after a newspaper reporter told him Mr Hani was dead.

Mr Hani, who often addressed three to four rallies a day, decided to take some time off over Easter.

He returned from Transkei after a day-long visit with ANC deputy secretary-general Jacob Zuma to see General Bantu Holomisa to discuss ways of reducing tension between Transkei and the SA government.

On Thursday night he appeared on SABC TV's *Agenda* with PAC secretary-general Benny Alexander.

On Friday his wife, Limpho, a Lesotho

□ To Page 3

CHRIS HANI
... collapsed
outside his
front door

Police hold 'right-wing' immigrant

By DE WET POTGIETER and EDYTH BULBRING

A FORTY-YEAR-OLD man of Polish extraction, allegedly with right-wing sympathies, has been arrested in connection with the killing of ANC Communist Party boss Chris Hani.

Police sources yesterday identified the man as Mr Jan Walus — a Polish immigrant with violently anti-communist sentiments and close links to the most militant wing of the Afrikaner Weerstandsbeweging.

They said Mr Walus fled Poland 10 years ago to "get away from the communists".

Meanwhile, a right-wing source said Mr Walus was unmarried and stayed on a farm outside Pretoria.

He is self-employed, selling glass and pottery.

He was described as a "concerned, active and registered" member of the AWB and the CP.

Extreme

Three weeks ago, in the wake of the shootings at Eikenhof, south of Johannesburg, AWB leader Eugene Terre' Blanche announced that an extremist white group, unconnected with his organisation, was setting itself up to wage civil war.

It is not clear whether the man being held by the police is connected with this extremist group.

No official confirmation of the man's identity was available yesterday.

The man was arrested by police half an hour after his car was spotted leaving the murder scene. Police, responding to an all-points

□ To Page 2

ANC calls for calm

By EDYTH BULBRING

THE ANC and the South African Communist Party yesterday appealed to their supporters to remain calm and restrained following the assassination of Chris Hani.

The ANC asked its members not to be provoked by those intent on wrecking the peace process.

ANC leader Nelson Mandela said Mr Hani, the leader of the SA Communist Party, was a martyr to the cause of justice and peace.

"His death demands of us that we pursue that cause with even greater vigour and determination," said Mr Mandela.

"With all the authority at my command, I therefore appeal to all our people to remain calm and to honour the memory of Chris Hani by remaining a disciplined force for peace."

Their call for calm was reiterated by Anglican Archbishop Desmond Tutu.

"I want to make a call to our people: Please, don't let them manipulate us.

"Don't let this tragic event trigger reprisals.

"It is what somebody wants to see happen."

Blacks taunted in streets

Sunday Times Reporter

ONLY hours after the slaying of SACP leader Chris Hani, four white men in a white bakkie cruised past the SACP headquarters in Johannesburg chanting "Up with the AWB".

Two men in the back of the open bakkie shouted abuse at black pedestrians.

Elsewhere, the communist leader's death was greeted with shock and, in some cases, anger.

The SACP reported spontaneous gatherings of supporters in the Eastern Cape and other major centres.

At the time of going to press, burning barricades were being put up in Khayelitsha in the Western Cape.

Tokyo Sexwale, a former MK comrade and now the ANC's PWV chairman and longtime friend of Chris Hani, stand in shock beside the SACP chief's body.
Picture: CECIL SOLS

between the ANC and the government, whose decisions were carried by a multi-party negotiating forum, which met from April 1993 to work out an interim constitution. It was agreed that the first democratic election would be for a parliament which would also become a constitutional assembly to draft a final constitution, which had to be in line with the 34 constitutional principles negotiated in 1993. Those negotiations took place while violence continued to ravage much of the country.

In April 1993 Chris Hani, popular leader of the Communist Party, was assassinated by a man linked to a leader of the Conservative Party (see Source E). In June the far right AWB attacked the World Trade Centre, where the negotiations were taking place. Covert forces, including the CCB in the SADF, continued to act as a 'third force', staging various 'dirty tricks' and trying to wreck the negotiations by staging acts of violence. But by late November 1993 the interim constitution had been agreed to, and the question then became whether Inkatha would participate in the election process, and whether the far right would take up arms to destroy the election. By this time the Pan-Africanist Congress had agreed to participate.

Had the government organised the election, it would have been able to influence the result. A Transitional Executive Council was therefore established, along with an Independent Electoral Commission (IEC) to work to ensure that the election was free and fair. Numerous foreign organisations and governments sent observers.

Activities

1 Summarise what Source E has to say about the death of Chris Hani.
   a How did he die?
   b Who was responsible for his death? (To answer this question you will need to look at more recent sources, particularly the reports of the Truth and Reconciliation Commission on his murder.)
2 What was the effect of Hani's murder on the political situation in South Africa?

The election and the aftermath

At the very last minute, Mangosuthu Buthelezi, leader of Inkatha, agreed to join in the electoral process, and the decision by General Constand Viljoen to participate did much to prevent an uprising by the far right. Violence continued, especially in KwaZulu-Natal, but the election was held peacefully in late April 1994. A sticker for the IFP was added to the ballot paper just before the election took place. Queues of people waited for hours to cast their vote. On 6 May the IEC declared the election 'free and fair'.

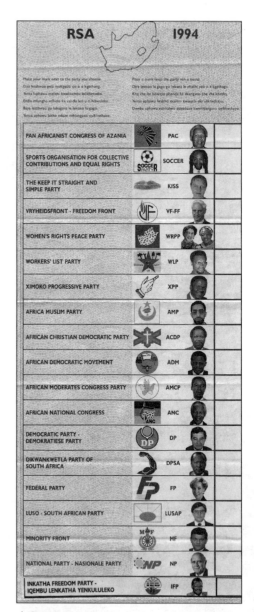

▲ Sample ballot paper

The ANC obtained just short of the two-thirds majority which would have enabled it to write the final constitution on its own. The National Party won 20,4 per cent of the votes, enough to give it a deputy president, and it won control of the Western Cape, one of the nine new provinces. The IFP won 10,5 per cent of the vote and control of KwaZulu-Natal, the Freedom Front of General Viljoen almost 2,2 per cent, the Democratic Party 1,7 per cent, and the Pan-Africanist Congress 1,2 per cent (see Source F showing election results). The ANC won control of the other provinces, and the former bantustans were re-incorporated into a united South Africa of nine new provinces.

Party	Votes	National percentage of seats	National Assembly seats
ANC	12 237 655	62,65	252
NP	3 983 690	20,39	82
IFP	2 058 294	10,54	43
FF	424 555	2,17	9
DP	338 426	1,73	7
PAC	243 478	1,25	5

▼ Map showing the nine provinces of South Africa and the capital of each

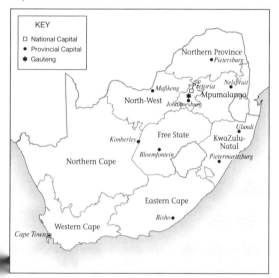

KEY
□ National Capital
● Provincial Capital
✷ Gauteng

Activities

Do some research to find out which parties control the various provincial legislatures, and the names of the provincial premiers.

The new government

On 10 May, Nelson Mandela's inauguration as president took place at the Union Buildings, Pretoria, before an audience which included many foreign heads of state. He swore the following oath:

> I, Nelson Rohlihlala Mandela, do hereby swear to be faithful to the Republic of South Africa, and to solemnly and sincerely promise at all times to promote that which will advance and to oppose all that may harm the Republic, to obey, observe, uphold and maintain the constitution and all the other laws of the Republic ...

In his speech he said, 'Out of the experience of an extraordinary human disaster, that lasted too long, must be born a society of which all humanity will be proud.'

Activities

1 What disaster was Mandela referring to?
2 What was his vision for South Africa for the future?
3 To what extent do you think that this vision has or has not come true?

Thabo Mbeki and FW de Klerk were sworn in as deputy presidents, and a Government of National Unity was formed. Mandela stressed the need for national reconciliation and nation-building. To deal with the legacies of the past, a Truth and Reconciliation Commission (TRC) was set up in 1995. The interim constitution provided for amnesty if full disclosure was made, and the TRC sought to provide a place where victims could tell of their sufferings, and where amnesty could, if appropriate, be granted. Reparations would also be discussed.

In 1996 the final constitution emerged from the constitutional assembly (made up of the newly elected Assembly and Senate together). The National Party then withdrew from the Government of National Unity, and in 1997 De Klerk resigned as leader of his party. The final constitution was referred back to the constitutional assembly by the constitutional court in 1996, and after amendments were made to bring it into line with the constitutional principles, the court approved it in December 1996 and it took effect in February the following year.

The constitution has many liberal democratic features, including, most importantly, a justiciable Bill of Rights. ['Justiciable' means 'could be tested in the courts'.] Any constitutional matter would be heard by the new constitutional court.

One of the provisions of the constitution which some said was undemocratic was the provision that members of parliament could not 'cross the floor', that is, they could not leave one party for another. All members were representatives of parties, and once a member ceased to be a member of the party he represented, he ceased to be a member of parliament. The ANC argued that this provision was necessary at a time when the new democratic order remained fragile.

Attempts were made to make the new government and parliament more transparent and accessible than the old one had been. The committees which met to discuss legislation were open to the general public, and appointments to commissions and to top judicial positions were made after a public process was undertaken.

◀ The leaders of the Government of National Unity

© i-Afrika/Eric Miller

Critics complained about the extent of corruption and misgovernment which they alleged occurred, to which the government replied that corruption, previously hidden, was being uncovered and dealt with.

The key question was whether the new democratic institutions could survive if the government proved unable to deal with the pressing social and economic problems that were apartheid's legacy. Unemployment was high, crime rising, and many people continued to live in shanty towns or in poverty in rural areas.

Questions that need to be asked

Let us end by asking some central questions about these years in our recent history and about the process of transition from apartheid to democracy. What happened in these years has often been called a 'miracle'. Mandela himself called it 'a small miracle' in May 1994. Some did not like the term because it suggested that some non-human agency had been responsible for the successful process, or because it implied that the process had been completed. The political transition, it was said, was only part of a much larger process of transformation which had to include economic redistribution, to end the inequalities in society. What are your views on these issues?

Activities ....

1 One of the reasons why the process was successful was that a degree of trust was built up between the major parties , and in particular between the chief negotiators, Cyril Ramaphosa of the ANC and Roelf Meyer of the NP.
  a How important do you think personalities were in the process?
  b Without a Mandela and a De Klerk, would it have succeeded?

2 It was necessary that the NP leadership should believe that the ANC would act 'responsibly' if it entered government, or that it would split, and so could be prevented from taking power on its own.
  a In what ways did the ANC modify its policies in these years?
  b Did it do so because of a new realism, or for tactical and strategic reasons?

3 At the heart of the transition was a compromise between the forces of the old order and those of the new.
  a What was the nature of that compromise?
  b Was there any other way in which the transition could have come about, other than through such a compromise, given the power which the NP retained?

4 The NP claimed credit for ending apartheid (see Source G: an ANC election advertisement of early 1994, critical of this view).
  a Was the death of apartheid inevitable?
  b Who or what, in your view, was responsible for the end of apartheid?

5 One of the main threats to the transition to democracy came from the far right. The Afrikaner Weerstandsbeweging (AWB) and other extremist groups spoke of fighting to maintain white supremacy.
  a How was this threat defused?
  b How serious was it in fact?

6 a What legacies of apartheid remained in South Africa in the late 1990s, and how did the new government attempt to address them?
  b With what success?

7 a How democratic was the new state born in 1994?
  b Explain the main democratic features of the constitution of 1996.
  c How democratic was South Africa in practice?

8 Consider the view that the democratic constitution meant little in practice, because crime and corruption were rampant. What was needed to consolidate democracy in South Africa?

Most of these questions have no easy or straight-forward answers. Consider the different sides to each argument, and then make up your own mind. Even the questions themselves may seem biased to some. If you are critical of the questions, make clear in your mind the grounds of your criticism. If you pass your opinions on to the publishers of this book, they will take your comments seriously, and consider whether to alter the next edition. In that and other ways you and other learners in your class may play a role in history.

Remember that history is, as the famous Dutch historian Pieter Geyl put it, 'an argument without end'. History does not end where we have to end this chapter on South African history. By the time you read this chapter, history will have moved on.

◀ **Source G**
An ANC election advertisement, 1994
(From: *The Argus*)

ACCORDING TO THE NP, YOU PLAYED NO PART IN CHANGING SOUTH AFRICA.

The National Party wants you to believe that they changed South Africa. That your years of struggle and sacrifice against National Party oppression had nothing to do with it.

But we know better. We haven't forgotten the past. And that's why only the ANC can build a better future for all.

ANC

Working together for jobs, peace and freedom - a better life for all

CHAPTER ASSESSMENT

In small groups write essay plans to answer each of the following questions. Then select one of the topics and complete the essay on that topic. The members of a group should write essays on different topics.

1 'I remember the result of that election as if it were yesterday. When the Nationalists came to power in 1948 blacks were appalled. They were worried that what had been said at election time, might in fact come to fruition.' (Nthato Motlana, Secretary of the ANC Youth League in the early 1950s)

   Explain why Motlana's fears about the National Party's policy from 1948–60 were valid or invalid. Explain, with reference to the concept of apartheid, the recommendations of the Sauer Commission, and the laws for the implementation of apartheid.

2 Discuss the ideology of apartheid as envisaged by the National Party government, referring to the various laws enacted to enforce this ideology between 1949 (Prohibition of Mixed Marriages Act) and 1959 (Promotion of Bantu Self-Government Act).

3 'The founding of Umkhonto we Sizwe was the beginning of a new phase in the struggle against apartheid and racial discrimination.' Review this phase of armed resistance until 1976. How did the government during this period act against armed resistance and with what success?

4 'Between 1951 and 1976 organised internal opposition against the National Party's apartheid policy took different forms.' Illustrate this by referring to the Defiance Campaign, opposition by the Federation of South African Women, opposition by white groups, the anti-pass campaign, the Soweto uprising and the student uprising of 1976.

5 'The Separate Registration of Voters Acts set the scene for a major confrontation between the government and the courts. The Nationalists were fairly certain that the Bill could be passed by a simple majority of both houses of Parliament, despite the provisions of the South Africa Act, which had entrenched the coloured franchise in the constitution ...' (Reader's Digest. *Illustrated History of South Africa*)

   Discuss the five-year-long constitutional struggle to place the coloureds on a separate voters' role and explain why the courts became involved in the struggle.

6 Why did FW de Klerk 'cross the Rubicon' in 1990, and what did 'crossing the Rubicon' mean? What kind of negotiated settlement emerged in 1993–94?

Further reading

H Barrell. *MK*. Harmondsworth: Penguin, 1990.

S Biko. *I Write What I Like*. New edn. Johannesburg: Bowerdean Press, 1996.

Constitution of the Republic of South Africa. Cape Town: Government Printers, 1994.

C Crocker. *High Noon in Southern Africa*. New York: WW Norton, 1992.

G Gerhart. *Black Power in South Africa*. Berkeley: University of California Press, 1978.

J Kane-Berman. *Soweto. Black Revolt, White Reaction*. Johannesburg: Ravan Press, 1978.

T Karis and G Gerhart. *From Protest to Challenge*, vol. 5. Unisa Press.

C Legum. *The Battlefronts of Southern Africa*. New York: Africana, 1988.

T Lodge. *Black Politics in South Africa since 1945*. London: Longman, 1982.

N Mandela. *Long Walk to Freedom*. Mcdonald, 1994.

N Mandela. *No Easy Walk to Freedom*. Oxford: Heinemann, 1990.

G Mbeki. *Sunset at Midday*. Braamfontein: Nolwazi Educational,1996.

G Mbeki. *The Struggle for Liberation in South Africa*. Cape Town: David Philip, 1992.

J Pampallis. *Foundations of the New South Africa*. Cape Town: Maskew Miller Longman, 1995.

L Price. *Steve Biko*. Cape Town: Maskew Miller Longman, 1992.

Readers' Digest. *Illustrated History of South Africa*. Cape Town, 1994.

A Sparks. *Tomorrow is Another Country*. Sandton: Struik, 1994.

P Waldmeier. *Anatomy of a Miracle*. New York: Viking, 1997.

Preparing for the Grade 12 final exam

Soon you will be facing your final exams in the Grade 12 history course. The ideas below are designed to help you prepare for these exams and perform at your best on the day.

Exam strategy

You should be clear about what is in the syllabus and the material that you need to have covered for the exams. You should find out if your Examination Board has excluded any themes of the syllabus from your exams. This is something that your teacher should be able to tell you.

The form of the exams

Try to find out as much as possible about the form that your exams will take. This knowledge will help you to prepare effectively for the exams.
- The exam will usually consist of two papers, one on each section of the syllabus.
- There will be essay questions and non-essay questions.
- Do you know how many essay questions and non-essay questions there will be, and how the marks will be divided between them?
- Take a look at recent previous exam papers. These will give you a good idea of what to expect in your exams.

The questions

1 Essay questions
Use a three-stage approach to answer essay questions (and look at the section on essay writing at the end of Chapter 1 on pages 41–42):
- understand the question
- plan your answer
- write your essay.

Remember to analyse the key words of the essay question. These will help you to focus on exactly what the examiners are asking so that you can answer the question correctly.

2 Non-essay questions
These will be a mixture of:
- multiple choice questions
- sentence or short paragraph questions
- source-based questions (which may be written or visual sources).

Look at how many marks have been allocated to a question and adjust the length of your answer to take this into account. Again, take note of key words and phrases in both the sources and the questions. When you answer questions based on sources remember the following points:
- Some questions may only involve reading and understanding the sources, but other questions could involve a comparison of sources, an analysis and evaluation of their reliability, and the use of information not given in the sources.
- You should be clear about the difference between primary and secondary sources.
- You might be asked to write an empathetic paragraph in which you respond imaginatively to the sources.
- Be careful to note details such as the date and author of sources and any captions which might

be given with the sources (especially in the case of cartoons). For statistical tables and graphs note what items are being shown, the units and scale used and the particular years which have been chosen. All of these are important clues to help you understand the sources.

Exam strategy

1 Before you even look at the exam paper you could make a few quick notes on the back of your question paper or answer book. These notes could contain any ideas, facts and other details you might have learnt, but are worried that you might forget. However, be very careful to spend only a few minutes making these notes.
2 Make sure that you have access to a watch or clock. Work out before you go into the exam how long to spend on essay questions and non-essay questions. Ask your teacher to help you with this.
3 Read and underline or highlight the instructions on the exam paper carefully, making sure that nothing is different from what you were expecting in the exam (for example, how many questions you have to answer).
4 Read through the question paper carefully and plan your time according to how many questions there are and the number of marks allocated to each. Stick to the time plan that you have drawn up.
5 Start by answering a question that you know well. You do not have to answer the questions in the order that they appear in the exam paper, and starting off confidently will help you with the rest of the exam.
6 Make sure that you number your answers very clearly and according to the question numbers so that the person marking your paper knows exactly in what order you have answered the questions. Do not waste time by rewriting the question in full. The question number is enough.
7 Remember to read the questions very carefully and direct your answer to what the question is actually asking, not what you think it should be asking. This is achieved through careful analysis of the question.
8 If you have made a mistake in a word or phrase simply use a neat ruled line to cross it out. Do not waste time tippexing the error out.
9 Try to plan your time so that you have a few minutes left at the end of the exam to read through the answers that you have written. You might be able to clarify an idea, add a point that you had missed, or improve your style and presentation by changing a few words. Good Luck!

Acknowledgements

Every attempt has been made to trace and contact copyright holders. Should any copyright infringement have occurred, please inform the publishers so that the error can be rectified in the next edition.

Special thanks to the following for granting permission to reproduce material not acknowledged alongside or within the sources used in this book:

p 8 questions about Source G Harper Collins; p 23 H Holt Rinehart & Winston; p 24 J Holt Rinehart & Winston; p 26 M Oxford University Press; p 32 B and C Penguin; p 33 E and F Penguin; p 35 I Oxford University Press; p 54 E Macmillan; p 57 B BT Batsford; p 59 E Cartoon redrawn by Walter Pichler, © McGraw-Hill; p 65 C Cartoon redrawn by Walter Pichler, source unknown; p 80 F Macmillan; p 85 G Heineman Educational; p 89 O Longman; p 124 F Longman; p 151 J and K Longman; p 152 L and M Longman; p 154 P Nelson; p 156 R Random House; p 159 G Press and Information Service of the Federal Republic of Germany, Bonn; p 163 L Hodder & Stoughton; p 172 L Macmillan; p 238 Reed Educational and Professional Publishing; p 248 photo courtesy of Peter Delius; p 273 photo courtesy of Peter Delius

Line illustrations on pages 2, 183 and 239 by Fiona Calder
Map on page 16 by Fiona Calder
All other maps by John Hall